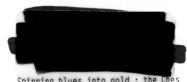

D1112681

SPINNING
BLUES INTO GOLD

Also by Nadine Cohodas

The Band Played Dixie:
Race and Liberal Conscience at Ole Miss

Strom Thurmond and
the Politics of Southern Change

NADINE COHODAS

SPINNING
BLUES INTO
GOLD

THE
CHESS
BROTHERS
AND THE
LEGENDARY
CHESS
RECORDS

ST. MARTIN'S PRESS ❌ NEW YORK

Title-page art courtesy of MCA/Universal Music Enterprises.

www.stmartins.com

Library of Congress Cataloging-in-Publication Data

Cohodas, Nadine.
    Spinning blues into gold : the Chess brothers and the
legendary Chess Records / Nadine Cohodas.
        p. cm.
    Includes bibliographical references and index.
    ISBN 0-312-26133-0
    1. Chess, Leonard, 1917–69. Chess, Phil, 1921– . Sound
recording   executives   and   producers—United   States—
Biography. 4. Chess Records (Firm) I. Title.
ML405 .C64   2000
781.643'149—dc21   00-025480

First Edition: May 2000

10   9   8   7   6   5   4   3   2   1

For Sylvia Cohodas,
who first put the music in my life,
and with a nod to Bessie Smith,
for Tracy Nelson, who got me going

CONTENTS

1. THE MEN ON THE CHESS BOARD   1

2. COMING TO CHICAGO   5

3. THE MACOMBA LOUNGE   22

4. IMMIGRANT TO ARISTOCRAT   33

5. MEMPHIS CONNECTIONS   51

6. CHECKERS, CHARTS, AND COPYRIGHTS   66

7. BLUES WITH A FEELING   81

8. THE BEAT HAS GOT TO MOVE   101

9. MONEY IN THE SONG   122

10. 2120 SOUTH MICHIGAN   136

11. ALL THAT JAZZ   151

12. PLAY FOR PAY   174

13. TRUST IN ME   183

14. BRANCHING OUT   194

15. VOICE OF THE NEGRO 212

16. THE SOUL OF A MAN 225

17. DON'T MESS UP A GOOD THING 245

18. 320 EAST 21ST STREET 267

19. FINAL TRACKS 280

EPILOGUE: LAWSUITS AND LEGACIES 302

DISCOGRAPHY 315

NOTES 318

BIBLIOGRAPHY 336

ACKNOWLEDGMENTS 341

INDEX 345

one

THE MEN ON
THE CHESS BOARD

By 1987 there was nothing remarkable about celebrating the life of an immigrant Jew who made good in America. This was, after all, the promise of the New World for those who came to it freely—men and women determined to surmount the barriers of poverty and language.

Success could come in unlikely venues through unexpected means, a combination of timing, place, luck, and instinct fused together by hard work. Why was it that thousands and thousands of Jews never made it more than a few miles beyond Ellis Island in New York, the central port of arrival, while others ventured out into new territory and new possibilities? Whatever the reasons, that first journey in America most often shaped what followed—the accident of location coupled with the necessity of making a living. Both were central factors in the lives of two immigrant Jews, Leonard and Phil Chess, who arrived in the United States in the fall of 1928 from Poland, made their way to Chicago to join their father, and ended up building a record company that influenced three generations of musicians.

Neither played an instrument. Neither had even a bent for music. But they were entrepreneurs, and through the indigenous sounds of America—blues and its progeny, jazz, rock and roll, and soul—they found their fortune. The Chess brothers didn't literally make the music in the studio, but they got it out the door and reaped the rewards.

Leonard was the older brother, the one with the vision and the presence. So the industry singled him out for an honor on January 21, 1987, when he was inducted posthumously as a "pioneer" into the two-year-old Rock and Roll Hall of Fame. He would have loved the scene in the Waldorf Astoria's grand ballroom, a full dress affair with men in tuxedos, women in sequins, long skirts, and high heels. He would have been perplexed only by the fact that Phil wasn't honored with him—the result of the political minuets that often accompany such awards events. Leonard's son, Marshall, who accepted the honor on his father's behalf, took care of the omission in his acceptance speech, reminding the audience that Chess Records had been a joint enterprise. Leonard was out front, it was true, but he couldn't have done it without Phil. Sometimes it came down to such simple things as knowing that his brother was watching the business while he was on the road making connections and making deals. The situation was often reversed: Leonard stayed home while Phil worked the road.

From the time he was a teenager, Leonard was determined to prosper. He just never dreamed that success would come through music. But from one small business venture to another, he stumbled upon the sounds of South Side Chicago, sensed an opportunity and built an empire.

It was particularly fitting on this glittery night at the Waldorf that another of the posthumous Hall of Fame inductees was McKinley Morganfield, the musician known worldwide as Muddy Waters. For it was Waters, nearly forty years earlier, who had made Leonard see a future in music. At the time, late in 1947, Leonard was operating a small club at Thirty-ninth and South Cottage Grove Avenue in Chicago, the Macomba Lounge. The music was primarily jump blues, ad hoc trios and quartets featuring lively horn players, a drummer, a piano player, and someone on bass. But in other venues—taverns, liquor stores, and cramped apartments—a different kind of music was finding an audience, the blues of the southern migrants, the black men and women who made their way from the fields of Mississippi and Alabama and Tennessee to Chicago and the hope of a better life.

Waters and Leonard got off to a rocky start. Leonard didn't understand his music and didn't want to record him. But Leonard learned quickly. The two men found what they needed when they found one another, and together they became the foundation of Chess Records, a company built on the convergence of outsiders—the Jewish immigrant from Poland and the black migrant from a cotton plantation in Mississippi.

At the turn of the century, when Chicago was a teeming mix of newly arrived foreigners, an Irish factory worker made an observation about one of his Jewish neighbors that was both compliment and fuel for the unflattering stereotype. "A Jew would rather earn five dollars a week doing business for himself," this man said, "than ten dollars a week working for someone else." Double-edged though it was, the comment captured

Leonard's singular ambition, except that he was confident he would make the other fellow's ten dollars and then some. Decades later, at the pinnacle of success, Leonard told one of his associates, "If you spend a dollar, make sure you get a buck and a half back."

The story of Chess Records, like the lives of the blues greats who were the label's anchor, is often approached with preconceptions built on misconception. The misinformation about the company's beginnings and the operation of its studios over the years hardened into myth, the stories embellished by the selective memories of participants and enshrined by writers who treated those stories as gospel. Leonard and Phil became stick figures reduced to unflattering emotional poses to further some other purpose. In so much writing the goal seemed to be less an effort to report on musical history and more the paying of homage to the musicians, who were given literary carte blanche. The universe of players, however, is broader, and the resources, such as the weekly trade journals *Cash Box* and *Billboard,* more extensive than the simple anecdote.

Hampering the effort to sort out myth from reality is the lack of company documents that could give so many of the stories evidentiary heft or show them to be untruths. But that in itself is a factor in the history. Independent record companies like Chess were never well-oiled corporate machines, even when they grew larger and more profitable. In the beginning they were seat-of-the-pants operations often run by daily improvisations; detailed paperwork was a secondary consideration, if that. Written contracts between label owner and musician were not yet the norm. Poaching between one label and another was common. The audience for the black music they produced was small. A "hit" did not mean a million seller; several thousand was a victory, enough to get back the costs and maybe a little extra to make the next record.

Equally important were the powerful emotional forces at work: first there was the music, which grew out of the life experiences of the musicians, then there was race, and then there was religion.

The early rhythm-and-blues companies were run by a fraternity of Jews who made money by making records, drawn together less by a common theology than by circumstances that kept them out of the American mainstream. Excluded from many commercial arenas because of anti-Semitism—both overt and covert—they found a home in the wide-open entertainment field. Pedigrees and formal education were not requirements. Religion was no bar. They were tough and they were shrewd—some said unscrupulous—and they were alternately loved, despised, respected, and feared. The deep bond of these cultural outsiders prompted one gentile, mild rebuke in his voice, to lament that "Yiddish was the second language of the record business."

The record producers were white, their talent for the most part black, many from impoverished backgrounds and few with much formal education, living in a society that regarded them as second-class citizens. The deals between the two parties were not the negotiations of peers. The relationships could be paternalistic, even condescending. At Chess it sometimes looked as though Leonard and Phil gave their musicians an allowance rather than a salary. Charges of exploitation were a common theme years later when some of the musicians reminisced. A few filed lawsuits over how much was owed to whom. But overall, discord was not the norm. In an otherwise segregated world, Leonard and Phil and their musicians found a racial comfort zone based on mutual need and respect and deepened by the fact that the Chess brothers made their living *in* the black community, not just *from* it. If they considered some of the talent like family, they didn't mean beloved servants. Musicians were guests at Passover seders and present at the Chess sons' bar mitzvahs. Chuck Berry stayed overnight at Phil's house and shared a room with his son, Terry. Willie Dixon came by whenever he wanted.

Leonard and Phil built their company on the blues, and the cultural impact of Muddy Waters, Howlin' Wolf, and Willie Dixon was felt most significantly through their influence on British blues aficionados, who in turn made that music popular with white America. When the Rolling Stones were breaking out as a premier rock-and-roll band, they came to Chicago to record at 2120 South Michigan Avenue, the home turf of their heroes—Waters, Wolf, Berry, Bo Diddley, and Dixon. But if Chess was built on the blues, it grew to be much more. In order to survive, Leonard and Phil had to adapt, and they did. The company not only put out well-received gospel and black comedy records but also popular jazz, rock and roll, and soul. Waters, Wolf, and Dixon may have captured a piece of the cultural consciousness, but they sold far fewer records than the successful jazz and soul artists.

By the time Leonard and Phil sold Chess early in 1969, the music business had changed. Competition was intense, and while the company was holding its own, Leonard was ready to do something else. The radio stations he and Phil had bought had proved to be lucrative investments; now Leonard wanted to move into television. His fatal heart attack on October 16, 1969, ended that dream, but the same sure instinct that had propelled him from the Macomba Lounge to the recording studio was still at play. The ceremony at the Waldorf early in 1987 honored that spirit and that achievement, recognizing a journey that began in a much humbler and distant place.

two

COMING
TO CHICAGO

Yasef and Cyrla Czyz and their three young children were a typical family in the small but close-knit Jewish community that
made up Motele, Poland, in 1920. Chaim Weizmann, Israel's
first president and perhaps Motele's most famous resident, once described
the village as "flat open country, mournful and monotonous." It was one of
hundreds of small communities that were home to the region's Jews, many
of them originally brought there under various Russian annexations and
then forced to live in what became known as the "Pale of Settlement." As
the twentieth century began, some five million Jews were concentrated in
this area, which encompassed the far western section of imperial Russia, parts
of Poland, Lithuania, Belorussia, the Ukraine, the Crimea, and Bessarabia.

Over the next twenty years more than two million would leave, the vast
majority of them heading for the new promised land of America. They
sought to free themselves from the pervasive anti-Semitism that not only
restricted their opportunities but also threatened their safety. Among those
who stayed behind were members of the Czyz and Pulik families—Cyrla,
Yasef's wife, was a Pulik. World War I had put an end to the wave of
migration that had begun before the outbreak of hostilities, and then
regional turmoil in the aftermath coupled with new, restrictive immigration
laws in the United States limited the number of individuals who would be
allowed to leave. But many still held on to the dream of coming to the
United States, and Yasef and Cyrla Czyz were no exceptions.

Like other young couples they experienced their share of joys and
tragedies. They had three children: Malka, in 1915; Lejzor, in 1917; and

Fiszel, in 1921 (memories and official documents differ on the precise dates, though Lejzor's was fixed at March 12). Three others had died. Life was difficult, hard work a requirement. It said something about the daily anxieties that the family told a story of Yasef tossing his infant son, Fiszel, into the river in one horrific moment of fear over feeding his family. The baby, the story had it, was quickly rescued and survived unharmed.

Another version—and probably the one more nearly correct—had it that after Fiszel was born, Cyrla was too ill to nurse him. A neighbor who had just given birth to her own child offered help but only for money, which Yasef didn't have. "What should I do," he asked her in exasperation, "throw him in the river?" Either way, the episode underscored the precariousness of their life in Motele.

Yasef was a shoemaker who traveled to neighboring towns, or *shtetls* as they were known in Yiddish, to find work. Cyrla took care of the children, a task sometimes made difficult because she was often sick, burdened by a weak heart and, later, tuberculosis. Many of a mother's chores consequently fell to Malka, who felt responsible for her younger brothers and for helping provide for the family. Sometimes that help came from an unlikely source. Malka had a lovely singing voice, and when soldiers came through Motele, she would stand outside and sing songs as they passed by. The soldiers tossed food to her—pieces of bread or vegetables they were carrying. Malka remembered them laughing, but she was glad to take the food and bring it to her family.

The Czyz home was both spare and typical for Motele—one large room with a cement floor, a sizable oven, no electricity and no running water. In cold weather, Cyrla would put blankets on top of the oven and let her children sleep there to stay warm. Sometimes one of the animals, most often the cow, would be brought inside to provide more warmth.

Motele did not have the amenities found in larger cities. There were no paved streets and no sidewalks, but there was enough land so that most families had their own gardens. In the Czyz plot were beets, carrots, cucumbers, green onions, and potatoes, which fit on a small parcel that was actually larger than the house. Like other Jews the family observed the rituals, particularly Cyrla and her mother, Dvera. Friday night—the Sabbath—was special. Candles were lit, prayers were said. Going to *shul*—a term of endearment for the synogogue—was important, as were customs associated with Orthodox Jewry. Small as it was, Motele had a *mikva*, a small enclosure that housed the ritual bath required of all married women. This was not lost on Lejzor and a few of his friends who would, once they were old enough to cause mischief, sneak around the *mikva* hoping to get a glimpse of the women bathing. It was one of the few memories of Motele that could make Lejzor smile. For most of his life, the little town became something to forget, a moment and a place to be left as far behind as possible.

The opportunity to get to America finally arrived for Yasef through Cyrla's uncle, Yossel Pulik. He had left for the New World in 1901 and settled in Chicago, by now a growing Jewish community that would swell to 100,000 by 1911. It was the second-largest Jewish population in the country, and in another fifteen years it would be the third-largest in the world. The vast majority of Jews had come from Eastern Europe, creating in Chicago an American version of the shtetls they had left.

Most of the Jews crowded into an area surrounding the intersection of Halsted and Maxwell streets, roughly two miles west of Lake Michigan and about three miles southwest of the center of the city. Wooden buildings crammed side by side gave the neighborhood the feel of a tenement district. A high point of each week was market day, when residents, Jew and non-Jew alike, would congregate to buy and sell their wares. The "smell of garlic and of cheeses, the aroma of onions, apples, and oranges and the shouts and curses of sellers and buyers fill the air," noted Louis Wirth, a writer enthralled with the scene. "Anything can be bought and sold on Maxwell Street . . . The sellers know how to ask ten times the amount that their wares will eventually sell for, and the buyers know how to offer a twentieth."

By the time Yossel Pulik was settled in Chicago, Jews had begun to move away from Maxwell Street, thousands heading farther west a few miles to a neighborhood known as Lawndale. Others, primarily but not exclusively German immigrants, headed south. The goal for both groups was the same: a more comfortable life and more economic opportunity. Such was the case with Pulik, who first settled at 2204 South State Street and then eventually moved farther south, to the 4300 block, a neighborhood of Jews and German and Irish immigrants that bordered on blocks filled with newly arriving southern blacks.

Like Yasef Czyz, Pulik was a shoemaker, a trade he continued in Chicago. He set up shop in the front of the building he bought at 4332 South State so he could rent out the second floor. Convinced of a more lucrative opportunity in dry goods, Pulik eventually gave up the shoe repair business to sell men's shirts, pants, and underwear and a few items for women.

By 1922 Pulik felt things were going well enough to send for two family members back home in Motele: his nephew, Moische Pulik, Cyrla's brother, and his nephew-in-law, Yasef, her husband. The men began their trip to America at the end of November. They arrived in New York on December 2, 1922, and were in Chicago a few days later. By this time Yossel Pulik of Motele had become Joseph Pulik of Chicago. After they arrived Moische became Morris Pulik and Yasef Czyz was now Joseph Chess, all the better to fit into this new American life.

In the years before Joe Chess's arrival in Chicago, so many "Motelers," as they were known, had left the old country for Chicago that they established their own synogogue: Anshe Motele, "the people of Motele." Many of the men had been carpenters back home and continued their trade in Chicago. So it was not surprising that the little synogogue became known as the "carpenters' shul," and it was likewise understandable that once he arrived in Chicago, Joe Chess traded in his shoemaking skills for carpentry work. As soon as he could, he started sending money home for Cyrla and the three children. The plan was to secure the necessary papers and passage so they could join him.

By now Cyrla's mother was living with the family. Cyrla would not leave Motele unless her mother could go, too. But by the time her papers were obtained, Dvera Pulik had died. Finally, in the fall of 1928, Cyrla and her three children, along with Morris Pulik's wife, Chaske, and their two daughters were ready to leave for America.

There was one big concern, however. Something was wrong with Lejzor's left leg. It was slightly paralyzed, making it hard for him to walk. His mother sought the best medical advice available, even trudging the twenty-five miles to Pinsk in a horse and cart so he could be treated by doctors there. They decided that Lejzor should wear a brace for support and outfitted him with a clumsy, heavy contraption made of two strips of iron held together with leather laces.

In late August, Cyrla and her children, along with her sister-in-law and nieces, set out by train for Warsaw to pick up their papers and begin the journey to the United States. When the two families arrived in the city, the children were awestruck. They had never seen such big and beautiful buildings and had never experienced the phenomenon of indoor plumbing. Malka was entranced. She was fascinated by the little room with a bowl of water, a seat, and a chain attached. She marveled at the fact that when she pulled the chain, water ran and emptied the bowl. She would be amazed to find the same thing in America.

From Warsaw the families continued on by train to Southampton, England, where they met the *Mauretania,* one of the Cunard Line steamships that ferried passengers on pleasure trips in the first- and second-class cabins and anxious but hopeful immigrants in third class. The Czyz and Pulik families took their place in the third-class quarters. It was crowded and unpleasant, with only rudimentary bunks for sleeping stacked one on top of the other. Malka somehow ended up on the top bed, and during a particularly rough night at sea she was hurled to the floor, one of many miserable moments during the bumpy six-day crossing.

The *Mauretania* was a floating Tower of Babel with a mixture of languages being spoken among the hundreds on board. Communication was difficult, prompting more than one fearful moment. Halfway through the voyage a loud whistle pierced the air in the middle of the night. Hearing the shrill noise, Cyrla feared the worst, sure that the boat was sinking and that she and her children would drown. She roused them out of bed and told them to put on all of their clothing. *"Schlim! schlim!"* "Help! help!" in Yiddish, someone yelled in the packed cabin. There was great relief when the frightened passengers learned that it was only a fire drill.

In the last moments of the journey Cyrla started to worry about Lejzor's leg. She knew that America wanted only healthy, strong immigrants, so she did the only thing she could think of. She told Lejzor to take off the brace, and she wrapped it in a comforter in the family's belongings, hoping none of the immigration officials would find it. Everything went smoothly. The family passed through the entry rituals without problem. There must have been something curative about coming to America, because Lejzor tossed away the brace at the first opportunity and never needed it again.

The two families stayed just one night in New York before taking the train to Chicago and their husbands and fathers. Cyrla and the children already had their American names picked out: Cyrla, Malka, Lejzor, and Fiszel Czyz became Celia, Mae, Leonard, and Philip Chess.

The arrival at Chicago's bustling railroad station was an especially significant moment for little Philip. *"Des es di tata"*—"This is your father," his mother told him in Yiddish, when the smiling, sturdy man swooped him up off the ground with his large, strong hands.

⋙

By the time he sent for his family late in the summer of 1928, Joe Chess had formed a partnership with Max Zisook and Gershon Weinstein and put up a building at 1425 South Karlov. It was divided into three- and four-room apartments, and one of them was to be the family's new home. It was in the heart of Lawndale, and this new haven for the growing community of Chicago Jews represented a significant step up, not only from the shtetls they had left with so much hope but also from the rudimentary settlements around Maxwell Street. In Lawndale there were no stifling tenements without plumbing, no peddlers with pushcarts. Instead there were substantial brick and stone "two-flats" or larger apartment buildings, some three stories, like the one Joe Chess had built. The area was full of children, and the several public schools had student populations that were 90 percent Jewish.

There were seventy synogogues spread out among the community, and Celia was comforted by the knowledge that Anshe Motele was just a few blocks away. It would offer her the chance to be in the New World but maintain a connection to the old. On top of that there would be a Yiddish newspaper to read so she could understand the world through a language she would never give up. For her children the transition would be different. They were starting a new life in the broadest sense—relatively new to the world at large and absolutely new to Chicago. Their main goal was to adapt, and the weeks and months ahead would be filled with trying moments, some of them amusing in the later retelling, once the embarrassment of an immigrant's gaffe was forgotten.

Chicago was nothing like Motele. Not only was Karlov Street paved, but instead of one room with no running water, there were four rooms in the apartment including a bathroom and a kitchen. And there was a boiler in the building to provide warmth for the winter. No one would have to sleep on top of the oven. By modern standards the family was crowded in the apartment, but compared to Motele, if this wasn't paradise, it was surely a step in the right direction. The boys had a couch to sleep on in the main room, Mae had an "in-a-door" bed that pulled out from the wall at nighttime, and Joe and Celia had the bedroom to themselves. Not only was there a new house to live in but new things to eat as well. The children had never before seen a banana or an orange.

Getting settled in school was one of the more difficult adjustments, even though Mae, Leonard, and Phil were surrounded by classmates with similar backgrounds. It was particularly hard for Mae, who was already thirteen but spoke no English. Concerned that she not fall behind, the teachers at Bryant Elementary put her in a class with much younger children, to her great embarrassment. She hated to be trotted out with girls seven and eight years younger than she for the hourly bathroom trips, so she found a way to avoid these moments by hiding in the coat closet. After a few months one of her teachers, sensing Mae's discomfort, took a chance and moved her into a class with boys and girls her own age. She made the transition successfully.

Leonard, who was eleven, and Phil, who was seven, were learning English—though still speaking Yiddish at home—and trying hard to understand the customs in their new country. In his first winter in Chicago, Phil had been taken with one of the little girls in his class and wanted to give her a valentine. But his ideas were ahead of his vocabulary, and when he stopped at a nearby hot dog stand that also sold school supplies, he ended up with a hot dog instead of a greeting card.

~~

As it did for most Americans, the Great Depression forced a change in the Chess family's lives. Carpentry work dried up. Money was tight, so much so that at his brother-in-law Morris's suggestion Joe took the candelabras that had come from Motele and had been in the Pulik family for decades and melted them down. Morris told him they were worth more as scrap metal than as a sentimental house ornament. Celia resigned herself to buying day-old bread, and she often told the children she was grateful they had that.

The children knew they would have to pitch in and help. In Mae's case, it required dropping out of school before she graduated to help take care of her mother, who had taken sick again. Leonard got a paper route, and soon bragged that he was one of the most successful paperboys around. He proudly showed off his growing list of customers, and it was only later that friends and family discovered he had made up some of the names and tossed these fictitious customers' papers under a porch. He wanted to beat the competition. Those who worked for Leonard in later years would, if they knew this story, ascribe much darker purposes to Leonard's deceit than the wish of a young boy to be the best.

When he was a little older, Leonard got a job delivering milk for the Capitol Dairy Company, which was run by a distant cousin. He would get up early in the morning, hitch a horse to a wagon, and bring the milk to customers. Phil occasionally helped out on weekends.

Leonard's leg didn't bother him anymore. He was able to participate in school sports at Crane Technical High School, a boys' school that served the whole west side of the city. But it was Phil who was the athlete in the family and excelled in sports at his school, Marshall High, which was known as "the Jewish school." His football exploits were captured in a four-column picture in the *Chicago Herald American* one November Sunday, showing him at halfback blasting through the line. It was a losing effort, though. Marshall lost 13–6 to rival Steinmetz.

A little heftier than his brother, Phil discovered that he was also a pretty good boxer, and when he learned that he could make three dollars fighting in matches at nearby Franklin Park, he decided this was a good way to earn a little money to help the family. He didn't tell his parents, knowing that his mother would never stand for it.

His first two bouts were easy, but in the third, the coach running the competition matched him against a bigger boy. The results were predictable, and when Phil returned home bloodied and bruised, he admitted to his parents that his opponent "beat the hell out of me." His mother was livid that someone would put her son in harm's way. One can only imagine the coach's reaction when he saw the now ample Celia Chess storming toward him, baseball bat in hand, chastising him in Yiddish for letting her son get hurt.

As a teenager Leonard worked as a stock boy at Berger's Shoes, a well-known store a few blocks east of South Karlov. After he graduated from high school, he worked full-time as a shoe salesman. Though he was more reserved than some of his friends, who seemed the more natural salesmen, Leonard nonetheless did very well.

A broken heart motivated Leonard to do even better, in the view of family and friends. He had hoped to marry Shirley Adams, a young woman he had been seeing for some time. But her parents didn't approve. They didn't think an immigrant shoe salesman, son of a struggling carpenter and his wife, was good enough for their daughter. So she broke off their relationship. Leonard vowed that someday he would show Shirley and her parents how wrong they had been.

There was a touch of irony in Leonard's disappointment over Shirley Adams. Joe Chess had used the same argument in trying to dissuade Mae from marrying the young man she was seeing, Harry Silverbrand. Joe wanted her to find somebody rich, a doctor or a lawyer, he instructed, and he was mad enough when Harry came to see Mae that more than once he chased him out of the house and down the alley. Mae stood her ground, however, and eventually married him.

While Leonard's distress over losing Shirley Adams may have inspired him, he also had a good example of drive and determination in his own home. Joe Chess always kept an eye out for the next opportunity, and when there was no more carpentry work by the mid-1930s, Joe decided that he and Morris should become junk dealers. They started out by renting a cart and a horse for three dollars a day and trolling for salvage. "Ragsoline"—a contraction of "rags and iron," the staples of the business—would ring out in the alleyways throughout the city as the junk men announced they were available and ready for offerings.

In 1935 the brothers-in-law had their own building and scrap yard— the Wabash Junk Shop, at 2971 South State—and plenty of competition. The city Yellow Pages for that year showed eighty-nine listings for junk dealers, so to make any kind of living required perseverance and long hours.

Old bottles were also of value, and on occasion, the bottle collection proved, if not lucrative, at least interesting. One of Joe Chess's customers was a man at the Michigan Hotel, which was the headquarters of what was left of the Al Capone organization. The bottles, as Phil understood it—he and Leonard often helped out at the shop—were used for bootleg liquor the organization was still manufacturing.

In 1940 a tragedy struck the extended family that changed everything. Morris Pulik was hit by a car and killed. Not only was it a heartbreaking loss for his wife and children, but it also meant that Joe Chess was without a business partner. If the Wabash Junk Shop was going to continue, then Leonard would have to join his father. Phil was not available. He had parlayed his athletic skills into a football scholarship at Bowling Green University in Kentucky and was away at school.

Leonard married Revetta Sloan in June of 1941. He had met her through his friends Marty Witzel and Millie Pincus, who had often gone out with Leonard and Shirley Adams. They had consoled him when that relationship ended, and Millie believed she helped cement this new romance because she and Revetta got along so well together. The four had become such good friends that they stood up at each other's weddings, which were just a few weeks apart.

After their wedding Leonard and Revetta moved south and east to Drexel Boulevard, where they rented a third-floor walkup apartment. It was primarily a white neighborhood with a sizable Jewish population that bordered on an expanding black neighborhood. The informal dividing line was one block west, Cottage Grove, with whites living to the east, blacks to the west. Leonard and Revetta's first child arrived March 13, 1942, one day after Leonard's twenty-fifth birthday. He was named Marshall, in memory of Morris Pulik.

Joe Chess had renamed the junk shop Chess and Sons in anticipation of Phil's return. It didn't take long. After three semesters at Bowling Green, he called it quits and came back to Chicago to join his father and brother. He told friends his father needed him. Once Phil returned, he displayed his own entrepreneurial bent, realizing there was money to be made from scrap cardboard. A military installation was located near the junkyard, and every week there would be a pile of used cardboard cartons that had held various kinds of bottles. Phil made a deal with the officer in charge to come pick up the cardboard every week, break it down, bundle up the material, and resell it as scrap.

By coincidence the junkyard was across the street from a small black church. Phil thought of the congregation fondly as "the hand clappers," and he and Leonard loved listening to the vibrant music that came out of the building "when they would get in a groove," he recalled later. The sound stayed with them, although neither brother realized then what a portent that church music was.

Musical accompaniment aside, Leonard was restless and unhappy as a junk dealer and growing tired of arguments with his father over how to run the business. This was neither where nor how he wanted to make his mark. What's more, he wanted to work for himself. When the opportunity arose to run a liquor store in the middle of the black community, at 5060 South State Street, Leonard decided to take it. He must have understood that the store was a good risk: liquor and music together, a place to come, to visit, and buy.

Cut-Rate Liquor was a sizable space that like many others in the neighborhood had a bar and a "soundie" machine—kind of like a jukebox that played music with pictures. Though friends like the Witzels thought Leonard was crazy and worried for his safety, he was not deterred. By choice he had already left the homogenous white enclave of Lawndale, both physically, when he and Revetta moved to Drexel Boulevard, and psychologically, when he joined his father in the junk business.

Phil helped out at State Street when he wasn't helping his father at the junkyard, but late in 1943 he was drafted into the Army. He remained in the service until the middle of 1946. He married his fiancée, Sheva Jonesi, while in basic training in Virginia, and then was shipped to the Aleutian Islands.

Why Leonard decided to leave Cut-Rate Liquor is conjecture. Those who could provide the best explanations are dead—Leonard, his father, and his wife. Phil was in the Aleutians and not keeping tabs on his brother's activities. Marshall was three years old then, and his father didn't speak later on about those days of struggle. Leonard, Marshall explained, was a man of the present who rarely even looked too far into the future, much less into the distant past.

Leonard most likely moved because he wanted to make more money. He found a spot on Forty-seventh Street, which was considered the crossroads of the "black downtown." The center of commercial and social activity was the intersection of Forty-seventh and South Parkway. At the corner was the Savoy Ballroom and the Regal Theater, and nearby was a major department store, residences, and small shops. Leonard's business was five blocks east of Forty-seventh and South Parkway and called simply 708 Liquor Store. He had transferred his liquor license from 5060 South State to this new location. The Forty-seventh Street business had a jukebox and probably some informal jams on weekends, so 708 was even more like a tavern than Cut-Rate Liquor had been. The clientele was a bit more prosperous than the customers who had patronized the State Street store, and given the location, more numerous. There was also plenty of competition. Forty-seventh east of South Parkway had a proliferation of small clubs and restaurants and at least one larger liquor chain, United Liquor stores, which had two outlets on the street, one directly across from 708.

Cook County, Illinois, liquor license information, old Chicago phone books, and newspaper ads in the *Chicago Defender* suggest that Leonard ran the 708 Liquor Store for about a year. One of the myths of the Chess story is that Leonard operated the "708 Club," which became a well-known blues spot. He did not. The 708 Club grew out of the 708 Liquor Store, but it did not evolve into a blues club until after Leonard had left the enterprise.

In 1946 Leonard moved on to the Congress Buffet, a little eatery at 3905 South Cottage Grove, a street that had become a magnet for black Chicagoans looking for spirited nightlife. Music, prostitution, drugs—all were easily available. He renamed the spot the Macomba Lounge and revamped the interior to include a bar and some booths. The club was up and running for a few months by the time Phil was discharged from the Army. Joe Chess had closed the junkyard and was now concentrating on real estate ventures. When Phil came back to Chicago, he went straight to the Macomba to work with Leonard.

In 1973 Mike Rowe wrote in *Chicago Breakdown* (later reprinted as *Chicago Blues*) that the Chess brothers "worked their way into the liquor business and by the '40s owned a small string of bars in [Al] Capone's territory on the black South Side." This description has been repeated and embellished over and over again, suggesting that the brothers were more successful and had more holdings than they actually did. Robert Palmer's well-regarded 1981 *Deep Blues*, for example, had the brothers owning "several bars and clubs."

Actually, Leonard operated three discrete entities between 1942 and 1950, none of them simultaneously: Cut-Rate Liquor, 708 Liquor Store, and then the Macomba Lounge. While they apparently didn't lose money, the Chess brothers were far from being wealthy men, and this period was a time of continuing hardship. "Whatever we did, we were partners," Phil often said. While that was accurate, it was Leonard who made the first moves and the major decisions and Phil who was his loyal lieutenant. It was true in 1949, and it would be true twenty years later at the height of the company's success. There was nothing formal and nothing in writing between the men, just an unspoken understanding. It was automatic that Phil would come to the Macomba when he got out of the Army, and the liquor license for the place, which was secured on February 16, 1946, was actually in his name. It cost twenty-five dollars. Leonard also had a small financial interest for a year or so in a little South Side deli run by his brothers-in-law.

It is not clear how Leonard knew the Congress Buffet was available and why he called it the Macomba, nor are there records to show how much he paid for it and from whom he bought it. What is clear is that the Macomba changed the brothers' lives.

◢◣

Cottage Grove Avenue is a north–south corridor that begins at Thirty-third Street and runs some ten miles almost to the edge of the city limits. The area around the Macomba hadn't always been a center of black nightlife, but it was one of the boundaries of the city's "black belt" that grew up with the migration of roughly 60,000 southern blacks to the city immediately after World War I. The black belt ran west of Cottage Grove beyond State Street to the railroad tracks, starting at Thirty-first Street and going south to Sixty-third. As more and more blacks streamed into Chicago—another 125,000 by 1930—to take advantage of work opportunities at the stockyards, the railyards and packinghouses, they needed to find places to live. When they encroached on previously all-white territory—the Irish to the west, Jews to the east near Lake Michigan—they were hardly given a neighborly welcome. One typical newspaper headline captured the alarmist atmosphere: "HALF A MILLION DARKIES FROM DIXIE SWARM TO THE NORTH TO BETTER THEMSELVES."

Whites made anxious by aggressive real estate agents sold their property for whatever they could get, and then the agents doubled the rents for the incoming blacks. Neighborhoods began to change from all-white to a mix of both and finally to all-black. These changes were not always peaceful; when the first blacks moved into an area they could expect harassment and sometimes violence, most often in the form of a firebomb tossed at their house. When a black Baptist congregation bought a synogogue on Michigan Avenue, another north–south corridor, the building was bombed repeatedly.

A full-scale riot had broken out in July of 1919, when a black boy swam across the imaginary color line at the Twenty-ninth Street beach. He was attacked by a group of white boys and drowned in the ensuing melee. His death set off six days of rioting that left twenty-three blacks and fifteen whites dead. Hundreds more were injured and property was destroyed during pitched battles between gangs of angry young white men and black residents. The riot ended only after the state militia was called in to take over from the ineffective local police.

Joseph Pulik was lucky that his store was not damaged, but his young son, Harry, just five at the time, never forgot the turmoil and the memory of being shooed off the street by soldiers sent to restore order.

The riot understandably shook the city. It also served to reinforce the reality for whites of a large and permanent black presence. The years right after, in fact, proved to be good ones for many black Chicagoans. A black professional and middle class evolved, and successful families were able to move into elegant stone houses and apartment buildings on fashionable streets.

The social center of the black belt by the late 1920s was on State Street, between Thirty-first and Thirty-fifth streets. The *Chicago Defender* was there along with a major life insurance company, the YMCA and YWCA, and a large funeral home. But a decision by a group of white New York businessmen determined to get an entertainment foothold in Chicago changed all of that when they decided to build the Savoy Ballroom some twelve blocks south, at South Parkway and Forty-seventh Street. A local white entrepreneur had already put up a department store on Forty-seventh Street just east of the intersection, and within months of the Savoy's opening, the ornate Regal Theater opened next door. In addition Sears Roebuck magnate Julius Rosenwald, a Jewish philanthropist, was putting up new apartments nearby for incoming black residents. A good many were familiar with his company, having bought clothes and furniture and their first guitars from the Sears Roebuck catalogue—treasured reading among rural blacks, along with the Montgomery Ward catalogue and the *Defender.*

While the Savoy and the Regal were entertainment centers built for black Chicagoans, they were also a reminder of how their social life was circumscribed by the white power structure and northern-style segregation. Clubs in white areas of the city were simply off limits—except for the black entertainers who performed for white audiences. Up until World War II, white-owned clubs in the heart of the black community also either were closed to blacks or had informal codes that relegated blacks, no matter how prosperous, to the cheap seats. The White City Ballroom and Casino was right next to a black neighborhood, but blacks were barred from entering. The same was true of the Pershing Ballroom, which was just across an alley from another black neighborhood. And the Coconut Grove ballroom, a half block north of the Pershing, kept blacks out even though street traffic in front of the club was 95 percent black. The famous Club DeLisa, which featured lively floor shows backed by local bands, operated a little differently. Black customers were allowed in but often were kept away from the best tables. Those nearest the stage were usually white patrons. The Club DeLisa's owner insisted that it was neither he nor his father, who built the place, who instituted the policy but rather their black bouncers who seated people according to the size of their tips. Whites tipped better than blacks, they claimed, so they got the best tables.

The ambiance in the 3900 block of South Cottage Grove, where the Macomba would be, was not as upscale as South Parkway with the Savoy and the Regal. Throughout the thirties, these blocks, still mostly white and still a racial boundary line, were filled with small retail shops—grocery stores, a shoe shop, a Walgreens. The racial dynamics on this part of the avenue began to change dramatically around 1941–42, when a hotel that had been a house of prostitution frequented by white men was sold and turned into a hotel for blacks. It was renamed the DuSable, for the man reputed to be the first black Chicagoan—Jean Baptiste Pointe du Sable, a trader from Santo Domingo who settled near the mouth of the Chicago River around 1790.

The hotel was an instant success, providing clean, decent accommodations for blacks, including the black performers who could not stay near the clubs or at the hotels they played at in the white downtown. Legendary piano man Fats Waller had a suite reserved for him, with a keyboard, whenever he came to town. Louis Armstrong and his wife were also frequent guests. The DuSable owners, who were white, decided to put a lounge in the basement, and that, too, was an immediate hit. An ad in the national edition of the *Defender* proclaimed the hotel "Chicago's finest," noting its "modern" rooms with "shower and tub baths" and its "world famous Cocktail Lounge, Bar & Dining Room." The fact that noted musicians and so many of their sidemen stayed there contributed to the energy around the place, prompting the *Defender* to marvel in one article that "there is always something going on there."

The hotel's success encouraged other entrepreneurs to open night spots in the neighborhood, and by the mid-forties the blocks between 3800 and 4000 South Cottage Grove and the adjacent blocks to the west were hopping, a magnet for all kinds of activity, legal and otherwise. The black belt now had a special moniker, "Bronzeville," traced to an editor at the *Chicago Bee*, one of the city's black-owned newspapers. At his suggestion the *Bee* sponsored a contest in 1930 to elect a "Mayor of Bronzeville." The post was symbolic, but the contest and the name stuck.

On any given night in Bronzeville one could stop in at the Congo Club for drinks, dancing, and the speciality of the house, fried chicken. Or drop in at Lillian's Chicken Shack, which also offered fried shrimp and oysters in season. Smitty's DeLuxe tavern claimed "the best people on both sides of the bar" with the added inducement of no cover charge and no drink minimum. Munchy Lewis's 113 Club, a few blocks east on Forty-seventh from Leonard's old place, promised "you are bound to meet someone you know here."

What helped to fuel all of this activity was another surge in black migration from the South to Chicago. Between 1940 and 1950 the city's black population increased 77 percent, from 278,000 to 492,000. A great number of the migrants were coming from Mississippi, eager to leave their difficult and dismal lives as sharecroppers on the cotton plantations of the Delta for better-paying work and a freer life, they hoped, in the "wide open" city. Many were drawn not only by the lure of new opportunity but by the plain fact that their jobs had disappeared with the advent of mechanical cotton pickers. They were pushed to leave their homes as much as they were pulled by Chicago's promise. The Illinois Central railroad became their *Mauretania*, the station at Twelfth Street and Michigan Avenue the Ellis Island for these new migrants. So many had come from the same towns in Mississippi that, like the Motelers who founded their own synogogue on the west side, these transplanted Mississippians formed their own community networks in the city to help former neighbors find jobs and housing.

The adjustment was often difficult, particularly when the reality of the move set in. Chicago was no paradise. One of the biggest challenges was finding housing in a city that by now was as rigidly segregated in its neighborhoods as any southern town. A shortage of housing citywide was particularly acute in Bronzeville. The number of suitable dwelling units failed to keep pace with the growing population. The result was a sharp increase in overcrowding. By contrast the white population actually decreased in the 1940s, while the number of whites moving into new housing actually increased by nearly 10 percent. Making the situation even more difficult in Bronzeville was the ability of real estate agents to inflate rents because of the high demand for housing. What evolved were essentially two markets, one for whites and one for blacks, with rents in the black neighborhoods running from 15 to 50 percent higher than in white areas for similar accommodations.

These difficulties served to underscore a significant difference between the white immigrant and the black migrant. Though one was a foreigner, the other an American, the fact of skin color, with the attendant judgments about culture, class, and heritage, was paramount. Jewish immigrants had flocked to their own ghettos and clung to the ways of the old country. Many felt the sting of discrimination and the wounds of ostracism. But they were not burdened by the legacy of slavery and its successor, Jim Crow, which had so effectively kept blacks "in their place." And they could, if they chose, more easily assimilate over time. It was always possible for Jews to lose their accents and change their names to fit in with the gentiles. Not so with Chicago's new black residents.

In the midst of their often trying adjustment to the city, it was essential for these southern migrants to hang on to the hopes and dreams that fueled the journey north. The difficult days could be eased by the camaraderie of others and by the knowledge that the folkways that had sustained them for so long in Mississippi need not be abandoned at the train station. A central element was the music, and that music was the blues. In the seminal *Chicago Breakdown,* Mike Rowe put it this way: "The two main features of black life in the United States were segregation and migration: the former providing the impetus for the latter. Musically, while segregation created the blues, migration spread the message."

That message was making its way through Bronzeville in cramped apartments and the small storefront clubs and taverns like 708 East Forty-seventh that sprang up to cater to the new population and provide venues for the musicians. Transplanted into a new setting, they were transforming the blues from acoustic to electric and adding drums to compete with the sounds of the city. The travails of daily living left no shortage of subject matter. There were so many musicians and so many who were good that not everyone could play in these neighborhood bars. One had to have something of a reputation or an informal sponsor to lend a helping hand. Even then playing in clubs was hardly easy work. The pay, if any, was minimal, and the crowd could be ornery. It was not unheard of for an errant beer bottle to be tossed toward the bandstand during one fracas or another. Fights were common.

For those who were not lucky enough to land a club date, there was the street. The place to find the largest audience was west of the black belt on Maxwell Street. The area had remained a street bazaar—a 1912 city ordinance officially proclaimed it the Maxwell Street Market—and it was still referred to by many blacks as "Jew town" well after most of the Jews had left. The street became, in Rowe's words, the "meeting place for all the newly arrived singers and the centre of amateur blues activity in Chicago."

Working on South State and then on Forty-seventh Street, Leonard was both eyewitness to and participant in the burgeoning black community. If he didn't fully understand the music he was hearing every day—not just the blues but plenty of swing, too—and if he didn't appreciate the fine points of migration patterns, he did understand a few important things. People loved music, and they would spend money for it. That would bode well for the Macomba.

three

THE MACOMBA
LOUNGE

From the outside the Macomba Lounge was nondescript. Its most distinctive feature was a long, vertical sign probably ten feet high that spelled out *Macomba* in bright lights. *Lounge* ran horizontally at the bottom in much smaller letters. The club was on a block and in a neighborhood with businesses owned almost exclusively by whites but now frequented largely by blacks.

Almost directly across from the Macomba was Walgreens Drug Store. Next door was Powers lunchroom, a favorite in the 1930s of Irish streetcar operators who stopped in after parking their streetcars in a barn one block north on Cottage Grove; blacks were not welcome. Just down from Powers was Neisner Brothers, a well-known five-and-dime store with branches all over the city.

Leonard, Revetta, Marshall, and now his younger sisters, Elaine and Susie, still lived a few blocks away at 4414 Drexel Boulevard, a stately street lined with substantial red brick apartment buildings and a median wide enough for a small park. As a toddler Marshall used to ride there on the back of the family dog, an Irish setter named Donny who would periodically scoop up dead pigeons and bring them to the doorstep. The apartment was just a few minutes by car from the lounge. Phil and Sheva weren't too much farther away, in an apartment at 4556 Greenwood Avenue, a building run by Joe Chess.

Given the status and proximity of Drexel Boulevard, many establishments incorporated the name into their businesses. A few doors down from the Macomba was the Drexel Furniture Mart and across the street and

THE MACOMBA LOUNGE | 23

down a half-block was the Drexel National Bank and Drexel Radio Services. Just north of the lounge was the Drexel Wine and Liquor Company.

The workaday world suggested by the surrounding businesses gave way in the nighttime to much livelier activity. The DuSable was still going strong, though by the late forties it had lost some of its luster. But the nearby Hotel Morocco had installed a new cocktail lounge, and the owners made sure its existence was known by taking out large weekly ads in the *Defender.* The Strode Hotel, barely a block away, had also put in a lounge, advertising it as "the coziest spot on the Lake Front." Spread out between the hotel lounges was one tavern after another. The streets were full of people, the atmosphere charged with an expectant buzz. Though he was talking about Brooklyn, prolific songwriter Doc Pomus could have been describing Cottage Grove when he wrote: "Everybody was out every night having a good time. It was a world of pimps, hookers, maids, chauffeurs, good-time whites, factory workers, white collar workers, musicians, entertainers, bartenders, waiters—everybody hanging out together . . . when a little money went a long way and there was no tomorrow." On Cottage Grove it was indeed difficult to separate today from tomorrow. The lights from tavern signs sparkled all night, a miniature Las Vegas off the shore of Lake Michigan. And prostitution was so common that Phil candidly described the neighborhood as home to "pimps and whores." Some nights so many women stationed themselves around the corner at Jimmy's Palm Garden that men referred to it as the "supermarket." Even the upscale DuSable was not immune from the trade, but the manager insisted that any business transaction take place in the hotel's popular basement lounge. He liked to joke that "nothing illegal went on above the second floor."

Cut-Rate Liquor and the store at 708 East Forty-seventh Street had been liquor stores selling packaged goods and offering some jukebox music and informal jams on the side. The Macomba, however, was a lounge, a place for entertainment, rebuilt by Leonard to suit this purpose. The entrance was on the left, and the first thing a patron saw was the long bar immediately on the right with a few stools at the front end. The place was so narrow that there was barely enough room for two or three people to walk in the path between the bar and the opposite wall. About halfway back the bar curved out like a horseshoe; a small bandstand, which was raised a few feet off the floor, was in this alcove. The bartenders handled their business on either side of the stage. A few tables were toward the back across from the bar; booths were added later. Bathrooms were near the end of the bar, and in the back Bob and Mary McNutt, a black couple, ran a barbecue pit serving "Bob's Ribs" out of the small kitchen. A second-floor apartment was rented to the janitor. Beer and other supplies were kept in the basement.

Whenever a place changed management, curiosity about the new owners attracted the public, so the brothers figured they would do all right financially in the short run. The unknown was whether patrons would come back after the novelty of a new place wore off. On the one hand they had a good location, Leonard's previous experience of running two South Side businesses and, perhaps as important, a willingness to put in the long hours required to keep a place running smoothly. The brothers had an informal pact: one of them would always be there when the Macomba was open. On the other hand, there was plenty of competition. While the other bars and lounges helped bring people to the area, there was no guarantee that barhoppers would like the feel of the Macomba. In Leonard's mind the key factor would be the music.

Chicago was full of good music and good musicians, not just the blues players found on the street corners of "Jewtown," but men and a few women who could play—or sing—jazz and swing and any other form of popular music. Many of these black Chicagoans had gotten their training at Wendell Phillips High School and many of the men had had their budding careers interrupted by World War II. By the end of 1946 most were back, anxious to pick up where they had left off, and willing to play in town or on the road if the job demanded.

The Macomba was hardly the only place that stayed open late and provided music, but from the beginning Leonard apparently had an instinct for the right musical mix. He hired musicians who were liked and respected by their peers, and the lounge became a magnet for other musicians. It developed a reputation as one of the best after-hours places on the South Side. Musicians would finish their dates at other clubs and then come over to the Macomba for drinks and a chance to jam. One of the pivotal hires was tenor saxophonist Tom Archia, a gregarious, talented player always looking for a good time. By the end of 1946 Archia was a mainstay in the club, and over the next few years he evolved into the leader of a loosely structured house band Leonard had put together. The makeup of the band was based more on the instruments for jazz—not the blues that would make the Chess name famous—rather than the particular individuals. There was always a horn player, sometimes two, piano, and drums. By 1947, a bass player would almost always be part of the group. Among the advantages to this setup was the draw for musicians. If no one lineup was locked in, anyone who came by had a chance to play. Often featured with Archia in these early Macomba days were Cozy Eggleston, another sax player, with Wendell Owens on piano and an array of drummers.

The fare was pretty much the standards of the time—Lester Young's "D.B. Blues," "Up & At 'Em," "Lover Come Back to Me," Lionel Hampton's "Flyin' Home," and Charlie Parker's "Billie's Bounce" and "Now's the Time." The musicians were more interested in urban bebop, reflecting both their training and city life, than the roots music of country blues or the gospel they'd heard in church. On most songs the sax man could take off, and every night the tunes would sound a little different. As the evening wore on, the sets got more improvisational and the songs longer. By midnight the place was usually packed, the crowd all the more responsive. Slow-turning ceiling fans aside, the lounge was sweltering during the summer—a steamy atmosphere no one seemed to mind. And in the winter all that body heat was a godsend, natural insulation against the harsh Chicago weather.

By the fall of 1947 Archia was part of one popular grouping that was regularly featured at the lounge: Robert "Hendu" Henderson on drums, Lowell Pointer on bass, and Bill Searcy on piano. Other groups would occasionally play in place of Archia and his bandmates. One that came to be known as "the off-night" group featured tenor sax player Claude McLin, with LeRoy Jackson on bass, Clarence "Sleepy" Anderson on piano, and Wesley Landers on drums. Like Archia, some of these musicians would later turn up on Chess recordings.

Though these men were the "regulars," they were often spelled for a portion of the night by other musicians who stopped by for the music and the ambiance. "People just liked to come in," remembered Charles "Truck" Parham, one of Chicago's talented bass players. By the mid-forties he had already been on the road with Fletcher Henderson and Earl "Fatha" Hines. Although work kept him out of town a good part of every month, whenever he came back to Chicago, he went to the Macomba "to see if any more of the cats were still livin' and still jammin'."

Silas "Buddy" Butler, a drummer, had been discharged from the army in 1946, and eventually he would be a staple in Roosevelt Sykes's blues band. He went to the Macomba every chance he could—"it was that jazz combo in there," he explained years later—and almost without fail, whoever was playing drums that night would ask if he wanted to play. He never said no. It was easy to sit in because the songs and styles were so familiar. "You had to know all those tunes," he said. Not everyone could play, however. A young Charles Walton, who had just gotten out of the service in 1946, was allowed to sit in not long after his return to Chicago, but he was asked to leave the bandstand because, as he recalled later, "I played so bad." He was embarrassed because his teacher, Oliver Coleman, was a prominent drummer who occasionally played the club.

Guest musicians could be a welcome relief for the house band. The schedule—though that may be too formal a word—generally called for the band to play six days a week: from 10:00 on Saturday evenings until 4:00 A.M. on Sundays and then 10:00 P.M. to 5:00 A.M. Tuesdays through Saturdays. Though 4:00 A.M. was the mandated closing time, the Macomba never really shut down. Instead either Phil or Leonard closed the blinds, and the music went on.

On Monday, the band's day off, there was still music from the "off night" band and from other musicians who came in for informal jams and played for drinks.

Years later Vernel Fournier, who went on to play the drums with jazz star Ahmad Jamal, asserted that "the Macomba was the most famous jazz house in Chicago." If that was a bit of hyperbole, Fournier was correct about its popularity. The relaxed atmosphere made it appealing. "Everybody who came in there knew each other," Eggleston recalled. "Leonard made everybody feel at home."

Though Walton wasn't much for drinking or carousing, he loved to go to Cottage Grove just to take in the scene. Standing room in front of the Macomba was a prime spot. He could hear the music and watch the crowd but stay clear of the smoke and jostling. He tried to absorb everything as people went in and out. Unobtrusive among the crowd of patrons, Walton often stood near Leonard and Phil when they came outside to talk things over, and more often than not it was about how to handle the drug dealers and the prostitutes they knew were looking for business inside. When they wanted to be sure that no one could follow their conversation, the brothers spoke to each other in Yiddish.

One false legend that grew up around the Macomba was that such major entertainers as Ella Fitzgerald, Louis Armstrong, Billy Eckstine, and Dinah Washington were booked to play there. The Macomba was a small neighborhood bar with a big local reputation. Well-known artists may have stopped by now and then, though accounts vary. Some stars came for an after-hours drink; a few may have stepped up on the tiny bandstand to play or sing. But none was hired to perform there. Phil remembered that Fitzgerald, who performed regularly at the Regal Theater a mile or so away, did drop in once or twice. Washington, who grew up on the South Side, also stopped by on occasion. So did drummer Max Roach. Other popular Chicago musicians actually performed there from time to time, including the piano player Albert Ammons, his son, Gene, the tenor saxophonist, and Eddie Chamblee, another tenor sax player.

Leonard rarely advertised the Macomba in the newspaper. He didn't need to. In June of 1947, though, an ad for the club appeared in each of that month's four weekly issues of the *Chicago Bee,* which was on its last legs. The paper would be out of business by the fall, so Leonard probably was enticed by a bargain price. Or perhaps, as Marshall thought years later, his father traded somebody drinks for ad space.

Under the heading "MACOMBA LOUNGE," the ad promised "continuous entertainment" by the Wendell Owens Trio: Tom Archia, sax, Wendell Owens, piano, and Glen Brooks, drums. The "trio," though, apparently was an advertising concept. There was no formal group fronted by Owens. Leonard had hired the individual musicians and packaged them for the *Bee* promotion. Right under a picture of the group was the caption "Jumping all night." Neither Leonard's nor Phil's name appeared on the ad, but it did list Odessa Morrow, a black woman and a "pillar" of the place, musicians said, as the Macomba's manager, and Gene Ross as assistant manager. It was not uncommon for a bar to advertise its bartenders—"mixologists" was the term of art. Some had developed reputations almost as big as a musician's. At the Macomba in the summer of 1947, the mixologists were Harold Johnson, Jutson Mitchell, and Willa Johnson.

Though Ross was given the title of assistant manager, he was really more bouncer and bodyguard and occasional bartender. Nearly six feet six inches tall, he was an imposing individual with a strong, sculpted face. Leonard had known "Big Gene" since his days at 708 East Forty-seventh Street. During a fracas not long after the Macomba opened, Ross helped break up a fight by stepping in front of Leonard and getting stabbed with a knife that was meant for his boss. It took seventy-five stitches to close the wound. Since that time, Leonard had made sure that Ross, who was in and out of jail for various scrapes, always had a job if he needed one. One time Leonard even loaned Ross his prized new car, only to have it impounded when Chicago police stopped Ross and found heroin in the glove compartment.

When Ross worked behind the bar, every now and then he would give the club a helping hand. After Archia finished a set, he liked to take a pint of whiskey for his break. One evening Eggleston noticed Ross writing it down on the tab as "two," double charging the sax player. Eggleston told him about it in the men's room between sets, but Archia just laughed. "When it's like that," he said, "it tastes better."

The only other known publicity for the Macomba was in July 1949, when a picture of Archia, Chamblee, and trumpeter King Kolax and one of their fans appeared in the *Defender*. Referring to Archia's Macomba sessions, the paper said, "His group has held the spotlight for moons."

Leonard always considered the bar business "a rough fuck"—the latter word having become a staple of his vocabulary. One of Leonard's nephews would say years later that "if Leonard didn't call you a motherfucker, it meant he didn't like you." Phil was certainly at home with street talk, but he was more circumspect in his language outside of the business setting. On occasion he was even embarrassed if an expletive slipped out in front of a stranger.

Phil remembered one rough incident at Cut-Rate Liquor with particular clarity. Two men were sitting at the bar when they suddenly got into a fight. Onlookers didn't know what started the fracas, but one of them pulled a knife on the other and cut him, leaving X's all over his body. Phil called the police and an ambulance, but by the time medical help arrived, the two men had stopped fighting and were back at the bar having a drink.

In recalling that incident, Phil shrugged his shoulders as if to say, "Well, these things happen." Leonard felt the same. Their days at the junkyard on South State Street in one of the tougher black neighborhoods were not that far in the past. They were comfortable with the business milieu they had chosen, and they had grown accustomed to their sometimes edgy dealings with blacks who were struggling with the harsh realities of ghetto life.

The brothers took whatever came their way. They didn't make judgments, but they adapted their behavior accordingly. They never underestimated the violence that could erupt when men, women, liquor, and drugs were mixed. "I used to tell my friends when I would go to work that I didn't know if I was coming back or not," Phil said.

There had been one frightening incident at 708 East Forty-seventh, when Joe Chess had gone down to the place on a Sunday morning to open up and let a cleaning crew in. Two men pushed him inside and demanded that he open up the safe to get the previous night's take. Joe told them he didn't know the combination, so they beat him up. The safe turned out to be open, and the men took the money. Some of it was recovered after Leonard called the police, who were able to track the robbers down.

Things could get rough at the Macomba, too. Though Gene Ross might have been the main bouncer, Phil did his share. Sheva learned not to be alarmed when he came home with blood on his T-shirt or a scratch on his arm. One time he leapt over the bar to separate two men who were going at it, and ended up with a hernia. The fights generally stemmed from too much drinking, though not necessarily at the Macomba; there were plenty of other places nearby. "Maybe they'd get drunk at Jimmy's, then come over and tear up your place," Phil once explained, referring to Jimmy's Palm. "Or get drunk at our place and go over there."

Occasionally Phil would have a tense moment with the men who came in and congregated along the wall across from the bar. The brothers didn't like any loitering, and if the men weren't going to buy a drink or sit down, they were asked to leave. Sometimes the request was made less politely than others. And it was always understood. Perhaps because they were foreigners and had had to struggle with English as children, Leonard and Phil listened closely to what they heard. They absorbed street language into their own vocabulary, and Phil had mastered the vernacular so well that one night a patron approached him at the bar to ask, "Is you black or is you white?"

Marshall went to the Macomba just once, when he was five, but it was a memorable visit. It was the night somebody fired a gun during a fight. His father threw him behind the bar like a football and lay on top of him for protection. Fifty years later Marshall could still remember his face pressed against the floor, taking in the pungent smells: a combination of beer, cigarette smoke, and damp wood.

Though the Macomba's clientele was almost exclusively black, whites would come by. The women among them generally fell into two categories, friends or family of the Chess brothers or prostitutes. Alyne Salstone was in the former category, the wife of Milt Salstone, a record distributor whom Leonard had gotten to know. The night they stopped by, they were the only whites in the club besides Leonard and Phil. Mrs. Salstone was advised in no uncertain terms to stand with her back to the bar and face out.

The matter of the police was a dicey one in two respects: getting help when it was needed but avoiding harassment for the illicit activity going on inside and around the club. It was no secret that club owners paid the police to leave them alone, both the cop on the beat and his superior. Whatever was paid depended on who the recipient was. The higher up the chain, the more money was required.

The Macomba was on a part of Cottage Grove Avenue where four different districts converged, and the police were very particular about the boundary lines. Phil was incredulous when he went outside to break up a fight but got no help from policemen who were having a cup of coffee at Powers across the street. He yelled for help. "Not our district" came the reply. Later one of them told Phil he should never have come outside and stood in the middle of the circle of angry men that had formed. "They get around you and one of them will stab you or shoot you," the policeman had explained, "and they tell you, everybody would tell you, 'We don't know anything about it.' "

Then there was the matter of drugs. In a long 1980 interview about the DuSable Hotel neighborhood, the drummer Vernel Fournier said the lounge was the place for "heavy traffic. . . . It was heavy dope. A cat used to just sit on a barstool and he used to make contact. Two pills, a boy and a girl (the boy was horse and the girl was cocaine), you could get a cap of each for a dollar and a quarter . . . Certain cats had certain barstools."

Fournier recalled that some dealers would sit in the club from 8:00 P.M. one night until four the next morning. They might spend "twenty-five or thirty dollars at the bar, but they might make two or three hundred dollars. . . . The police and everybody knew it. It was all sanctioned." Nobody thought Leonard was involved in drug dealing, Fournier added, just that he knew it was going on.

The brothers were certainly aware of the drugs, but it would be bad for business to crack down, not to mention futile. "You throw five guys out, five more come in," Phil said. Sometimes dealers would tape their goods under a barstool or the seat of chair. In case there actually was a raid, the drugs would not be on their person. Either Leonard or Phil checked under the seats every day, and whatever was found was flushed down the toilet. Every now and then the help asked for the goods, looking to make a profit on the street. The brothers refused. Phil's standard reply was that the drugs were going where they belonged, down the drain.

It was not unusual for band members to indulge. One bass player "stayed high all the time and stayed happy," Walton recalled. "There was nothin' but dope in the place."

Dave Young, another sax player who regularly worked in the area, remembered that prostitution was a financial boon to the club. The women would get their customers inside and make them buy a drink before leaving for the business at hand. "So you see," Young said, "if five hundred guys came in there, you knew all they wanted was the contact, 'cause a lot of times he'd paid for the drinks and he was in a hurry to get out. He wouldn't even drink the drink."

The bar business was a cash business, and most nights or early mornings when Leonard was ready to take a break, he would gather up the day's receipts and bring them home. Aware that he could be easy pickings for a robber, he bought a chrome-plated, pearl-handled .44 revolver for protection. He strapped the gun to his waist and made sure that it was visible when he went outside. He always told Marshall that a gun in the pocket would "do you no good."

The gun was a source of fascination to Marshall. He knew his father's routine well. He would come in the house, unstrap the gun, and put it high on top of a cabinet in the front hallway that held the family's good dishes. Marshall and Elaine often scrapped with each other, and one day he managed to climb on top of the cabinet, get the loaded gun and smack his sister in the head. Fortunately the gun did not go off.

Despite the hard work these were still lean times for the families. Marshall remembered one Hanukkah when he was given a secondhand wagon. Right before the holiday, he saw his parents repainting a used one in the bathtub. He had wanted a squirt gun, which many of his pals were getting, and though they only cost a dollar, his mother told him they couldn't afford it. Disappointed but undeterred, Marshall went to a nearby store and stole one. When his parents found out, they were horrified. They made him take the squirt gun back and apologize to the owner.

While Phil and Leonard initially shared much of the responsibility for the Macomba, Phil was the more relaxed of the two. Leonard was the driven one, determined to make sure the place would earn a profit. By this time— he was barely thirty years old—he worked all the time and was a heavy smoker. There were times when Leonard's family only got a glimpse of him, and then he was stretched out on the sofa for a few hours' sleep. Once he dozed off with a cigarette in his mouth and set his hair on fire. Sometimes, to spend time with Marshall, he would forgo sleep altogether, waking his son at dawn after a long night at the lounge so they could go fishing on the rocks at Lake Michigan, just a mile away.

The pattern would repeat itself. When the family shared a vacation with the Witzels at a rented lakeside cottage a few hours out of the city, Leonard often showed up on the last day, and then he was so tired he used the time to catch up on sleep.

Sheva looked forward to election days because that meant the bar would be closed and Phil would have time for the family. "We were never able to go out, except on rare occasions, if there was a wedding to attend or if somebody had a bar mitzvah. I had to wait for those times," she remembered, "otherwise he was busy all the time."

Though the Macomba was a consuming enterprise, the brothers had guessed right about one thing: music would keep them in business.

four

IMMIGRANT TO ARISTOCRAT

Evelyn Aron had the good taste, good manners, and relaxed sense of style that comes with old money. Her grandparents had come to Chicago in the 1880s, early members of the city's growing Jewish community. By the 1940s the family was both well established and sophisticated, a far cry from recent immigrants like the Chess brothers. In one of those intersections of a good idea and a sensed opportunity, Evelyn and Leonard would become the most unlikely of business partners.

Evelyn had grown up around music. Her father was a concert pianist, and her mother occasionally sang classical songs on local station WBBM under the name Claire Lewis. She had given her daughter both an appreciation of the arts and the encouragement to chart her own territory. At sixteen Evelyn had her own canary yellow convertible. She loved to drive around town bathed in Shalimar perfume, smoking Kools. By any conventional measure she was attractive—slender, medium height, with striking red hair. Before finishing high school she entered into an impetuous short-lived marriage to Milt Salstone; it was annulled within six months. About a year later Evelyn married a handsome Romanian immigrant fourteen years her senior, Charles Aron, who had a painting business on the South Side. They seemed opposites—he the cautious businessman, she the vivacious risk-taker.

The Arons were part of a group of South Side Jews who liked to gather at each other's homes for poker games. Past relationships seemed not to get in the way of present good times. Milt Salstone, for example, had remarried, too, and he and his wife, Alyne, would see the Arons at some of these gatherings. Evelyn stood out for more than her good looks. No slouch at the poker table, she frequently bested her male competitors. Years later her reputation as a high-rolling gambler prompted Las Vegas casino managers to fly her out to Nevada to play at their tables. Leonard knew the Salstones from the tavern business, and he was invited to these parties a time or two, providing him entrée into a new circle that would soon prove worthwhile.

Though he had not grown up with music, Leonard now appreciated the city's vibrant music scene because of the Macomba. For anyone living in Chicago, it was hard, if not impossible, to miss. Race dictated where you lived and what you did for a living, but music was transcendent. There were no boundaries for what you could listen to and what you liked, though white Chicagoans had many more places they could go than blacks. *Billboard* and *Cash Box* magazines, two mainstays of the music industry, each had a category for "race" music. It was not based exclusively on who the musicians were—black or white—but rather on who they imagined to be the audience. "Race" music was bolder and less refined, more obvious in its sexual themes than anything Dinah Shore or Vic Damone might sing. Some black entertainers would frequently turn up on the "popular"—or white—music charts, though the reverse was almost never true. In March of 1947 songs by Ella Fitzgerald and Count Basie were on one of *Billboard*'s top ten lists along with tunes by Guy Lombardo and Shore. Basie also showed up in the number three slot of the "race records" with "Open the Door, Richard," right behind Louis Jordan in first place with "Ain't Nobody Here But Us Chickens," and competing versions of "Open the Door, Richard" by Dusty Fletcher and Jack McVea, which tied for second. It was not unusual for record companies to have a "popular" music division and one for "race records." Typical was Mercury, which recorded such white stars as Damone in their "hit tune" category, along with Albert Ammons doing "St. Louis Blues" and "Shufflin' the Boogie," and Dinah Washington singing "Mean and Evil Blues."

Leonard and other tavern owners knew that the live music in their clubs was essential to making money. Radio was showing that records by musicians who were so popular in clubs and theaters could be a new source of revenue. People could hear a song they liked, then buy the records and listen in their own homes. Evelyn Aron apparently had the same thought, and turning a hunch into a business plan she found the resources to get started. In the spring of 1947, Evelyn and Charles and another couple—Fred and Mildred Brount—decided to start a record company and formally incorporated as Aristocrat Record Corporation. Art Spiegel, one of Evelyn's high school sweethearts, helped them with the initial financing. There were a few necessary steps that required about $2,000. The most basic element was getting a license from the musicians' union, which spelled out the musicians' pay scales and studio requirements—$41.25 for a three-hour session; twice that for the bandleader. Then there was the studio time, between $25 and $40 an hour, and finally money for the record presser and the printer who made the labels. Distribution could be handled in house simply by putting the records in the car, driving to the various stores and radio stations, and dropping off the product. Money for advertising, while helpful, was considered discretionary.

Billboard announced the formation of Aristocrat as "a new general catalog record label" in its April 26, 1947, issue. The first artist signed was bandleader Sherman Hayes and "a girl singer, Wyoma." The article listed the founders as the Arons and the Brounts. Spiegel, a silent partner, was not listed. "Corporation intends to stick to pop and race records," the magazine said.

The first ad for the company appeared in *Cash Box* on May 5, the second several days later in *Billboard*. These magazines weren't aimed at the retail customer but to the trade, and each was an important outlet for news and promotion. Both kinds of information surfaced in stories and columns devoted to one part of the industry or another—*Cash Box* was geared to the jukebox owners and operators, *Billboard* looked at the industry as a whole. Each weekly published charts of bestselling music and reviewed records calibrated by their own award system. The chart placements and reviews were important barometers of how a label was doing. The eventual changes in both the descriptions of the music surveyed and the names of the columns to cover it would later reflect the ongoing change in the music world.

The first Aristocrat ads in *Billboard* and *Cash Box* were roughly identical quarter-page displays trumpeting "The ARISTOCRAT of Songs!" Underneath was "Sherman Hayes and his orchestra featuring 'Chi-Baba Chi-Baba'—the novelty sensation of '47." (By the summer it would be recorded by ten other artists, including Louis Prima—who had the biggest hit—Perry Como, Peggy Lee, and Lawrence Welk.) On the B side was a vocal by Wyoma, "Say No More." The address for the company was 7508 South Phillips Avenue, Charles Aron's painting shop. The record had been made at Universal Recording Studios, by now one of the prominent recording spots in the city and one the company would use often.

Through the spring and summer four more Aristocrat ads appeared in *Billboard*. The one on July 5, which advertised Hayes's new release, "Get on the Ball Paul," was notable because it listed ten distributors around the country who were carrying the record, in places as diverse as Jackson, Mississippi, Denver, St. Louis, New York, Cleveland, and Milwaukee. It lent a kind of seriousness to the label, suggesting that this two-month-old company was for real. But at the same time it was a sign that this was still a small operation; the big companies—Mercury, Decca, Columbia—didn't have to announce who sold their records. They distributed their own. The September Aristocrat ad listed an additional three distributors. The company also benefited from ads by the music publishing company that owned the rights to "Chi-Baba Chi-Baba," Oxford Music Corporation. Oxford took out its own *Billboard* ads citing all the artists who had performed the song. Tiny Aristocrat was packaged in the ad with some of the majors: Decca, MGM, Capitol, Columbia, and Mercury.

Equally helpful were brief mentions in *Billboard*'s gossip column, "Music—*As Written*," which noted what new artist the little label had "inked"—the magazine's term for signed. Typical was the May 17, 1947, item announcing that "Billy Orr, Negro organist inked to an Aristocrat Record pact," and one the next week saying that "Jackie Cain, promising swing chirp" had been signed.

Leonard had been in the Macomba about a year when Aristocrat was formed and issued its first record. He seemed to be intrigued by the notion of making records even before he opened the lounge. At one of those South Side gatherings when Leonard was still at 708 East Forty-seventh Street, Alyne Salstone remembered him "pumping" her husband for information about the record business. Salstone by then had opened MS Distributing Company. It seemed to Mrs. Salstone that Leonard had more than just a passing interest.

The crowds in the Macomba and the popularity of Tom Archia and some of the other musicians were certainly an indication that a market for their music existed. And the increasing presence of black radio, principally because of disc jockey Al Benson, "the Swingmaster" at WGES, meant that black music could have an even larger audience. Around this time—the spring of 1947—Leonard got to know Sammy Goldberg, who had been a talent scout with some small labels—Savoy and Aladdin among them. He had been in Chicago since the mid-twenties, and he apparently started doing some work for the Arons shortly after the company started recording. He was listed as a co-composer for Jump Jackson's "Not Now Baby," which was recorded in June of 1947 and released a few months later.

During the summer Goldberg went to New Orleans scouting for talent and brought Clarence Samuels, a young blues singer, up to Chicago to record. Closer to home Goldberg had been struck by a young man who was singing around the corner from the Macomba at Jimmy's Palm Garden. His name was Andrew Tibbs. Actually it was Melvyn Andrew Grayson, but because his father was a well-known South Side minister, the Rev. S. A. Grayson, who didn't approve of nightclub singing, Tibbs used his middle name and the maiden name of his grandmother. So did his older brother, Kenneth. Both had started singing as children in their father's church, which gave them the opportunity to sing with Mahalia Jackson and a South Side neighbor, Ruth Jones. Jones eventually changed her name to Dinah Washington, and for a brief time she was married to Tibbs's older brother, Robert. They had a son together.

Tibbs was a tenor. The sweet sound of his voice and his genial personality belied a zest for adventure and a good time. "I didn't say 'no' to nothin'," he used to say. "I just enjoyed myself." Goldberg was interested enough in Tibbs that he brought him over to the Macomba to meet Leonard. It was a good fit, and Tibbs ended up singing at the lounge in between his sets at Jimmy's. Even more important, he proved to be the catalyst for Leonard's entry into the record business.

When he learned that someone else wanted to record Tibbs, Leonard, as Phil remembered it, decided he should make a record himself with this gentle, engaging singer. Why let someone else grab the opportunity? But Leonard knew nothing about the business and needed to find a label. It was Bill Putnam, cofounder of Universal, in Phil's version, who told Leonard to see the Arons. But as Alyne Salstone had noted, Leonard knew of the Arons beforehand from one or two social gatherings on the South Side. And when he decided he wanted to record Tibbs, he most likely got in touch with them himself. He would have known of the label in any event because Aristocrat had already made several records with Archia, the mainstay of the Macomba, and Jump Jackson, who had also played there.

The addition of Archia, Tibbs, and Jackson to the Aristocrat label was in keeping with *Billboard*'s observation that the company "intends to stick to pop and race records." Goldberg, himself black, apparently took a prominent role in developing the "race" roster. A notice in *Billboard*'s encyclopedia for 1947–48 noted that he was "in charge of building its negro talent." Leonard's name was not mentioned.

As Tibbs remembered it, both Leonard and Goldberg wanted him to record and gave him a contract. Because he was only seventeen, his mother had to sign it. When Goldberg asked him whether he had "lyrics" Tibbs didn't know what he meant. Songs he had written, Goldberg explained. At that moment Tibbs did not, but his mother helped him with the first song he took to Aristocrat, "Union Man Blues." It was the conventional theme of romance on the rocks. The union came into the picture because the man wouldn't take the bad treatment anymore " 'cause I'm in the union." The B-side, "Bilbo Is Dead," was a sarcastic take on the death of Theodore Bilbo, United States senator from Mississippi and one of the country's most virulent racists. Tibbs and Archia had scribbled down the lyrics on a brown paper bag in a cab on their way to the recording studio. The punch in the song came from the fact that a black man was singing "my friend Bilbo is dead" and that "since Mr. Bilbo is dead, I feel like a fatherless child." Tibbs was backed on both tunes by the Dave Young orchestra, which played for a long session that also included four sides with Samuels. In fact, Young recalled, Tibbs got his chance to record that August day only because there was time left over from the Samuels session. Beforehand Tibbs had been put up at a South Side hotel and kept out of sight because, he said, his new sponsors were afraid somebody else might sign him.

When the Tibbs record was finally released in December 1947, Leonard had taken a writing credit. It's not clear why, but doing so would have protected a financial investment at some later date had the record taken off. At this moment there was no in-house publishing company that controlled Aristocrat tunes; few were copyrighted. But being a songwriter was one way to get money out of a record, and later a number of companies would assign such credits as a way of funneling cash to influential people such as disc jockeys and record company executives. The writers themselves were occasionally willing to trade some of the credit for money.

Marshall, who was only five when "Union Man Blues" was made, repeated a story he had heard about the record for one interviewer in 1970. The Teamsters were so angry about the song that they destroyed some of the records. "We had to pack the shipping cartons with bricks and smuggle out the record ourselves," he said. After it was printed, the story took on a life of its own, becoming one of the cornerstones of dubious Chess lore. It is almost certainly apocryphal. "Union Man Blues" was about a man and a woman, not the Teamsters. Moreover, Aristocrat didn't need and couldn't afford truckers. New records were sent to distributors in other cities by rail or bus, sometimes directly from the record-pressing plant. On occasion Charles Aron and Leonard just loaded up their own cars. Norman Leftwich, Charles's nephew-in-law, used to help his uncle pack up the inventory at Aron's painting shop on South Phillips Avenue and go on distributing runs around the city.

Though a minor hit among blacks, "Bilbo Is Dead" was too inflammatory to be put in jukeboxes in the South and to get what little airplay was available for black music.

Leonard had little to do with recording these first Tibbs songs except for taking that writing credit. "He didn't know one note from the other," Samuels recalled. What Leonard brought to the Aristocrat operation, however, was his own connection to popular Chicago musicians, acute business instincts, and the drive to make money. From his perspective, Aristocrat was an opportunity to expand his enterprise beyond the Macomba. In its October 11, 1947, issue *Billboard* noted that Leonard had been added to the label's sales staff—the most modest of beginnings in the record business.

His first major trip was that fall, to Pittsburgh, in a Buick loaded with one hundred copies of Tom Archia records in the trunk. Leonard's first stop was to see a Mercury distributor, Irv Derfler, the salesman responsible for the city. Derfler's boss told him the company would carry the record only if he could find a buyer. So Derfler and Leonard headed to one of the outlying black neighborhoods and stopped at a hardware store that also had a record rack. Derfler put the disc on the owner's turntable. The reaction was everything Leonard had hoped for.

"You've got a hit record there," the owner told his visitors.

Leonard grinned and got right down to business.

"How many would you buy?" Leonard wanted to know.

"Well, I'll buy a hundred," the proprietor said.

"I'll be right back," Leonard said, taking just a few minutes to unload his trunk full of records in the store.

The trip marked a turning point for Aristocrat. There would be a few more records by white artists—the accordion player Lee Monti and his Tu Tones was one of the last—but with the continuing influence of Goldberg, the label was becoming more interested in the "race music" made by Archia, Tibbs, and Jump Jackson and a new sound—piano-based blues. Aristocrat signed one of the notable practitioners, Sunnyland Slim, a native Mississippian born Albert Luandrew. Like Tibbs, Sunnyland became a pivotal figure in Leonard's life, not so much for his own music but for providing an introduction to a guitar-playing musical partner named McKinley Morganfield. Thanks in part to Leonard, the music world would soon know him by his nickname: Muddy Waters.

If Leonard's partnership with Evelyn was unusual, the relationship that developed with Waters was extraordinary. Waters would later say that his friendship with Leonard was one of the things he was most proud of. On the surface they had little in common—a white immigrant Jew and a black southern migrant, one who didn't know anything about music, one who had made it his life. The men were united, however, by a fierce determination to succeed. Once they discovered this bond, their friendship would shape the lives of both and through music influence the cultural tastes of generations.

"Wonderful things happened to me because of my success on records," Waters told the *Louisville Defender,* that city's black newspaper, a few years after his first hits. "The first was that a friendship developed between Leonard Chess and myself for which I wouldn't take a million dollars. Here was a guy who had blind faith," Waters went on. "He didn't believe in my blues but believed in me as a person when we started out. I got a big kick out of proving myself to him as a performer. I got more of a kick out of the fact that we became more than business associates, real intimate friends. I tell everyone who asks that the one person responsible for my success is Leonard."

Leonard could have said the same thing in reverse. Waters was always welcome at his home, and Marshall never forgot the first time he met the man he'd heard his father speak of so often. Eight years old then, Marshall was playing in the yard when a black Cadillac pulled up. A man in an electric green suit got out, his hair slicked back on the side, a three-inch pompadour on the top. Marshall was transfixed by the man's shoes: buckskin toes, with the fur still on them.

"You must be young Chess. I'm Muddy Waters," he said, gazing down at the boy. "Is your daddy home?"

Marshall nodded and went to get his father, "and that's how I met Muddy Waters," Marshall recalled years later, adding, "we were tight ever since." Marshall sometimes called him "Grandfather," and one time Waters gave him a poem to give to a girl. He was always thrilled when Geneva, Waters's wife, brought him her homemade fried chicken wrapped tight in tinfoil to stay fresh.

Waters came to Chicago from the Mississippi Delta in 1943. He had left the drudge work of the cotton fields as so many others had, but unlike most of them, he was not simply looking for a better-paying job in a factory. Waters was a musician, and he set out to find a niche in the varied and bustling musical world of Chicago. He started playing at informal "house parties" on the South Side and quickly gained a reputation as someone special. With his friend Jimmy Rogers (his real name was James A. Lane), another Mississippian, he moved on to some club work. Though Waters and Sunnyland had known each other slightly in the Delta, they got together musically at the Flame Club on Indiana Avenue, another well-known South Side night spot. Waters had been performing there with piano player Eddie Boyd, but the two didn't mesh. The fit was better with Sunnyland, both of them letting their Delta roots come through in the music.

Waters's first paid recording session came in 1946 for Columbia Records under the auspices of Lester Melrose, a white man who had parlayed a small music store on Cottage Grove into a publishing company and deals with Columbia and RCA. For a time Melrose had been the dominant recording figure for Chicago blues, though his brand of homogenous, highly produced music was losing popularity. Sunnyland and Waters preferred a rawer sound, and they soon found an avenue to pursue it through Goldberg, the talent scout.

Sunnyland and Goldberg ran into one another at the musicians' union hall in Chicago in the late summer of 1947. After Sunnyland talked up his friend, Goldberg wanted to hear Waters play, but he didn't have his instrument. For years after Waters delighted in telling anyone who would listen how Goldberg urged a reluctant Lonnie Johnson, already a celebrated performer, to let him use his guitar.

"I don't loan my guitar to *nobody*," Johnson said.

"Let the man play one piece," Goldberg retorted. "What he gonna do to it? He can't *eat* it."

Muddy played, and Goldberg liked what he heard. A month or so later Sunnyland arranged an Aristocrat session for himself on piano and Ernest "Big" Crawford on bass. But plans changed when the group in the studio decided to add a guitar. Sunnyland wanted Muddy, but when he went looking for him, Muddy wasn't home. It took a few hours to track him down at his day job delivering venetian blinds. The rest is legend: Muddy was determined not to let the recording opportunity get away. He told his boss that a cousin had been found dead in an alley, and he had to get off work. He headed right to Universal for the session.

Up to now, Aristocrat's black artists had been recording the more urban, swing sounds of Archia, Jackson, piano player Jimmy Bell's trio, and the Sax Mallard orchestra. Sunnyland marked a stark shift—no horns, just piano, guitar, bass, and drums, and no written arrangements either. Trouble with a girlfriend was still the dominant theme, but Sunnyland's first song—"Johnson Machine Gun"—was, as critic Robert Palmer put it, "a violent urban fantasy with a touch of sinister humor." The singer boasts of buying a Johnson machine gun "and a carload of explosive balls" and threatens his wandering girlfriend: "If you don't be makin' whoopee with the Devil tomorrow, you'll be surprised." It was a long way from "Chi-Baba Chi-Baba," and even the biting lament for Bilbo's death. Sunnyland's B-side tune, "Fly Right, Little Girl," was a more conventional blues song.

"Let me do one by myself," Waters told Goldberg when Sunnyland finished.

Though Sunnyland's familiar chords started things off, when Waters sang "Gypsy Woman," about a "bad luck child" girlfriend, the vocals were decidedly different. His strong voice and particular phrasing resonated over the piano and his own guitar work. And when he took a guitar solo, he alternated between complementing Sunnyland and competing with him chord for chord. Then he sang "Little Anna Mae," about a "good little girl" but one who "liked to run around."

"This is my kind of stuff," bass player Crawford exulted when they finished.

The musicians had found their sound, but it wasn't yet the sound for Leonard and the Arons or the buying public. The records sat on the shelf for months. Waters never forgot the slight, or the disappointment he felt when the records were little noticed after their release in February 1948.

Leonard and the Arons remained committed to race music, however. They ran an ad in *Billboard* during a January 1948 music convention in Chicago that for the first time listed one of Aristocrat's "race" records right beside a white offering: Tibbs's "Union Man Blues"/"Bilbo Is Dead" and Lee Monti's "Wabash Blues"/"Have You Ever Been Lonely." The company also made a noteworthy change in distributors in the fertile southern market of Jackson, Mississippi. In the summer of 1947, when Sherman Hayes's "Get on the Ball Paul" was released, the Jackson distributor was one who handled "popular" music. In 1948, distribution was handled by a company in the heart of Jackson's black community.

Aristocrat now had company making race records. *Billboard* attributed the trend to "the growing demand for platters in Negro urban areas and in the South and Southwest and to the discovery of the idiom by the general record buying public." But when the magazine named the labels with race records to their credit—Apollo, Savoy, Aladdin, King, Modern, Specialty, and Miracle—there was one notable omission. Aristocrat had not yet made its mark.

As the label's music changed, so did its structure. In the spring of 1948 there was a major shakeup triggered by the Arons' divorce. Charles Aron left; Leonard bought out his share and the shares of three other partners. By the middle of the year he and Evelyn were running the company together from a new office at 5249 South Cottage Grove. Leonard's father, making money now operating South Side rooming houses for blacks, provided financing. He lent his son $10,000, according to Nate Notkin, a childhood friend who later became one of the brothers' principal lawyers. And when that investment failed to yield a return, the senior Chess put in another $10,000. "His father had confidence in him," Notkin said.

Evelyn and Sammy Goldberg were certain the music Waters and Sunnyland wanted to make would find an audience. Leonard was not, and remained skeptical as they got ready for an April 1948 session. No one expected anything special. Instead it turned out to be historic. Waters would recall the moment with bemused satisfaction. Leonard would chuckle at what he almost missed.

The session started off with "Good Lookin' Woman," which opened with Sunnyland's piano and then Waters's vocals. Big Crawford was keeping the beat on the bass. Though Waters provided some guitar work in between, the piano was dominant. Alex Atkins provided alto sax in the background. Next came "Mean Disposition," with Waters taking the lead on the vocals and then offering a guitar solo where Sunnyland had done the same on the previous tune. Crawford and Atkins again provided the backup. The next two songs were a dramatic departure, spare arrangements with only Waters's guitar and Big Crawford's bass. The first opened with Waters's deliberate picking of his amplified guitar. Crawford's bass provided a simple two-step beat. And then Waters began to sing with fervor the first of his many classics, "I Can't Be Satisfied," about "goin' back down South." His intricate guitar work only deepened the story of disappointment and longing. The next tune, "I Feel Like Going Home," was similar in style. Precise single-string picking led into a series of chords; Crawford continued to provide that simple bass line as Waters sang about "wakin' up this morning and all I had was gone."

He had recorded these same songs years earlier for the Library of Congress when Alan Lomax found him in Mississippi. But those recordings were done with an acoustic guitar. These were with an electric guitar that added another dimension to the music, giving it body and bite.

Leonard didn't get it. He was mystified, even irritated by Waters's indecipherable drawl. "What's he saying? What's he saying?" Leonard asked in frustration. "Who's going to buy that?"

This lean emotional sound was new to Evelyn, too. But she felt its power. "You'd be surprised who'd buy that," she told Leonard.

"She dug me," Muddy recalled years later.

Her own romantic life a melodrama—an annulment and one divorce already—Evelyn seemed to understand blues. Besides, she was willing to take some chances. The last several months had been difficult, she confided to Jonathan Benjamin, a younger cousin, who was a student at the University of Chicago and already a blues fan. Distraught, she was concerned about the company's finances, and her own marital troubles aside, her partners, the Brounts, wanted out. Benjamin told her to trust her instincts. He agreed that the label should turn to black musicians. Leonard heard the same message from another source. Record distributor Ernie Leaner, who was black, told him Waters was "the best talent you have."

Leonard's failure to appreciate Waters's music was understandable. He had been making records for barely four months and hardly knew his way around a studio. He was a businessman interested in making money, not a musical innnovator. He didn't see a market yet. But he would in a hurry.

Waters's tunes got in line for pressing and eventual release. Three thousand copies of "I Can't Be Satisfied" with "I Feel Like Going' Home" on the B-side were pressed and then delivered to various locations in Chicago on a Friday in June 1948. There weren't many stores that sold only records; instead a variety of outlets—beauty salons, little grocery shops, and the like—would have a few records for sale. By the end of the next day none was left. "They sold 'em out," Muddy recalled, "the people buyin' two or three at a time." One entrepreneur over on Maxwell Street—the hot spot for street blues—had hiked the list price of 79 cents to $1.10 and put on a limit of one to a customer, even for Muddy, who explained to no avail that he was the singer.

The success of the record was crucial for both Waters and Aristocrat. It established Waters for good as a blues presence and solidified the label's evolution to race music. It also shifted the label's orientation from the jazz-flavored tunes of Tibbs and Archia to the blues of Muddy Waters. Most important, sales spoke the language Leonard understood. Now he could see that Waters was a bankable artist, and he let him know it. "Then he was my buddy," Waters recalled years later. "Chess began to come close to me."

The changing black population in Chicago contributed to Waters's new prominence. By 1948 the city's black population had swelled to nearly 500,000. And the lion's share of those migrants had come out of the cotton fields of the South, particularly Mississippi. At the same time, black radio in Chicago was becoming a presence through Al Benson—himself a Mississippi native. Benson, whose real name was Arthur Leaner, was the uncle of Ernie Leaner, the distributor. He was one of only sixteen blacks among an estimated three thousand radio announcers nationwide. As important, he made no attempt to "sound white," as a number of the successful black announcers had. They "tended to be conservative in their programming choices, leaning as heavily on Count Basie and Sarah Vaughan as on their vowels," one commentator observed. Not Benson. "When I got into radio it was my very ambition and intention to let people know who I was," he once said. "I used certain terms that we black folks are accustomed to using. Slang—and that alone picked up my identity." He was happy to play Muddy Waters and other down-home blues, well aware that it would satisfy the musical longings of the recent southern migrants.

So there were two important factors that helped Waters achieve his first success—the sheer number of people who might like this music and a new way to popularize it. The moment was a marriage of commerce and culture, the kind of moment that tapped into Leonard's business instincts. He didn't know Delta blues any better than he had known the urban swing of Tom Archia, but if it sold, that was good enough for him.

Billboard offered a clue about how much Waters's record was selling. By late summer he had landed in the number eleven spot on the magazine's "Most-Played Juke Box Race Records" for "I Feel Like Going Home." It was the first time an Aristocrat record earned national recognition, but it registered on only one of the magazine's two tallies for race music. The other was top-ten retail sales. Waters held the spot for two weeks in September before dropping off the chart.

Cash Box had its own survey system for race music—the "hot charts," which were top ten records, based on weekly surveys the magazine conducted, in various cities around the country. The listings had such stylings as "HOT in Harlem," "HOT on Chicago's South Side." A couple of weeks later the record showed up in the number ten spot in *Cash Box*'s weekly chart of race records in four locales: "HOT in Harlem," "HOT on Chicago's South Side," "HOT in New Orleans," and "HOT on Central Ave.," the heart of the black community in Los Angeles. Waters's record garnered the tenth position in these four cities.

Neither "I Feel Like Going Home" nor "I Can't Be Satisfied" got very kind treatment from *Billboard*'s reviewer—an indication that this was indeed a new sound and not well understood. The cryptic comment about "I Feel Like Going Home" was "poor recording distorts vocal and steel guitar backing." That latter comment was mystifying; there was no steel guitar on the recording. It was Waters using a slide. A more conventional blues rendering by Tibbs was praised.

Often when a company's record landed on one or another of *Billboard*'s charts, the label took out an ad to boost the release with jukebox operators, radio stations, and music stores. Aristocrat chose not to, despite Waters's record being the company's first to make a splash. Right now there was little or no extra money. Dwight "Gatemouth" Moore, who made his first gospel recordings for Aristocrat in 1948, periodically stopped by the Cottage Grove office and found Leonard by himself packing up the latest releases for delivery. "He had no help," Moore remembered.

There were many dicey financial moments in the company's early days. Cash flow depended on getting paid by distributors, and distributors had the right to return what they didn't sell. The record presser had to be paid up front, and it was not unusual to have some tense times between label and presser until some sort of understanding was worked out. "The label had some financial difficulties. We had to work through those . . . to get comfortable with each other," said Art Sheridan, one of Aristocrat's first record pressers. "They didn't have a lot of money in the business, and they would wind up owing significant amounts to the pressers."

Sheridan, who had been pressing records for his father since the early forties, was surprised when he first ran into Leonard at Aristocrat. "How in the world did he get in the business, I wondered." He considered Leonard "a ruffian in the nice sense—just pretty crude . . . the constant use of street language." But after getting to know him, his feelings turned from surprise to respect. "He attacked the business like a hardworking yeoman," Sheridan said.

The hard work was apparently paying off. By the end of the year, Leonard and Evelyn decided it was worthwhile to advertise in the year-end edition of *Cash Box*. The text of the ad was continuing evidence of the label's new direction. The three songs listed were all in the "race" category: Waters's "I Feel Like Going Home," Tibbs's "I Feel Like Crying," and Archia's "Swinging for Christmas." The company's outside distributors had now grown to twenty-two. In addition he and Evelyn had set up a distributing arm to handle not only their own records but whatever other independent labels they could get. The company listed itself in the ad as handling only the "race" records in Chicago, another indication of the label's emphasis. "White records only" were available from North Side distributor James H. Martin on Diversy Parkway.

~~

The new year, 1949, started off in the best way possible. Tibbs's "I Feel Like Crying" was number twelve on *Billboard*'s "most played juke box race records" in the week of January 26. But it must have been a disappointment at the Aristocrat office to discover that the magazine had listed the label as "Savoy." The company's increased visibility was apparent when *Cash Box* mentioned Aristocrat releases two weeks in a row in its regular record gossip column, "Round the Wax Circle." The column was unabashed boosterism, frequently made up of paraphrases from a company's own press release. But at the very least, Aristocrat was now part of the industry conversation. On February 26, the magazine noted that Evelyn had just returned from New Orleans "with some very good reports"— Waters's newest Aristocrat record, "Mean Red Spider," released about ten days earlier, was "sellin' like mad there." *Billboard* hadn't thought much of this record either: "Slow blues item with nothing much of anything happening."

Evelyn's travels were an indication of the more aggressive person-to-person contact around the country that was to become a staple of Leonard's eventual stewardship of the company. In a time of still-tight budgets, her trip to New Orleans had been made easier by the fact that she could stay with relatives, who not only provided free lodging but also gave her contacts within the city.

The second mention in *Cash Box* touted the good reaction to Tibbs's new release, "I'm in a Travelin' Mood." "Looks like Evelyn has that hit on her hands," the magazine said. Once again, *Billboard* was dubious: "Failure to find a unifying conception holds this one down." It was also noteworthy that both *Cash Box* items cited only Evelyn. Leonard had not yet surfaced publicly as part of Aristocrat even though he had been working there for eighteen months and had been Evelyn's only business partner since the previous summer.

Hoping to build on the free publicity, Leonard and Evelyn sprang for an ad in the March *Cash Box* touting "Aristocrat HITS." The ad included the Tibbs song, Water's "Mean Red Spider," and records by two new groups, the Dozier Boys, a harmony vocal group, and the Jimmy Bell Trio. The next week, April 9, the label got some more good news. "I'm in a Travelin' Mood" was number five on the *Cash Box* chart of "HOT on Chicago's South Side." The record stayed there for the rest of the month, though it dropped to number nine.

Tidbits about Aristocrat's latest releases continued to pop up in the *Cash Box* record column. *Billboard* paid attention too, but often with criticism. Where *Cash Box* predicted that a record by Eugene Wright and his Dukes of Swing, "Dawn Mist" backed by "Pork and Beans," was "headed for the top," *Billboard* was unimpressed: "Screamer opens with honking one-note bary bus, then a bop trumpet and tram take solos. No unity or build here."

It was difficult to gauge how much publicity affected sales. The negative reviews from *Billboard* were hardly a boost; on the other hand the label was getting noticed. By the summer of 1949 *Billboard* listed Aristocrat as number twenty-six in its survey of thirty-two labels and their sales over retail counters in the "rhythm and blues" category. This was the magazine's new name for the "race" records, and a category that embraced both the spare blues of the Mississippi Delta and the more uptempo music found in the city. The list offered no clues about staying power, however; within two years Leonard would overtake several competitors, and one of them, number nine Miracle, would be out of business by then.

Evelyn and Leonard suffered a setback in August when a fire broke out at the Cottage Grove office. Damage was reported to be around $12,000. *Billboard* reported that the fire apparently was set by burglars who broke in and started the blaze after they failed to open a safe. The company found temporary quarters a few doors away, and Evelyn, acting as spokesperson, told the magazine that operations would not be interrupted. Aristocrat's latest disks would be distributed without interruption because they were going to outlets directly from the pressing plants.

Early in October another Aristocrat release was on the *Cash Box* race record charts. The Dozier Boys with "Big Time Baby" was number ten on the South Side. While this was good news, it was a modest accomplishment in comparison with the label's competitors. Dinah Washington's "Baby Get Lost" for Mercury was number four in Harlem, number three in Chicago, number six in New Orleans, and number three in Los Angeles. Memphis Slim's "Blue and Lonesome," for Miracle, was number nine in Chicago, and number four in New Orleans and Los Angeles.

In the meantime Leonard was doing what he could to promote the label. He recognized that Waters had tapped into a market, and even though

Aristocrat was recording many other sides that could not be described as Delta blues, Leonard was looking for other musicians who could play that kind of music. At Waters's suggestion, Leonard agreed to record Robert Nighthawk, an Arkansas musician who came to Chicago with his piano player to make a record. This would prove to be a significant session. It was the first time Leonard used Willie Dixon as the bass player, and it was the first step in an enduring relationship.

The Nighthawk record was released in November—"Annie Lee Blues" with "Black Angel Blues" on the B-side. *Billboard*, this time much kinder, offered a prophetic observation: "moody blues could pick up business in the Southern market."

That is exactly what Leonard had in mind. As the record was being distributed, he was on one of his increasingly frequent road trips to make Aristocrat more widely known. A typical stop was the one he made in Shreveport, Louisiana, in the fall of 1949 with traveling companion Lee Egalnick of Miracle, who was still reveling in the success of a number-one hit, "Long Gone" by Sonny Thompson.

Their first stop in Shreveport was at Stan's Record Shop. Stan Lewis had opened the store about a year earlier with his entire savings of $2,500, painstakingly collected from odd jobs cutting grass, selling used goods, and fitting in paper routes when he could. At twenty-two, Lewis was considerably younger than Leonard and Egalnick and pretty much of a small-town boy. He had only been out of town once, to Kansas City to visit relatives. So his eyes opened wide when he saw a long, dark Chrysler pull up to his shop at 728 Texas Street and two men in topcoats and fedoras get out of a car with Illinois plates. For a moment he thought a couple of organized crime toughs were paying him a visit. A closer look at the car revealed that it was packed with records, stacked on the back seat, floorboards, and in the trunk.

Leonard took an immediate liking to Lewis, and the feeling was mutual. He did exactly what Leonard had hoped, showing him around town to the taverns with jukeboxes that would play his blues records, particularly the new one, "Annie Lee Blues," and the local five-and-dimes, H. L. Green, W. T. Grant, and Woolworth's, which might stock the records. Leonard reciprocated by giving Lewis one hundred discs to dispense. By this time, Lewis had learned about radio packaging—buying time to sponsor a fifteen-minute show with a particular musical theme like rhythm and blues and then giving the disc jockeys the records to play during that show. Now acutely interested in building up his blues line, Leonard reminded Lewis that "if you see any talent, be sure and send him my way."

The trip to Shreveport was the first of many for Leonard, the start of another lifelong business friendship. But as that relationship was beginning another one was ending. In December, Evelyn Aron decided to leave Aristocrat. She wanted to stay in the record business, but not with Leonard. The two were cut from a different cloth. She was sophisticated and stylish. He was neither. So Evelyn turned her attention to distributing. She had gotten to know Sheridan, the record presser, and suggested they start a company together. American Record Distributors had been formed in late fall, and parlaying her *Cash Box* connections into the new company, she secured a bit of publicity for their venture in the December 17 issue: "New firm that opened here, American Record Distributors Inc., owned by Art Sheridan and Evelyn Aron, already under way with a very big show room." Sheridan and Evelyn were married by now, but it was to last only a year or so, slightly longer than a previous marriage to Gene Rolf, after the divorce from Charles Aron.

Evelyn's departure from Aristocrat left Leonard in control, but it was too much to handle for one person. Phil had been holding down the Macomba, and being in the tavern business hadn't gotten any easier. It was tough and sometimes unpleasant work, but by now, with the right managers, the bar was running smoothly. So shortly after Evelyn left, Phil joined Leonard at Aristocrat, beginning a new phase of their partnership. Two weeks into the new year, 1950, he showed up in both *Billboard* and *Cash Box* as company spokesman. He was able to dispense good news. In *Cash Box* he touted a new release by the Blues Rockers, "Times Are Getting Hard." The record had been purchased from disc jockey Al Benson's small label, and it was doing well on the South Side. Phil told *Billboard* that a buyers' preview of an instrumental by the sax player Gene Ammons had generated advance orders of 2,500 records and several queries about writing lyrics for the music.

The Chess brothers were now more than just siblings. They were a company.

five

MEMPHIS CONNECTIONS

Fire trucks arrived at Thirty-ninth and South Cottage Grove on a chilly fall night in 1950 as patrons and musicians were scrambling to get out of a burning Macomba Lounge. Bobby Blevins, barely old enough to get in the place but already a skilled keyboard player, had grabbed the upright bass that was on the small bandstand and was struggling to carry it out of harm's way. By the time Leonard got there—one of the managers had called him at home—firemen had things under control, enough so that a few of them formed an assembly line to take unbroken boxes of liquor out of the basement and onto their truck. Phil came as soon as Leonard called him.

Although the fire occurred at a fortuitous time, an insurance investigation turned up nothing untoward. Marshall sat with his father in the master bedroom of the Drexel Boulevard apartment while Leonard counted the insurance settlement, carefully laying out the stacks of cash on the chenille bedspread.

While the building at 3905 South Cottage Grove survived, the Macomba did not. The brothers closed it down, happy to be out of the tavern business and happy with a cash settlement that netted them as much, if not more, than they could have gotten from a sale. They were free now to focus their energies on making records, and the next few years would be a whirlwind of activity—recording new artists, buying master session tapes from other companies, traveling the country to promote the product. There was no business plan, no grand strategy. They learned as they went along.

Waters's success with "I Can't Be Satisfied" had turned Leonard into a blues believer, at least for the blues formula that had worked—Waters and his guitar and Big Crawford on bass. He was willing to make more records that fit this mold, and several more tunes, each modestly successful, followed: "Rollin' and Tumblin'," his version of an old Mississippi Delta song, and "Rollin' Stone," the song that would inspire the Rolling Stones. Waters's "Rollin' Stone" was no rock song, however. It was in the same spare style of "Satisfied" and "Feel Like Goin' Home."

Waters had put together a band and was chafing to bring them into the studio: "Little Walter" Jacobs on harmonica, Jimmy Rogers on guitar, and "Baby Face" LeRoy Foster on drums and occasionally guitar. Waters was sure a record would capture the sound that made them so popular in local clubs, but Leonard would have none of it. "Chess wouldn't upset things," Waters said. "He wouldn't mess with the harp or the extra guitar. He wanted to keep the combination that had made the hit record—just Big Crawford's bass and my guitar."

From Leonard's perspective that made sense. He still didn't know a great deal about music, and unpersuaded by Waters's success in the clubs, he was not convinced that there was a market for this different sound. Each record, after all, was both investment and risk. If one failed badly, it would put him behind for making the next one. On top of that, Leonard was superstitious. He believed in omens, for good and bad, finding his own talismans for deciding whether to record this song or that musician. Sometimes he emptied his pockets of change before going into the studio to remind himself of the times when his pockets were empty. Despite the repeated urging of Nate Notkin, his lawyer and friend, he refused to sign a will, even though Notkin had prepared three different versions and made one appointment after another so Leonard could make the final decisions. He always found an excuse to postpone. "Nate, why are you pushing me?" he groused, as if the mere act of signing would hasten his death.

Waters stayed with Leonard despite their disagreement, though he made some surreptitious recordings with his friends on an even smaller Chicago label. He was not the front man and was not mentioned on the record, but his guitar work was unmistakable. It wasn't too long before Leonard found out what his main bluesman had done. He was not happy, but he didn't punish Waters. Instead, he yielded, and in the summer of 1950 Leonard let him bring Jimmy Rogers on second guitar and Little Walter on harmonica into the studio to record. But it would be October before he let a drummer in on the session. The results with this bigger group were all that Leonard could have hoped for. "Louisiana Blues," with Little Walter on the harmonica, Elgin Evans (also known as Elga Edmonds) playing drums, and Big Crawford on bass, was an instant success when it was released at the end of the year. The addition of Little Walter's harp complemented Waters's vocals and shadowed his slide work during the instrumental passages, giving the music a new and warmer dimension. For a week early in January 1951 the record was number ten on *Billboard*'s top ten R&B sales list, though it did not crack the jukebox tally.

That was encouraging enough for Leonard. Now Waters had no trouble getting his band into the studio to make records. Four more followed that went right onto the *Billboard* R&B chart. One song, "She Moves Me," was noteworthy for two reasons: it marked the first time Little Walter used an amplified harp, giving the instrument a richer, more resonant sound, and it was Leonard's debut—and farewell performance—on an instrument. Waters's drummer was having trouble getting the beat on a long verse, putting a turnaround flourish where the straight beat should have continued. "He couldn't hold it there to save his life," Waters said, but Leonard knew what to do. "Get the fuck out of the way. I'll do that," Leonard said, his impatience obvious as he provided a steady, serviceable thud.

Candid about their lack of musical training, Leonard and Phil believed in their instincts. "If you put the scale on the wall and ask me which one was *do re mi,* I couldn't tell you," Phil once said. "Neither could Leonard. But," and he motioned to his ear, "this could tell you. That's what told us." Phil was becoming another set of eyes and ears for his brother, relying on his own instincts for what would make a good record. He demonstrated as much in a session with Eddie Johnson, another of Chicago's talented saxophone players he recruited early in 1951. Phil liked the soft-spoken young man, who had been playing with well-known bands around town, and he offered him a chance to record under his own name. At one session there was some studio time left over, and Phil suggested that Johnson try a popular tune, "This Love of Mine." But he wanted Johnson to pick up the beat. "Play it faster, and give me some kind of boom, boom, boom," he told the drummer. Though he didn't know the terminology, Phil was referring to a backbeat, "and," Johnson said, "he turned out to be right. Don't you know that was the bestseller I made." It was such a hit in Chicago that a prominent local disc jockey used it as a theme song for his show.

Getting the music out beyond Chicago was Leonard's prime concern. A tireless promoter, he was constantly on the road, cementing his relationships with distributors, meeting disc jockeys, and learning more each time about the business itself. The South was still his prime territory, Memphis a key city. His distributor there was Buster Williams, who was also a record presser. Though their backgrounds were different—Williams was a solid son of the rural South, a Mississippi native who had worked as a young man in Louisiana—the two became fast friends. More important, Williams would end up giving Leonard a piece of advice that would change the course of his business.

A self-made man, Williams was quiet and serious but with a taste for adventure. He flew his own private planes, and on one trip in 1957 he landed in Cuba with his wife and a few friends only to get caught in the outbreak of the revolution against the Batista government. He showed his first creative spark when he was fourteen years old by figuring out how to preserve roasted peanuts in wax paper bags: he rigged up a drawstring at the top of the bag. This was no aimless effort. As a way of earning money, Williams's mother roasted peanuts before high school football games in their hometown of Enterprise, Mississippi. Prior to her son's innovation, she had to spend hours in front of the stove on game day roasting the nuts to keep them fresh. Her son's creation allowed her to spread out the roasting over a few days. By the time he was sixteen, Williams had saved enough money from peanut sales to buy a small drugstore. He earned a profit from the coin-operated machines inside—some sold snacks, others were rudimentary slot machines—and the experience eventually led him to jukeboxes. He moved to Louisiana in his early twenties, a college dropout with plenty of ideas and energy. In his job as a mechanic on a cotton plantation in northeastern Louisiana, Williams made a lifelong friend in Ed Newell. Before long the two of them were putting slot machines in country stores, making their money on the commissions. Though the machines were technically illegal, the police never gave the young men any trouble. Both were well known—Newell's great-grandfather had settled the area in 1860. Flush with success, Williams, with Newell as a helping hand, opened a Wurlitzer jukebox distributorship in nearby Monroe, Louisiana, and the Service Novelty Company was born. Before long, they were handling accounts in four states, Louisiana, Mississippi, Arkansas, and Tennessee.

After the outbreak of World War II, Williams joined the Army Air Corps and was stationed in Memphis. He felt instantly at home in the city and parlayed his zest for business into running a record distributorship along with the jukebox business while still in the service. The decision to open Music Sales, as the company was called, made good sense. If Williams became a record distributor, he could get the records he needed for his jukeboxes more cheaply. Music Sales prospered—Newell had relocated to Memphis to help his friend—and the two opened offices in other cities, shipping records throughout the country. But Williams had still other ideas. Much of his clientele in the mid-to-late forties were the independent labels—Aladdin, Modern, King, Savoy, Specialty—and there were few record pressers available to them. They had to deal with the majors—Columbia, Decca, RCA—to get their records pressed, and because the independents were never first in line, they were never sure when their product would be available.

Williams recognized a need and the chance for profit by opening a pressing plant, Plastic Products. For $40,000, a chunk of it spent on Army surplus sheet metal, he put up a Quonset hut on the outskirts of the city in 1949 to house the machinery and supplies for pressing, packing, and shipping the records. Once again it had taken ingenuity to get the operation going. None of the majors would let Williams look at their pressing plants to see how the machinery worked. But he found help from an unlikely source, a school for the blind in Kentucky that made records for its students. They welcomed Williams to their plant so he could watch and learn. By the process of trial and error he designed his own pressing machine and had it built by a locomotive company. It took more experimenting until he got the right combination of ingredients for the compound needed to make the records. But Williams made it all work to his advantage. He started by pressing a thousand records a day, gradually upgrading and expanding by adding three more Quonset huts so he could press fifty thousand a day. Now Williams had a hand in the manufacture, distribution, and consumption of the music. It was a business model Leonard would come to appreciate in the years ahead.

Music Sales had become one of Aristocrat's first distributors, and by 1949, Plastic Products was pressing some of the label's records. One thing was critical: Williams pressed on credit—and the rate varied between ten and fifteen cents per record. There was an understanding that Leonard would pay when the money came in from record sales. This was really the only way the independents could survive because the cost of making a record couldn't be recouped until the product was sold, and even then, the numbers were not huge. As a result, the independents were generally strapped for cash. To his wife's astonishment, Leonard opened a charge account at Baskin's department store and came home one day with a new three-piece suit and complete accessories, shoes to hat. He would find a way to pay for it later, he told Revetta. He knew his chances of succeeding were better if he looked the part of the prosperous businessman.

On one of Leonard's trips to Memphis early in 1950, Williams took it upon himself to offer some advice. "Aristocrat" was not the snappiest name for a record company, Williams said. Why didn't Leonard think about using the family name. It was a good sound, "Chess," crisp like the downbeat that kicks off a song. And the possibilities for art were obvious, playing off the board game that everyone knew.

Leonard agreed, and by June the label was renamed and its color scheme changed from the original white with red accents to blue and white. Framing the word "Chess" were the knight, the bishop, and the king. (Leonard and Phil, who were operating with not so much as a piece of paper between them, would not formally incorporate as Chess Records for another two years. They finally did so at Notkin's urging, with Leonard, Phil, and Revetta as equal stockholders.)

The first Chess record was not Waters's Delta blues but the sounds of Thirty-ninth and Cottage Grove—Gene Ammons and his tenor saxophone doing a version of the current hit "My Foolish Heart." The brothers gave the record a special number—1425, in honor of their first home in the United States, 1425 South Karlov Avenue. It was a moment of great excitement when Leonard came home with the first record that said *Chess.* Marshall was particularly tickled—he had been at the "Foolish Heart" session, though he had fallen asleep in a corner of the hot, smoke-filled studio to the sweet sound of Ammons's sax.

The second record, Chess 1426, was one by Waters, "Walkin' Blues," backed with "Rollin' Stone." These first two Chess releases were an appropriate pairing—each reflected a different kind of "race music." Indeed, the last ads that ran under the Aristocrat label in the trade magazines highlighted the variety, touting the label as home to the "biggest jazz and blues" tunes of the day. Jazz was the mainstay, however. One-third of the songs recorded in the first six months of 1950 featured Ammons, and several more featured two other sax players—combined they represented just over half of the songs recorded in that time period.

Although the straight-ahead jazz players and the blues musicians worked under the same label, they had almost nothing to do with each other, even when they had back-to-back studio sessions. They didn't fraternize much at the union hall, either. It wasn't a matter of overt hostility from the more entrenched sax players and their bands, just lack of interest. "We were worlds apart," Eddie Johnson said. "We really ignored that type of music. It said nothing to us." "We didn't think it was going anywhere," added Bobby Blevins, the keyboard player who had rescued the bass from the burning Macomba.

Ammons, who occasionally sat in at the Macomba, had signed with the label in January and had scored a modest hit in Chicago with "Pennies from Heaven" and then "Rockin' Rocker." But "My Foolish Heart," that first Chess song, caught on right away, landing on *Billboard*'s top ten R&B charts for two weeks after its release, an auspicious beginning for the renamed label. It was part of the trend of taking a popular song and retooling it as a rhythm and blues or jazz tune. While *Billboard* called the Ammons version "an outstanding instance" of the genre, the magazine took a swipe at the label: "a comparatively slight diskery called Chess Records."

Though Waters's "Rollin' Stone" was doing well in the South, Leonard was still following the Aristocrat formula. In the second half of 1950 most of the releases were the sax-based music of the Macomba. The first Chess ad in the trade press didn't mention blues—it was for another saxophone player, Claude McLin, doing "Mona Lisa" backed with "Benny's Bounce." Two-thirds of the company's first catalogue, issued early in 1951, was devoted to sax players, though three Muddy Waters records and three by Jimmy Rogers were offered along with one gospel record by Reverend Gatemouth Moore.

"Catalogue" was really too fancy a term for the Chess offering. What Leonard and Phil had put out was really a leaflet, one piece of pink paper, folded in thirds, with the pictures of a half-dozen artists on the outside flap and their records listed inside. The final panel offered blanks by each numbered record where the distributor could fill in how many he wanted.

In addition to the Chess musicians, the catalogue also included three records by Al Hibbler, a singer who had just left Duke Ellington's band. Leonard had picked up his masters from another company in February of 1951. They were indicative of Leonard's broader strategy now of getting music from other labels or producers he thought would find a market. He would be proved right many times over in the coming years, and in the immediate future some very good luck was about to come his way a few hundred miles south.

✹

Music Sales, Buster Williams's record distributorship in Memphis, was a gathering place for the area's music community. Disc jockeys from radio stations in the region came in regularly, and Williams took good care of them: he put in a separate shelf with bins of records labeled station by station and stocked the bins every week with the newest releases. Local musicians and those just passing through town dropped in, and so did label representatives like Leonard and his counterparts at the other independents. They liked to gossip, hoping to get a fix on what their competitors were doing, hoping to get a jump on the next hit.

Sam Phillips was a local producer who had concentrated on making country blues music with musicians he felt had raw talent neither influenced nor programmed by contemporary tastes. He challenged himself to understand their sound and then deliver it in the studio. Phillips had started his own recording business and then his own label, but that venture lasted barely two months. In the meantime, Phillips began producing records for the Modern label in Los Angeles, owned and operated by Jules, Saul, and Joe Bihari. Like Williams, the Biharis had been jukebox operators, and when they started having trouble finding enough new suitable records, Jules told his brothers they should make their own. By 1951 they started a subsidiary, RPM, and looked to Phillips to produce more inventory. They made a handshake deal that the Biharis regarded as exclusive and giving them the right of first refusal on anything Phillips made. He didn't see it that way, and in early March of 1951, he sent his most innovative material, "Rocket 88," to Leonard, whom he had initially met at a radio station during Leonard's promotional swings through Memphis. Phillips liked him well enough, but he didn't agree to do business with him before checking with Buster Williams. "Does he pay his bills?" Phillips wanted to know.

Williams gave his blessing, and Phillips went forward. Helping him make the decision was unhappiness in his relationship with the Biharis. While there "wasn't any great split" with the brothers, Phillips remembered, "I just decided to see what kind of an association I could build with Leonard and Phil."

The Chess brothers almost missed hearing "Rocket 88." A purist and a perfectionist when it came to sound, Phillips had sent the song on a special sixteen-inch disc rather than the more conventional twelve-inch disc. "I wanted all the little nuances to be conveyed for them to listen to," he explained. The disc had barely arrived in Chicago when the phone rang at Phillips's office. The brothers were on the line, distressed because they couldn't play it. They didn't have the machinery to handle the larger disc, so Phillips had to redo the song on the twelve-inch version, the kind used to make a master tape. Leonard and Phil snapped up the song as soon as they heard it.

"Rocket 88" was a fast-paced tune named after the new Oldsmobile coupe. Jackie Brenston sang vocals; on the keyboard was Ike Turner, a talented musician from Clarksdale, Mississippi, who brought his six-piece band to record for Phillips. The men put the song together on their trip north, looking forward to getting the twenty dollars per person Phillips would pay them. Despite some equipment problems that required on-the-spot innovation—the speaker on the guitar amp had broken—everyone was pleased with the result. The song was rhythmically similar to some of the Aristocrat tunes, and it echoed the harmonies of those Chicago jump blues. But in "Rocket 88" there was no trumpet, just guitar, bass, tenor sax, drums, and Turner playing a boogie-woogie piano. The guitar provided the same fill that a second sax did in the more familiar urban blues. All of it provided a swing to support Brenston as he sang about his new car: "You've heard of jalopies, you've heard the noise they make. But let me introduce my Rocket 88. . . . Everybody likes my Rocket 88, Baby, ride in style, movin' all along." Though "Rocket 88" was touted by some, including Phillips, as the first rock-and-roll song, music critic Robert Palmer made the persuasive point that musically, even though the song had a driving beat and a heavily amplified guitar, "there was nothing particularly startling about the way 'Rocket 88' moved." Some West Coast R&B musicians, he noted, had made records "that rocked just as hard" even if they had less amplification.

"Rocket 88" was on *Billboard*'s best-selling retail and most-played jukebox R&B charts by May 12, and was number one on both before the end of June—a first for Leonard and Phil. It was also number one in several of the cities monitored by *Cash Box,* including Chicago, New Orleans, Dallas and Los Angeles. No doubt an intensive ad campaign in the trade papers helped. One quarter-page ad in *Cash Box* was particularly striking. It broke the mold of the usual box with print and no graphics. Instead the ad featured a woman clad in a bathing suit straddling a rocket with "Rocket 88 by Jackie Brenston" written on the side. "Climbing to the top," she was saying, with a wave of her hand. Unconcerned about hyperbole, Leonard now advertised the business as "the Hottest Little Label in the Nation."

The success of "Rocket 88" was only one piece of good news for Chess.

Waters's "Louisiana Blues" and "Long Distance Call" were still in the top ten *Billboard* R&B charts, and "Long Distance Call" was still registering on the *Cash Box* hot charts, as was Al Hibbler's "What Will I Tell My Heart." The flip side of "Louisiana Blues" was an instrumental, "Evans Shuffle." The title was instructive: it was Waters's homage to disc jockey Sam Evans, one of Al Benson's counterparts at WGES who was also playing Waters's music. More than once Waters attributed his early success to the radio play, and he seemed to be right. "Honey Bee," another 1951 release, went on the *Billboard* jukebox R&B chart in the summer.

～～

With Phil now in the record business full-time, the brothers established a routine. Phil stayed in Chicago handling the orders; Leonard went out on the road to promote the product and look for new music. He followed the same pattern he had a few years earlier in Pittsburgh and Shreveport, only now he was better known. His trips to such places as Jake Friedman's Southland Distributing in Atlanta combined business with a social visit— usually lunch, maybe dinner, and sometimes even an overnight stay at the distributor's house. He was well liked by his business associates. They admired his directness. Like a good politician, he looked someone straight in the eye when he talked to them, shook hands with a firm grip, and in that moment made them feel special. It was something Leonard passed on to Marshall, tutoring him on their first plane ride together when the boy, barely a teenager, accompanied his father on a promotion trip. "You have to learn how to shake hands properly," Leonard told him. "You'll be meeting people." The two spent the first hour of the plane ride practicing a firm grip.

Once Leonard hit town, business always came first: taking samples from the couple of hundred copies of his latest releases he had packed in the car and playing them on the distributor's turntable. Friedman and his assistant, Gwen Kesler, generally knew from the first few bars what would sell. And they almost never turned down something Leonard offered. Like Williams, the Memphis record presser and distributor, Friedman operated on credit. He paid Leonard up front for what he had brought without waiting to see if his customers, the jukebox operators and small record shop owners, were going to take them. It was a combination of trust between the two parties and a belief in the music. The latter came from an appreciation for the market that had developed with the growth of radio play for rhythm-and-blues music. Not only were local stations, such as WGES in Chicago and WGST in Atlanta, important, but critical to the increasing popularity of the music were powerful, clear-channel stations like Nashville's 50,000-watt WLAC. At night, the station could be heard in some thirty states, and three disc jockeys—all of them white—became fixtures in the rhythm-and-blues community: William "Hoss" Allen, Gene Nobles, and John Richbourg.

Nobles had been the first to play R&B music, responding to requests from black students at local black universities to play "some of our music" in between Tommy Dorsey and Jo Stafford. Nobles gave it a try, and it proved to be a popular decision. In the beginning the music primarily found a southern black audience, but little by little whites tuned in to the station and were captivated by music they had never heard before. They wanted more. Richbourg and Allen then followed his format. In the meantime, Nobles had asked his friend Randy Wood, an enterprising young businessman in nearby Gallatin, Tennessee, to sponsor these nighttime shows at six dollars a night, and it led to one of the first mail order businesses for R&B music. Randy's Record Shop, which by 1950 was selling thousands of records around the country, became a model for other ambitious shop owners throughout the South.

But it was local disc jockeys who were the most important connection for label owners. Leonard made sure to visit them every time he stopped to see his distributors. Like his counterparts at the other companies, he regularly left twenty-five or fifty dollars when he dropped off his newest records. The distributors usually followed up Leonard's visit with phone calls, reminding the jockeys about the new product. "They started banging the records away, and we started selling them," Southland's Kesler explained.

Joe Bihari, who would occasionally run into Leonard on the road, called the money a "thank you" and an insurance policy. It wasn't that you needed to pay money to get your record played, Bihari said, "but without it you wouldn't get it played as often as you wanted."

Though the stench of scandal would not come for another eight years, the industry was already talking about the practice in negative terms. "R&B JOCKEYS RIDE PAYOLA" blared a *Billboard* headline early in January 1951. The story said that a survey of the R&B market showed "that payola has permeated the field to the core." The jockeys themselves did not start the practice but were "conditioned to take it by some of the publishers and diskeries." First came the free records. Then came the cash gifts. And now, the magazine said, jockeys were were used to getting twenty-five or fifty a month. In some cases they were essentially on salary with the distributors. One unnamed label head itemized his costs: two New York "spinners" at twenty-five dollars a month each, one in Newark at twenty-five dollars, two in Philadelphia at fifteen dollars each and a third at twenty-five, one in Pittsburgh got fifteen dollars and a distributor in Washington got 150 free copies of each record, and in return he bought local radio airtime. Another ten dollars was paid each month in Detroit for "a specified drive on a given record." One disc jockey, unnamed, was unapologetic about the practice, saying he didn't ask for anything up front, but if he was given something after he played a record as a thank-you, he accepted. "Also I declare every dime on my tax return. In my best year the whole deal amounted to $2,200 in payola . . . I don't need it," he added, because he already got a percentage of ad revenues from his station.

Noting the variety of ways to pay off the jockeys, the story concluded that "there's little prospect for a cure."

~

Even though he had a wife and three young children—Marshall was not yet ten, Elaine was seven, Susie was a toddler—Leonard was gone more than he was at home. But his travels were helping the business to grow. Things were going so well by the summer of 1951 that the brothers decided they needed larger quarters. They moved to new space at the corner of Forty-ninth Street and South Cottage Grove, announcing their businesses with signs in the windows that framed the entrance: CHESS RECORDS and ARISTOCRAT RECORD DISTRIBUTING CO., INC.

Leonard's music deal with Sam Phillips in Memphis proved to be worthwhile, though there were tense moments among three parties over the right to record certain musicians: Leonard, Phillips, and the Bihari brothers at Modern. The Biharis eventually signed Ike Turner to be their talent scout and producer, and the conflict between Phillips and the Biharis only intensified when Phillips sent Chess a musician who would become one of their signature performers. He was born Chester Burnett in eastern Mississippi, but the world came to know him as "Howlin' Wolf," an appropriate nickname given his distinctive and compelling rasp of a voice.

The Wolf was a commanding figure. It wasn't just that he was well over six feet tall. It was his overall presence. He took over a room when he walked in, took over the stage when he performed, even sitting down and dressed in the overalls of the farmer he was. Marshall was awestruck when he first met him. He wanted to shake his hand, but just nine years old, and diminutive at that, found it an impossible task. He extended his small hand and took Wolf's, but his tiny fingers couldn't grip those large ones. Even adults were taken aback. "His thumbnails to me looked as if they were as big as half dollars," said Nate Notkin, the brothers' lawyer who had occasion to shake Howlin' Wolf's hand after one transaction or another. Even the largest size shoes could not accommodate the Wolf's feet. So to keep himself comfortable, he took a razor blade and slit the outside soles from the toe down toward the heel, giving his toes the room they needed. His trademark white socks peeked through the opening.

Howlin' Wolf's association with Chess had complicated beginnings. He had come to the Memphis area in the late 1940s from the Mississippi Delta, where he had been a farmer most of the time, a harmonica player, a guitar player and singer some of the time. Before World War II, when he served four years in the Army, Wolf learned from and played with some of the legends: guitarist Charlie Patton, his primary influence; the immortal Robert Johnson; and harmonica player Rice Miller, better known as Sonny Boy Williamson II. Initially, after the war, farming was Wolf's primary activity. But gradually making music—on the harp, the guitar, or just singing— became more important than tilling the soil, and he moved to the city to further his career. In 1950 he got a fifteen-minute, six-day-a-week spot on KWEM, playing his blues and pitching grain and fertilizer. While the chords may have been the familiar blues progression and the theme the well-treated one of bad woman/good man or vice versa, the presentation was unique. There was a fierce energy that transformed the music, enhanced by Wolf's husky, deep voice.

At the suggestion of a local disc jockey, Phillips finally listened to Wolf's show, and he was entranced. "When I heard Howlin' Wolf, I said, 'This is for me. This is where the soul of man never dies,' " he said years later. And when Wolf came to the studio, Phillips saw that same intensity. "He would sit there with those big feet planted wide apart, playing nothing but the French harp and I tell you, the greatest sight you could see today would be Chester Burnett doing one of those sessions in my studio. God, what it would be worth to see the fervor in that man's face when he sang. His eyes would light up, you'd see the veins in his neck and, buddy, there was *nothing* on his mind but that song. He sang with his damn soul."

More than a decade later, Chess engineer Malcolm Chisholm had a similar experience. A guitar player had recorded some instrumental tracks—six minutes' worth—and when some lyrics eventually were written, everyone agreed Wolf should sing them. There wasn't time for him to learn anything that was written down, so Chisolm rigged up a mike in the control room that was attached to headphones Wolf was wearing out in the studio. Every four bars, the producer told him the words. "He sang it wonderfully," Chisolm said, remembering that magical moment. "He was an enormous musical talent, the damnedest thing."

Wolf's first recording for Phillips had the same drama as Waters's "I Can't Be Satisfied." It was spare and emotional, but where the opening notes of "Satisfied" were Waters picking his amplified guitar, Wolf opened with a deep and mournful moan—the song was appropriately titled "Moanin' at Midnight"—that rose to a howl. Then Willie Johnson started in on his amplified guitar, quickly joined by the solid drumming of Willie Steele. Wolf switched to his harp, which shimmered above the steady beat from Steele and Johnson's lively ornamentation. Alternating the harp with each verse, he gave the song drive and feeling. The flip side, "How Many More Years," was different. Ike Turner offered up a fast string of two-fingered piano chords and then Wolf sang, "How many more years do I got to let you dog me around?" He followed each verse with a blistering harp solo, whose long wails and short blasts punctuated the story of the romantic troubles described in the song.

The record took off right away after it was released in September. "Moanin' " found its way onto *Billboard*'s top ten jukebox chart early in November. "How Many More Years" followed a few weeks later, and stayed on the journal's R&B charts for nearly three months. It also did well in the *Cash Box* "HOT" chart listings in several of the cities that were monitored.

Leonard and Phil were ecstatic. But keeping Howlin' Wolf at Chess was not easy. The Biharis considered Wolf their property because of their relationship with Phillips. So for the next few months, Wolf seesawed between the two labels. He would finish up a session for Phillips and then go over to a radio station in West Memphis, Arkansas, to record slightly revised versions of his Chess releases—one was "Morning at Midnight"—for the Biharis until they finally gave up their claim. Leonard then signed Wolf to an exclusive contract. In exchange the Biharis got the exclusive rights to piano player Roscoe Gordon, another musician Phillips had produced and who also had releases out on both labels.

Phillips's own relationship with Leonard and Phil lasted barely a year.

The end came over a disagreement about who was to pay the bills for a bus tour Jackie Brenston and the Delta Cats were taking to promote "Rocket 88." Years later, Phillips recalled, Leonard would make the bittersweet joke that "if I hadn't a messed up, I could've had Elvis and Jerry Lee Lewis," a reference to two major stars Phillips produced when he started his own Sun label.

"Yes, you could have," Phillips always replied, only half in jest.

The disputes among these men were largely a result of the informal nature of the contracts, the wish by all parties, label, producer, musician, to make the most money, and the evolving nature of the R&B music industry. Sure they were irritated with Leonard, Joe Bihari said of the flap over "Rocket 88." "But we would have done the same thing." On top of that, "contracts didn't mean nothin,' " according to Turner. "We would play for anybody who gave us twenty-five dollars." That was particularly true in a place like Memphis, where there was no union that could, at least in theory, set pay standards. The conflicts among the label owners usually were resolved with a few phone calls, maybe the threat of a lawsuit, because the independents regarded themselves as members of a fraternity. They were competitive—Phillips once said they acted like "jealous children"—but they were not hostile. At bottom there was a shared sense of enterprise.

Like Waters, Howlin' Wolf would develop a special relationship with Leonard and Phil, and if it wasn't quite as personal as Leonard's friendship with Waters, there were good reasons. Leonard had grown up musically with Waters—he had been a critical part of Leonard's musical learning curve. And they had shared their first success on Aristocrat's "I Can't Be Satisfied." It was only three years later that Howlin' Wolf had come along, but Leonard had packed a lot into that time—many, many more hours in the studio, thousands of miles on the road, countless conversations about the music business. He was no longer a novice, even though neither he nor Phil had reached their peak.

six

CHECKERS, CHARTS, AND COPYRIGHTS

D espite the press-release tone of many of its dispatches, there was a good bit of truth in a short *Cash Box* item that ran in the November 17, 1951, issue: "Leonard and Phil of Chess Records have staunchly established themselves this past year." The success of "Rocket 88," the signing of Howlin' Wolf, and the continuing popularity of Muddy Waters had raised the label's visibility, attracting more distributors and new artists and giving them the confidence to keep expanding. In the spring of 1952 they borrowed from their counterparts at the other independent labels and created a subsidiary, Checker Records. The expense for new label graphics was expected to be offset by the opportunity to cut a wider swath through the market. Now that radio play was becoming a factor in sales, disc jockeys often limited the number of records from any one label that they would play on their program. So more labels offered the chance for more airplay and with it the possibility of greater sales.

The first publicity for Checker actually appeared in the trade papers before the brothers formally opened the label. "IT'S YOUR MOVE NOW to get to Checker Records," said an ad in the April 5, 1952, *Cash Box*. It featured records by two of Chicago's jump blues artists: Sax Mallard, who had recorded for Leonard since the earliest days of Aristocrat, and singer Arbee Stidham, backed by musicians who had appeared on several Aristocrat and very early Chess records. A few weeks later the formation of Checker was officially announced. The brothers told *Cash Box* they intended to use the label not only to promote their R&B artists but also to start a country-and-western line—an idea that never panned out despite a few releases in the genre. The company did not incorporate for another four years, which fit the pattern of the brothers' very informal business operation. When Checker did become a company, Sheva, Phil's wife, was added as stockholder along with Leonard, Revetta, and Phil.

The label on each Checker record was another play on the board game: a maroon backround with a checkerboard superimposed on it, a few gray checkers randomly placed on the squares, and *Checker Record Co.* sweeping across the top.

In the meantime, the Chess label was continuing to turn out records—several more Muddy Waters tunes with Jimmy Rogers, Little Walter, and Elgin Evans still backing him, and a few more by Eddie Johnson, the sax player Phil brought to the label. Leonard had also picked up several master tapes by an unorthodox guitar player who was recording in Detroit, John Lee Hooker. Hooker favored an unusual beat often accented by his stomping foot and used spare, distinctive chord progressions in his music. He had had a hit with the Biharis on their Modern label, "Boogie Chillen," and that only encouraged his entrepreneurial bent. He didn't consider himself bound to any one company, and he made records for a number of labels at once, changing his name as needed to accommodate each backer: "Booker," "Cooker," "Texas Slim," and "Little Pork Chops" among them. Leonard signed Hooker to make some records in Chicago, and one of his tunes was a variation on the successful "Boogie Chillen," "Walkin' the Boogie."

Before their split, Leonard had also bought more masters from Sam Phillips, not only more tunes by Howlin' Wolf but also records Phillips produced by two men who would go on to important R&B careers, Rufus Thomas and Bobby Blue Bland. All of this was alongside the main enterprise, producing records in Chicago that would bring out the best in the musicians and provide a salable product. Leonard and Phil got more than they hoped from a May 1952 Muddy Waters session, when Little Walter, the young harp player, took center stage in the studio for a few hours.

⋘

Walter was born in a small Louisiana town in 1930 and started playing the harmonica as a street musician and in clubs in New Orleans and Monroe. He moved to Helena, Arkansas, when he was fourteen to absorb what he could from that small community's band of prominent musicians, among them Rice Miller—Sonny Boy Williamson II—and guitar players Robert Junior Lockwood and Robert Nighthawk. These more seasoned pros ignored Walter in the beginning, regarding the slight teenager as little more than a street urchin. He spent his share of nights sleeping on a pool table and scrounging for meals wherever he could. Determined to survive and persistent about his music, Walter went to the small local clubs night after night, taking the bandstand when the regular musicians would leave for a break. He started to build a following, and musicians began to take note, particularly Williamson. Listeners appreciated his tone and were impressed by his technique. He played the harp like a horn. Drawn naturally to the blues of his surroundings, Walter also listened to jump blues, particularly that of the popular singer and sax player Louis Jordan. With his good ear and natural skill, Walter began to imitate Jordan's saxophone solos on his harmonica, giving the small instrument a new and dynamic resonance.

In 1945, barely fifteen years old, Walter got a radio show on the local Helena station. On occasional short trips to Chicago, he surveyed the music scene and finally moved there for good in 1947 with his friend guitar player Honeyboy Edwards. On their first full day in the city, Walter insisted they head straight for Maxwell Street to play their music for spare change on the crowded corners. They took in more than fifty dollars. Over the next year Walter made a couple of recordings for a small local label, but they didn't sell very well. He continued to work Maxwell Street and caught the eye of Jimmy Rogers, the guitar player who was one of Waters's sidemen. The two teamed up, going from club to club in the evening, sometimes playing six taverns in a row for whatever they could get. On a good night they would net fifteen or twenty dollars.

It was Rogers who then mentioned Walter to Waters, providing the introduction that eventually led to "Louisiana Blues" and "Long Distance Call." "When I run up on Little Walter, he just fitted me," Waters recalled. "He had a thing on the harp that nobody had . . . He was much younger than me, but he could really understand the blues and he knew what to put in there and when to put it in there."

When Waters's band returned to the studio in May of 1952 for another session, there was time left over after the main work was done—Waters's "Please Have Mercy." So they decided to record an instrumental that had been the band's break tune and consequently was played several times a night in clubs at the end of each set. It had proved quite popular with the audience, so it was worth a try to make it into a record.

As was still the practice, Chess was using Universal Recording studios, now located on Ontario Avenue. Either Leonard or Phil was present at the recording sessions, watching over the process even if neither was participating. Time was money, and they were conscious of not wasting either. Tape was expensive, too, and more than once Leonard reused old tape for new sessions, the previous items, like commercials from a radio show, occasionally popping through in between takes of the current recording work.

The band's instrumental—as yet unnamed—began with Walter's sweet tones ascending the scale punctuated with Waters's quickly struck guitar chords, and from drummer Elgin Evans, a soft brush background with just the right amount of ornamentation. A few bars from Rogers added a boogie woogie bass line.

Even though the band knew the song backwards and forward, it took some time to get it right in the studio. A minute or so into the first take, the musicians stopped, unhappy with how the sound was meshing because of an uneven start. "I'm watchin' your foot," one of the men said to Walter. "When you start, I'm gonna start this time." The band went through the song three more times, finally deciding that the second take was the best and would be kept for the master.

The B-side featured Walter singing one of his own compositions. By now, despite his lack of musical know-how, Leonard was beginning to use his instincts to good effect. He told the musicians he wanted a certain punch at the end of the first line: "Crazy about you baby—wham bam," his shorthand for a solid drumbeat. The band got just a few bars into the first take when they stopped abruptly. Leonard was not happy, telling Walter, "There's a squeak on that on the harp. I don't know why." Five takes later they got the song where they wanted it, preserving the sixth try for the master.

Each of these songs had a temporary title. Universal's preproduction report listed the instrumental as "You Pat Will Play," a slight miscue for the song's onetime title, "Your Cat Will Play." The B-side was listed as "Ever Think of Me," one of the lyrics in Walter's tune.

Leonard did not release the record right away, but he kept it around the office on Cottage Grove and played it now and then. One warm, rainy day in late spring, he had it on the small turntable in the office. The door was open because there was no air conditioning, so the sounds could easily be heard out on the street. Marshall, by now ten years old, happened to be at the office that day, and so was Phil. Both saw Leonard's eyes light up as they watched an older black woman standing at the corner, dancing joyfully to Walter's snappy opening notes while she waited for the bus. That was enough market research for Leonard. He decided to release the record on the Checker label, calling the A-side "Juke," the shorthand for jukebox, and with it an evocation of the lively atmosphere in the clubs and taverns where patrons used the machines. The flip side was renamed "Can't Hold Out Much Longer," another of the lyrics from the song.

"Juke" was an immediate hit in the R&B world. By the time the band got to Shreveport on a southern swing, the record was in jukeboxes everyplace they went. Walter was delighted to see customers drop their coins in the machines and play the song over and over. Back in Chicago, Leonard told *Cash Box* a week after the record had been released that his first five hundred were gone in an instant. He had Buster Williams send him another five hundred by air freight—an extraordinary expense at the time—and told the magazine he expected to sell a thousand copies a day around Chicago. It was the kind of hyperbole expected when a label got good news, just like their ads: "Juke—from any angle it looks like a hit." The small ad showed the song title skewed sideways on the page.

By September the record was on the *Billboard* jukebox and bestseller charts, where it stayed for twenty weeks. It was number one on September 27 and stayed there for five weeks. On November 15, *Cash Box* put Leonard and Little Walter on the cover—a first for the label. The picture had been taken in the studio at WGES with the disc jockey Al Benson holding the record while a smiling Walter, harp in hand, sat between him and a grinning Leonard. The record "has gone into the smash category," the magazine said.

Waters and Jimmy Rogers regarded Walter's success with some bemusement. They didn't exactly begrudge him, but they believed they were largely responsible for his getting the credit. "Juke" wasn't really his tune, they maintained for years, but they let him have it because each had had successful records out under his own name, and Walter had not.

Despite the record's success, Walter left Waters's band. It was an incident at the Club Zanzibar, another Chicago night spot, that apparently persuaded Walter to join a group where he would be the star. A patron had asked for "Juke" and dropped some coins on the stage as a tip for the band members. He gave Waters and Rogers double what he gave Walter. That was the ultimate insult. Not long after, he hooked up with a group that called themselves the Four Aces: Louis and Dave Myers, guitar-playing brothers, Fred Below on drums, and Junior Wells on harp.

Walter's arrival meant Wells's ouster, and the band, picking up on the success of "Juke," became known as Little Walter and His Jukes. Leonard got them into the studio in October, anxious to build on Walter's popularity. They recorded "Sad Hours," another instrumental but without the bounce of "Juke." The flip side was "Mean Old World." The results were rewarding: both made it onto the *Billboard* charts in a matter of weeks, and "Sad Hours" also did well in several cities, including St. Louis and San Francisco as tracked by *Cash Box*'s HOT charts.

From the time of the Macomba, Leonard had appreciated the importance of the piano, which was an integral part of the combos that kept his little club packed every night. His nascent recording efforts with Evelyn Aron at Aristocrat featured plenty of keyboards. So it was no surprise that as Waters and Little Walter were making their marks, the Chess brothers turned their attention to piano players.

Benson, whose radio shows helped popularize the Chess brand of blues, also dabbled in recording ventures. Among the musicians he signed was a twenty-six-year-old piano player from Memphis, Willie Mabon, who had been in Chicago since 1942, learning to play jazz and meeting as many other musicians as he could. He was part of the Blues Rockers, who had recorded for Benson. Leonard bought a handful of masters from the deejay, and the group had had a minor hit in Chicago in 1950 on the Aristocrat label.

A handsome, stylish man who looked good in his tuxedo, Mabon considered himself an all-around entertainer but was most comfortable with the breezy touch of jump blues. In the fall of 1952 Mabon wrote "I Don't Know," a wry take on romance with the hook of "I Don't Know" as the answer to each little argument presented in the lyrics. Mabon's piano work was complemented by sax, bass, and drums, and the tune was popular in the clubs he played. Benson recorded "I Don't Know," giving Mabon about $500, according to a friend. But Benson quickly sold the record to Leonard, and it was released on the Chess label in late November 1952. By the first week in December it was on the *Billboard* charts where it stayed for nineteen weeks. The *Cash Box* city-by-city HOT charts put it as number one in several locales.

Hymie Weiss, a brash young man from the East Bronx who would later run his own small label, was the Chess distributor in New York. He took credit for the record's success in Harlem, which, he claimed, spawned its nationwide run. "I was the best salesman, period. I walked in and told them, 'This is a record.' I did not ask," though he conceded that every now and then, money could help. "I was the one who created the fifty-dollar handshake," he boasted, though other record men also claimed to be the first to lay out cash-for-a-play. Weiss's relationship with the Chess brothers started when he met Phil for the first time in the lobby of Manhattan's Edison Hotel to get his sample copies of "I Don't Know." Phil offered Weiss some money as advance encouragement for working the record, but Weiss refused, certain he was going to profit from the commissions he would get from the jukebox and record store sales in his territory.

◆◆

The end of 1952 was a promising moment at Forty-ninth and Cottage Grove. Leonard and Phil had produced three simultaneous R&B hits, "Juke," "I Don't Know," and "Sad Hours." The publicity from the trade magazines buttressed by radio play boosted the company's profile. Less clear was how well the labels were doing financially. While hits might make money, it did not always mean that the profits from these records would offset losses on the discs that didn't. Joe Bihari often joked that label owners trumpeted their sales as "boxcar numbers"—those several-digit numbers painted on freight trains. But often, he said, they suffered "platinum returns" when distributors sent back most of the records unsold. Their costs had to be absorbed by the label.

The prevailing wisdom in the early fifties was that sales of forty thousand for an R&B record were exemplary—enough to get you on the charts, maybe even the number-one slot. Sales of eighty thousand would be a huge success. The sales in turn determined how much money was coming back into a company, and then it was a separate matter how much of that, beyond having been paid for a session, would go to the artist. Accounting procedures were anything but formal and precise, and the label controlled the tallies, both for costs and sales. Though contracts were now more common between label and musician, they were still ad hoc affairs, and the label owners exercised the power. They had the facilities to make the record and promote it, and if they couldn't do business with one musician, there were others to choose from. The musicians, on the other hand, had fewer options because not that many labels were making R&B records. For them it amounted to take it or leave it.

None of the early artists' contracts or any Chess or Checker financial documents survive in company files, so it is not possible to know, for example, what Leonard paid Benson for Willie Mabon, and then what Mabon was supposed to have received, if anything, by way of royalties. Also not available is the exact number of records "I Don't Know" sold and what Leonard's costs were. What has survived, however, are allegations of exploitation by the Chess brothers. And no one was angrier in the retelling than Willie Mabon, who was unhappy about a $3,700 royalty check he believed should have been much bigger.

According to Eddie Boyd, another Chess piano player, Mabon was so angry at Leonard and McKie Fitzhugh, a prominent black disc jockey who was the go-between to get him to Chess, that he stormed down to the office with a gun to shoot them both.

In his retelling in a long 1978 interview with the magazine *Living Blues*, Boyd said Mabon was dissuaded only when Boyd told him the better strategy was to hire a lawyer and take Leonard to court. The story made its way into blues legend. Guitar player John Brim, a Mabon friend who was living in nearby Gary, Indiana, claimed to have heard about the incident. Buddy Guy, who didn't come to Chicago until seven years after the alleged event, was sure it was true. Dixon said Mabon "and the Chess company had some kind of complicated situation."

Beatrice Burnett Mabon, his widow, said no such incident happened. Her husband didn't fool with guns, she said. While it was true that Mabon would come home from a road trip and talk about all the musicians who grumbled about their pay, she said they never had problems with the Chess brothers. She never saw her husband squabbling with either Leonard or Phil when she came to the studio with him, and she recalled the brothers taking care of their rent if need be and sending baskets of food at Christmastime.

Marshall never heard his father talk about what would have been a frightening moment. Phil didn't remember it at all. "I never knew Willie Mabon to do something like that," he said.

Whatever the royalty arrangement between Mabon and the Chess brothers, "I Don't Know" was good to Mabon. In this time of a still small R&B market, musicians wanted to get a record out to enhance their marketability. The money was in the club dates, not in making records. Mabon provided the evidence. Prior to the release of "I Don't Know" and the promotion the company put behind it, Mabon had made union wages when he played, and he usually got club dates only on weekends. But as soon as the record came out, Mabon was turning down jobs for $200 a night—good pay for any musician in 1952. Talent scouts were coming to Chicago hoping to sign him up. On January 24, 1953, his picture was on the cover of *Cash Box* with his wife. The week before he had played a sold-out engagement in Philadelphia that led to a booking at New York's famed Apollo Theater.

Boyd's relationship with Chess was another rocky one. He never forgot Leonard's initial snub when, he said, Leonard used a 1951 session as a demonstration in order to get material for Waters. On top of that he told Boyd he didn't have much talent anyway. Another of the many Mississippi migrants, Boyd went ahead and recorded for a different Chicago label. His "Five Long Years" wound up as a national hit, and Benson eventually got his contract. Then he turned around and sold it to a now-interested Leonard.

Early in 1953, Boyd recorded "Twenty-four Hours" for Chess. It was a lament for a missing girlfriend who had been gone "twenty-four hours and that's twenty-three hours too long." Boyd's spare piano work and straightforward vocals were accompanied by a wailing sax. The song turned into another hit for the label. This time Leonard used a new marketing tool, sending letters out to disc jockeys around the country, "We guarantee '24 Hours' will be a hit in 24 hours."

Though he recorded other records—one called "Third Degree" hit the charts in July—several others were not released. Boyd's relationship with the company soured, and he subsequently blamed Leonard for squelching his career in Chicago. By 1965 he had relocated to Europe, where he remained until his death in 1994, still angry at Leonard.

The matter of unreleased songs was a sore point with some of the musicians. Jimmy Rogers, who had his own deal with Chess beyond backing Waters, complained that too many of his tunes wound up on the shelf and bottled up his opportunities with other labels because he was considered Chess property. Rogers complained to *Living Blues* in 1973 that he would make four songs in a session, Leonard would release one and put the others on the shelf. "The next time you'd record again, see, and he'd release one more. See now he got four songs on the shelf and four in the street. That's the way he would do. He was just tyin' you up, steady tyin' your material up there." When he asked why the record wasn't released, Rogers said Leonard told him, "Well, it's not too good."

Late in 1997, not long before his death, Rogers had his own doubts about the unreleased material. He told *Living Blues:* "I made a lot of stuff. I hope they don't ever release it. I hear some stuff they released on Muddy Waters, it's terrible, man."

⌁

While other labels may have had better studio facilities or owners with more knowledge of music, none worked any harder than Leonard and Phil. Just back from a fall swing in the South, Leonard had headed out again in December 1952 on a spur-of-the-moment trip to Buster Williams's pressing plant in Memphis. "Juke" and "I Don't Know" were at the top of the charts, and Leonard wanted to ensure that his records were being pressed promptly and sent out to distributors. He spent the night at the plant just to be certain. Months earlier he had taken Waters south with him to introduce his prized artist to disc jockeys and distributors. White and black men did not travel together as equals in Tennessee, Mississippi, Alabama, and Georgia. Where Leonard could eat Waters could not; where Leonard could stay, Waters could not. But more than once Leonard stayed in hotels in the black neighborhoods. They were convenient for business; most of the distributors, although white men, operated in their city's black quarters, and having spent a decade in business on Chicago's South Side, Leonard was not uncomfortable in such locations.

However, there could be safety concerns if some white man in authority took umbrage at this breach of "custom and tradition," the benign euphemism for segregation. Joe Bihari, who traveled the South as much as Leonard, was threatened twice by sheriffs in Mississippi who objected to his chummy relationship with his label's black musicians.

By this time Phil was on the road almost as much as Leonard. It not only reflected the growth of the company but also the brothers' understanding of how best to use their talents. Two could cover more territory than one, and they knew by instinct who should go where, based on whose personality meshed better with a particular disc jockey or distributor. Leonard was the driven one, all business and with an edge. Phil was the more jovial younger brother. Recalling the arrangement thirty years after his father's death, Marshall was certain that Chess "might never have reached the level it did had not Phil been there. There was an alchemy between them."

Because Chess was still a two-person operation, Leonard and Phil couldn't be gone at the same time. They also had to schedule their trips around recording sessions. Phil often had an ambitious itinerary that took him east, first to Detroit, then to Cleveland, north to Boston, and then stops in Buffalo and Syracuse before hitting New York, Philadelphia, and maybe Baltimore. Places like Syracuse and Buffalo were a challenge: because of the small black populations, there was no built-in market for the music. "But you had to do the ground work," Phil said, with the hope that it would pay off down the road.

Now that Marshall had turned eleven, Leonard decided he was old enough to take on the road. Marshall's first trip in the fall of 1953 was a short one by his father's standards: Chicago to Gallatin, Tennessee, for a stop at Randy's Record Mart, a sponsor of those WLAC R&B shows; Atlanta, to see Jake Friedman at Southland and Zenas Sears, an influential white disc jockey who played black music; and then home. By this time, Leonard had bought a Cadillac—it was roomy, sturdy, and most important for a man who hated the heat, it had air conditioning. It seemed to be the car of choice for these independent record men. Joe Bihari had had two in a row, one green, the other black; Leonard's was two-tone blue.

Precocious by nature and encouraged by his father, Marshall sometimes was allowed to drive on isolated country roads. He had learned the rudiments behind the wheel on the dirt roads near Miller Beach, a modest resort area a couple hours outside of Chicago where Joe Chess had bought a cottage. For a boy who missed his father when Leonard was on those promotion trips, the chance to go with him now was doubly special. And there would be a particularly gratifying moment a year or so later, when Leonard showed his trust in Marshall by curling up in the backseat for a nap as his son, perched on two pillows, drove down one of the back roads his father had come to know so well.

That first stop at Randy's in Gallatin was an eye-opener for Marshall. It was the first time he saw a white teenager buy a rhythm-and-blues record. The moment was both a testament to the influence of nearby WLAC in Nashville and Randy's advertising and a hint of what the market could be. There was also a culinary surprise for this Jewish boy from the city: eating a hamburger literally made of ground-up ham.

Marshall's sister Elaine also got to dabble in the business. Though only eight, she became one of her father's informal record testers. After listening to a passel of songs, she'd tell Leonard which ones she wanted, and, he boasted to Cash Box, she picked songs that became hits.

◆◆

One of the by-products of Willie Mabon's success with "I Don't Know" was the interest it generated among other musicians anxious to record it. In its first month on the charts, two entertainers decided to do their own versions, one of them Tennessee Ernie Ford for Capitol Records. With the right kind of business setup, generally a separate publishing company, this could generate additional income for the writer and the publisher, depending on whether the song was copyrighted, who owned the copyright, and whether the song and the writer had registered with the organizations that monitored "public performances" of these works. A "public performance" included radio play or a live performance in a club or theater—owners paid yearly license fees for the right to have live music, and radio stations paid yearly license fees for the right to broadcast copyrighted songs. Until 1978 jukebox play, despite the popularity of the medium and its particular importance in the R&B field, was not considered a "public performance" unless admission was charged to enter the premises with the jukebox.

The first of the performance rights groups was the American Society of Composers, Authors and Publishers, ASCAP, which had been formed in 1914. The second, Broadcast Music Inc., BMI, started operating in 1940 as a direct result of disagreements between broadcasters and ASCAP over licensing fees for radio play of ASCAP songs. The creation of BMI proved to be beneficial to black artists—ASCAP wanted little to do with the kind of music they were writing and performing, focusing instead on what members considered to be mainstream popular music. One illuminating case was the long struggle Jelly Roll Morton, the prolific and talented jazz musician and writer, endured before he was granted membership in ASCAP and allowed to collect the royalties due him from his work.

BMI realized there was a large and fertile field open to them, and they advertised themselves as welcoming the talent ignored by ASCAP, including the black rhythm-and-blues artists. By 1950 it was not unusual for every song on the *Billboard* R&B jukebox and sales charts to carry the BMI designation. An ASCAP song made only a rare appearance. Significantly, however, there was no radio play chart for R&B music, evidence of the paucity of broadcast outlets for it and because of that, greatly reduced potential for income from the songs.

In the first years of their record operation, Leonard and Phil paid no attention to copyrights and performance rights. They were concerned about making records and selling them. They weren't alone among the independents. The Bihari brothers at Modern were three years into their operation before they set up a publishing operation. Evelyn Aron, though, knew about copyright. She and one of her original partners, Mildred Brount, secured the copyright to "Bilbo Is Dead" in 1947. The writing credit on the application went to Tom Archia. Clarence Samuels, with help from Sax Mallard, had protected three of his songs, including the popular "Boogie Woogie Blues," by securing his own copyright. But that was only one step in the process. Copyright protected the holder from infringement—somebody stealing the words or music—but in order to collect those performance rights fees, the copyright owner (usually the publisher) had to join either BMI or ASCAP and register the songs with the organization. When either organization's respective monitoring system determined that the song had been performed, it paid a share of royalties to the publishing company that registered the song and to the songwriter as long as he or she was registered with the group. Though ASCAP always had provided for writer-members, BMI did not do so until 1950. In its first ten years of operation, the organization relied on publishers to get the money to the writer. By 1950, if a writer was not a member of BMI or ASCAP, then the writer's share of the royalties was lost unless he or she had a separate agreement with the publisher to share in the performance royalties paid to the publisher.

In these early days few of the blues writers registered with either BMI or ASCAP. Most were probably unaware of the procedures and expected to get their money from record deals and club dates where they performed their songs.

The lax attitude about publishing was apparent from the *Billboard* charts. Typically the charts included the association designation for each song listed, but in the R&B section there were occasions when only the artist and the label were listed. This was the case when Waters and Andrew Tibbs made their first appearance on the jukebox charts in 1948, an indication that neither Evelyn, Leonard, nor an independent publisher had registered the songs. In many cases their tunes were not registered with BMI until several years later.

By 1951 some Chess and Checker material was being copyrighted and registered with BMI, but not because of Leonard or Phil's direct involvement. The brothers had hooked up with John Henry Burton, a black Chicago lawyer who had formed his own publishing company, John Henry Burton Ltd., with an address at the Chess offices at 4858 South Cottage Grove. As a publisher, Burton had secured the copyright for a number of songs on the labels. Among the more prominent were Howlin' Wolf's first two songs, "Moanin' at Midnight" and "How Many More Years," Little Walter's "Juke," and Eddie Boyd's "Twenty-four Hours." They were also registered with BMI, so whatever performance fees were collected accrued to Burton. Burton also acted as in-house counsel for the brothers. He was on the payroll and did a number of things such as looking over union contracts prior to a session and helping out a musician who might be in some kind of trouble. "We got to know each other," Phil explained. "He started to come around, and we said, 'What the hell, give him an office.' "

Burton stayed with the Chess brothers for many years, though in the mid-fifties, while still associated with Chess, he ran a succession of small labels, including Parrot, which he had purchased from Al Benson. A man with the reserved air of a business lawyer, Burton was something of a trailblazer in his private life, moving to the white upper-echelon suburb of Glencoe when there were just a handful of other black families there.

Though Leonard was blasé about copyrights and performance rights, the potential value of the Chess catalogue was not lost on two New York businessmen, and early in 1953, Gene and Harry Goodman, by coincidence Chicago natives and also Benny Goodman's brothers, came to see the Chesses. They already were successful music publishers in Manhattan. Now they had a proposal for Leonard and Phil: Create a new publishing company divided equally among the four—two Goodmans, two Chesses. Each set of brothers would get half the profits coming into the company.

His own boss up to now, Leonard nonetheless accepted the deal, deciding not to follow the practice of several of the other independent labels and start his own publishing company. Jerry Wexler, the energetic executive at burgeoning Atlantic Records, told Leonard he was crazy to hand over half of his potential profits. Wexler offered to have Atlantic handle the copyrighting of the company's material for a small service charge, 15 percent. "I can't bother with that," Leonard told him.

So Leonard accepted the Goodmans' deal. "He's not making any money anyway," Marshall explained, recalling his father's thinking, "so to make fifty percent of something is better than 100 percent of nothing." Allen Arrow, one of the Chess brothers' lawyers, explained further. In these early days, Arrow said, "Leonard and Phil never understood, never cared about the music publishing business at all." With the nonchalance that marked his style, Phil put it this way: "We had a couple of records that started to make some noise, so we decided to do it."

Arc Music was formed in August of 1953, and the Goodmans' first mission was to comb the catalogue to copyright as much material as possible and register it with the appropriate performance rights society. The bulk went to BMI. Eventually they bought the copyrights and publishing rights to the Chess and Checker songs that Burton had controlled. Another mission was to market the company songs for "cover" versions to yield even more income. The latter could be especially lucrative. Indeed, Leonard's lack of appreciation for the value of a song was apparent when he had sold "I Don't Know" to another company, Republic Music. Had there been an Arc to publish Mabon's song, the money due from the sales of Ernie Ford's version would have been paid to the company and Mabon directly, had he signed up with BMI. Under industry practices, Mabon, as the writer, would get half the "mechanical" royalty of two cents that came in, or one penny, and the remaining half, the other penny, would be given to the publisher.

The Chess brothers and the Goodmans made their own deal concerning the "mechanical" royalties involving songs first put out on Chess and Checker records. The four Arc principals agreed that Chess would pay the one-penny "mechanical" fee on the sale of these records directly to the writer. But Arc would not get the other penny even though it was the publisher of the song. That penny per record remained at Chess and Checker. One provision of the early Arc songwriting contracts said specifically that "no royalties are to be paid on these recordings" for the Chess and Checker labels. The writer would get mechanical royalties through Arc only from the sales of subsequent versions of a song on other labels.

The Arc songwriting agreements, which had provisions typical of the time, spelled out the revenue breakdowns between publisher and writer for selling copies of the sheet music and orchestrations, and for licensing the music for movies and broadcasts in the United States, Canada, and foreign countries. Generally, these license fees were to be split fifty-fifty between the publisher and the writer.

None of this mattered much until Mick Jagger and his English mates came along and turned so many of the songs in the Chess catalogue into worldwide hits.

seven

BLUES WITH A FEELING

Willie Dixon, the big, cheerful bass player, had kept up an informal relationship with Leonard since playing on those few Aristocrat sessions in 1948. The two men got to know one another from the Macomba, when Dixon would stop in to hear Tom Archia after finishing work with his group, the Big Three, at the El Casino. It was just around the corner. "Once in a while I'd bring my bass in there and jam with them, so they found out I was a pretty good bass player," Dixon said.

Dixon had been surrounded by music as a boy in Vicksburg, Mississippi, both the spirituals he heard in church and the more profane, alluring blues and honky-tonk from musicians who passed through town. He loved to write poetry, drawing on the drama of his own life for material. One of fourteen children with an absent father, who had already served time at state prison farms by the time he was sixteen for stealing plumbing supplies and hoboing on a freight train, Dixon put his poems to music and peddled the songs to traveling hillbilly and country-and-western groups. Dixon's own first musical experience came when he sang bass with a local gospel quartet, but it was his athleticism, not his musical ability, that propelled him out of Mississippi to Chicago and the career that would make him famous.

Dixon headed to Chicago in 1936 to become a boxer. At six feet plus and nearly three hundred pounds, he was something to be reckoned with, and not long after his arrival, he won the novice division of the Illinois Golden Gloves. He never abandoned music, though, and sang with various vocal groups in the area. One of his singing partners was Leonard "Baby Doo" Caston, who became a good friend as soon as they met. As important, he made Dixon his first bass—a one-string affair attached to a tin can—and convinced him to give up boxing for music. He promised it would be more lucrative, and he knew it was easier on the body.

For a time the two were part of a group called the Five Breezes, making whatever money they could going from corner to corner around Chicago and passing the hat. They didn't look like much, Caston remembered, "but we had good harmony." They had the best luck on Maxwell Street—"Jewtown"—making as much as fifty dollars apiece after one day. It was better money than a job at the stockyards.

By 1946, Dixon and Caston had reconfigured their musical lives, creating the Big Three Trio: Dixon on bass, Caston at the piano, and Ollie Crawford on guitar. No longer scruffy street musicians, they now dressed in suits and polished their stage presence for work in clubs, especially those frequented by whites. Their music was light and jazzy, not the hard-edged blues of other Delta migrants or the jump blues favored by the sax-dominated bands.

Dixon himself, though, never strayed too far from the blues. "As far as I'm concerned, blues is the greatest music on earth 'cause it speaks the facts of life, for somebody in the past or somebody in the present, somebody in the future 'cause it's telling the truth," Dixon said. He linked that truth to the history of his people, reminding any audience that blues grew out of slavery, and that the conditions of black Americans were still grim. So strong were Dixon's views on racial matters that he had refused induction into the armed services. "Why should I go to work to fight to save somebody that's killing me and my people?" he told authorities. "I wasn't a citizen, I was a subject." Dixon spent ten months in jail for his refusal to serve, and when he was discharged, he was given a new classification that kept him out of the draft for good.

When Baby Doo Caston's persistent marital problems forced the Big Three to break up in 1951, Dixon was on his own. Now he was free to accept an offer from the Chess brothers to work for the label. It was a good match: Leonard was looking for someone who could find musicians, help with arrangements, and write songs; Dixon found an opportunity to meld his musical talents and beliefs into business. He had paid attention to how recent migrants like Waters were adapting their music to the hustle of Chicago. He was sure he could contribute to their enterprise.

Like Waters and Howlin' Wolf, Dixon had a special relationship with

Leonard, and like those two men, he was also a presence in Marshall's life. The boy thought of the jovial big man as Santa Claus, and if Dixon didn't give Marshall actual presents, he gave him the gifts of experience and camaraderie. They were pals, driving around the South Side together in Willie's Chevrolet station wagon, which always tilted leftward because he was so heavy and Marshall was slight. Sometimes they went to the bank where Willie cashed his Chess check, or they'd stop by to see Willie's family, which was an eye-opener for a white teenager, even the son of the street-smart Leonard.

"Willie had two wives and families," Marshall said. "He would talk to me about that . . . It was very strange for me. I mean, how many people would have wives and families that both knew of each other? It was like from another era."

Dixon explained it this way: "You see most people have always tried to make it some type of disgrace because a man has more than one woman. . . . I don't feel it's no disgrace for a man because it's forty cows to one bull, one male fish to a hundred females, ten hens for one rooster, and if there's one tomcat in the neighborhold, he has everything in full bloom."

In later years Leonard referred to Dixon as "my right arm." The relationship between the two men, however, was not to be without its problems. Often centered on money, the disagreements were rooted in different views of how the business operated, how much money the company had in those early days, and most important, who was entitled to what.

Dixon remembered that he had to wait a long time to get paid for his 1948 Aristocrat work with Robert Nighthawk, but Leonard eventually came through with sixty dollars, roughly the union amount for a sideman who played two sessions. At the time, the delay was a fact of life in the nascent business: Leonard couldn't pay out money until money had come in from sales. Later on, the disagreements would become much more complicated, when royalties for songwriting were at stake and the amounts in question were much more substantial. For now, however, Dixon found a home, and Leonard and Phil found someone to help fill the gaps in their musical knowledge. It was another step in building a successful business.

~

Little Walter was the first Chess musician to work with Dixon, on two tunes recorded in March 1953 and released a month later, "Tell Me Mama" and "Off the Wall." The Myers brothers were still on guitar;

Dixon played the bass, and Fred Below was on drums. Each of the songs had a brief stay on the trade paper charts.

Although Leonard banked on the blues in its various permutations—with harmonicas, guitars, and pianos—he was always shopping around for something else that might sell. And so it was in this same month of March that the company released "Let's Go Down to the Tavern" by singer Buddy Moreno. It was one of the few Chess records by a white musician, and Leonard and Phil must have known that it had a natural base of support. A half-page *Cash Box* ad said the tune was "backed by the National Tavern Owners Association." There was one other noteworthy aspect to the ad. For the first time in a year or so, Chess listed its distributors—now an impressive list of twenty-eight with representation in every part of the country.

With these early spring releases out of the way, Leonard left on a three-week southern swing in early April 1953 to lend his personal touch to the Chess promotion. He made his usual stops—Memphis, to check in with Buster Williams, his distributor and record presser; Atlanta; New Orleans; and Shreveport, where he made a point to be especially attentive to Stan Lewis. It was not uncommon now for a Chess record to get its first big break—airplay or promotion—through Lewis's growing enterprise. The spirit of camaraderie-despite-competition was evident when Leonard and Jerry Blaine of the Jubilee label found they had the same itinerary and traveled the last few stops together.

In Shreveport, Leonard learned that Lewis was about to start sponsoring a new one-hour R&B radio show in Little Rock. It was a promising development given that R&B got relatively little radio play. *Billboard* still declined to publish a radio play chart for the music, as was done for popular and country-and-western songs. Despite the obvious audience for the music—the vast majority of them black listeners—and the proliferation of labels in the past year—though several were short-lived—the music still accounted for less than 6 percent of the record business.

Nonetheless a radio station tried to find the broadest possible audience, and R&B music presented the stations with a dilemma. They weren't sure whether to have shows devoted exclusively to the genre or to weave the music into shows that played a mix of tunes. Much depended on the tastes of each particular disc jockey and whether he knew the music and his potential audience. Picking the tunes to play was more difficult than in pop music or country and western, because in these genres there were many more well-known artists and songwriters recording on bigger labels. Well-entrenched companies could provide the deejays with plenty of background material on pop and country and western music. The smaller R&B labels provided few such aids. But the new Arkansas program was evidence that the music Hoss Allen, Gene Nobles, and John Richbourg had played on Nashville's WLAC seven years earlier was here to stay.

⌁

Phil headed east to meet with his distributors as soon as Leonard got back to Chicago, the brothers now resembling an entrepreneurial tag team. Leonard then turned his attention to the next batch of releases—an eclectic bunch including a new disc by Eddie Boyd, "Third Degree"; a woman's answer to Mabon's "I'm Mad" by local club singer Mitzi Mars called "I'm Glad"; and a new Mabon recording, "You're a Fool," recorded in New York under Leonard's supervision. The out-of-town production didn't mean much commercially, though. The record made little splash.

If Leonard and Phil had a philosophy, it was to make a hit, and, they told *Cash Box* "the key to a hit is to give the people what they want to hear." Figuring that out was the hard part, a combination of experience, a hunch, and knowing how to give a song a boost. The brothers didn't always guess right, but Leonard was willing to try anything. After a chance encounter with veteran bluesman Washboard Sam at Chicago's Midway Airport, Leonard convinced him to make a few sides for the company, and released "Diggin' My Potatoes" late in the summer. He put out "Watermelon Man" on the Checker label because he liked the idea of the song, which was about the days when men went house to house selling watermelons from the back of their trucks. It was written and performed by Browley Guy, a young man who had never recorded before, and the record didn't sell despite a positive mention in *Cash Box.*

When the vocal group the Orioles had an R&B and pop hit with a tune called "Crying in the Chapel" on Blaine's Jubilee label, Leonard wanted to get his own vocal group. He found one through a recent acquaintance, Alan Freed, a young disc jockey in Cleveland who was starting to shake up the radio world. Before long, Freed would become one of the most powerful men in the business. With the muscle to make or break a record, he would influence how label owners did business not only with disc jockeys but with their own artists as well. For now, though, Freed was a friend and fellow music enthusiast who first came into the Chess brothers' orbit when Phil met him at a small station in Akron.

The two men hit it off and became close enough that when Freed had a serious car accident, his wife Jackie asked Phil to come to Cleveland and help her out. Phil had actually been a secret but important part of their courtship. Freed was still married to his first wife when he met Jackie, and he needed some cover to see her on the job at a dance studio. When Phil was in town, Freed recruited him to go to the studio on the pretext of dance lessons. In time Leonard became an equally good friend of the Freeds. On occasion, his home in Chicago provided a respite for Jackie during the turbulent moments with her husband.

Freed had discovered the Coronets, a group of high school friends from Cleveland, when they brought him a dub of an original song, "Nadine." He liked it enough to send it along to Leonard. Friendly as they were, the nod to the Chess brothers was not unique. Freed had many deals and arrangements with many labels, sending songs to various label owners in return for gestures of appreciation. Art Sheridan, Leonard's first record presser, had made Freed, his wife, and brother partners in a distributing company. Others gave the disc jockey pieces of songs, banking on their ability to earn royalties from Freed's promotion. Phil and Sheva made sure to send Baccarat crystal to Freed and his wife, for their anniversary. This was all more sophisticated than slapping some bills into a waiting hand, though Freed never overtly asked for anything. The idea of each party taking care of the other was implicit.

In the studio in Chicago the Coronets' original version of "Nadine" was scrapped in favor of a more traditional sound, with Sax Mallard's combo backing the singers. Released the first week in September, the record lasted nearly three months on *Billboard*'s jukebox chart and landed on several of the HOT charts in *Cash Box*. Leonard bragged to the magazine that he was shipping 25,000 records a week, even before its official release date. Whether that many were selling was another matter.

The Coronets' success was tempered by the fact that they had to share a writing credit with Freed. It meant he got a share of the mechanical royalties, one penny for each record sold. Sam Griggs, one of the singers, said Freed got the credit because he had "the necessary influence" within the record industry. Besides, Griggs said, he and his singing mates were told that without Freed "nothing else would happen" with the song.

By now either Leonard or Phil or the company were regulars in *Cash Box*. It was rare to find an issue that didn't have some piece of news about the brothers' comings and goings or some mention of a new release, either as an "award-o'-the-week" or a "sleeper." Other label owners and their records were mentioned—the Biharis, Syd Nathan at King, Wexler and

Ahmet Ertegun at Atlantic, Blaine at Jubilee—but few, if any, with the frequency of the Chess brothers. While the Chess and Checker records were reviewed regularly in *Billboard,* gossip about the company was much rarer. *Billboard* cut a wider swath through the entertainment world—and charged much more for advertising. It covered television, radio, and movies, not just music, and in the big picture, Leonard and Phil were still small-time players. *Cash Box* was devoted to the jukebox industry and paid particular attention to the small independent labels. The free publicity for Chess and Checker in the chitchat columns came from Leonard's boldness in pushing Chess Records as well as the interest of young, ambitious writers at the magazine looking for copy to fill their weekly columns. All the free mentions were in addition to ads the brothers regularly took out in both magazines, along with their sponsoring a short weekly *Billboard* column with other label owners, "Rhythm and Blues Tattler," about the latest R&B happenings.

~

Little Walter and Muddy Waters remained the heart of Chess and Checker music. When Walter went back in the studio in July, the Myers brothers and Fred Below were still behind him. The group turned out another hit in the fall of 1953, "Blues with a Feeling." The accented interplay between Walter's opening harp solo and Below's drum strokes hinted at the stop rhythm that would be used so successfully in a few months on Waters's upcoming records.

When he came into the studio for his September session, Waters had some new musical ideas, and now neither Leonard nor Phil got in the way. For the first time since his Aristocrat days Waters brought a piano player in to record, twenty-three-year-old Otis Spann, another Mississippi native. Spann's father was a preacher who also played the piano; his mother played the guitar. Touched more by the profane than the sacred, young Otis wanted to play blues, not spirituals. When he was eight, he won a blues contest in Jackson, and by the time he was fourteen he was playing with a band in juke joints and house parties around the Mississippi capital. He moved to Chicago in 1947, served a stint in the Army, and then joined Waters early in 1953 after his discharge from the service. Waters and Spann had "fooled around," as Muddy put it, before Spann went into the Army. Now he wanted him to be part of the bigger sound he was looking for. "If you get that piano in there you get a whole full bed of background music," he explained. "I had it in my head that the piano always was a blues instrument and belonged with my blues. . . . Spann and I had a thing together," Waters added. "I felt very close to him." It was that unspoken communication that helped propel their first record together, "Mad Love," onto the *Billboard* bestseller chart and the *Cash Box* HOT charts. Spann's piano work was unobtrusive but carefully wrought, complementing Waters's vocal and the harp accents provided by Walter Horton, filling in for Little Walter.

As in "Blues with a Feeling," the opening stop-time accents that alternated between Horton and Spann prefigured the great success that would come in a few months when Waters and Dixon found their musical common ground. The flip side of "Mad Love," "Blow Wind Blow," showed off Spann to much greater effect with a spirited solo full of rapid-fire passages that mimicked the guitars.

Apart from Waters's sessions, Leonard was on the road for most of September 1953. He made his usual stops in Louisiana, Tennessee, Florida, and Georgia and this time added a swing through Alabama. Early in November he was on the road again, back to New Orleans to record four songs with a new discovery, James "Sugar Boy" Crawford. Crawford's first song, "I Don't Know What I'll Do," had done well enough for Leonard to want more. He was trusting his instincts now. As soon as he heard Crawford, he signed him to the label and cut the record on the spot. On this November trip to New Orleans, Leonard's interest in making a new dollar surfaced when he briefly contemplated buying a radio station in the city. He talked to Stan Lewis about putting in a bid for local station WMRY, whose studio Leonard had used to record Crawford, but the general manager publicly squelched rumors of any negotiations. He said the station was not for sale and that while he had met Leonard, there had been no talk about buying the station. It could be that Leonard was not financially ready to branch out. In fact, the manager took a swipe at him for apparently not paying his bills. Leonard had used the studio and some of the employees, he explained, adding, "I understand that promises of reimbursement were made but not fulfilled." While this opportunity failed to materialize, Leonard did not give up on the idea of owning a radio station. It would just have to wait until the right opportunity meshed with the right time.

Nineteen fifty-three ended well for the brothers. Six songs had made it onto the *Billboard* charts, and most of them were also on the *Cash Box* HOT charts. In an end-of-the-year jukebox poll Willie Mabon garnered several mentions for the label: he was number three on the "most promising artist" list, number four on "best artist," and number five on "best record" with "I Don't Know."

Company financial records from this time are not available, but there were two good indications that the brothers were now making money. Both had left the neighborhood near the Macomba and had moved some forty blocks south to the Jewish enclave of South Shore; their sister Mae and her family had also moved there. Each family bought a sturdy, two-story brick home with a small yard, and the three families were just a few blocks from one another. As important, Leonard was looking for new office space to accommodate the expanding business. He found it in the spring of 1954, a block and a half north at 4750 South Cottage Grove.

The space the brothers rented in a one-story red brick building was at the south end of the block, nicely situated among several other small businesses. Victory Stationery, a printing shop, was next door. It was owned by Russ Fratto, who printed the Chess and Checker stationery and who also owned the building that housed his business and what were to be the new Chess offices. He agreed to let the brothers convert it from unused space for his printing operation. A carpet company, an automobile accessory shop, and a tire company were across the street. In a few months, another local record company would move in, Vee Jay Records at 4747. Up the block at the corner of Forty-seventh and Cottage Grove was Pappy's Liquor Store, the scene of weekly spats late in the night that occasionally turned ugly. More than once passersby would see bloodstains on the sidewalk on their morning walks. And catty-corner from the liquor store was South Side Bank and Trust, where Leonard and Phil did their business. Right across the street from the bank was a small restaurant run by another set of Jewish brothers, Hymie and Jay Deutsch and their father, Sam—Deutsch's Kosher-Style Restaurant. It reflected the time when Cottage Grove and Forty-seventh had been primarily Jewish. There were still some Jews around—most of them businesspeople like the Chesses—but now the neighborhood was primarily black.

Marshall came to know these landmarks well. Just shy of his thirteenth birthday and just as precocious as his father had been, he started coming to the office after school and daily during the summer, whizzing north on Cottage Grove on his motor scooter—a Cushman Eagle that he parked right inside the door. He did the scut work—sweeping the floors, picking up

trash, running the addressograph machine, where every disc jockey, distributor, and radio station owner the brothers knew had his own nameplate,
and then stuffing big canvas mail bags with the latest Chess and Checker
releases. They were packed in special envelopes, big enough to accommodate the record and two pieces of cardboard on either side for protection.
Leonard also let his son literally handle the money—the boy made regular
trips up the block and across the street to the bank, carrying the day's or
week's proceeds in a paper bag. Often it was cash from the record sales in
Chicago the brothers handled themselves. A few checks might be sprinkled
in from distributors sending in the proceeds from their sales. The banking
completed, Marshall would go across the street to Deutsch's to pick up coffee and buttered kaiser rolls for his father and uncle, plain, no poppy seeds,
because Leonard didn't want any stuck in his false teeth. His had been
removed years earlier as a result of gum disease, but he was determined that
no one, not even his wife, see him without his teeth in. He had two pair
made so that one set could soak while he wore the other one.

The Chess operation was still a small one, but by now Leonard and Phil
had some clerical help for billing and other administrative chores. The
women Leonard hired—Idell Nelson and Carri Saunders, both black—were
smart and efficient and, perhaps most important, not cowed by his aggressive personality and penchant for swearing. Sonny Woods, a young black
man, had known the brothers since the Macomba, when he did odd jobs
around the club as a teenager. He moved with them to Forty-ninth and
South Cottage Grove and moved again with them to 4750. Now he helped
with the shipping and distributing, and over time he evolved into an informal record tester. "What do you think?" Leonard would ask. If Sonny gave
it a thumbs-down, Leonard usually put it on the shelf, having had his own
suspicions confirmed. On the other hand, Marshall said, "No one would
stop my father if he had the feeling about a song."

When Leonard told *Cash Box* about the move to 4750, he said the idea
was to bring in state-of-the-art recording equipment and make the records
right there. For the moment that turned out to be wishful thinking. However, 4750 was amenable to making some music on the premises. The inside
space was set up like a railroad flat, one room behind the other. Inside the
doorway, which opened onto Cottage Grove, was a little reception area
with a desk. A narrow hallway ran along the right with a door opening into
one room, Leonard and Phil's office, and then right behind it was another
room. There was a window on the wall that connected the two rooms.

Over time the back room evolved into a rehearsal space and a primitive studio with a few chairs for the musicians, a microphone or two, and the necessary backup equipment. The tape recorder sat on a table in the adjacent room in front of the window. It wasn't much, but the brothers had taken the first step toward making their own music.

Russ Fratto became more than just a landlord and business associate. Soon he was one of Leonard's best friends, so good a friend that he would get songwriting credits on a few Chess and Checker tunes, some of them, Phil said, in exchange for giving the writers cash on the spot. Later on, there would be disputes about that assertion. Fratto also became one of the regulars at 4750, joining Leonard for amiable games of casino in the evenings when he was finished with the day's business.

The administrative details of moving an office could not be allowed to interfere with making music. Leonard and Phil were determined to make 1954 an even better year than the previous one. They got off to a good start when Little Walter's "You're So Fine" made it onto the *Billboard* jukebox and bestseller lists by the first week of January, just ten days after its release. By February it was on the HOT charts in eight of the twelve cities polled by *Cash Box,* including Chicago, San Francisco, New Orleans, Dallas, and Nashville.

"You're So Fine" was another up-tempo blues tune featuring Walter's prodigious talent in mixing up different harp sounds in the same song. It was one of the last records he made with the trio that had served him so well—the Myers brothers and Below. Though they were putting out the records, neither Leonard nor Phil could control the relationships among the recording artists, much as they would have liked to keep a good thing intact. Dave Myers felt that the combination of him and his brother was the perfect backing for Walter. Before Willie Dixon came, Myers had played the bass parts with his creative guitar work, which earned him the nickname "Thumper." He liked the loose atmosphere at Chess. Neither Leonard nor Phil interfered with the music, letting the musicians play and imposing no scripted arrangements. "We didn't actually have no charts from Little Walter because he was unable to tell us what he really wanted to play," Myers explained. "But whatever he jumped on, we could fit with it because we knew how." Though the three musicians melded into a musical whole, they eventually broke apart over disagreements with Walter about what he promised to pay them.

With the Myers brothers and Below gone, Walter would now record with a mix of guitar players and drummers, with Dixon often playing bass. Though the two had a distant and testy relationship, their time in the studio together would nonetheless produce a few more hits.

At the same time as "You're So Fine" was making its mark, Dixon came up with a new tune that he felt was perfect for Muddy Waters. It featured the stop-time rhythm Waters had already used in "Mad Love" and incorporated that same "gypsy woman" Waters sang about in his first recording for Aristocrat in 1947. Dixon's new song, "I'm Your Hoochie Coochie Man," again combined the mystical with the sexual, weaving together fortune tellers, mojos, and the magic of number seven—"on the seventh hour, on the seventh day on the seventh month the seven doctors say he was born for good luck"—into a driving blues. Leonard told Dixon that if Waters liked the song, he could have it.

Dixon had no doubt it would work. On a cold December night he found Waters and his group at the Club Zanzibar, and at the break Dixon told him to get his guitar. The two of them stood in front of the bathroom, Dixon explaining the song. "Now here's your riff: 'Da-da-da-Da,' " Dixon said. "The gypsy woman told my mother, Da, da da Da," and he went through the verses. After going back and forth with it for about fifteen minutes, Waters decided to perform it on the spot. He and the band had an impromptu rehearsal and then played it for the audience. It was an instant smash and became as identified with Waters as his pompadour and guitar. "He was doing that song until the day he died," Dixon said later.

On January 7, 1954, Leonard gathered Waters and his band in the studio to record the song. It was released at the end of the month, and Phil bragged to *Cash Box* that four thousand copies sold in the first week. At the same time, Leonard took off for one of his southern swings to boost the record and look for new talent. By the time he got back, he was trumpeting "Hoochie Coochie Man" as Chess's number-one seller. The national R&B charts indicated that he and Waters had a hit. By March 13, the song was on the *Billboard* jukebox and sales charts and was listed as number six on *Cash Box*'s "Rhythm and Blues Top 15," an expansion of the magazine's recently added top ten R&B tunes, itself an indication of the music's growing popularity. Right above the Waters tune was Little Walter's "You're So Fine," still selling in a number of cities across the country. The one place that neither song did particularly well in was the Northeast. Even though "Hoochie Coochie Man" and "You're So Fine" stayed on the charts in the Midwest and South, they did not crack the Philadelphia and New York markets, which seemed more attuned to vocal groups and jazzier presentations than the pulsing blues coming out of Chicago.

Getting the musicians to tour to support the music was an important ingredient in a record's success. Though booking agencies handled such things for the most part, Leonard stepped in on occasion. When he left on his southern swing in May, his first stop was Memphis, where he and popular local disc jockey Dewey Phillips cosponsored a dance at the city's Hippodrome Ballroom featuring his three main blues stars, Little Walter, Muddy Waters, and Howlin' Wolf. The Memphis dance meant good exposure for the musicians. They were already known in the city, but the Hippodrome, which was actually a skating rink for black Memphis residents, offered the chance, because of its size, to reach a large, live audience all at once and one that was more upscale than those in small, local clubs.

The timing was especially good. A live show would surely be a boost to the new songs the three had just released: Waters's "Just Make Love to Me," Walter's "Oh Baby," and Wolf's "No Place to Go" and "Rockin' Daddy." Wolf was living in Chicago now and was backed by a snappy young guitarist, Hubert Sumlin, with Otis Spann on the keyboard and Dixon on bass.

Dixon was not only writing songs for Chess—"Just Make Love to Me" was his and he had coauthored "Oh Baby"—and playing the bass. He was also putting sessions together. He had a terrific network of contacts throughout the city's blues community, and when it came time to go into the studio, he could find an errant musician. Not everyone had telephones; even if they did, they didn't always answer them, and they didn't always stay at home. Dixon not only knew them but also knew their friends, their girlfriends, and their habits. Leonard knew the South Side as well as any white man, but Dixon's ability to gather the necessary personnel made Leonard's work that much easier.

∾

Waters's reward for the success of "Hoochie Coochie Man" was a new red and white Oldsmobile 98. The gesture was instructive, a window into the relationship that was evolving between the Chess brothers and their artists. It was an amalgam of culture, commerce, and custom that tried at once to be both family and business. The musician would be taken care of, but he would also be held to account. One kind of record was made; another was kept. On the surface it looked uncomfortably close to sharecropping; the label was the company store, the musician the employee/sharecropper. But Chicago was not the plantation, and musicians were not held hostage to the company. They were paid for making records, and they didn't have to give the money back even if the record flopped. The issue was how much profit they could earn from their music. Here the label owners had the upper hand. They controlled the product, its promotion and the books. The royalty rates on the sales of each record were fairly standard in the business—paid in pennies, they were between 1 and 3 percent—but only Leonard and Phil knew how much it actually cost to make a particular record, and only they knew how many records had sold.

Giving a musician a car was not an uncommon form of payment at the time, particularly if the tender was a Cadillac. Taking care of musicians' other needs—clothing, rent, medical and legal bills—was all part of the mix. In Waters's case, more than once Leonard made available his personal lawyer, Nate Notkin, to handle Waters's paternity suits. There were at least half a dozen, Notkin, said, and he never lost one. A particularly memorable case involved a woman who claimed that Waters had signed an affidavit acknowledging paternity. Was Waters the father? Notkin asked. Waters wasn't sure because he said the woman was married, something she denied.

To catch her in a lie, Notkin asked Waters to call her from his office and make a date to come over. He listened in on another phone. When Waters offered to stop by for a couple of hours, she said no because her husband was home. Notkin became a witness in the case to testify about the phone call. He also unraveled the woman's case when she presented the alleged affidavit, all handwritten. It had to be false, Notkin told the judge. Waters had learned to sign "McKinley Morganfield," but beyond that he could barely write. The paper was a hoax right down to its fraudulent notary's seal. Notkin won the case, and Waters never forgot Notkin's help. Years later when he was performing on the college circuit, Waters was stopped by a fan in Eugene, Oregon, home of the state university. He presented his father's business card and introduced himself as Joey Notkin. A smile broke across Waters's face. He grabbed the young man by the shoulders and gave him a huge handshake. "Boy," he said, "your dad got me out of more scrapes than I can remember."

Leonard made sure that Notkin got paid for his work. In his mind, the lawyer's fee was just like a loan, a house payment, or a medical bill. It was a legitimate expense that could be charged to the artist and deducted from the royalties he was due. Leonard was a stickler. He even got into a fight with Lillian McMurry of Trumpet Records over who should pay for a bottle of whiskey during a recording session with Arthur "Big Boy" Crudup in Jackson, Mississippi, where McMurry lived. Crudup wanted the whiskey before the session, and McMurry provided it. After the session was over and it was time to pay the musicians, Crudup and Leonard almost came to blows when Leonard said he was deducting the cost of the whiskey from Crudup's pay. McMurry intervened in the escalating exchange of expletives. She told Leonard in no uncertain terms that the whiskey was a gift to Crudup—she also told him never to speak like that in front of her again.

One of the best illustrations of the financial entanglements between artist and label comes from McMurry's files. Tutored by an accountant her husband hired, she kept meticulous records of her musicians' expenses and credits, earning a reputation for honesty and fairness in a business where few others won such praise. Trumpet's best-known artist was Sonny Boy Williamson II—Rice Miller—who would eventually become a Chess artist in a deal with Buster Williams.

Williamson was constantly in debt to Trumpet. Between January 1951 and December 1953, McMurry made sixty separate loans or cash advances to him. They varied from ten to fifty dollars. Some were for his wife's driving lessons; others paid for travel for band members, for repairing equipment or paying a furniture bill. Each was entered on a ledger sheet, as were expenses McMurry incurred for such related work as printing posters or taking Williamson's collect calls from the road.

"He spent money like water," McMurry said. "He'd take $100 out in the morning and come in 'fore noon again wantin' another. That afternoon he'd want another $100 and another $100 before six o'clock." Sometimes Williamson wouldn't feed his wife, Mattie, and on occasion McMurry let her stay at her house in Jackson until Mrs. Williamson got her strength back. More than once McMurry interceded in squabbles between the couple. At one point Mattie Williamson wrote McMurry asking to get Williamson's contract "fixed so he can't get any money without my signature."

Recorded against all the loans and expenses were the credits due Williamson from the royalties on his recordings and the loans he repaid. The rate in his contract was one and one-half cents per record, so when "Mighty Long Time," for example, sold 49,536 copies, Williamson's debts were reduced by $743. At the end of 1953, McMurry's ledger showed Williamson still $672.01 in arrears.

Equivalent documents from the Chess and Checker labels do not exist.

Without them it is impossible to determine how well the brothers kept their books and whether they were fair. The lack of paperwork has not prevented powerful perceptions from taking hold years after the fact, when another generation gloried in this music and made it worth more money than Leonard and Phil and their musicians could have imagined. The prevailing view became one of exploitation, of fictional expenses used to offset royalties, of artistic property in effect stolen through unfair deals.

The truth is in some amorphous middle ground, shaped by the differing viewpoints of each side. The musicians believed they deserved more than they got. Leonard and Phil believed they treated them fairly. They played by the rules of the time, not questioning whether their practices and those of every other independent stacked the deck against the artist. Race was an element in the conflict, not because of Leonard and Phil's behavior toward their musicians but because of what it meant to be black in the mid-fifties, particularly for a migrant from the South in Chicago. There had been little opportunity for formal education and no training in the intricacies of business. In their place were strong and creative ways of surviving and thriving in a white-dominated world. It was a day-to-day proposition, celebrating the joy of the present with not much thought for the future. The money these musicians made was often the most they had ever seen. It could slip through their hands in a day.

In 1983 Phil spoke about these issues in a conversation with Charles Walton, the South Side drummer who had known the brothers since their days at the Macomba and who was now an informal oral historian of the South Side music world. Neither expansive nor apologetic, Phil gave his account of how the company took care of home payments, car payments, and medical bills on a monthly basis, just like a bank with its mortgage books.

"You almost treated them like they were your children," Walton observed.

"Well, they wanted to be," Phil replied. "They used to come to you whenever they had a problem. If one had his wife having a baby in one hospital and his old lady in another, they come to you to pay the bills so his old lady wouldn't know."

"They didn't do it in a business way," Walton said. "They did it almost like a family coming to a father, getting money."

"It would be an advance royalty," Phil replied. "That's what you gave them. . . . People forget." At the time, the musicians were appreciative, he said. As time went by it was, "You know this wasn't right, that wasn't right, which I'm not gonna dispute. I'm not gonna defend. I know in my mind what it was and that's it."

♦♦

Despite the obvious success with their blues artists, Leonard and Phil wanted to make the company more than a one-note operation. That was part of the reason both brothers, particularly Leonard, were on the road so much. A month after Waters's "Just Make Love to Me" and Little Walter's "Oh Baby" hit the charts, the company released its first—and almost its last—country-and-western song. It was recorded in Louisiana and featured Jack Ford, a cast member of the radio show *Louisiana Hayride,* singing "I Understand Just How You Feel." The B-side was "That's All You Gotta Do." The sales were modest. One of the few existing early royalty statements showed that between its release at the end of June and December 31, 1954, 1,642 records sold, not counting 183 given away for promotion. Ford got two cents per record for a total of $32.84. This was paid against $288.75 for the session to produce the record. So Chess was still entitled to collect $255.91 before Ford would get any royalties from the disc.

Louisiana was fertile territory—not just Shreveport, where Stan Lewis continued to be one of Leonard's strongest supporters, but also New Orleans. In the spring Leonard recorded Crawford again and then in late summer he signed Paul Gayten, a piano player and arranger whom he had known, albeit slightly, since the Macomba days. Gayten was a teenager who used to hang around the club but had moved to New Orleans. He helped with some Chess recordings in the city before doing his first record for Leonard in August 1954, cementing what would be a lifelong friendship between the two men. On that same summertime swing, Leonard signed Lowell Fulson, a singer and guitar player whose blues featured horns and piano arranged with a lighter touch than the more feral sound coming out of Chicago. His "Reconsider Baby" was recorded in Dallas with Lewis, who came over from Shreveport to be the executive producer.

"Reconsider" was released in November and was an immediate hit—another good hunch that paid off.

The Fulson and Crawford recordings were examples of the Chess brothers' unusual relationship with Universal Studio. Most clients used the facility for the entire process, from rehearsal to recording to mastering the final tape that would be sent to the record presser. Leonard sometimes followed that procedure for the important sessions because 4750 had inadequate equipment. But now that he was on the road so often getting new material, he would come back home with tapes and use Universal for the final technical work before the pressing. It was one more instance of his creative determination. He learned the rules and customs and then found ways to adapt them to further his own enterprise.

~

By 1954 Alan Freed had become increasingly important in the R&B world. He called himself the "Moondog," a moniker that grew out of a stunt he pulled in his early days on radio when he pretended to converse with a howling dog on the record "Moondog Symphony." His popular radio show in Cleveland and his "Moondog" balls, the huge dances for young people, catapulted him to new prominence when he was hired by New York City's WINS to bring his high-energy R&B show to Manhattan. Leonard and Phil remained friendly with him, as did every other independent producer. When Freed had hosted a party in Cleveland before taking his new job, both Chesses made sure to attend, as did their old record presser, Art Sheridan, who was now running the Chance label, and an assortment of other disc jockeys, record men, and distributors.

Freed was continuing to keep his eye out for talent, not only promoting it but supplementing his own income from the profits his discoveries made. It could come from management fees, record sales, distribution deals, or songwriting royalties, as the Coronets had learned. Earlier in 1954 Freed found another vocal group called the Moonglows, built around the dynamic baritone of Harvey Fuqua and the sweet tenor of Bobby Lester, boyhood friends from Louisville. The other members were tenor Pete Walton and Prentiss Barnes singing bass. Freed signed the Moonglows to Sheridan's Chance label, but their recordings under his tutelage were only modestly successful. Phil had actually been in Cleveland to watch part of a Chance recording session with the group and liked their sound. He was interested in getting them to Chicago. Freed helped put the deal together—the brothers paid Sheridan $500 for their contract.

In October the Moonglows went into the studio to record, and in December Leonard released their first record, "Sincerely." It opened with a deep and mellow "bah bah doh" from Barnes, the bass, who was then joined by Fuqua and Walton with their own harmonizing wordplay—one writer described it as "the owl-like 'voo-it.'" Lester, the lead tenor, came in to plead "Sincerely, oh yeah, sincerely, 'cause I long for you. Please say you'll be mine." The interplay of harmonies continued until the end. The song concluded with what became the Moonglows' signature "ooh-wah"—a note that seems to explode sweetly into silence. It was a technique called variously called "blow harmony" or "blow notes."

The record was all that the brothers could have hoped for. It went right on the charts and stayed there for twenty weeks. But even more important for the label, Phil had gotten the song to the McGuire Sisters, a popular trio. By coincidence he was on the same plane as the sisters and their manager while returning to the Midwest after one of his sales trips. During the flight, he told the sisters' manager that he had a song he thought they would like. They ended up staying at the same hotel in Detroit, and after everyone got settled, Phil sent one of his copies of "Sincerely" up to the sisters' room. They loved the song, and six weeks after the Moonglows' original was released, the trio made their version on Coral Records. It rose to the top of the pop charts in less than a month.

Freed had taken a writing credit with Fuqua, though Fuqua always insisted that the disc jockey did not contribute 50 percent of the effort even though he got "fifty percent of the action." Indeed, when the original copyright for the song was filed October 28 by Arc Music, the partnership with the Goodman brothers, only Fuqua's name appeared as the author of the words and music. Two months later the document was amended to add Freed's name. Fuqua was realistic about the situation: "I can understand what the deal was"—Freed could, and did, make things happen.

The McGuire Sisters' success was a boon for Arc. The year-old Chess-Goodman partnership got one penny from each sale of their record plus a share of the performance royalties from BMI. It was the first clear indication for Leonard and Phil that a song could be valuable, and it was a lesson they would not forget.

~~

Leonard and Phil ended 1954 in a good position. An end-of-the-year poll in *Cash Box* found three Chess/Checker artists in the top twenty male R&B musicians of 1954. Little Walter was fifth, with 39,767 votes, just ahead of Waters, who had 38,206. Walter would have his biggest hit yet in three months, "My Babe," written by Dixon and modeled after the popular spiritual "This Train." Willie Mabon was sixteenth with 11,582. He would have another good seller in January, "Poison Ivy," which had the catchy tag line "I'm like poison ivy, I break out all over you. . . ." Howlin' Wolf made it into the top twenty of "most promising new R&B artist," an irony given that he was the oldest among the Chess group and hardly new to the business at all.

Despite the relative success of these bluesmen, there was a recognition in the business that things were changing. A *Cash Box* essay by Atlantic's Jerry Wexler and Ahmet Ertegun highlighted the expected trend. With prescience they observed that the rhythm-and-blues sound was changing to a more pop feel in response to the growing potential of the white teenage market—principally "southern bobbysoxers." These fans called it "cat music." In New England, they wrote, pop disc jockeys were showing up at local high schools with a satchelful of Eddie Fisher and Jo Stafford, only to be asked by the teenagers for Fats Domino or the Clovers, a popular vocal group that had a hit with "Lovey Dovey" and "Good Lovin'." "For every two or three [Perry] Como's and Patti Page's the record hop jockeys now have to put on a cat record so that the kids can swing out."

Wexler and Ertegun offered a concise definition of what this "cat" music was: "the up-to-date blues with a beat, with infectious catch phrases and highly danceable rhythms. . . . It has to kick," they wrote, "and it has to have a message for the sharp youngsters who dig it."

Leonard and Phil didn't know it yet, but two musicians were about to knock on the doors of 4750 South Cottage Grove and fill that prescription.

eight

THE BEAT HAS
GOT TO MOVE

From the day he got to Chicago's South Side in 1934, six-year-old Ellas McDaniel, a transplant from Macomb, Mississippi, was absorbed in music. There were lessons in school and at Ebenezer Missionary Baptist Church, which was not far from young McDaniel's home at Forty-seventh and Langley. Attendance was mandatory. Gussie McDaniel, who had adopted Ellas as an infant, was a devout Baptist who taught Sunday school there. As soon as McDaniel was old enough he joined the choir, where his distinctive voice often drowned out his choirmates during the hymns. He learned how to play the violin in the Ebenezer Baptist Sunday School Band and Orchestra, intrigued when he saw some older children play the instrument. But McDaniel didn't want to play the classics favored by Professor O. W. Frederick, his teacher and orchestra leader. Instead of "Drink to Me Only with Thine Eyes" he wanted to play blues and jazz, even if it meant getting smacked on the back with a violin bow by an irritated Frederick.

McDaniel got his first guitar at age twelve, and he adapted to six strings what he had learned from the violin's four. His mechanical bent was encouraged at Foster Vocational School, where he made his first instruments—a violin, stand-up bass, and a guitar. He was especially proud of the bass—he cut and shaped the wood with such care that it was scarcely distinguishable from a store-bought instrument. It convinced McDaniel that he had special talents and prompted him to start experimenting with his own molds for the oddly shaped guitars that would become one of his trademarks. His natural aptitude for fixing things also turned him into the neighborhood handyman. "Go find Ellas" was the standard suggestion when anyone complained about a leaky faucet or some other mechanical malady.

Busy with odd jobs and more interested in music than studies, McDaniel quit school when he was barely fifteen and formed a trio. They first called themselves the Hipsters, but then McDaniel renamed the group the Langley Avenue Jive Cats to cash in on the popularity of "jive," which was a catchall description for all things popular. Venturing over to Maxwell Street to compete with other street musicians, the group on a good day made fifteen dollars, collecting the nickels, dimes, and quarters in a cake bowl McDaniel had spirited out of the house. They played their own versions of what was big on radio. "Caledonia," "Hey! Ba-Ba-Re-Bop," and "Honeydripper" were particular favorites. Still underage and anxious to learn, McDaniel sneaked into South Side clubs to hear Muddy Waters whenever he could. The man was his hero. McDaniel always tried to find a spot in the corner between the jukebox and cigarette machine that was close enough to the door to make a quick exit if the manager saw him. More times than not he was forcibly thrown out.

That McDaniel and the Jive Cats were improving was evident from their weekly victories on amateur night at the the Indiana Theater on Thirty-ninth Street. They won so many contests in a row that the manager finally told the musicians they could play but not compete so other groups had a chance to win.

Over the next few years, McDaniel mixed his music with a stint as a boxer and catch-as-catch-can work—truck driver, elevator operator, manual laborer. It was tough to make a living, and by now he was married and a father, so the nights and weekends out on the street corners provided important extra money. In the summer of 1950 McDaniel picked up another young Chicago musician, Billy Boy Arnold, a self-taught harmonica player who modeled himself after John Lee "Sonny Boy" Williamson, the city's most revered harp player, whose legendary career was cut short in 1948 by a street thug who beat him to death in a robbery.

When the group got good enough to move off the streets and into the clubs, McDaniel started experimenting with new sounds, building an amplifier out of old radio parts to get a bigger sound and adding a maraca player to produce a penetrating shuffle. He was writing his own material now, humorous, suggestive songs like "Hey Noxema," which was in the tradition of black vernacular rhymes. Playful and verging on the ribald,

"Noxema" talked of "me an' my baby . . . playin' in the bushes" when a pesky mosquito bit her on the thigh. They were sitting on the grass when the bug went further and bit her "on her big fat . . . / Hey Noxema."

By the fall of 1954 McDaniel had to put together a new group. One of his original bandmates had been drafted, another left to work with Howlin' Wolf. He reconnected with Arnold, who had gone out on his own for a while. Arnold liked the new configuration and suggested the group make a demo tape to shop for a recording contract. With McDaniel's rudimentary machine they cut two of his original tunes, "Uncle John" and "I'm a Man." By February 1955 they were ready to make the rounds. The first stop at United Records went nowhere. The second company, Vee Jay at 4747 South Cottage Grove, turned them down. Figuring they had nothing to lose, the musicians went across the street to see the Chess brothers.

Arnold had met Phil a couple of years earlier when he inquired about a record deal for himself. Phil didn't sign him, but he encouraged Arnold to stay in touch. He recognized the young man right away when the group came in. As soon as he heard the music, Phil realized it was something new. Though he now signed artists and bought records on his own when he was on the road, Phil wanted Leonard to hear the demo. He told the men to come back the next day around 2:00 P.M. with their instruments. It was the Chess operation in microcosm. Phil was the talent scout and sounding board for his brother; together they would decide whether to sign a new act.

The next afternoon the group set up in the small back room that functioned as a makeshift studio. Leonard listened intently, nodding his head. He liked McDaniel's guitar. It had an unusual sound because of the way he rigged it up. "Turn that up a little bit," Leonard told him. "Let me hear some more of this stuff."

Ready to do business, he had the group come back the following day to rehearse. Then they would go to Universal to make a record. The rehearsal sessions started out with Ellas McDaniel's band, but they ended up with something entirely different. How the name "Bo Diddley" came into being has been the subject of much conjecture. There had been at least two other performers named "Bo Diddley," one, according to a British magazine, who performed in China in 1929 and another who performed in Chicago in July 1935, according to an announcement in the *Chicago Defender*. McDaniel told one biographer that the name was given to him by a grammar school friend and he had no idea what it meant. He has told music writers other versions: that the name came from his days as a boxer, that it evolved from his penchant for the strange-looking guitars he built—"I guess that's why they call me Bo Diddley 'cause I always jump out of the bag with some new crap"—and that the nickname was a scat phrase to describe his unusual rhythm.

Arnold had another version. There was no "Bo Diddley" until the rehearsal sessions at 4750, when Leonard wanted a new name for the group and different lyrics for McDaniel's "Uncle John." The original began, "Uncle John got corn ain't never been shucked / Uncle John got daughters ain't never been . . . to school." Older folks won't like it, Leonard said. Disc jockeys won't play it. Find some new lyrics.

Arnold said "Bo Diddley" popped into his head when he recalled seeing a circus clown on the street who used that name. He joked with the band about its funny sound. "How about 'Bo Diddley'?" he suggested in the studio.

Leonard wasn't sure. He didn't know what the phrase meant, and he worried that it might be something derogatory toward blacks. Assured that was not the case, he let the band go ahead and play around with the song, keeping the same rhythm—"Bo Diddley" fit the cadence of "Uncle John"—but changing the words. Now it started, "Bo Diddley bought his baby a diamond ring. . . ."

When the group gathered at Universal to record on March 2, 1955, Leonard brought in Otis Spann on the piano to augment Diddley's band—Arnold, James Bradford on bass, Clifton James on drums, and Jerome Green on maracas. The session was a long one; getting "Bo Diddley" the way Leonard wanted it took several takes. Telling Diddley where to play his solo and to turn up the tremolo on his amplifier, he was at his most provocative. "Motherfucker, sing like a man," he ordered. "The beat has got to move at all times."

On the second tune, the boastful "I'm a Man," about the prowess of the singer, Leonard brought Dixon in on bass to replace Bradford. Then he decided Diddley should spell out "man" slowly and with an edge "M . . . A . . . N." It took several takes before Diddley got it right, finally angrily spitting out the letters, which is what Leonard had wanted all along. The song had the same "da da da Dum" of "Hoochie Coochie Man," but Bo Diddley spiced up the pattern with the distinctive maracas and wailing harp accents from Billy Boy Arnold.

Ellas McDaniel was now "Bo Diddley," and "Bo Diddley" the song was on its way. There hadn't been a sound on Chess or Checker quite like this before. Bo Diddley played his guitar like a percussion instrument, propelling the music forward. The Bo Diddley beat became his signature: "a 4/4 beat shoved slightly off center, like 'shave and a haircut, two bits'," as one writer put it. The ubiquitous maracas in the background gave the music a Latin feel. The staccato lyrics added to the overall effect of a constant, infectious rhythm.

Paired with "I'm a Man" on the B-side, "Bo Diddley" made an immediate impact. "Diddley is a talent to watch," said the April 9 *Cash Box* review, praising the song's "danceable beat." *Billboard* was equally enthusiastic about the "down-to-earth rattling rhythm," and its sales charts reflected the record's popularity. It was moving well in the South, Midwest, and in Buffalo—that unlikely territory cultivated with such care by Phil. The brothers had guessed right again.

Though "Bo Diddley" would register immediately on the *Billboard* sales and jukebox charts, where it would eventually take the first and second spots, respectively, it took a few more weeks before the song registered on *Billboard*'s tally of disc jockeys' favorites. This was a new R&B category reflecting the increased number of radio stations that played black music. Two years earlier there had been only a handful; now there were dozens. Not surprisingly Alan Freed, by now at WINS in New York, was leading the way on behalf of the new Checker record. He played it right away, giving it the kind of plug Leonard and Phil loved: "Bo Diddley, Checker Records. What a tremendous beat." By the middle of May, "Bo Diddley" was also moving up on the *Cash Box* listing of "Rhythm and Blues Top 15," and it was making its mark in the dozen cities around the country monitored in the HOT charts. Anxious to include a rising star on his roster of talent, Freed promptly recruited Bo Diddley for a live music stage show he was taking through New England. Diddley shared the stage with fellow Chess and Checker artists Little Walter and the Moonglows, and Mercury Records star Dinah Washington. Later in the year, Tommy "Dr. Jive" Smalls, another popular disc jockey, included Bo Diddley on some of his stage shows, keeping the new Checker star busy through the spring, summer, and fall, including one stint on Ed Sullivan's television show as part of an R&B package Smalls put together.

That it all turned out so well was a fluke in Arnold's view. "The reason I say it was a fluke is had we recorded for any of the other record companies, the word 'Bo Diddley' would have never come about because they would have recorded exactly what we had. They wouldn't have sat down like Leonard did and sort of like made the record what it was."

Though there would be later disputes between Bo Diddley and Chess

Records, this was an important collaboration: the musician with ideas and the new sound and the company willing to record him. Not only that, the record emerged at an important time, in the midst of an evolving cultural approach to the music that was broadening its audience beyond black America. What the music was called was of more than superficial importance. The vocabulary helped free the music from stereotype, loosening spoken and unspoken taboos. It was only in June 1949 that *Billboard* had changed its "race music" category to "rhythm and blues," leading the way for others to follow. But even this new term carried a particular connotation—it was still considered black music, a stew of blues shouters, jump bands, vocal groups, straight-ahead jazz and torch singers, in all an edgier, earthier sound than the crooners and songbirds with their polished bands who recorded the popular music that was aimed at white America and still dominated the airwaves.

But the younger white audience captivated by "cat music" was growing, and more than anyone, Freed was showing that "rhythm and blues" programming could be profitable for a radio station. New York's WINS posted a 42 percent rise in advertising sales in 1954, his first year. It was the kind of thing that got an owner's attention and made him receptive to more of the same. Station owners in other cities were watching, too. As important, Freed popularized a change in terminology. He called the music "rock and roll." Though the term had not previously been used to describe a kind of music, "rock" and "roll" had appeared in lyrics. Not always paired, the words were nonetheless understood by singer and audience as a euphemism for sex. In 1922, blues singer Trixie Smith recorded "My Daddy Rocks Me (With One Steady Roll)"; countless other blues songs through the thirties and forties featured "rockin' " or "rollin' " as a part of their stories. In 1951, the Dominoes had a hit with "Sixty Minute Man," which included the boast, "they call me lovin' Dan/I rock 'em and roll 'em all night long, I'm the sixty minute man." But with its light, jazzy feel—there was no driving beat or heavy electric instruments—it was not rock-and-roll *music.*

Freed had the stage, figuratively over the airwaves, literally in big auditoriums, to make the term a synonym for the music he was playing, giving it a certain respectability, even innocence. And it was catching on. *Billboard* referred to Freed as a "rock and roll" disc jockey. So did *Variety* in its passing attention to the R&B market. The magazine noted in one short piece on Freed that the term "designates the type of music he plays on his WINS show." Mercury adopted the phrase in a March ad featuring singer Dinah

Washington and saxophonist Red Prysock: "Mercury Rocks 'n Rolls With 2 Smash Hits!"

Freed's early Moondog Balls in Cleveland had drawn mostly black patrons. His new rock-and-roll shows, which grew large enough to fill such big-city stages as New York's Paramount Theater, drew crowds equally divided between white and black. This fusion of black music and white audience meant a potentially huge market. The challenge for a record company was to understand this cultural shift and figure out how to meet the demand. Leonard and Phil weren't sociologists, but they certainly knew how to straddle two cultures.

✹

Though firmly entrenched in America, Leonard and Phil had not given up the rituals and traditions of Judaism, even if they were more lax in practice than their parents. They were raised in a kosher home where Yiddish was preferred over English and worship at Anshe Motele was a given. Each of the boys had a bar mitzvah, the religious coming of age for Jewish boys, each had married a Jewish woman, and each was raising his children accordingly. If Leonard and Phil didn't go to worship services every week as adults, they did observe the high holidays of Rosh Hashana and Yom Kippur, always held a Passover seder, and lit the Hanukkah candles. So when Marshall turned thirteen, there was no doubt that he, too, would have a bar mitzvah.

Leonard and Phil made little distinction between office and home. Family was business and vice versa. So it was not surprising that Marshall's bar mitzvah on April 17, 1955, turned into something more than a traditional worship service. A centuries-old ritual combined with present-day business, the event resembled an R&B convention, Hebrew chants mixed in with blues. Ertegun and Wexler from Atlantic Records and Freed and his wife came from New York. Randy Wood of Randy's Record Shop and Dot Records came from Gallatin, Tennessee; disc jockey Zenas Sears came from Atlanta, WLAC's Gene Nobles came from Nashville, Buster Williams and his wife came from Memphis, and so did a host of Chicago area music makers, including prominent black disc jockeys Sam Evans, Al Benson, and McKie Fitzhugh, and George and Ernie Leaner, black record distributors. Some of the Chess musicians were also there. It was one of the few times blacks came to a worship service at Agudath Achem, the family's synogogue.

The service was conservative, in Hebrew with a little bit of English. Marshall chanted the important prayers and read from the Torah. He made the traditional speech, thanking family, friends, and rabbi, before receiving the final blessings that made him a man in the eyes of the congregation. Now he could be part of a *minyan*, the mandatory ten men required for a worship service.

When Marshall first stepped up to the altar to begin the service and turned to the congregation, he nearly broke out laughing at the unusual sight. Halfway back in the sanctuary was a row of black guests, yarmulkes, the traditional skullcaps for men, perched precariously on their pompadours.

The day before the bar mitzvah, WGES disc jockey Sam Evans and his wife hosted a cocktail party at their home for the family and visiting guests. Such a biracial gathering would have been impossible in the native state of so many Chess musicians and business associates. It was 1955, less than a year after the monumental Supreme Court decision ending segregated public schools, *Brown v. Board of Education.* Back in Mississippi, white businessmen were preaching white supremacy, not having dinner with their black neighbors. The social mixing at the Evans home was not all that common in Chicago either, particularly when the host was black. But such things didn't faze the Chess brothers. Family was business, business was family, and the Evanses were part of the Chess circle. The brothers on occasion visited the couple at their vacation home in Idlewild, Michigan, a resort community for blacks.

In the evening after the bar mitzvah, Leonard and Revetta invited 350 people for a dinner in the Cotillion Room of the Morrison Hotel, a favorite for such events. Marshall's was one of two bar mitzvah celebrations on the seventeenth, along with the B'Nai Jacob Sisterhood Dance and another dance sponsored by the West Rogers Park congregation. The evening was one of Leonard's few indulgences, just like his purchase years earlier of the three-piece suit bought on credit. He believed then that to be successful, he had to look successful. Now that he was, it was important to throw a good party.

The dinner was a formal sit-down affair. Floral centerpieces at each table added zest to the traditional white tablecloths and silver place settings arrayed for the multicourse meal. The table assignments mixed race and record politics. The family's black cleaning lady and her husband sat with Chess relatives; label owners sat with disc jockeys; record pressers sat with distributors. A small dance band provided music but took a break for the evening's special treat—a performance by the Flamingos, another doo-wop group that had just been signed to Checker.

Not one to miss an opportunity, Leonard wove business into his after-dinner welcome. In the already effusive atmosphere he boasted, "We will do bigger and better this year. We will be in first place throughout 1955 in the R&B field." It may have been the only bar mitzvah ever written up in both *Billboard* and *Cash Box*.

The complicated dynamic between blacks and Jews in general and the Chess brothers in particular was at play here. Leonard and Phil's comfortable relationships with their black counterparts, both the artists and businessmen, was obvious. They treated them like they treated everyone else—flattering when necessary, helping when necessary, getting angry as tempers flared, and using street language with impunity. "There was nothing derogatory about it," Billy Boy Arnold said. "It wasn't like Leonard was putting you down. He would tell me, 'Play that harp, motherfucker. You want to be another Little Walter, don't you?' "

Sometimes, said Paul Gayten, Leonard's main music connection in New Orleans, acquaintances thought Leonard was black before they met him "because that's the way he talked. You talked to him on the phone, you didn't know he was white, because he was around black people all his life."

Leonard and Phil weren't averse to using Yiddish insults either, but when they did, it was really the same as swearing in English. The crude moments sometimes grated on such better-educated Jews as Wexler, who found the Yiddish terms, in particular, inappropriate under any circumstances. It reflected the greater distance Wexler kept from his musicians, even if the business relationships looked identical on the surface. Wexler and Ertegun considered themselves fans of the music even as they produced it, and to them Atlantic was not a synonym for family. They handed out plenty of advances, "poured them out," Wexler said. "But we didn't make their car payments, we didn't pay their mortgages . . . we didn't dress them. We were not lords of the manor." Atlantic may have been less paternalistic than Chess, but it faced the same charges of underpayment of royalties that were made against Chess and other record companies, though Wexler resented being lumped in with labels he said operated with a very different style.

To many blacks, Jews were a separate category of whites, different, though not always in a positive way, from gentiles. They were not themselves a separate race, but neither were Jews just a religious group. There was something else bound up in their long history and distinct culture that set them apart in some palpable way. C. Eric Lincoln could have been talking about Leonard and Phil when he wrote about blacks and Jews in *Coming Through the Fire,* his spare but eloquent discussion of race. "For better or worse black conventions almost never indiscriminately lump Jews with Caucasians. The conventional reference in black folklore is to whites *and* Jews. In most instances this has permitted an interpretation of racial attitudes and behaviors toward Blacks in which the Jew consistently appears less vicious and less brutal, if more cunning and deceitful." Thus the story of the black entertainer angry at his Jewish agent who he is sure is exploiting him. He tells friends how angry he is, but then admits, "If the Jews didn't get us bookings or parts, we wouldn't work—they make a gold mine out of us."

This stereotype of the crafty, even rapacious Jew played into the disputes that arose later over royalties and contracts: Jews were about money, smart but not to be trusted. "To me every nationality has a reason for bein' here, an' mostly all the Jewish people own everything," said Bo Diddley. "They got all the money. Give him a thousand dollars, he'll turn it into ten million. How the heck they do it, I don't know."

If the double-edged sentiment was leavened by the feeling that Jews were "less vicious, less brutal" than their Christian counterparts, perhaps it was because they, too, were outsiders. There were in the best moments a sense of common cause and an appreciation that to large segments of white America, both black and Jew were "the other." Recalling how Alan Freed helped popularize his music, Little Richard, the exuberant rock and roller, said it was "a little Jewish boy" who had played his songs when so many mainstream radio stations refused. Freed's being Jewish was the salient factor, not his white skin. Had Freed been a Methodist, it is hard to imagine Richard praising the "little Methodist boy" who played "Tutti Frutti."

⋙

There may have been a new sound evolving at Chess, but Leonard still believed in his old methods: daily attention to detail and face-to-face contact with distributors and disc jockeys around the country. When Revetta and the children joined other northern Jews in the traditional exodus to Miami Beach for the holidays at the end of 1954, Leonard went to Cleveland to do business and then made his way to Florida to join the family for New Year's. Their accommodations were modest, the nondescript Prince Michael Hotel across the famed Collins Avenue from the beach and the high-end hotels. It would be a measure of success years later when the family moved uptown and back across Collins to the much fancier Thunderbird.

By mid-February Leonard was on the road again, this time to Memphis to supervise the pressing of "My Babe" and make sure that Little Walter's hit got out to the radio stations and stores. The only significant break in his travel was in the weeks before Marshall's bar mitzvah. Right after the event, Phil left for Detroit and other Midwest stops, and when he returned, Leonard was on the road again, this time for a two-week swing through the South. It was June, and school was out, so he took Marshall with him, something of a bar mitzvah present for a son who cherished the time he could spend with his father. They had an ambitious itinerary that included Nashville, Charlotte, Houston, Dallas, and New Orleans and smaller places in between.

At a stop in an Alabama town, where Leonard knew a local black tavern owner, he went out in the field to tape a local musician on the small machine he had brought from the office on Cottage Grove, one of the rare times—contrary to myth—that he did so.

From Alabama, Leonard and Marshall headed to New Orleans. While Leonard slept in the back seat, thirteen-year-old Marshall took the wheel of the Cadillac, driving the back roads until they got to the outskirts of the city. The most trying moment came in a wooded area so overrun with locusts that Marshall had to turn on the windshield wipers so he could see.

On the one hand, it was irresponsible to let a teenager drive; on the other, it was Leonard's way of showing confidence in Marshall and letting him know he could handle himself. He did so in even more dramatic fashion in New Orleans. The first day in the city Leonard gave Marshall a ten-dollar bill and left the boy on his own while he did his business. The money covered two movies—they were barely a dollar—and all the food he wanted. When Leonard got back for dinner and put him to bed, Marshall didn't question his father about where he had been or where he was going once Marshall was asleep. He understood that his father always kept some associations private. Occasionally this "other life," as Marshall called it, came to light in one special circumstance or another. No one knew that Leonard had friends in a black motorcycle gang in Chicago, but when he had been hospitalized with jaundice a few years earlier, the result of a contaminated mumps vaccination, the family went to visit in him in the hospital only to find the motorcycle men in full leather regalia chatting with Leonard at his bedside.

Leonard and Marshall returned home to Chicago and some good news. A *Cash Box* disc jockey poll named Bo Diddley in a tie with Nappy Brown of Syd Nathan's King label as "up and coming male vocalist." He was in first place in the category of "most promising" male vocalist. It was a helpful boost for his second Checker record, "Diddley Daddy," which included the Moonglows chanting "diddle diddle daddy" and "diddle diddle dum dum" in the background. The record was released in early June to good notices in *Billboard* and *Cash Box*. The Moonglows, who had followed their hit "Sincerely" with another good seller, "Most of All," won the *Cash Box* award as "up and coming vocal group" in recognition of their newfound success after singing for almost two years, though only eight months with Chess. And Little Walter placed sixth in the category of male vocalists most played on radio. "Sincerely" and "My Babe" were number seven and number eight on the most-played records, which meant a mention for both Chess and Checker. The magazine's poll was a good indication of how well the brothers were tuned into their market. Chess was now more than just a blues label.

Leonard didn't stay in Chicago very long. The first week of July he was in New York and then Philadelphia before returning home for what turned out to be one of the most important periods in the company's history, when past, present, and future came together.

◆◆

Though Muddy Waters had made several more records after the popular "Hoochie Coochie Man" and "Just Make Love to Me," he hadn't had a song on the R&B charts since October of 1954. That changed in July, when he made "Mannish Boy," a sly takeoff on Bo Diddley's "I'm a Man." Repeating the same "da da da Dum" beat throughout, the song boasted of finally being twenty-one and ready to "have lots of fun" to the happy shouts of a female chorus. *Cash Box* and *Billboard* put it in their spotlight, the latter calling the tune "an exciting deep south parody" of Bo Diddley and praising the "wonderfully wild chorus of yowling fems in the background."

Waters was a hero to many aspiring guitar players, not just those in Chicago who could see him regularly at his favorite clubs, but others around the country who heard him on the radio or on local jukeboxes. He was a major influence on one young St. Louis man whose eventual short meeting with the popular musician would result in one of the storied marriages between performer and company.

The sounds of the St. Louis Antioch Baptist Church choir surrounded

Charles Edward Anderson Berry from the day he was born on October 28, 1926, to Henry and Martha Berry. Chuck, as he came to be known, and his five other siblings were steeped in their parents' religious traditions. Music was a central element. Choir rehearsals were held in the living room of the Berrys' small home, the group gathering around the family's spinet as Mrs. Berry provided accompaniment. Even when there wasn't choir practice, she often sang her favorite gospel tunes while doing the housework and encouraged her children to join in.

It was no surprise that the six Berry children, three boys and three girls, loved music. But it was only a matter of time before their tastes would change, when they listened to St. Louis's only black radio station and heard the deep blues of Tampa Red and Big Maceo, the smooth and soothing Nat King Cole and Ella Fitzgerald and the sweet sizzle of Louis Jordan and his sax. After that, hymns came in a distant second for Chuck, even though Berry sang in the choir and was part of a gospel quartet. He used to argue with his sister Lucy about what to play on the family victrola. He wanted to hear Big Maceo's "Worried Life Blues" or Fitzgerald's "A Tisket a Tasket." Lucy preferred "Ave Maria" and "God Bless America."

By the time Berry was in high school, the secular had won out over the sacred. Already full of stage presence, he stopped the show at a high school production with an insouciant version of Jay McShann's "Confessin' the Blues." The students loved it; not so the teachers, who were used to the much tamer "Danny Boy" and "Old Man River." The performance brought Berry new popularity, which in turn brought a gift that would alter his life. One of his newfound friends gave him an old four-string tenor guitar, and Berry was hooked.

He taught himself the essential blues chords and then realized that with a change in tempo or a different stroking of the strings, he could expand the sounds to fit different songs. He picked up *Nick Mannaloft's Guitar Book of Chords* to build his repertoire and honed his technique playing backyard parties. He looked for playing tips wherever he could, even from friends at the local barber shop.

Berry's carefree and sometimes adventurous life came to an abrupt halt before he turned eighteen. Not long after graduating from high school, he and two friends, on a youthful swing across the state in Berry's 1937 Oldsmobile, went on a robbery spree. They were arrested after one of their heists and spent nearly a month in jail before pleading guilty to the charges against them. They were sentenced to ten years each at the Missouri reformatory for young men.

Settling into reform school, Berry appreciated that music could be a saving grace, and not just at the mandatory Sunday morning church worship. Seizing the opportunity to make use of his music background and knowledge, he organized a singing quartet to bring some life to an otherwise pedestrian service. The quartet became so popular that the group was invited to sing at the white services as well. Eventually the black inmates were allowed to perform outside the prison farm, even going to St. Louis where Berry could see his family. The lead singer, known as "Po' Sam," was a professional guitar player. He and Berry started a boogie band that was as popular for nighttime entertainment as the quartet was for church services.

The painting skills Berry had learned on construction jobs with his father also came in handy, and he scored valuable points with the authorities by painting the dormitories. That, combined with the success of his music endeavors and his clean record, resulted in his release three years after his incarceration and just a few days after his twenty-first birthday.

Back in St. Louis, Berry returned to music, playing private parties on solo guitar and working in small clubs for six or eight dollars a night. By now he had developed the rudiments of the style that would make him so famous, adopting gestures, as he explained it, that complemented the lyrics—"squatting low to do a passage in a song that was sentimental and bluesy" or making facial expressions "that pronounced the nature of the lyrics."

Married by 1950 and the father of a baby daughter by the fall, Berry took another job as a janitor at radio station WEW. It turned out to be a fortuitous move. Joe Sherman, one of the city's better-known guitarists, played for the station's *Sacred Heart* program and offered Berry his old electric guitar for thirty dollars—paid in weekly five-dollar installments. A few months later he bought his first tape recorder and started recording his own improvisations, both words and music. He was making a name for himself as an engaging entertainer, and at the end of 1952, he had a stroke of good luck. Piano player Johnnie Johnson, leader of the Sir John Trio, invited him to play the group's New Year's Eve show at the Cosmopolitan Club in East St. Louis, Illinois, across the river from Chuck's home. It was four times bigger than any place Berry had performed and provided him just the kind of opportunity he had been waiting for. Playing a variety of styles, he grabbed the limelight, getting the biggest response from his country-and-western music. Clubgoers left the "Cosmo" wondering, "Who is that black hillbilly?" The group was such a hit that the club owner asked them to come back for a long engagement.

A genial and modest man, Johnson didn't mind that Berry got the glory. When Berry asked him if he could be in charge and rename the trio, Johnson acquiesced. He didn't like the business end of the music. Besides, "Chuck was a go-getter . . . and I figure with him as the leader we would have more jobs and a better success."

There was instinctive communication when Berry and Johnson played together that made their music seem effortless—the same kind of easy flow that Waters had with Otis Spann. "Johnnie and I became so tight in feeling each other's direction," Berry explained, "that whenever I played a riff with any pause in it, he would answer it with the same melodic pattern and vice versa." In live performances Berry tried to outdo Johnson by slurring the guitar strings for a sound completely distinct from the piano, but Johnson always seemed to find a way to answer back. It never failed to bring an ovation for the piano player.

Johnson's instinct about Berry's business acumen was right. The group expanded its work beyond the Cosmopolitan Club and played in cities around St. Louis. Anxious for more, Berry wanted to get to Chicago. The first week of May 1955 he loaded up his new cherry-red Ford Esquire station wagon and headed for the city, accompanied by high school friend Ralph Burris, who was visiting his mother there. They made a beeline for Forty-seventh Street, still the home to many clubs, and feasted on the music: Howlin' Wolf, Elmore James, and most important, the revered Waters. When they got to Waters's venue, the men inched their way to the front of the bandstand. After Waters finished playing, Burris yelled out to him so they could get his autograph. Berry seized the moment. He wanted to make a record. Could Waters suggest anyone in the business?

"Yeah," Waters said. "See Leonard Chess."

Though Berry had planned to return to St. Louis the next day, a Sunday, he changed his plans. Early on Monday morning he drove over to South Cottage Grove, parked the car and waited in a storefront across the street until the office opened. He watched a white man go in and then crossed the street himself, walked in and asked the receptionist to see Leonard. In fact Leonard had just arrived, and when he saw Berry, he motioned him into the office. Berry explained that Waters had sent him; Leonard wanted to know if Berry had any tapes. Not with him, he replied, but he could come back with some music. Fine, Leonard said.

Berry hurried back to St. Louis, called Johnson and got the group together to start working on new material. Within the week he wrote four songs and was on his way back to Chicago to play his tapes.

Leonard was immediately taken with a country-sounding song called "Ida Red," though he seemed surprised that a black man could sing "a hill-billy song." He told Berry he wanted him to bring the band up to Chicago and he would consider a recording contract. They would have to make one change, though. There already was a song called "Ida Red," so the tune needed a new title. As Johnson remembered it, Leonard suggested "May-bellene" when he noticed a mascara box made by the Maybelline cosmetic firm sitting in the windowsill at the Cottage Grove office near where the secretaries sat. "Maybellene" fit rhythmically with "Ida Red" so it was easy to make the change.

Leonard set the recording session for May 21 at Universal. He brought Willie Dixon in to play the stand-up bass to get a fuller sound. It was not an easy session. Leonard had a specific idea of what he was looking for, and it took thirty-six takes to get the sound he wanted, even though Berry thought several of the previous ones were good. But the band was willing to trust Leonard. After all, he had done this many times before; they were novices, and they quickly realized that playing before a live audience in a club was different from being in the studio. "We had no idea what to do," Johnson explained.

With "Maybellene" out of the way, the group spent a few more hours at the studio and recorded three more originals: "Wee Wee Hours," "Thirty Days," and "You Can't Catch Me."

After the session, as Berry remembered it, he and Leonard went back to the office to sign a recording contract—a standard form with no company name on it—and a publishing contract with Arc Music that would cover the copyright matters relating to the songs. Later the meeting would be the source of controversy, but for now Berry was happy to have a record under his belt with a legitimate company; Leonard and Phil were hoping that once again they had tapped into a successful new sound. They didn't have to wait long to find out.

"Maybellene" was released July 30. With its opening guitar run—a rapid mixture of notes and chords—the song had a relentless energy, a similar feel to Bo Diddley's first single but with a different style and a lighter sound. And then there were Berry's unconventional lyrics, unusual words, perhaps, but creating an unmistakable mood: "As I was motorvatin' over the hill, I saw Maybellene in a coupe de ville." *Billboard* appreciated that the song was special, but even its praise—"ace showmanship and expressive good humor . . . catchy rhythm and a solid driving beat"—couldn't capture the record's spirit.

Just prior to the official release of the disk Leonard took out an ad in the magazine's July 23 issue promoting Waters's "Mannish Boy" and "Maybellene." Though it was the routine two-column display, this one was pivotal, for it reflected where Chess had been and where the company was going.

Muddy Waters still had many more records to make and more fame to enjoy, but the high point for his brand of blues had passed. He had helped make Chess Records a viable company; Chuck Berry could take it to a new level. "Maybellene" was selling well all over the country, in places where the more traditional Chess blues had failed to make a significant mark: Boston, New York, and Philadelphia, in addition to prime Chess territory in Detroit, Nashville, and Atlanta. Berry was becoming a star. He was signed by the Gale Agency, which handled his bookings, and Freed recruited him for his "Big Rock and Roll Show."

But the best was yet to come. Leonard had made sure that Freed got a copy of "Maybellene," going to New York to deliver it personally. The strategy paid off, because Freed gave it enormous airplay. By the first week in August, the record was in high gear. So much so that Phil had to interrupt a short vacation to Eagle River, Wisconsin, where he was joining his family. They had a daughter, Pam, and a son, Terry; another son, Kevin, would arrive in 1958. Phil knew something was happening when he turned on the radio in this small northern Wisconsin town and heard "Maybellene" wherever he turned the dial. Then Leonard phoned: "Get your butt back here."

Phil rushed home, and he and Leonard and the half dozen Chess employees in the office packed and shipped records hour after hour through two weekends to meet the orders. Emergency calls had gone out to Buster Williams in Memphis, to Nate Durhoff in California, their West Coast presser, and to a small outfit in Chicago to get the records made as fast as possible.

By August 13 "Maybellene" was on the *Billboard* bestseller chart, the jukebox chart, and the all important "most played jockeys" listing. By September, the song had won the R&B trifecta: it was number one simultaneously on all three *Billboard* tallies and would remain there until mid-October. It was number one in sales in most of the cities surveyed by the magazine and also in *Cash Box*'s HOT chart cities. But there was even better news. The record had moved on to *Billboard*'s top ten tunes in the nation, starting at number ten, and then climbing the pop chart up to number four in sales, number eight in the jukebox category, and fifteen in the category for pop disc jockeys. The song even made a brief appearance in *Billboard*'s country listing as a "best buy" October 8. It also surfaced in *Variety*'s listing for the "top talent and tunes," its survey of bestselling discs. At the same time "Maybellene" even spawned some "answer songs," most prominently "Come Back Maybellene" by John Greer on the Groove label, and another by the same name from Mercy Dee on the Flair label.

In his darkest days, when prosecutors in New York indicted him, when the Internal Revenue Service squeezed him in audits, Alan Freed would insist that he never pushed a song on the radio that he didn't like. If it was clear that he liked "Maybellene," it was also clear, when the first Chess royalty statements came out, that he stood to gain from the song's success. Freed was listed with Berry as coauthor along with Chess landlord and friend Russ Fratto. It hadn't always been so. When Arc Music first filed a copyright application for "Maybellene" on July 5, 1955, Chuck Berry was the only name on the line for "composers, authors, etc." When Arc received its official certificate of registration dated August 2, 1955, however, Freed and Fratto had been added. Likewise, the sheet music to "Maybellene" carried their names. (Copyright records suggest that Freed and Fratto were prolific songwriters, which no doubt would have surprised those who knew them well. Freed was credited with some twenty-eight songs for a variety of companies, Fratto a dozen.)

Berry maintained that he never knew at the time that he was sharing "Maybellene" with anybody. He said in his 1987 autobiography that Leonard told him the song would "get more attention with big names involved."

Phil said that Fratto bought a piece of the song, paying either $500 or $1,000 to Berry when he came to Chess. Giving Freed credit was plainly a way to get him money in exchange for helping the song. Some companies, like Atlantic, actually had Freed on the payroll, providing him with steady income that they cut off at their peril. Atlantic's Wexler never forgot Freed's response when he and Ertegun asked him if he would forgo their payment for a month or two because the company was in a slump. "I'd like

THE BEAT HAS GOT TO MOVE | 119

to help you out," he told them, "but that would be taking the bread out of my children's mouth." And, Wexler said, "he took us off the air."

Leonard knew what a Freed play meant. He had gotten orders for three thousand records in one day a few months earlier after Freed played "A Toast to Lovers" by Danny Overbea just a single time.

Three of the principals in the "Maybellene" dispute are dead—Leonard, Freed, and Fratto—and the one living person, Berry, is adamant that he was never told that two-thirds of his song proceeds were being given away. "What you need," Marshall said, "is my father and Chuck in the same room and they can fight about it, what went down that many years ago." The Freed aspect, he said, "was a strict payola situation. Everyone would have done it. If I had a rock act, and I could give the publishing of one song to MTV to play it seven times a day, I would do it today, right now—bag the writer. I would do it in a second."

Perhaps he learned that from his father. In 1959, when Leonard brought Etta James to the company from the Biharis' label, she said he showed her some royalty information for Berry so she could see how well Chess took care of its people. Noticing Freed's name, James asked him what it was doing there. "Look darling," he said, patting her gently on the arm, "certain deals you have to make."

If Leonard was making deals in the service of success, he apparently did not tell the individuals most directly affected—the recording artists—what he was doing. This was paternalistic at best, deceitful at worst, even if neither was Leonard's intent. In the case of "Maybellene," the money was not diverted from Berry into his pocket or Phil's. But it was nonetheless diverted from Berry. While Freed's enthusiasm no doubt gave "Maybellene" a huge boost, and while Leonard and Phil were not alone among the record companies in their practices, this way of doing business opened the brothers up to severe criticism and later litigation. When the original copyright held by Arc Music expired, Berry secured the rights to "Maybellene."

Leonard and Phil hardly coasted with this new success. They knew you could be hot one month and cold another. That helped account for their frenetic fall pace: Leonard took a six-day trip through the South in October. As soon as he returned, Phil took off for the East, stopping in New York for a personal visit with Freed and area distributors. When he got back, Leonard headed to Memphis and Nashville. That trip over, Phil made an early December trip to Cleveland and Detroit.

The brothers wanted to capitalize on Berry's popularity, and when they quickly released his "Thirty Days," there was the promotional work to do on the new record along with others that were coming out, including a new Dixon record—not one of his originals but a version of "Walkin' the Blues"; a new Moonglows record, "Starlite" backed with "In Love"; and new discs from the Chess piano players, Mabon and Eddie Boyd, who was still making records for the company even though he had not had a good seller for two years.

There was also a new musician on the roster, Sonny Boy Williamson II. His arrival at Chess was a cautionary tale in itself, a striking example of the vicissitudes of the business. Williamson came to Chess from Lillian McMurry's Trumpet label in Jackson via Buster Williams. Struggling to keep her business afloat, by 1955 McMurry was losing the battle. She owed Williams $6,000 in pressing costs and knew she couldn't pay the bill. They settled the account for $1,000 and Williamson's contract (she had originally paid him $10 to record in 1950 with a royalty of one and a half cents per record sale). Williams turned around and sold the musician's contract to Leonard and Phil. Williamson's first release on the Checker label was "Don't Start Me Talkin'," with Waters and Jimmy Reed backing him on the guitar. It proved to be a good start; the record made all three *Billboard* R&B charts.

The Chess brothers' relationship with Williamson would also be touched by controversy, this time McMurry's twenty-year battle with the brothers about their right to re-record material Williamson had done for Trumpet. She was incensed to see the Chess version of a song she insisted belonged to her company. What made McMurry even angrier was her belief that Leonard was partly responsible for Trumpet's decline, using his clout with certain distributors, she was sure, to discourage them from carrying her records. McMurry would eventually settle with Arc Music in 1982 for $84,000, $4,000 of which went to Mattie Williamson, the musician's widow.

Though Gene and Harry Goodman were handling all the publishing matters at Arc, Leonard was getting involved bit by bit. He made a quick trip to New York in mid-December to attend the year-end banquet of BMI, the performance rights group that administered the royalties on the public performances of Arc songs. With the increased radio play and the sheet music sales, publishing was taking on new importance to the company. Money was coming from a song now, not just the sale of a record.

The year-end industry year polls confirmed the obvious for Leonard and Phil: 1955 had been the best yet. Berry had won both the *Cash Box* and *Billboard* "most promising new artist" award and he was number fifteen in *Billboard*'s favorite artist category. "Maybellene" had broken out of the R&B niche to become a pop hit. Bo Diddley was right behind Berry in the *Cash Box* new artists poll. The Moonglows' "Sincerely" had placed high in both magazines' most popular/best-selling song category, and the group had placed third in *Cash Box*'s "most promising new R&B vocal group." The more established Chess/Checker musicians still commanded an audience: five of them—Little Walter, Waters, Lowell Fulson, Willie Mabon, and Howlin' Wolf—were in the *Cash Box* top twenty-five R&B male vocalist of the year category. Chess had done better than most of the other independents, like Herman Lubinsky's Savoy label, Syd Nathan's King, the Biharis at Modern. But they still trailed Atlantic, which routinely had four or five musicians or songs on the charts and had great success with something not yet represented on the Chess and Checker roster, successful female singers. The brothers, though, had kept up with a changing market. They were positioned to build on their success—and to branch out in new directions.

nine

MONEY IN THE SONG

N o town in the South was too small to escape Leonard's interest if it had a radio station, a distributor, a record store, or a tavern with a jukebox. Crowley, Louisiana, was no exception, and one of Leonard's periodic stops was the store run by Charles Redlich. He went by the provocative nickname "Dago" and stenciled it in big letters on his front window. Leonard made his standard request during every visit: *If you know of any new talent, let me know. Call collect.*

In the spring of 1955 Dago believed he found someone special. He had stopped by the Crowley High School senior prom to hear the band, which was from nearby Abbeville and featured a teenage singer with an unusually appealing voice, Bobby Charles Guidry. When the group took a break, Dago found Guidry and told him about Leonard's standing offer. The next day Guidry went to the record store and the two of them made a collect call to Chicago. Over the phone Guidry sang a song he'd written that was a local favorite, "See You Later Alligator." Intrigued, Leonard told Guidry he wanted him to go to New Orleans to record the song. Paul Gayten, who handled New Orleans business for Chess and Checker, would produce it.

An excited Guidry accepted the offer, and after taking care of the necessary paperwork long distance, he and his band headed to New Orleans in early fall to make the record. They used the tiny one-room studio that Gayten liked, which was in the black part of town, behind a small shoe shop. Leonard and Gayten wanted to use seasoned professionals—the same musicians who played with Gayten and recorded with Fats Domino—but

Guidry insisted on using his bandmates. He was working for them, he explained, not vice versa.

"Alligator" opened with a breezy instrumental reminiscent of the jump blues from the Macomba Lounge days. Drummer Kenneth Theriot and Ed LeBlanc on the piano set the pace for Guidry, whose easygoing vocals were a perfect fit for the tune's catchy hook: "See you later alligator, after while crocodile." While it had a more gentle overall sound, "Alligator" had the same danceable beat that made Chuck Berry and Bo Diddley's music so popular. The song had come to Guidry in a flash, the product of a late-night visit with LeBlanc to a roadside diner in rural Louisiana. The two had stopped for something to eat, and when Guidry got up to leave, he made a little joke. "See you later alligator," he said on his way out. "After while crocodile," yelled a tipsy patron in a nearby booth. Guidry walked on by and out the door. But instead of getting in his car, he went back in and aproached the woman who had spoken.

"What did you say?"

"After while crocodile."

When he heard it again, Guidry knew he had the makings of a song. He dashed it off in twenty minutes as soon as he got home.

Before the record was released on Chess early in 1956, Guidry dropped his last name because people had trouble pronouncing it, "Gi-dree." Now he was known simply as Bobby Charles.

"Alligator" registered only modest sales in its initial weeks. Things did not look as promising as the Chess brothers hoped. But then Bill Haley, the white rock-and-roll sensation, decided to do his own version on Decca Records, and everything changed. Haley's recording took off. It landed on the trade paper R&B charts before Charles's version had a chance to find an audience; by the end of March Haley was number six on *Billboard*'s pop chart. By April he had sold one million copies. At two cents a record for the "mechanical" royalty paid to a publisher, this was an easy $20,000 for Arc Music, which published "Alligator," to divide with the songwriter. Leonard and Phil had learned how to make records. Now they were learning about publishing.

As part of his recording deal, Charles had also signed a songwriting agreement with Arc. The company would publish the song, becoming the copyright holder and in essence the funnel for all the revenue generated. Charles was listed as the writer. The setup was not unique; most of the labels had publishing arms by now. On the one hand, the writer gave up half of his potential royalties to the publisher. On the other a company was promoting the song with the chance of making more money than the writer could on his own. Under the agreement a publisher like Arc handled such administrative details as registering "See You Later" in Charles's name with BMI to collect any performance royalties from radio and television play. It also handled the "mechanical" royalties collected from the sales of the "cover" versions. In addition to Haley on Decca there were two other versions on small labels. The standard practice was for the publisher to split the two-cent "mechanical" royalty on each sale with the writer—that meant $10,000 for Charles, though later he would contend that he didn't see all the money he was entitled to.

Proper publishing was more important than ever. By now "cover" versions of R&B songs were commonplace. The major labels realized that the independents were a rich source of material. Their artists could do the same songs, but with larger budgets for advertising and promotion and greater access to the airwaves, they had the potential to sell many more records than the original. Some were so successful that much of the public wouldn't know that the major-label cover was not the original, as was the case with "Alligator." This was a boon to the songwriter, who stood to gain from any sale of his song, but it cut into the earning potential of a performer who had recorded someone else's song and therefore stood to make money, beyond being paid for the session, only from the sales of the record.

Atlantic's LaVern Baker was so upset about the "note for note" cover of "Tweedle Dee" that Georgia Gibbs made early in 1955 that she wrote to the House of Representatives asking for a change in the copyright law to prevent such copying. She claimed it was "thefting my music." While the law protects the author of the song, it does not protect an arrangement, and there was nothing to prevent such cover versions. Baker claimed she lost an estimated $15,000 in royalties because buyers flocked to the Gibbs cover and not her original version.

The proliferation of R&B covers meant that the interests of an independent label like Chess and its publishing arm, Arc, both converged and diverged. The publisher gained but the label was hurt. When a musician such as Bill Haley covered an Arc song and sold one million records, Arc got 50 percent of the two-cent "mechanical" royalty from each sale, and Leonard and Phil split that penny per record with their partners, the Goodmans. Charles was entitled to the other penny as the songwriter. But Haley's version dwarfed Charles's on Chess, depressing his sales and reducing the revenue that came directly into the label. The less money Chess earned on the sales the less Charles earned in royalties.

Both Arc and Charles also made money on the sheet music, and the Haley version, with his picture—rather than Charles's—on the cover was a good seller. "Alligator" had climbed quickly onto *Billboard*'s Honor Roll of hits, which monitored several measures of a song's popularity: sales, radio and jukebox play, and sheet music sales. It reached number eight by March 10 and stayed on the Honor Roll for three months.

Covers not only cut into the earning potential of nonsongwriting performers, they also diminished the earning potential of the independents' distributors. Sometimes the distributors would be promoting a new original, which was how they earned their money, while at the same time the label-publisher was pushing for a cover version by one of the majors. Noting the apparent conflict of interest between label and publisher, one music writer sniped that the record companies were sometimes "more eager to promote the ditty than the platter."

From Leonard and Phil's vantage point "Alligator" was a success, and they wanted more from Charles. This time, though, they wanted him to record in Chicago. They made the arrangements for him to fly into the city; Phil would meet him at the airport. Everything went smoothly until the first face-to-face meeting after Charles got off the plane. Phil's jaw dropped when he saw the blondish, blue-eyed young man approach him. "Jesus," he said, "Leonard is gonna shit." Neither of the brothers knew Charles was white. They never asked and no one in Louisiana said otherwise. They just assumed from his soulful sound that he was black.

When Charles walked into the South Cottage Grove office, Leonard had a one-word reaction: "Motherfucker."

"What?" asked the startled Charles, who had never heard the word before.

"You're not black."

"I know," Charles replied.

It wasn't going to be a secret for long. After his recording session was over, Charles appeared on a local television station to promote his music. And shortly after that, Chess took out ads in the trade papers featuring Charles's picture and his new record, "Don't You Know I Love You." The label rarely put pictures of its artists in the ads, and it is possible they were trying to capitalize on the fact that he was white.

Though Leonard always tried to make the most of what was working at the moment, not every idea was a good one. One of the more obvious post-"Alligator" flops was "See You Soon Baboon" by Dale Hawkins, another white singer who was also from Louisiana. "I was trying to get in the door," Hawkins explained years later, "and that's the reason I wrote the song. I said, 'Well, if he can, I can.' "

Charles was making a name for himself now. By early spring he was a regular on the various rock-and-roll shows that were going around the country, one of the few white performers on entertainment bills that featured such performers as Berry, Al Hibbler, teenage sensation Frankie Lymon, and Della Reese. The company also kept him busy in the studio, recording a half-dozen more singles in the spring and summer. They did modestly well, and one of them, "Only Time Will Tell," made it onto the *Billboard* charts for three weeks in August.

The song had another benefit. It brought Leonard together with a young promotion man, Dick LaPalm, who was working for Nat King Cole. The Chess brothers and La Palm disagreed over who would publish "Only Time Will Tell." Gayten claimed part credit, and he had a relationship with Cole's company, Muirfield Music. It eventually got the publishing, and while Leonard and LaPalm got off to a stormy start, a friendship was born nonetheless. Leonard realized LaPalm knew a lot of disc jockeys on Top 40 radio because of Cole's popularity. He had been trying to make inroads with one of them, popular Miami jockey Milton Smith, who was known as "Butterball." When he learned that Cole would be performing in the city, he asked LaPalm to get Butterball good seats for Cole's upcoming show and to make sure Butterball knew they came through Chess. LaPalm obliged. It was the first of many such arrangements LaPalm made for Chess as a consultant before he joined the company full-time a few years later.

That kind of hustle made Leonard confident in the promises he could make to a musician he believed had talent. He told Charles in their first meeting that Chess would make him rich and famous and he could have all the women he wanted, though Leonard had expressed the latter sentiment in far cruder terms than the seventeen-year-old was used to.

Leonard's gruff exterior and penchant for street language was part of what intrigued Charles. Sometimes he was taken aback, but he was also drawn to the man by the sheer force of his personality. Perhaps because he was only seventeen when they met, Charles was more captivated than the older musicians. "Just being around him you could feel his presence and you could watch the way things happened," he said. The apparent contradictions were endearing and instructive—a man who could be so crude in private yet so concerned about public perception, always mindful of what might help or hinder sales. Charles never forgot a Little Walter recording session in the summer of 1956 that ground to a halt over language.

Walter was at full throttle, blowing the harp with his usual intensity and singing his heart out in the vocal passages. But Leonard stopped everything and came out from the control booth.

"You can't say that," he told Walter. "You can't say 'my pants are coming down.'"

No, no, Walter told him. "It's 'my pains is coming down.'"

Everyone in the studio—technicians and musicians alike—burst out laughing, including Leonard. "Just a Feeling" was released two months later with "my pains is coming down."

~~

Charles had come to Chess as an unknown quantity. Not so another of their vocal groups, the Flamingos, who, the brothers hoped, would have as much success as, if not more than, the Moonglows. Leonard and Phil had had their eye on the five-member group for some time. They listened to their records on Art Sheridan's struggling Chance label and then later on Parrot, the label that disc jockey Al Benson operated.

The Flamingos had formed in the fall of 1952, an outgrowth of friendships formed in the church choir and the neighborhood. The group was two sets of cousins: Zeke and Jake Carey and Johnny Carter and Paul Wilson. They were eventually joined by Sollie McElroy, who was the lead singer, and when he left, Nate Nelson. At first the cousins were just singing for their own enjoyment, but their efforts took a more serious turn when Fletcher Weatherspoon, one of Zeke Carey's friends from work, insisted he come to a party with him. He would even provide transportation. Zeke Carey and his friends agreed to go. After they arrived, Weatherspoon turned off the music and told the audience his pals were going to sing. "The people went crazy," Zeke Carey said, and by the next week Weatherspoon had lined up a few parties for them. Word spread and the group started to get requests to perform for one private event or another. They eventually started singing in cabarets and small clubs, doing their versions of current hits but in very close harmony, which set them apart stylistically from other groups. When Sollie McElroy joined the other singers a short time later, the Flamingos were officially born.

Early in 1953 the group signed with Chance, and while Sheridan put out several Flamingos records, they never sold much beyond the Chicago area. The men moved to Parrot in 1954 as Chance was going out of business. Benson was happy to get them notwithstanding their disappointing sales. In Chicago they were the hottest group.

The Flamingos had only modest success in their year-plus at Parrot. Their manager wanted them to move on. His first choice was the ever-expanding Chess. Their signing in the early spring of 1955—with lead McElroy now replaced by Nate Nelson—proved to be particularly good timing, given the religious backdrop to their appearance as new Chess musicians at Marshall's bar mitzvah party. The four cousins—the two Careys, Carter, and Wilson—were black Jews. This didn't mean that they were Jews in the traditional sense only with dark skin. Rather they were members of the Church of God and Saints of Christ. The congregation worshiped at a small storefront church at Thirty-ninth and South State streets, not far from the brothers' club, the Macomba Lounge. One of the singers' core beliefs was that they were descendants of Jews in the Holy Land. Their liturgy, however, was a combination of several elements, some from Judaism, others influenced by Pentecostal beliefs and black nationalism. The church services featured a choir but the music was not traditional Christian gospel. Instead it was infused with minor-key chants found in Jewish praying, or "dovening." The choir sang its songs in English, translations of the Five Books of Moses. The trinity they revered was Abraham, Isaac, and Jacob, not the Father, the Son, and the Holy Ghost, and they would not work on the Jewish holidays. Though business was business with Leonard and Phil, the Flamingos believed their common religious beliefs created a special bond.

The Flamingos' first release on Chess was a ballad, "When," which was backed by the up-tempo "That's My Baby (Chic-a-Boom)." The record was not the blockbuster they had hoped for, but the group and the Chess brothers persevered. Several more songs were recorded and released over the next few months. One of them was "I'll Be Home," released in January 1956. The Flamingos finally got what they hoped for—a bona fide hit that made it onto the trade paper charts and stayed there for weeks.

The song was written by Ferdinand "Fats" Washington and Stan Lewis, Leonard's good friend. Washington lived in Shreveport and knew Lewis, often stopping by the record shop on Texas Street to visit. Washington had a gift for lyrics and melodies, and Lewis suggested they form a partnership to publish the music. Their deal, set out in a contract, was a simple one:

Washington wrote the songs; Lewis took care of the expenses to promote them and get them published. When they were sold and the money came in, Washington would repay Lewis's costs, and anything left over would be split fifty-fifty.

"I'll Be Home" was published by Arc and made available to the Flamingos. The opening bars of the ballad featured lead singer Nate Nelson, who set the theme: "I'll be home my darling. Please wait for me. . . ." The rest of the group joined him in their tight harmony, creating a sort of vocal cushion underneath his lead. Falsetto highlights from tenors Zeke Carey and John Carter gave the song added poignancy.

The group had actually recorded the song twice, once in the rudimentary office-studio at 4750 South Cottage Grove and then at Universal. Leonard didn't like the more professional version—it came out "too clean," Zeke Carey remembered—and he decided to release the first version. That it turned out so well was remarkable given the setup—just two mikes with the group arranged around them and a big tape recorder.

Although "I'll Be Home" got airplay on a number of Top 40 stations, the record never made it onto the pop charts. But a different version did, when Pat Boone cut the record on Randy Wood's Dot label. It skyrocketed into *Billboard*'s top ten, just three slots behind Bill Haley's "See You Later Alligator." Wood and his Dot label had learned how to mine the R&B field for record gold: the flip side of Boone's "I'll Be Home" was a very tame version of Little Richard's "Tutti Frutti."

Boone's "I'll Be Home" severely depressed the sales of the Flamingos' record. The singers were devastated. They believed the hit was theirs to have, and Zeke Carey was sure that Leonard, who had known Wood for years, encouraged the much larger label to make the Boone version. Not only were the Flamingos losing recognition and sales royalties, they didn't get writers' royalties either. That was a particularly bitter pill to swallow. Zeke Carey and Nate Nelson maintained that while Washington and Lewis were the registered writers, they provided only the bare bones. The song that was recorded was changed and improved by the group. They had worked many hours to get the sound and the feel they wanted from the basic tune that Leonard first gave them.

"I'll Be Home" also turned up on *Billboard*'s Honor Roll of Hits, which meant its sheet music sales were also doing well. That meant more money for the Arc coffers. So while Checker revenues were depleted by the Boone version, the publisher's were not. And half of what came into Arc went to

Leonard and Phil. If the brothers hadn't known the value of a song before, they surely did now.

Years later it was some measure of comfort to the Flamingos that the version of "I'll Be Home" that was best remembered and then played on "oldies" stations was theirs and not Boone's—the same for Little Richard's "Tutti Frutti."

The Flamingos had another popular tune in the R&B market by June, when the ballad "A Kiss from Your Lips" reached number twelve on *Billboard*'s radio play chart. The song was also noteworthy for the writing credit: the Chesses' good friend and landlord, Russ Fratto, shared it with Roquel "Billy" Davis, a young Detroit musician and songwriter. Once again Carey believed he was shortchanged. He deserved a writing credit, he said, for retooling the melody and writing the bridge between sections of the song. "We were cheated," he said.

Davis disagreed. While he acknowledged that the Flamingos did their own arrangement of his song, he pointed out that a Detroit vocal group, the Ames, who later became the Four Tops, had recorded it as a demo. The dispute was not uncommon among musicians, a reflection of differing views on who contributed what and how much, if anything, it was worth under copyright law.

The Flamingos were understandably dispirited by their loss of sales on "I'll Be Home," but the exposure they got from the record nevertheless enhanced their concert opportunities. In June they went on an extended tour with Bill Haley that took them all around the country. Perhaps most important, within a year they would be signed by a big label themselves, Decca Records.

At the same time the Moonglows, the company's other prominent vocal group, was doing well with two songs that registered on the R&B charts in *Billboard* and *Cash Box*, "We Go Together" and "See Saw," also written by Davis. It was renewed confirmation for Leonard and Phil that they had made good choices in their effort to keep up with a changing market.

Leonard didn't dwell on the past, and he didn't like to look too far into the future. He believed in the present moment. But in his rare times of reflection there was satisfaction in the fact that he and Phil were a success. They had been on their own in the record business for barely five years. When they started neither had known anything about music, but they had shown that they could not only compete but prosper. Part of their success could be attributed to hard work and relentless drive. Another part was instinct—the ability to recognize an opportunity and seize it. The brothers were not visionaries, but Leonard, in particular, was as good as anyone at making the most of someone else's new idea.

The proliferation of pop versions of R&B songs prompted the next move: Why not get some of the pop market directly for themselves? On December 17, 1955, Leonard and Phil announced that they were going to start up a new subsidiary to focus on pop material. It would be called "Marterry," a combination of Marshall and Terry, the names of their sons. They planned to use some of their current roster of artists, such as singer Danny Overbea, and to bring in new musicians who would do material not then associated with Chess or Checker. The brothers also decided to line up new distributors to concentrate only on Marterry. The hope was that fresh faces would bring a new energy and new visibility to the products.

Leonard made a week-long visit to the West Coast in mid-January 1956 to look for new material and came back with the entire catalogue of one small company, the Crystalette label, which included the master tapes of singer Kay Starr. In addition, Leonard announced the signing of singer Savannah Churchill and a vocal group, the Daps. He told *Billboard* that the first Marterry records would be out by mid-February, but the first one, the Daps' "Down and Out" backed with "When You're Alone," wasn't released until the end of the month. With his typical bent for promotion, Leonard got them a spot on a local television show to push the record.

The disc turned out to be one of only two that carried the Marterry name. Bandleader Ralph Marterie objected to a label name so close to his, so by the end of March the brothers came up with a new name, "Argo." Though it wasn't another play on board games, the brothers and everyone else in the office liked the sound of it, Phil said, and so the name stuck.

The first Argo releases appeared the week of May 12, one by Savannah Churchill, the other by Danny Overbea. In the meantime, Leonard and Phil took turns calling the trade magazines with updates about the label's signings. Typical was a short *Billboard* piece that appeared at the end of April reporting the "stepped up" activity of signings, which included the Ravens, a group that had been popular in the late forties and early fifties and had most recently recorded for Jubilee, the jazz musicians Ahmad Jamal and James Moody, and another woman singer, Pinky Winters.

When the Ravens released their first Argo song, "I Can't Believe" backed with "Kneel and Pray," the half-page ad Leonard and Phil took out in the trade magazines showed they intended to push Argo with the same gusto as Chess and Checker.

Their good friend and New Orleans coordinator, Paul Gayten, made his own record for Argo in late summer, "The Music Goes Round and Round," and the company took out a quarter-page ad in *Billboard* to promote this disc too. Added to the basic information of name, address, and phone number was a new slogan: "Where you expect the hits—and you get them." It might have been wishful thinking, but the brothers knew they were on the right road with Argo when they finally got on the *Billboard* charts early in December 1956 with another New Orleans production, Clarence "Frogman" Henry's "Ain't Got No Home." Gayten produced the record, a fast-paced number that didn't sound too different from the songs put out on the Checker label. The novelty feature was Henry's playful vocals, a falsetto he used to "sing like a girl," a deep growl to "sing like a frog." Though Argo was supposed to be a "pop" label, "Ain't Got No Home" registered on the R&B charts, but Leonard and Phil weren't complaining. It was important to get the subsidiary established and visible. That they had accomplished, even if Argo hadn't yet found its true identity.

~~

A large company ad in the December 1, 1956, *Billboard* was instructive: three columns wide and a half-page high, it was divided into nine squares, each showcasing a new release. Stripped across the bottom was the label name *Chess-Checker-Argo*. Displayed most prominently were a new Muddy Waters release, one by Little Walter, and one by Chuck Berry. While the nine discs were a reminder of the effort to diversify, they were also a reminder of the company's roots in the blues and its growth into R&B during the preceding months.

Waters had started things off, getting on the R&B charts in January with two new numbers, "Sugar Sweet" and "Trouble No More." Berry's new release, "No Money Down," went on the charts at the end of February. "Smokestack Lightning," Howlin' Wolf's latest, was on the charts by the end of March. Though music was changing around him, Wolf remained constant. The short *Billboard* review could have been written about his first Chess records five years earlier: "a hard-driving primitive chant." Little Walter with "Who," a slow, rhythmic blues, also spent a few weeks on the charts in March. Waters followed with a third release, "Forty

Days and Forty Nights," which found its way onto the trade paper tallies by early May.

Berry hit his stride again in June with the witty "Roll Over Beethoven," a song about change in the music world: "Roll over Beethoven and tell Tchaikovsky the news." The record stayed on the *Billboard* and *Cash Box* chart for nearly two months, though it failed to cross over to the pop charts as "Maybellene" had. Waters's "Don't Go No Further" was released in the summer and made a modest splash for a couple of weeks in September. It had one of the more unusual opening phrases for an R&B song: "You need meat. . . ." Both sides of Berry's third record of the year, "Too Much Monkey Business" backed with "Brown Eyed Handsome Man," wound up on the *Billboard* and *Cash Box* R&B charts by the end of October, and each stayed almost two months in the limelight.

Sonny Boy Williamson, one of the label's newer blues artists, got his own taste of success by the middle of November. His "Keep It to Yourself" on the Checker label was on the *Billboard* R&B bestseller chart for a week. Down in Jackson, Mississippi, Lillian McMurry was incensed at the release. Globe Music, her publishing company, still held the copyright. But the Checker disc listed the publisher as Arc. She contested the company's claim that it had properly obtained the copyright and was therefore entitled to the benefits from sales and performances. Twenty-six years later she received a share of the royalties as part of her eventual settlement with Arc.

The Chess, Checker, and Argo songs that registered in *Billboard* and *Cash Box* were the successes, but they were only part of the company's inventory. For each record that sold well there might be four, five, or six that went nowhere. The hope was that the costs for these unsuccessful discs would be recouped by the revenue coming in from the ones that clicked. Competition was as intense as it had ever been. Some weeks, the top fifteen songs on *Billboard*'s R&B charts were divided among thirteen different companies. Usually it was only Atlantic or Chess and Checker that had more than one successful record at a time. When it came to radio play, which meant exposure for the musician and label and performance royalties for the publisher and songwriter, the difference between the most-played artist or song and the second or third on the list was considerable. A mid-year *Cash Box* poll of R&B disc jockeys found Fats Domino the most-played artist—21.1 percent of the time. Ray Charles was number two—with just over half the play, 11.1 percent. Chuck Berry, who was sixth, was played just 5 percent of the time, Muddy Waters and Little Walter, who were several notches down the list, were played on the radio less than 2 percent of the time. While the Moonglows were number five in most-played vocal group, that meant they got on the air only 5.3 percent of the time—barely a quarter of the Platters at number one, with 20 percent of the play.

Though such figures were sobering for a label, they were not the complete measure of visibility for the musicians. Even if the record wasn't a smash, there was a reciprocal relationship between making a record and performing live—a new disc almost always yielded new bookings, just as it had in 1948, when Muddy Waters's first recording for Aristocrat propelled him into the forefront of Chicago blues. It was also the gateway to getting a booking agent. Saxophonist Gene Barge was "desperate," as he put it, to get a record made in 1956 so that he and his quintet could move out of the small musical confines of Norfolk, Virginia. He was more than willing to let Checker put out an instrumental he wrote, "Country," that Phil bought after hearing it just once over the phone. Barge and his group had recorded the song in a Norfolk radio studio, and the disc jockey, who knew Phil from his many trips through town, told Barge he wanted to play it for Phil. Though Barge, who was a professionally trained musician with a college degree, found the entire process most unusual, he agreed to make the deal, even though there was no contract, just some cash from Phil a few months later. The record was released and while "Country" was not a hit, it was enough to get Barge signed with an agent. It was also the start of much bigger things to come that would eventually bring him back to Chess as a senior producer/arranger.

At the end of 1956, Alan Freed provided Chess and five other labels with a bonus. He produced a special long-playing record to go along with a rock-and-roll film, *Rock, Rock, Rock,* that he was producing. Chess was represented in the movie and on the record by Berry, the Flamingos, and the Moonglows, each singing songs written for the movie and published by Freed's own company. That meant that Freed would share the performance royalties along with the writer. The record was not for sale to the public. Instead copies were sent to some six hundred disc jockeys around the country as a promotional device for the film. In exchange for the use of their musicians, the labels were allowed to display their own records in the movie theaters showing the movie. Leonard and Phil got an extra filip when they put out a special long-playing record with songs from the movie by Berry, the Flamingos, and the Moonglows and filled out by some of their earlier records including "Sincerely" and "Maybellene." The nod from Freed was one more example of building business into friendship and vice versa.

A by-product of Leonard's early days on the road for Aristocrat was connections in dozens of cities. Detroit was always prime territory, and even though Phil had now taken over the Midwest, Leonard still retained important friendships there. One was with Joe Von Battle, a black entrepreneur who had a small record label, JVB, a publishing company of the same name, and a retail store, Joe's Record Shop.

One market niche in the black community was religious fare, not just gospel music but sermons that could be packaged on records and then sold across the country in small towns and rural areas where residents thirsted for the kind of spiritual uplift that comes from a powerfully preached lesson of faith. There were few better practitioners of the craft than the Rev. C. L. Franklin of the New Bethel Baptist Church. Von Battle recorded many of Reverend Franklin's sermons, but without being hooked up to a distribution network like the one the Chess brothers had established, it was hard to do much with his product. So in the spring of 1956, Von Battle made a deal with Leonard and Phil to lease his master tapes to Chess, which then put out the sermons under their label. It was another stream of revenue, to be sure, but Leonard also saw this as providing a service to part of the black community that otherwise would have little or no access to such things. It was also another example of the brothers' gift for recognizing a good deal.

By the late fall of 1956, there were visible new signs that the company was making money. One benchmark was Leonard and Revetta's decision to move from their small but comfortable house on South Yates to the northern suburb of Glencoe. This time they settled into a much larger house on a corner lot with a two-car garage, 1076 Oakridge Drive. An equally significant sign of the company's growth was the brothers' announcement in October that they were going to move the office again, this time to South Michigan Avenue, where their Cottage Grove neighbor, Vee Jay, had already relocated. They wanted space that would allow them to build a real studio with bona fide recording equipment and enough room for offices, a reception area, and a packing room.

Before long their new address would become synonymous with Chicago blues.

ten

2120 SOUTH
MICHIGAN

By the time Leonard and Phil bought a narrow, two-story build-ing at 2120 South Michigan Avenue, the surrounding neighbor-hood already was known as "record row." Vee Jay was down the block and across the street at 2129. Milt Salstone's MS Distributing Company was at 2009, Garmisa Distributing was two doors away at 2011, Mercury Records' distributor was at 2021, Paul Glass's All State Distribut-ing was at 2023, United Distributors was near the end of the block at 2029. One of the city's prominent publishing companies, Brandom, was at 1323 South Michigan, one block from Capitol Records' distributor at 1449. So the move was a logical one, and Leonard and Phil must have hoped for the same kind of synergy among like-minded neighbors that existed for a few years around Cottage Grove, the previous home to ten or so record operations.

Twenty-one twenty had been constructed in 1911 as a commercial investment property. It was only twenty-five feet wide and was sandwiched between the two-story Standard Supply Company, which dealt in machin-ists' equipment, and a seedy roominghouse, the seven-story Fairview. The majority of the Fairview's clientele were truck drivers making a one-night stop on their way to and from the stockyards. Though narrow, the building ran deep, roughly 125 feet back from Michigan Avenue to an alley. Over the years, consistent with the neighborhood, 2120 had been occupied by a number of commercial tenants. Prior to the Chess brothers' purchase, the building had housed a furniture slipcover manufacturer and a tire company but was vacant when the brothers bought it. While they put up the money,

Leonard and Phil instructed Nate Notkin, their lawyer, to draw up the papers so that the building would be in Joe Chess's name. They would pay him rent every month. It was a way to give their father and mother additional income.

The new building was not in particularly good shape; that probably appealed to Leonard because it meant he could get a good deal. Though it would take some work, 2120, with its substantial interior space, could be turned into the kind of offices the brothers wanted. It would, however, have to fit within a budget. More than one set of plans was required before architect and owner were in agreement about what to do. The choice was between what was optimum and what was minimally acceptable weighed against Leonard's wallet.

Leonard was going to be forty years old on March 12, 1957. Up to now he had seemed indestructible despite the days on end of long hours, little sleep, and bad habits—too much coffee, too many cigarettes. His family noticed that occasionally he looked uncomfortable, panting while he was chasing the dog or lifting something heavy, grimacing at shooting pains in his arm. The last week in January, in the midst of running the business from Cottage Grove and planning the move to Michigan Avenue, Leonard felt so bad he went to see Dr. William A. Brams, one of the city's prominent cardiologists. Brams did a routine test in his office, and the news wasn't good. Leonard was having a heart attack.

The doctor ordered him to go immediately to Michael Reese Hospital, insisting that Leonard not even stop at home for a change of clothes, let alone stop at the office to make arrangements for his absence. He would have to rest for six weeks, at least two in the hospital. When they learned Leonard was in Michael Reese, friends sent get-well cards and letters. More than one was signed "Mother," a joking reference to Leonard's favorite nickname for everyone. (One friend even sent him a Mother's Day card at the appropriate time, "To My Favorite Mother.")

Asking Leonard to lie down and take it easy was asking the impossible. He was a man in motion, even on the weekends at home. If he wasn't doing business, he was fixing things, drinking one cup of coffee after another, a cigarette hanging out of his mouth. The heart attack made him angry because it interfered with his plans. His life had momentum. Things were moving and moving fast, and now he was in a hospital bed disconnected from the phone and the business. The anger made an impression on Marshall. It wasn't that he had never seen his father mad before, but it was the boiling, almost helpless frustration that made it different.

Leonard was allowed to go home to Glencoe by mid-February, but then he had to stay there for another few weeks. Right after his birthday on March 12 he started coming back to the office for a few hours every day. At the end of the month he and Revetta took what was supposed to be a short vacation to Florida, though it turned out to be a working one. He was monitoring the business long distance, checking in with the office and his magazine contacts to make sure Chess was a weekly presence in their R&B chitchat columns. *Cash Box* duly noted a report from Florida in its April 6 issue.

Neither Leonard nor Phil knew anything about studio construction but they knew people who did because of their long relationship with Bill Putnam at Universal Studio. Putnam and his crew handled most of the Aristocrat, Chess, and Checker work. One of the youngest men at the studio was Jack Wiener, a self-taught eighteen-year-old who worked on mastering the tapes that would be turned into records, refining them for sound and musical mix. Wiener had seen Leonard and Phil coming in and out of the studio and had worked on some of the tapes they made in the small Cottage Grove office—and he always considered these a challenge because to his ear the quality was terrible. But the first time he actually met one of the brothers was when Phil bought the young engineer a cup of coffee. They had a reputation for being very frugal, so the small gift was noteworthy. The extra coffee was a small celebration because one of the Chess tunes was about to be covered by a white artist on a major label.

Wiener was gradually getting to know Leonard and Phil, but their budding friendship was put on hold when Wiener accepted an offer in 1956 from Randy Wood, the head of Dot Records and one of Universal's major clients. The job was in California, where the label was moving. Wiener stayed barely a year. He came back to Chicago early in 1957 after his father had a heart attack. It was fortuitous timing for Leonard. He offered Wiener, now only twenty-two, a wonderful opportunity: the chance to build a studio and bring in his own recording clients. It would be a joint venture. Wiener would have a one-third interest; Leonard would put up the construction money and Wiener would pay back his one-third from the proceeds.

While it sounded appealing, Wiener needed to think about it, and the brothers had to make more than one entreaty. They finally hashed out the deal over coffee at Deutsch's, the informal extension of the Cottage Grove office. Leonard and Phil had very limited space at 4750, and if they couldn't do business on the telephone and needed to do it in person, Deutsch's was the place.

When Wiener saw 2120, his heart sank. "A lousy choice," he thought, "too small and too narrow." The space on the second floor designated for the studio was roughly twenty feet wide and thirty-seven feet long. But it was all he had to work with, and Leonard told him to do it right. There was more than the wish for a good sound; Leonard knew that any improvements stayed with the building, and by extension, him as the owner. The first thing Wiener did was cover the original wood floor on the second story with two inches of cork. Then he laid concrete over that. He designed the walls, which were painted beige, to float on resilient springs for complete isolation from the adjoining rooms. This was to maximize soundproofing. On one wall were nine adjustable panels that could be opened for greater absorption of sound. When all the panels were closed, they presented a hard surface. And perhaps most important, there were no parallel surfaces in the room. The idea was to eliminate any rumbling that might occur from the low resonance of the drums, the bass, or heavy traffic from Michigan Avenue. Sound engineers knew that such low frequencies would bounce off parallel walls and hinder the recording process.

Wiener also built two echo chambers for special effects, running wires from the second floor studio down to the basement on either side of the room. A microphone and speaker were attached to each wire in the basement. He also built a specially designed twelve-channel console for the control room, turning the makeshift studio at Cottage Grove into his shop during the construction process. The rest of the equipment at 2120—tape machines, microphones, amplifiers—was up to the standards of any other independent studio. The control room was at the east end of the studio, nearest Michigan Avenue. Behind it were two rooms with the machinery to make the record masters.

Though the original plans called for large men's and women's restrooms on the second floor, they were eliminated. In their place was a small washroom with just a toilet and sink—a setup entirely in keeping with Leonard's no-frills approach: functional and not fancy. There was also a smaller rehearsal studio on the second floor and a small office, which Wiener used.

Behind that was empty space. Within a year or so a vault was built to hold the company's tapes.

While Wiener was putting the studio together, Leonard hired Bernard Chalmers and Associates to do the renovation work. By the time Wiener started on the studio, the first floor had been gutted and was being rebuilt, including the front. Twenty-one twenty needed a fresh face, and a new aluminum recessed storefront was installed, framed by dark artificial stone slabs. Set back behind the show windows was a partial wall of ornamental ribbed glass.

Although some extras, like the big bathrooms and fancy wood display shelves in the front, were eliminated from the original plans, the brothers did spring for California redwood trim for the first floor interior, including their side-by-side offices, and for the small office on the second floor. The redwood was one of the last things to be installed, a detail mentioned in *Cash Box,* which provided readers with periodic updates about how the move into 2120 was going.

The first few days in the new studio operation were a blur to Wiener. With so many things to think about on those warm summer days it was hard to remember who was even coming in to record. For good luck he had put up a small wall-hanging in his second-floor office, a gift from his parents. It was the theater masks, tragedy and comedy, and he already knew there was a good chance he would experience a little of each.

~~

It was fitting that the first sessions at 2120 were with the musicians who had given Leonard and Phil their first taste of success: Muddy Waters, Little Walter, Howlin' Wolf, and Chuck Berry. The brothers would be missing one of the fold, however. Upset about money he believed was owed him, Willie Dixon had left Chess to go to work for a small local label, Cobra Records, run by Eli Toscano. Dixon would come back now and then, however, to do a session.

Though Leonard didn't play golf, that didn't stop him from going to an out-of-town golf outing sponsored by bandleader Fred Waring. Even though the studio was just getting up and running, Leonard no doubt knew he could do business at the function. There were going to be lots of industry people there, and he was most adept at making new connections and reinforcing old ones at these kinds of events. Besides, Phil was in Chicago looking after things.

According to his agreement, Wiener was recording the Chess musicians as well as outside clients he brought in. He operated as "Sheldon Recording Studios," using his middle name for the business. In the first few months of operation he did work for Atlantic and some local talent sent to him by another prominent Chicago disc jockey, Daddy-O Daylie. Wiener also made himself useful to Leonard outside the office, picking him up at his Glencoe home, which was not far away from Wiener's own house, and dropping him at Midway Airport when he went out of town. The first time Wiener picked Leonard up on Oakridge Drive there was a shock of recognition when he got to the door. He knew the house; it had been built for his father's employer and Wiener and his brother had wired a speaker system inside.

Leonard appreciated getting a ride from Wiener, though he wasn't crazy about the cramped quarters of the MG the young man drove. But it was still better than going by himself: he worried that something might happen to his Cadillac in the parking lot, and it rankled him to have to pay a parking fee. It was one more example of Leonard's penchant for saving money. There were others. When Wiener wanted to hire his father to keep the books for the studio, Leonard said absolutely not. Wiener hired his father anyway but paid him out of his own earnings.

It didn't take long to establish traditions at 2120. If Deutsch's had been the informal commissary for 4750 South Cottage Grove, Batts Restaurant, in the New Michigan Hotel across the street, became its successor. The restaurant's motto was "Next to Home . . . It's Batts," and that seemed to be true for Leonard and Phil and their associates. Sometimes they went there for breakfast, lunch, and dinner. Most days the same choices were offered for the latter two meals: chop sirloin steak (with baked potato and salad), soup (clam chowder or beet borscht), and homemade blintzes (cheese, cherry, strawberry, or banana). And there was always a weekday businessman's special—perhaps soup, baked perch with Spanish sauce, potato and vegetable, all for $1.50. Phil's son, Terry, by now ten years old, loved to go to the office with his father on weekends because it meant breakfast at the restaurant.

Batts was also convenient. There was a back door to the hotel lobby right across from the Chess offices. Not only that, it was efficient. If any of the men needed a shoe shine or a haircut, they could get either on the way in or out. The shoe shine stand and the barber shop were a few feet from the restaurant's back door.

On Cottage Grove, Carri Saunders was the receptionist, only now she had new power, conferred on her by the ability to buzz people in and let them go upstairs to the studio or to the back of the first floor to see Leonard and Phil. Idell Nelson also moved over to 2120 to continue to handle clerical matters, and within a year or so, Ruth Brown, a white woman and no relation to the popular Atlantic singer, was also hired. Sonny Woods continued to supervise the stockroom and still served as Leonard's in-house record reviewer.

Musicians had to get used to the new studio, and in general it was a happy adjustment for those who had done their rehearsing and some of their recording in the cramped quarters of 4750. Even though the place was new and modern, it almost immediately had character. Whenever Waters and his band came in, they commandeered the back part of the studio, sitting in folding chairs and talking among themselves far from the control room. "I remember the smell of Muddy's sessions," said Marshall, who was nearly sixteen now and spending more time learning the business. "There was sweat. Not because he didn't take a shower, but sweat . . . you take a shower and fifteen minutes later, you sweat. You get four or five guys in there in an unair-conditioned place, recording in the summer in Chicago. I'm not saying it was a bad smell," he added. "It was a smell." He called it "funk."

Mixed in with the "funk" was the occasional waft of marijuana coming from the upstairs bathroom. It was the musicians' informal hangout, the place to share a joint.

∿

The first ads with the new company address had appeared in *Billboard* even before Leonard and Phil and their small staff moved in. One of them, a full page on May 20, 1957, was instructive not just for the information on the whereabouts of the "Chess Producing Corp." but also for an update about where Chess was musically. It was the first ad to give prominence to albums, one by Berry on Chess and three on the increasingly active Argo label, each of them more jazz oriented than the first Argo releases, which were the singles by "Frogman" Henry and Paul Gayten. Leonard and Phil were moving into long-playing records, but they were doing so with caution. Their bread and butter was the R&B market, which was based on the fast fading 78 market and the growing market of the smaller 45s and extended-play 45s. The latter had two or three songs on each side but was still a small disc. Leonard told one music writer that 45s were outselling 78s "seven to three," but he was reluctant to phase out 78s altogether because he knew they were still popular with his southern customers, who still had phonographs that played these records. Atlantic told the same writer that 75 percent of its singles were 45s.

Chess was not the only R&B company taking its time with long-playing records. The prevailing feeling among the independents all through 1956, and reinforced by their dealers, was that only the biggest pop stars could carry a long-playing record of vocals. Artists such as Dinah Washington, who crossed over into different categories, could carry an LP of jazz or pop standards, but one that was all blues was not likely to work. Rhythm-and-blues instrumentals had a better chance, and in fact the few R&B long-playing records that came out in the last quarter of 1956 were instrumentals with the exception of Fats Domino on Imperial Records.

Chess did have one LP under its belt, *Rock, Rock, Rock,* which had been issued at the end of 1956 in conjunction with Alan Freed's movie. The majors, by contrast—RCA, Columbia, Decca—already had committed to the long-playing records, and it was possible to buy classical fare, Broadway show tunes, movie soundtracks, some pop compilations, and jazz. There was enough LP activity that both *Billboard* and *Cash Box* ran sections each week about what was going on in the album field or, as *Billboard* called it, "packaged records." The trend was unmistakable. In the February 16, 1957, issue the magazine reported that sales of LPs had risen to 26 percent of all sales in the first three quarters of 1956 from 15 percent from the same period in 1955. The actual dollar increase jumped to 60 percent of total revenue spent on records in 1956 from 44 percent the previous year.

⋙

As the *Billboard* ads suggested, Chess production hadn't slowed down even though the brothers were in the midst of a construction project and Leonard was sick for more than a month. The releases coming out of 4750 were a mix of everything in the Chess stable: new blues from Muddy Waters, Sonny Boy Williamson, Howlin' Wolf, Little Walter, and Jimmy Rogers; more Chuck Berry, Bo Diddley, Lowell Fulson, Bobby Charles, and the Moonglows. Perhaps it was hyperbole, but Leonard got a kick out of one disc jockey, who he said was so anxious to be the first to play "I'm Afraid the Masquerade Is Over" by the Moonglows that he played a broken copy. It was the flip side, though, that was the more unusual of the two numbers. "Don't Say Good Bye" had a lush string backing. "You'd never believe this came out of the Chess studios," *Billboard* said, "but there it is."

Leonard continued to have good luck picking up music from other labels. His decision to lease and then release two songs from the J&S label by the duo Johnnie and Joe, "I'll Be Spinning" and "Over the Mountain, Across the Sea," proved to be a good one. Both made it onto the *Billboard* charts, the latter popular enough to register for four months.

The Argo subsidiary was also more productive, beginning to move into the pop-jazz arena and doing so with LPs. That made sense from a marketing standpoint; other companies had already led the way, and the jazz customers were becoming accustomed to the twelve-inch disk.

Productivity was also synonymous with Chuck Berry. He not only stayed busy all the time, he had also been a success from the beginning of his relationship with Leonard and Phil. Most everything he recorded since the release of "Maybellene" in the summer of 1955 had done well—seven songs on the trade paper charts, one right after the other. They were witty and easy to grasp, and he never lost that danceable beat. Berry was also a popular attraction for the big rock-and-roll shows that toured the country, good for him and good for the label.

Berry's newest release in the spring of 1957, "School Day"—which actually had been recorded the previous December—was no exception to the trend. It opened with a lively chord repetition and one of Berry's classic rhymes: "Up in the mornin' and out to school, the teacher is teaching the golden rule. American history and practical math, you study 'em hard hopin' to pass." The trade papers predicted great things for it, and they were right. By mid-April it was on the charts. By May, Berry was battling for the number one spot on *Billboard*'s three R&B tallies—sales, radio play, and jukeboxes—with a young musician who seemed to be reshaping and redefining the musical landscape every time he stepped to the microphone, Elvis Presley. His "All Shook Up" and Berry's "School Day" alternated between number one and number two on the R&B charts for most of the month. The competition in *Cash Box* was similarly intense, though on the pop charts, Presley was invariably three or four notches above Berry.

Presley came out of Memphis, nurtured by Sam Phillips, the same record man who had given Chess Records Jackie Brenston and his "Rocket 88" and the one-of-a-kind Howlin' Wolf. Presley knew from the time he was a teenager that he wanted to make music, but it had not been love at first sight between Phillips and the shy young man. He first stopped in at Sun Records in the summer of 1953, but it took Phillips nearly a year before he summoned Presley back to his studio for some work with local musicians who had already made a none-too-successful record at Sun. Their studio time on that hot July day in 1954 was not going very well, but when Presley and guitarist Scotty Moore and bass player Bill Black started into an old Arthur Crudup tune, "That's All Right Mama," Phillips heard something special. It was the same visceral feeling he had when he first heard Howlin' Wolf. There was something fresh here, he was sure, even though the song was not original and the musicial arrangement was ragged. Its raw honesty made it work.

Phillips was right. And he also believed he might have the key to unlocking a new and potentially large market for the music of the Howlin' Wolfs and other black performers he cared about so much, even if it wasn't performed by them. He knew their music appealed to "white youngsters," he told a Memphis reporter in 1959, reminiscing about his first days with Presley. "But there was something in many of those youngsters that resisted buying this music. The southern ones especially felt a resistance they probably didn't quite understand. They liked the music, but they weren't sure whether they ought to like it or not. So I got thinking how many records you could sell if you could find white performers who could play and sing in this same exciting, alive way." Disc jockey Alan Freed believed the same thing, only he was cultivating a white market for the black performers who made the music he loved as much as Phillips did.

"That's All Right Mama" was an immediate hit in Memphis. *Billboard* gave it a boost with a short review that called Presley "a potent new chanter who can sock over a tune for either the country or R&B markets."

The magazine was two-thirds right. What they hadn't predicted was that within eighteen months, Elvis Presley would capture the pop market, too.

Slightly more than a year after his breakthrough with Phillips and Sun Records, Presley signed with RCA Victor, which bought his Sun contract for $35,000—more than had ever been paid before for a popular singer, let alone one who was not fully tested. While the majors had had little success with conventional R&B and its largely black audience, Bill Haley on Decca had shown that this hybrid "rock and roll" could be lucrative.

Along with his RCA deal Presley signed a songwriting agreement with the well-established company Hill & Range, which set up a separate publishing firm for Presley. The headline in a December 3 *Billboard* story about Presley was right on the mark: "DOUBLE DEALS HURL PRESLEY INTO STARDOM." The story explained that RCA intended to "push his platters in all three fields—pop, r&b and c&w." Within a month of his signing, RCA announced that Presley would perform on four consecutive segments of *Stage Show,* produced by Jackie Gleason and hosted by Jimmy and Tommy Dorsey. It was Presley's entry into television, opening the way for him to break out of country and western. RCA even took out a full-page ad in *Billboard* announcing Presley's arrival as "the most talked about new personality in the last 10 years of recorded music."

It had been a great moment at Chess when "Maybellene" spent a month as number one on all three of *Billboard*'s R&B charts and led the *Cash Box* HOT charts in a dozen cities, and then when it crept into the top ten on the popular charts for a couple of weeks. But that was nothing compared to Elvis Presley. His first million seller was "Heartbreak Hotel," and it was followed by seven more million sellers within a year. He was topping the charts in all three genres, just as RCA had hoped. He was so popular by the beginning of 1957 that when *Billboard* ran its annual chart of bestselling artists for the previous year, Presley, listed in first place, had four songs after his name, not just the usual one. On top of that he was in first and seventh place in bestselling albums—the only one from the rock-and-roll/rhythm-and-blues field to be represented in the top fifteen list. It was another tribute to his stunning popularity.

This was one of those transformational moments, the kind that caused the most astute observers in the industry to rethink and revise their assumptions and ideas. This had to be more than just a fluke. Maybe it was the moment when musical boundaries would disappear. *Cash Box* thought so. "Rock and Roll May Be The Great UNIFYING FORCE," the magazine trumpeted in inch-high letters in a March 1956 editorial. Citing "Heartbreak Hotel" and "Blue Suede Shoes," by Carl Perkins, another Phillips find who had burst on the scene, the magazine said, "The overwhelming sensation in the record business this week is the fact that two records which started essentially in the country field have become hits also in the pop and rhythm and blues area." This success, the editorial went on, "demonstrates clearly the possibilities that exist—and which are becoming more definite all the time—of bridging all three markets with one record."

Over at *Billboard* the talk was about "the integration of chart categories," and by the time Presley had garnered his fifth and sixth bestsellers early in 1957, the magazine called him "something of a trend all by himself." But the editors also sensed a pivotal change, one important enough to prompt a change in how they covered the industry.

From now on there would be no more "Rhythm and Blues Notes." Instead the column would be expanded and renamed "ON THE BEAT—

Rhythm & Blues—Rock and Roll." Gary Kramer, the columnist, said that the new format, introduced February 16, "will cover not only rhythm and blues—but also the other musical areas that have developed in the past few years under the inspiration of the unusually wide acceptance of the R&B idiom. 'Rock and roll' and what has come to be called 'rockabilly' are the most important of these. No abstract categories prevent the teenager today from buying records by Fats Domino, Elvis Presley, Bill Haley, Carl Perkins or Little Richard at one and the same time. The trade, therefore, must revise and perhaps abandon some of its old boundary lines."

Kramer credited the independents with spurring the trend: "They pioneered and nourished rhythm and blues—and rock and roll—and are still its vanguard."

Presley and Perkins had shown the possibility of enormous drawing power across the spectrum. Writing in a subsequent column, Kramer suggested the reverse was true as well. Once, he said, "rhythm and blues" meant a black market. "Today for almost no rhythm and blues manufacturer, however, is the Negro consumer the prime target. His operation is typically geared economically to anticipated sales to both white and Negro customers . . . Indeed it is significant that recent releases of artists like Ruth Brown and Fats Domino hit pop charts as soon as R&B." Kramer called this "an interesting case of integration of the tastes of the majority into the minority."

Record men like Leonard and Phil, who operated on instinct and intuition, would never have considered these matters in such conscious, intellectual terms. They knew Presley was good for business. He brought customers into the record shops. They weren't in a headlong rush to get their own Elvis. Rather the Presley phenomenon meant, as Kramer suggested, the continuing promise and possibility of new markets.

One of the many musical "what ifs" has been the question of whether Chuck Berry could have been Presley had he been white. That frames the question backward. It was because Elvis Presley was white that he had such an impact. He was exciting, alive, sexual, sensual, threatening, even dangerous to some, and he came in for his share of criticism and vilification. A black performer doing the same things in that moment and in a highly public forum was unacceptable. Muddy Waters at his most provocative, in a club before an enthusiastic black audience with a Coke bottle stuffed in his pants, to be popped open when his song hit a fever pitch, would not be tolerated. He would have violated every racial-sexual taboo. Berry himself appreciated the racial-sexual borders, if for no other reason than his occasional scrapes with southern sheriffs angry and unsettled by his popularity among young southern white women only too happy to share his company. Sam Phillips had also understood, and perhaps in their own way Leonard and Phil had too. They were more interested in doing what they knew how to do, making records that might capture some of the market that Presley opened up. With their own studio they felt ready to compete with even more energy.

～

Leonard and Phil had made more good decisions than bad since becoming full-time record men, but if they had forgotten that precarious days always loomed on the horizon, a July 8, 1957, story in *Billboard* reminded them all over again. "Indies Feel Money Pinch Despite Hits" said the headline. The story was a discussion of "a general tightening up" among the independents, even those who were considered successful. "A number of indies state that in spite of the apparently thriving condition of their business they are hard pressed for ready money," the magazine explained. "Some blame the distributors, claiming that the average distrib meets his bills promptly only on those lines he needs—lines which are currently hot. Often an indie, when he needs money most, gets back a flock of records instead." The surest way to avoid this, the story went on, is to have at least two hits in a row. That way the distributor can't get the newest hit without paying the bills on the previous one.

Leonard was both particular and demanding about his distributors. Harold Lipsius of Universal in Philadelphia knew that only too well. One of his salesmen, Harry Finfer, paid Leonard a courtesy call late in 1956. When Leonard asked how things were going, Finfer spent all his time talking about the releases on Universal's new in-house label, Jamie. Leonard listened quietly. After Finfer left, he called Lipsius and told him he was pulling Chess out of Universal. All he heard, he said, was about Jamie, nothing about Chess.

Lipsius was flabbergasted. Despite a few entreaties, including one in person in Chicago, he could not get the label back. Finfer, he realized ruefully, was wearing two hats, Jamie salesman and Universal distributor. In Leonard's office, he had forgotten which one he had on.

Such tough-mindedness surely contributed to the success of Chess. The brothers also considered themselves lucky that they were making enough music now so that at least one or two of their musicians would have a hit to carry them through the lean days of the others. But stories like the one in *Billboard* were constant reminders that they could never let up.

The new and more sophisticated setting of 2120 did not change Leonard's way of operating when he involved himself in the straight blues sessions. Sonny Boy Williamson had recorded five tunes earlier in 1957; in September he did his first session in the new studio backed by a four-piece band including Little Walter's former drummer, Fred Below, and Willie Dixon, who was making one of his periodic appearances. Warming up for one of the takes, Williamson hummed a few notes and set the rhythm. After several bars of harmonica introduction, he started to sing: "Little village, too small to be a town." He repeated the line.

"What's the name of that?" Leonard interrupted from the control booth.

"Little Village, Little Village, motherfucker," Williamson said, his voice rising.

"Little Village."

"There isn't a motherfuckin' thing in there about a village, you son-ofabitch," Leonard shot back to the laughter of the musicians. "There's nothin' in the song that has anything to do with a village."

"Well, a small town."

"I know what a village is," Leonard retorted.

"Well, all right, goddammit. You don't, you don't need no title," Sonny Boy yelled. "You name it after, after I get through with it, you sonofabitch. You name it wha'ch you want. You name it your mammy if you want."

That broke Leonard up. "Take one," instructed the engineer, who was so distracted he misspoke for the start of the second take. "Rollin'."

It seemed like a good omen and a blessing for the new offices and studio that the cover of the August 3 *Cash Box* featured Chuck Berry. He was dressed in a dark suit and bow tie, crouched with his guitar in a ready-to-play mode. The caption underneath said he was "one of the country's top recording artists." Within six weeks he would have another solid hit, "Rock and Roll Music." The lyrics, about a backbeat "you can't lose it any old time you use it," were an apt recognition of the musical moment.

At the same time the brothers had another stroke of good luck when a master they bought from the Casa Grande label, "Happy Birthday Baby" by the Tuneweavers, turned into a hit. The song stayed on the charts nearly three months. There wasn't too much hyperbole in the breezy observation *Cash Box* made about the brothers in its R&B chat column: "Proves they can pick 'em." The truth of that observation was borne out again with the success of "Long Lonely Nights" by Lee Andrews and the Hearts, which the brothers had picked up from the Main Line label. These things weren't done completely by chance, however. Leonard and Phil had what they considered pseudo–talent scouts, disc jockeys at various stations around the country who played new material and then gauged the response. If there was good, instant feedback, they'd call Chicago to let Leonard or Phil know, and then the two would decide, usually after checking with a few record stores, whether to buy the disk and put it out on Chess. In other words, "there had to be some action" on the record to get their interest.

The Andrews record caught the attention of Atlantic as well, and there was a race to buy the master that went literally down to the wire. Leonard beat his competitors by about an hour, but Wexler and Ertegun were not deterred. In a few days, Clyde McPhatter cut a version for the label, and he and Andrews each sold well.

While Chess and Checker were turning out records, the brothers were also tending to Argo. But it was evolving now from the pop-blues flavor of "Frogman" Henry into jazz. Leonard and Phil were beginning to bring in other individuals, at least part time, to help keep the company moving forward musically. Though they didn't sit down and plot these moves according to a business plan, they did have the sense to hire people who knew more substantively about the music than they did and could increase the likelihood that the new things they were trying would find a niche.

In the wake of Leonard's heart attack, the brothers also realized they needed help in publicity. They were fond of a young promotion man who worked for the distributor David Rosen in Philadelphia. Max Cooperstein had been handling Chess and Checker records for a couple of years and had an affinity for the product. He used his good connections to Dick Clark, host of a popular Philadelphia-based television show, *American Bandstand*, to get Bobby Charles, Dale Hawkins, the Moonglows, and Chuck Berry on the air, and that made an impression on the brothers. Cooperstein started his Chess tenure traveling with Phil to Boston, Buffalo, Detroit, and Pittsburgh. Before long he would be summoned to Chicago to handle the promotion work right out of 2120. Chess Records was no longer a little family operation.

eleven

ALL THAT
JAZZ

Leonard and Phil first met Dave Usher at Universal Studios in 1951 when Usher was recording Dizzy Gillespie, his friend and partner in Dee Gee Records, Gillespie's own label. A young, committed jazz enthusiast, Usher had come in from Detroit, Gillespie from New York, to use Universal's facilities. Their session ran late, and Usher bumped into the Chess brothers, who were waiting their turn for the studio. The three talked briefly as Usher was leaving, but there was nothing remarkable about the short interchange. In the small world of independent record labels, however, people remembered such brief encounters, and they had a way of turning into important relationships.

By 1953 Usher and Gillespie folded Dee Gee, and from then on, Usher nurtured his love of music as spectator rather than participant. He kept current through acquaintances such as Detroit disc jockey Mickey Shorr, by now one of Phil's important contacts in the city, and by reading *Down Beat*, a Chicago magazine devoted to jazz. Every now and then he noticed a mention of Argo releases that featured Chicago musicians, and they caught his eye because he knew the artists, among them pianist Ahmad Jamal and bass player Chubby Jackson. There were some bigger names, too, like sax players Zoot Sims and James Moody. Usher saw Phil every now and then on his trips to Detroit, so the brothers were on his mind early in 1958 when a young, talented piano player, Bess Bonnier, came to him seeking help.

Frustrated that her career was stagnating in her hometown, Bonnier thought she would have better luck in Chicago, but she didn't know where to start. Go see the Chess brothers, Usher told her.

Bonnier made the trip, and during her visit to the Michigan Avenue studio, Phil had an idea. If Dave Usher is so high on her, why doesn't he come to Chicago to run the session? They called him on the spot, and Usher said yes, even though by now he was working in his father's oil reclamation business and had a wife and children. Intending to come to Chicago just to do the sessions, Usher stayed five days. The five days blossomed into a new position, A&R man—artist and repertoire—for Argo. His mission was to expand the line: find new talent, organize sessions, and produce the albums from the music to the cover design to the advertising and promotion. What helped cement the deal was running into his friend Ahmad Jamal in the hallway.

Usher's arrangement was an unusual one. Instead of moving to Chicago he commuted every week from Detroit, sometimes staying at the Conrad Hilton Hotel, about a mile north on Michigan Avenue, but more often than not bedding down at 2120 and becoming one of the three-times-a-day regulars at Batts. Occasionally Usher slept on a couch in Leonard's office. Sometimes he stayed on an army cot he brought into the second-floor office. Jack Wiener was gone. He was drafted in August of 1958, and he and Leonard decided to end their business relationship. Leonard got the studio setup; Wiener took his mastering equipment that had been in the second-floor room overlooking Michigan Avenue. Usher turned the space into an office for album production.

A number of the earlier albums that had caught Usher's eye were put together by Joe Segal, a young jazz fan who used to frequent the Macomba Lounge as part of his nighttime circuit through the city's music haunts. He was self-taught, motivated by his love of the music and his urge to share it with others—he put on jazz sessions at Roosevelt University where he was a student and wrote a jazz column for the school newspaper. By the time he was twenty-five he was presenting musical acts wherever he could find a forum. Leonard and Phil wanted to hire him to head their fledgling jazz operation, but that didn't pan out. However, Segal brought his talents to bear on several sessions between 1956 and 1958 that helped get the Argo label going; *Down Beat* had taken note in a short August 1956 article: "Chess Waxes Chicago Jazz."

To help establish the Argo line, Phil and Leonard bought masters from Al Benson to release on their label, among them records by Jamal. He knew the brothers from the Macomba Lounge because he occasionally played solo piano at Jimmy's Palm Garden around the corner. He first met the man who would become his drummer, Vernel Fournier, when he stopped in at

the Macomba to listen to Tom Archia and his friends. Over a few months in 1956 and 1957 two Jamal albums were released, *Chamber Music of the New Jazz* and *Count 'Em 88*, and Jamal was signed to Argo.

He had come to Chicago from New York, where he won attention and acclaim for his technical skills although he was barely twenty. Aside from his occasional solo work in Chicago, Jamal was the first part of a group called the Four Strings: bass, guitar, violin, and piano. The quartet eventually became a trio, and the guitar player was replaced with a drummer, Fournier. Veteran club musician Israel Crosby played the bass. In addition to recording for Benson and Argo, Jamal and his trio found steady work at the Pershing Lounge, the club room in the well-known hotel of the same name.

Toward the end of 1957, Jamal and Leonard talked about what he should do next. One of their friends, WGES disc jockey Sid McCoy, happened to be at 2120 at the same time, and as the conversation developed, an idea took hold for a live album. Why not do it at the Pershing Lounge? It was a place Jamal knew and liked and an atmosphere that could provide a kind of immediacy to the recording that would not be possible in the studio. Though Wiener ran the Chess recording studio, the decision was made to use Malcolm Chisholm, an experienced engineer from Universal who had worked on a number of Chess/Checker tunes over the years. Jamal, though, would be in charge of the musical part of the evening. There would be no additional producer.

On the evening of January 16, 1958, Jamal, Crosby, and Fournier set up on the Pershing Lounge stage; Chisholm loaded his equipment from Universal into a station wagon, drove the few miles south to the hotel, and got everything in place. Because the lounge was so small he had to put the recorder on a table in the liquor room, a small, enclosed space away from the bar. He hooked up two sets of earphones and alternated between them: one for the high end of the musical scale, the other to pick up the dynamics of the low end so he could get the best possible musical mix. Neither Leonard nor Phil could make it to the Pershing, so Phil asked Max Cooperstein and Howard Bedno, a young West Side distributor who liked to hang around 2120, to go down to the lounge and watch the session.

The trio played forty-three songs over several sets. Jamal selected eight for the album, *Ahmad Jamal Trio at the Pershing: But Not for Me*, among them George and Ira Gershwin's "But Not for Me," one of his most requested songs at club dates, "Surrey with the Fringe on Top" from the Rodgers and Hammerstein musical *Oklahoma!*, and a seven-and-a-half-

minute jazz tune "Poinciana." Independent of the song selection and the instrumentation, documentation on the album made clear that this was different from Chess blues and R&B. Each of the songs was registered with ASCAP, the established and establishment performance rights group, and not the upstart (by comparison) BMI, which handled nearly all of the material put out on Chess and Checker.

Down Beat didn't think much of the album. "Apparently this is being marketed as a jazz record," it began. While acknowledging Jamal's skill at the piano and his influence on other jazz musicians, notably Miles Davis, the reviewer said Jamal played "cocktail" music. "The trio's chief virtue is an excellent, smooth light but flexible beat," he wrote. "Throughout the music is kept emotionally, melodically, and organizationally innocuous."

The critic and the jazz fan seemed to be looking for different things. *But Not for Me* was a smash. It sold five thousand copies in one day right after it was released. Usher knew that competitors could scoff at the numbers, so he told Leonard he should let a *Billboard* reporter come over to 2120 and look at the sales figures. "Leonard looked at me like I was nuts," Usher said, but he did it.

"Argo, Buoyed By Jamal Hit, Plans Big Fall" read the headline on an article in the magazine's August 25, 1958, issue. An album that sold 15,000 or 20,000 copies "was big," the story said. Jamal's had already sold 47,762. In addition, a single from the album, "Music, Music, Music" backed with "But Not for Me" sold 27,500 copies while the extended-play 45 from the record sold another 11,362. By December, according to *Down Beat*'s poll of three hundred retail outlets, the album was the number-one jazz bestseller.

Marshall knew firsthand that the Jamal record was doing well. Now sixteen years old, he had graduated from doing mail runs and getting coffee for his father and uncle to assembling the LPs for delivery. It was a cumbersome process. The cover, generally with some color, was printed in one place. The liner notes, which were black and white, were done separately. Then they had to be glued onto the cardboard that protected the record. The cover fabricator would deliver the finished covers to 2120, and the pressing plant delivered the records. Then the records had to be put in the jackets and shrink-wrapped. While the pressing plants did a good deal of the assembly, there was always some that was done on Michigan Avenue, particularly for a record that was as popular as Jamal's. Distributors were coming in day and night, weekends too, to pick up their copies.

But Not for Me ended up staying on *Billboard*'s album chart for an

astonishing 107 weeks—more than two years. While it didn't register quite as long on the *Cash Box* tally, the journal also showed it to be one of the year's strongest sellers in 1958.

~~

Phil's interest in jazz and his growing responsibility for building this part of the Chess operation resulted in another gifted piano trio joining the Argo roster. This one was headed by Ramsey Lewis, a Chicago native and, like Jamal, something of a star by the time he was a teenager. Lewis joined a group called the West Side Cleffs that had been formed by drummer Red Holt and his friend Wallace Burton, who played the piano and sax. The two men recruited talented friends until they eventually had seven members. A couple of piano players moved on, and Lewis, who had known Holt since both were children, joined the group. By 1956, the Cleffs had been whittled down to a trio: Lewis, Holt, and Eldee Young on bass. They were getting steady work at the Lake Meadows Lounge, a popular spot on South Thirty-fifth Street in the midst of an apartment complex and shopping mall. One fan was a policeman—"George the Cop," they called him—who talked up the trio to anyone who would listen. Eventually Daddy-O Daylie, the prominent disc jockey, came by the club, and he, too, was impressed. He told them they should make a record, and Daylie was most likely the one who told Phil he should go and hear the trio. Phil obliged, taking his wife, Sheva, one evening and coming away equally impressed. He had the trio audition at 4750 South Cottage Grove in the fall, and they played well despite an equipment problem. Holt had a hole in his snare drum, but Leonard came up with a solution. He dispatched one of his employees to the stockroom to get a piece of cardboard from one of the record boxes and told Holt to tape it on the drum. He finished the audition with brushes rather than his sticks.

Holt and Lewis had a good feeling just watching Leonard and Phil nod their heads to the music in the small, makeshift studio. "You guys are pretty good," Phil said, calling in Sonny Woods to get his opinion. He liked them, too. Phil agreed to record the group, and within a few weeks he set up an appointment at Universal to cut the tracks.

The Gentlemen of Swing: Ramsey Lewis and His Trio was released early in 1957. Although the three men had formed a partnership—each had a one-third interest—Daylie told them that Lewis's name should be out front.

It was the style for trios to have the piano player in the lead, he said, and he told them that club marquees were not big enough to accommodate all their names. A quarter-page ad in *Billboard* touted Lewis as "a new recording star." The ad was more than a boost for Lewis, however. It was a nice plug for the Argo line, listing eight other jazz musicians who were on the label, most of them talented local artists like Sandy Mosse and bass trumpeter Cy Touff, though Zoot Sims, who had made an album the previous October, and Jamal were also mentioned. Lewis's release coincided with a short *Down Beat* review of the trio's two-night stint at the SRO Club. Referring to three jazz greats, editor Jack Tracy wrote, "This group could hit the heights of acclaim achieved by such as Shearing, Brubeck and Garner with proper handling, and if they continue to play with the simple, communicative honesty they now show."

The Chess operation in all its permutations—Chess, Checker, Argo—was running quite smoothly now. While there was still an air of informality and spontaneity, there was also a regular order to the procedures needed to get a record out the door: contracts for the musicians, union clearances, song selection, and obtaining the appropriate licenses for payment of royalties on the songs recorded. A six-hour union-approved recording session with four musicians—a leader and three sidemen—now cost slightly more than $400. The sidemen each got $82.50, the leader got double. The musician got a royalty of roughly three cents on a single, ten cents on an LP on 90 percent of the records sold. The 10 percent of the records not counted reflected the number given away for promotion. The royalties accrued would be paid against the costs of making the album—any advance plus the associated studio expenses. And if a musician brought in his own composition that had not yet been recorded, there were songwriting agreements to be executed with Arc Music.

Until Usher came there was no specific plan for putting out the Argo releases and publicizing them. He changed that to give the label a higher profile and, he hoped, boost sales. He hired a young art director, Will Hopkins, who helped him develop a distinctive spine for all the LP jacket covers, a small black-and-white checker pattern that would stand out when the releases coming out of 2120 South Michigan were lined up on store shelves. Usher also came up with a slogan for the jazz line, "Audio Odyssey by

Argo"—a journey through music. The small checkerboard started showing up in the trade paper ads as an identifying mark for the "Chess Producing Corporation."

There was another important change on the technical staff. With Wiener's departure, Leonard needed another full-time engineer, so he hired Malcolm Chisholm. The engineer became available when Universal denied his request for a raise and Leonard agreed to the sum Chisholm asked for—roughly two hundred dollars a week, enough for Chisholm to buy himself the Alfa-Romeo sports car he had always wanted.

Like Wiener, Chisholm didn't think much of 2120 when he first walked in the door. "I'm gonna die in the goddamn control room. It's too bloody small," he thought to himself. And he didn't care for the configuration of the studio either, wondering aloud, "How the hell am I going to set up a rhythm section?" But then he realized that while the studio was narrow it was also deep and probably could accommodate the musicians and instruments that would be needed for the company's repertoire. And when Chisholm clapped his hands a few times, he liked the liveliness of the sound. It convinced him that he could survive. There was also the matter of pride. Regardless of the room, he told himself, "I won't do bad work."

Despite the rigors of the commute and missing his family in Detroit, Usher loved what he was doing. Leonard and Phil were pleased, evident by the free hand they gave him creatively and the promotion he got in September 1958 to A&R man for all Chess material, not just the Argo division. Max Cooperstein was named national sales manager, expanding his territory from the East. Paul Gayten, the brothers' friend and associate from New Orleans, became the national promotion man.

The brothers' confidence in Usher was demonstrated further when they backed his idea of including a free extended-play 45 with four tracks on it into a standard LP package, which would sell for $3.98, a dollar less than the usual package. Usher called his creation a "Kangaroo Split Pack." The idea was to get more of the Argo product out to listeners, even in sample form. The test LPs included one by prominent drummer Max Roach, who came to Argo in an exchange with Mercury, his label, for one LP by Ramsey Lewis, and one by the Jazz Exponents, a quartet popular in Michigan. To promote the concept Leonard sprang for a two-page ad in *Down Beat* featuring kangaroo drawings to demonstrate the concept and a mail-in coupon to order the records.

Usher also convinced Leonard to take out a half-page ad in *Billboard* touting the "Audio Odyssey by Argo." While Jamal's album was featured prominently, the ad also listed the twenty-two albums that had been released in the previous eighteen months and five new ones, including an LP by Bess Bonnier, who had been the catalyst for Usher's coming to Chess.

In the fall Usher had another success, this time a remote session at the London House, one of Chicago's more prominent jazz clubs, with noted pianist Marian McPartland. Compared to the Pershing Lounge, the London House was a snap for Chisholm. He could engineer the recording right in the performing space. He had done so many sessions at the place while he was at Universal that the owners knew what kind of coffee he liked. Usher also put together an innovative album with Jamal backed by a fifteen-piece string ensemble that was done in New York City at the Penthouse studio. He insisted that Chisholm handle the job, so Leonard agreed to fly the engineer out to do the technical work. *Cash Box* designated *Jazz at the Penthouse* one of its favorites.

The magazine devoted its December 6 cover to the pianist. He and Leonard were shown separately in side-by-side pictures, a smiling Leonard in a striped polo shirt and slacks with Dave Usher, whose back was to the camera, in the control room. In the adjacent frame, Jamal, dressed in an open necked, short-sleeved shirt and dark slacks, relaxed on a stool, a huge grin on his face. The caption said Jamal and his trio had "turned into one of the hottest properties in the music business." Not only were his records selling, he was also in demand as a performer. One date in Alaska netted the group $6,500 plus expenses for two concerts.

Leonard and Phil's partnership with Gene and Harry Goodman at Arc also paid off. Their brother Benny agreed to make a jazz album for the company, *Benny Rides Again,* although this one was released on the Chess label, rather than Argo.

It wasn't just the musical freedom that Usher enjoyed at 2120. It was the overall atmosphere, a hum of activity as soon as the doors opened in the morning: answering phones, meeting musicians, handling orders for new records, setting up studio sessions, developing artwork and liner notes for albums, seeing the constant flow of individuals in and out of the place, including salesmen and disc jockeys looking to give something to Leonard and Phil and maybe get something in return. Every now and then Joe Chess would come by, and some of Usher's favorite moments were those he spent chatting with the elder Chess in Yiddish, still his first language.

Though it wasn't a requirement to be Jewish to work in Chess management, or to run an independent record label, for that matter, one could be forgiven for thinking so. Along with Leonard and Phil, most of the "indies," as they were known, were operated by Jews, either immigrants or the children of new arrivals a half-century earlier: the Bihari brothers at Modern, Syd Nathan at King, Herman Lubinsky at Savoy, Hy Weiss, Leonard and Phil's onetime distributor, and his brother Sam at Old Town, Morris Levy at Roulette. Vee Jay's Vivian and Jimmy Bracken and their partner, Ewart Abner, who were black, were the exceptions. So was one white gentile, Sun's Sam Phillips.

For most of the men, running a label was the next logical step from an earlier job as a jukebox operator, a distributor, or a nightclub owner. They had been handling the product; why not produce it? Self-made, most had a coarse streak born out of their rough climb from difficult childhood circumstances. It was no wonder that Lillian McMurry with her Trumpet label down in Jackson often felt, for all of her own moxie, uncomfortable among these streetwise, unpolished men. That so many were brought up as Jews had cultural rather than religious importance. Their shared ethnic background was more common ground than a set of precepts to be followed. In fact, to outsiders they were subject to the same kind of stereotypical thinking that applied to race. In this case it was the oft-repeated view that Jews were shrewd at business, probably untrustworthy, and almost always successful.

Like the Chess brothers, these other label owners worked largely with black musicians and in their minds those relationships were for the most part positive. "We were people who had an understanding," said Usher. "Look, we got along very well with the *shvartzehs*," he added, no trace of condescension or derision as he used the Yiddish slang for blacks.

⌁

Leonard would have considered it a compliment if someone called him "a record man," but that didn't mean he was a *music* man. To him this was a business, and music was his product. His goal every day was to figure out how to make that business as profitable as possible. He had admired Buster Williams in Memphis from the beginning and never forgot how Williams expanded his own enterprise from jukeboxes to a distributorship to a pressing plant. The latter was a pivotal part of the process. A good recording session and a master tape are of no use if the tape can't be turned into a record and sold.

By now Leonard had a network of pressing plants that handled the

Chess product, including Plastic Products in Memphis, Southern Plastics in Nashville, and an RCA plant in Indianapolis. Periodically Usher would stop in on his way from Detroit to Chicago, particularly if the company was having a hard time getting its orders filled. If he hadn't understood the importance of Elvis Presley before, he did every time he walked into the RCA plant. Presley's picture was on the wall of every room, as though he were president of the United States. Sometimes there would be Chess backlogs at Plastic Products as well. Williams's main client was Dot Records, the Randy Wood label, and Dot was taking up an increasingly large part of the Memphis plant's operation.

As the business at 2120 continued to thrive, Leonard decided he needed his own plant in Chicago. On one of his visits to Nashville, he explored the possibility with John Dunn, the owner of Southern Plastics.

"Why don't you put one in?" Dunn asked.

"I need somebody to run it, and I don't want to mess with it," Leonard replied.

"Okay," Dunn countered. "We'll go fifty-fifty. We want fifty percent and you can have fifty percent. I've got the man to go up and do it for you." He motioned to James Gann, his top assistant, who was sitting in on the conversation.

Leonard liked Dunn and had confidence in him. Otherwise he wouldn't have agreed to put up half the money. Their agreement was $7,500 each, though Dunn brought in two partners for his share, providing a total of $15,000 to buy six presses at roughly $1,500 each, and the other needed materials. They made a deal with Leonard and Phil's good friend Russ Fratto to put the plant at 4750 South Cottage Grove, site of the old Chess offices. Although Fratto's Victory Stationery printed company stationery and the like, he couldn't do the labels for the records. Instead Leonard and Gann found an unlikely printer, the Croatian Franciscan Fathers, who operated a printing plant out of their parish at 4851 South Drexel Boulevard. The priest in charge was Father Salistine, a Croatian immigrant who published a newspaper for the Croatian community in Chicago.

The pressing plant was called Dunn Record Pressing Inc. In the beginning the machines only did 78s, cranking out between seven and eight hundred an hour, and eventually running twenty-four hours a day in three shifts. While the bulk of the business came from 2120, Gann did solicit work from other labels. It was to his advantage. Leonard offered a modest salary but promised Gann 10 percent of the profits from the plant, whose books were kept separately from the record company. "He didn't believe in overpaying anyone," Gann said.

$$\sim\!\!\sim$$

While the initial push on LPs was in the jazz line, the brothers were moving into long-playing records with their established stars and starting to put some of the jazz out on stereo, the latest sound technology. In March 1958 they announced the release of a Chuck Berry album, *One Dozen Berries*, which included his newest single hit, "Sweet Little Sixteen," and five previously unreleased tunes. To give both artist and album a boost, Leonard did something he almost never did: buy a full-page ad in *Billboard* on April 7 devoted exclusively to one musician. Included in the ad was a plug for Berry's newest single, "Johnny B. Goode," which followed "Sweet Little Sixteen" onto the charts.

The "Sweet Little Sixteen" session had taken a little longer than usual. Phil's son, Terry, now eleven years old, was almost like a studio mascot, allowed to sit with the musicians while they were recording as long as he behaved himself. If Berry was in town so much the better; he was treated like a member of the family. Occasionally, Phil would have him stay at the house on South Phillips, where he would sleep in the other twin bed in Terry's room and join the family for breakfast the next morning. Berry was so fond of Terry that he gave him one of his old guitars. When Berry and his band gathered in the studio on December 29, 1957, to record "Sweet Little Sixteen" and a few other songs, Terry came down with his father, found an empty chair out in the studio and waited for the music to begin.

Berry kicked off the song, the band members joined in, and Terry, an aspiring drummer, picked up two empty record crates that were sitting on the floor and started to beat what he thought was the time. "Get him out of here," came a growling voice over the intercom. The chastened youngster was hastily escorted out, and the session resumed.

Rock, Rock, Rock, with songs from the 1956 Alan Freed movie, had been the first blues/R&B Chess LP. Over the next eighteen months, the brothers had put out a few more long-playing discs, generally compilations. One was of Berry's music, with one or two previously unreleased tunes, a "best of" for Muddy Waters and Little Walter, and albums by Dale Hawkins and the Moonglows. None of these sold very well, however. The market for this music was not yet attuned to albums, and few buyers of singles had the equipment that could play LPs, though that was changing. The big push for *One Dozen Berries* reflected the change, and at the same time such moves by Chess and the other labels were also encouraging it. The more LPs there were, the more fans would buy new equipment to play the music of their favorite musicians.

At the same time Leonard and Phil relied on their network of unofficial talent scouts to pick up masters from other labels. They made another good guess early in 1958 with the Monotones' "Book of Love," which they bought from the Mascot label and which turned into a bestseller. So did another Mascot tune, "Been So Long," by the Pastels. Both were put out on the Argo label. The brothers also made deals in the spring to distribute two other small labels, Cosmic and Singular, which was headquartered in Philadelphia, though the latter would be closed down and a third, Fenwick, picked up. A few months later they would pick up a fourth label out of Detroit, Anna, which was run by the young songwriter-arranger Billy Davis and Gwen Gordy, the sister of his friend and producing partner, Berry Gordy. Anna was named for another Gordy sister. While these distribution deals were more evidence of the brothers' interest in new ventures that might yield a profit, they were also evidence that Chess was established well enough nationally that it was attractive to a smaller label looking to get its product out. Chess sold the records manufactured by the smaller labels and then paid them a royalty on the sales.

In the midst of all this activity the bluesmen—Waters, Wolf, Walter, and Williamson—were still making records, even though they were not hitting the charts regularly. Walter and Waters, though, did have good sellers at the end of 1958, Walter with "Key to the Highway," and Waters with "Close to You." In terms of the business this was the gravy. The blues records were a steady baseline for Chess, twenty, thirty, maybe fifty thousand records every time out, that Leonard always appreciated. "Fuck the hits. Give me thirty thousand on every record," he periodically told Chisholm.

Once he got his driver's license—in March 1958—Marshall was often given the task of loading up a car with the latest blues releases and driving them over to the Oak Park Arms hotel, where popular WOPA disc jockey Big Bill Hill would play them on his morning show, which was geared to factory workers getting off the night shift. It amazed Marshall to see Hill drinking scotch or bourbon out of a hotel water glass at 7:30 in the morning as he got ready to go on the air.

◣◣

By the industry measure, Chess, in spite of its staying power and continued growth, had not yet had a million seller. Even "Maybellene," which topped all three R&B charts for a month and which broke into the pop and country charts, didn't reach that mark. When *Billboard* published its tally of million sellers in March 1958 that encompassed the previous few years, Chess was not represented. However, Arc Music was, by virtue of the cover versions of songs in the company's catalogue. It was another reminder of the importance of publishing as a means of revenue. Three Arc songs were listed: the McGuire Sisters doing "Sincerely" on Coral, Pat Boone doing "I'll Be Home" on Dot, and Bill Haley doing Bobby Charles's "See You Later Alligator" on Decca. Under the "mechanical" royalty rate at the time, each of those songs, if the system worked, should have brought at least $10,000 to the publisher and yielded $10,000 to the songwriter.

Although Berry couldn't claim a million sales on any of his records yet, he still was a popular recording artist, enough so that he was among the handful of nonjazz performers invited to be part of the 1958 Newport Jazz Festival. Billed as "Blues in the Night," the special attractions included Ray Charles, Joe Turner, and Big Maybelle. Mahalia Jackson was also invited to do a gospel set. *Billboard*'s Ren Grevatt, who had taken over the "On the Beat" column, paid close attention to the experiment and offered his review in the July 14 issue. It was not a success.

"Let it be said here and now that all of the performers involved here, Ray Charles, Joe Turner, Big Maybelle and Chuck Berry, performed splendidly. The failure of rapport between them and the audience (except in the case of Berry who did get a reaction) was not wholly the fault of the artists." Grevatt blamed the planners, who for "some inexplicable reason" had Charles start with jazz selections before he played any blues. "Charles is a good jazz man," Grevatt said, "but he did not play well that night and the same can be said about his group. By the time Charles had finished playing jazz he had lost the jazz part of his audience and not enhanced his position with those who had come to hear Ray play and sing the blues." As for Berry, it was a generational thing. The younger members of the audience loved him; the older ones were far more restrained when he sang his string of hits. They were well performed, Grevatt wrote. "But a straight rock and roll singer like Chuck was out of place on a blues or jazz show." To a jazz man like Usher, Berry stood out for more than his music. Though he had been the contact to get Berry on the bill, he was unprepared for the musician's arrival in the rarefied atmosphere of Newport: in a hot pink Cadillac with a venetian blind on the back window, air horns on the fenders and a raccoon tail tied to the tailpipe.

As *Billboard*'s Grevatt noted, Berry did better than most at reaching a broad audience, and a few weeks after the Newport festival he was featured again on the cover of *Cash Box*, which noted his continuing success. This time he was pictured with Max Cooperstein; Dick Clark, who had given Berry a symbolic gold record for three bandstand hits; and Mattie Singer, a Philadelphia distributor for the label. Though *Cash Box* was not a magazine for the record-buying fans, its audience of distributors, jukebox operators, club owners, and disc jockeys remained an important one. They were the ones who got the music to the public, and getting their attention via a cover was always a boost. Berry was one of three Chess representatives on the magazine's year-end list of top R&B singles, earning recognition for "Sweet Little Sixteen" and "Johnny B. Goode," the same two that showed up on the year-end *Billboard* tally. Also listed from the 2120 studio were the Monotones on Argo for "Book of Love" and the Moonglows, now known as "Harvey and the Moonglows," for "The Ten Commandments of Love," which had been on the charts for two months.

As further evidence of the growth of R&B as a commercial force, *Billboard* expanded its chart listings at the end of October to include the top thirty songs each week. Instead of surveying bestsellers in stores, radio play and jukebox play, it now ran a single listing under a prominent two-inch-high banner "Hot R&B Sides."

The initial challenge for the Chess brothers a decade earlier had been starting a business. The next one was keeping it alive. Now the challenge was to build on the momentum of the last eighteen months. Berry and Bo Diddley were helping to do their part. Between mid-December 1958 and the summer of 1959, Berry had three more big sellers, "Sweet Little Rock and Roll," "Almost Grown," and "Back in the U.S.A." Diddley found success with "I'm Sorry" and "Crackin' Up," and two versions of "Say Man," the second, "Say Man, Back Again," a sort of answer to his first. As an advertising ploy for the latter, the company took out a full-page ad in *Cash Box* showing what was apparently a telegram from a Los Angeles distributor who reported that 8,600 copies of the record had sold in two days and requesting another 10,000.

Diddley also put out his first original album, *Go Bo Diddley,* which registered on the charts for several weeks. *Cash Box* put him on the cover of its October 31, 1959, issue, noting the success of his two singles and the album. The magazine described Bo Diddley as playing "a major role in the development of rock and roll in its early stages"—an indication that the magazine apparently thought that the genre, barely four years old, was out of its infancy and already had musical elders. Leonard and Phil also put out LPs by Howlin' Wolf and Sonny Boy Williamson in the early part of the year, which were compilations of their previously released singles, as well as a second one by Berry.

The brothers could see that Usher was a good investment, not only for what he brought to the jazz line but also for helping get a unified design and packaging concept for all the albums. Don Bronstein, a photographer who had gotten his start with Hugh Hefner's *Playboy,* was shooting most of the cover art for the LPs, giving another element of consistency to the products.

They were learning from the jazz sessions that they could give musicians free rein in the studio and good music would result. Ramsey Lewis praised the freedom in the liner notes he wrote for his third album, *An Hour with the Ramsey Lewis Trio,* which was recorded April 22, 1959. Already a fan of Chisholm, Lewis explained that the engineer "got a good balance on the trio then just sat back while we played. Occasionally he'd leave the control booth and let the tape run. There was no one else in the studio or the booth," Lewis continued—most likely the first time since Leonard started making records that something like that had ever occurred and probably the last. "We were free to play as long (and whatever) we wished," Lewis explained. "Because the recording studio atmosphere was so informal, we played everything just once, then went on to something else. A few days later we listened to it all and began selecting the things we were happiest with for this album. We think it comes closer than anything we've yet done to give an idea of how the group sounds in person at a jazz club."

Some of the hands-off attitude with jazz also reflected the fact that Leonard and Phil knew what they didn't know, although they understood what they liked. "Boy you sound good when you play at the high notes," Phil told Lewis. "Why don't you play up there more?" And Holt cracked up when Leonard came into the control room during a session and tried to send instructions with a note scribbled in black ink on a big piece of cardboard: "Blues, blues . . . get more bluesy." He was serious, Holt explained, operating on an instinct to get the instruments to sound like the blues singers, particularly when there was a solo. "He was right in most instances," Holt said. "Get a little more blues in it . . . go into that funk thing."

♦♦

Leonard and Phil wanted to keep a good thing going, so they were disappointed when Usher told them in the summer of 1959 that he needed to return to the family business in Detroit. Leonard didn't help his own case by refusing Usher a raise when he asked for one. "What do you think, you're one of my family?" was his reply.

Phil had a line on Usher's replacement, Jack Tracy, whom he had gotten to know when Tracy was editor of *Down Beat*. Phil had recruited him to write liner notes for the album by sax player Zoot Sims, and the two men kept in touch after that, even after Tracy left the magazine to work for Mercury Records. The brothers were lucky that Tracy wasn't all that happy at the label, so he was willing to meet them when Phil asked him to lunch at a spot far away from Record Row. None of the men wanted anyone else to know about their meeting. The record community was small enough that rumors would have been flying right away. Indeed, the first thing Leonard said when Tracy came in the restaurant was, "I suppose you know why we're here."

Tracy accepted the offer to come to Chess on the spot. Like Wiener and Chisholm, he, too, had an initial laundry list of complaints when he saw the studio. It was much more rudimentary than what he was used to at Mercury, where he recorded in New York and on the West Coast. But before long he realized, as the others did, that good music really could come out of the room.

Though Leonard still sought to pay the minimum salary he could get away with, Tracy negotiated a producer royalty for himself—a penny on each single, a nickel on each album sold that was made by an artist he brought to the label. Leonard wasn't happy about doing this, but he wanted Tracy, and this was his price. Tracy began to understand when Leonard did something that he didn't really want to. He would be sitting behind his desk, listening, thinking, and finally deciding. When he gave his reluctant "yes," it was usually accompanied by "goddammit" and the sound of his heel hitting the floor. After a short time with the company, Tracy noticed that this little routine generally occurred when the request involved spending money.

At the end of Tracy's first year, his producer royalty amounted to $750.

Tracy was tickled. Leonard was not. "We're going to change things," he announced. "You won't be getting a royalty again." Tracy didn't argue. He knew it was fruitless.

The atmosphere around 2120 that Usher found so invigorating was likewise a source of fascination to Tracy. Some days it was like a circus with activity in every room on both floors. Jamal considered the building his "family gathering place." Even if he wasn't recording—and many of his projects were done on location at a club—he still liked to come over when he was in town. "I found it very, very exciting and very wonderful to go there," he said. Musicians came in and out, disc jockeys still stopped by to get the latest and, not infrequently, to ask for something. Maybe one of them needed new carpeting in an apartment. Leonard would take care of it. Maybe another needed help finding an apartment. He would see what he could do. Tending to their needs was part of the business landscape now.

When Leonard put in a swimming pool out at the house in Glencoe, it was less for his own relaxation and enjoyment in the hot Chicago summers and more to give him a place to entertain the deejays and business associates who came to town. Leonard was handy around the house and liked to fix and build things when time permitted. He had constructed a small brick barbecue near the pool, and his specialty was grilling hamburgers for these gatherings, where there were usually eight or ten people. Though neither he nor Phil, or their wives, drank much, Leonard made sure to have plenty of liquor around for the guests. It was rare that anything got out of hand because of too much drink, but there was some commotion one summer evening when Paul Glass, who ran All State Distributing, was emboldened to try a dangerous stunt after several rounds of cocktails. Everyone was aghast when they saw him up on the balcony outside Leonard and Revetta's bedroom launching a dive into the pool.

He made it, but Glass would have died if he missed.

Like Marshall's earlier bar mitzvah party, the swimming pool was also an apt metaphor for how business and family intersected in the Chess brothers' lives. Similar to so many marriages in midcentury America, the Chess husbands kept the details of the business away from the Chess wives. There were no dinner-table discussions about who was signed, who had a session, or how much money the company was making. If a question was asked, it was answered, but very little was volunteered.

Sons could work at the studio after school and on weekends. Daughters were a different matter. Leonard was happy to let Elaine pick the A-side of a record for him, but she could not have a part-time job at 2120 South Michigan. "He wouldn't have wanted her exposed to the 'motherfuckers,'" Marshall said, certain of his father's reaction.

But if Leonard and Phil kept the hard facts of the business separate from family, there was nonetheless an important role for the wives. Revetta and Sheva were expected to keep the nice houses their husbands provided them and handle most of the details of child rearing. Even as a child Marshall understood a clear division of responsibility between his father and mother: "He took care of Chess Records, she took care of the children." If Elaine or Susie was having trouble in school, that was Revetta's problem to solve. She also took care of Leonard in ways that seemed unlikely for a man so self-sufficient. Whenever he went out of town, she packed his bags. No matter how early Leonard got up, Revetta got up with him to make his coffee and breakfast. It was the couple's time together because Leonard so often came home late in the evening, too tired to do anything but sleep for a few hours.

The wives were also expected to be gracious hostesses at their homes when the disc jockeys and distributors and their wives came in from out of town. Sometimes it meant providing a nice dinner; other times the visitors were overnight house guests. That went for musicians as well. Paul Gayten stayed with Leonard and Revetta; Chuck Berry continued to stay at Phil's house, even when the family moved to Highland Park. It was a source of delight to Terry and Pam and their friends when Berry, guitar in hand, would do his famous duck walk across the stair landing in front of Phil and Sheva's bedroom. The children got a kick out of watching Berry's nighttime ritual: putting a tight nylon stocking cap over his hair, knotted just so, before he went to sleep.

There was another dimension to the brothers' work and their families: As the business did well, the wives did too. The day Revetta got her first mink coat was, in its own way, as important as the day Leonard brought home that first Chess record in the spring of 1950. And while it would be overstatement to say that every hit meant a new ring or bracelet, an astute observer could tell how well Chess Records was doing by the new jewelry Revetta and Sheva wore with each passing year.

Around the same time he put in the swimming pool, Leonard bought a gray Thunderbird, "a weekend car." It arrived just after Marshall's sixteenth birthday, and he all but gave it to his son. Within a few weeks, Marshall crashed the car into a tree. He was showing off for a girlfriend and lost control. Nobody was hurt, but the car was badly damaged. Marshall told his father a tire had blown. Though Leonard accepted the story, he didn't let his son off the hook. He convinced the police to suspend Marshall's license for two months, so instead of squiring his friends around in a snappy car, Marshall had to go everywhere on his bicycle.

If it looked as though Leonard was indulgent with his children, he didn't see it that way. Buying them nice things was one of the rewards of success. He had been poor as a child and struggled as young man with a growing family. When Marshall was a toddler, the boy had to make do with a secondhand wagon repainted to look new. But those days were gone. When Marshall was bar mitzvahed, he didn't have just any new suit. His was a custom-made light blue outfit from "Max the Tailor," as the family called him, and he had custom-made shoes to go with it.

More than Leonard, Phil carved out special time for his children, making up for all the time he missed when he was on the road so often. In the early days it always seemed that as soon as he went on one of his ten-day swings, either Terry or Pam got sick—one time it was the chicken pox, another time the flu—and Sheva was left alone to handle things. Now that he was home more, Friday evening became the time for a family dinner in the city. Sheva would bundle up Kevin, the baby, and Terry and Pam would get dressed up—Pam loved to wear her dainty white gloves—to take the train into the city. From the station they would go to the studio and wait for Phil to finish work. Then the five of them would drive the few miles north to Trader Vic's in the basement of the Palmer House hotel for a fancy dinner.

Once Pam started to take ballet lessons on Saturdays, Phil drove her downtown, dropped her off for class, did a few hours' work at the studio, and then picked her up. Most of the time they went for something to eat afterward at Batts. Pam's favorite waitress called her "Twinkle Toes" and always wanted to know what she learned in class. After Pam obliged with a pirouette or plié, the reward was a sundae on the house. On the way home father and daughter stopped to buy fudge on the pretense, Phil always said, that "your mother would like some." Most of the time, the fudge had been eaten before they reached the Highland Park border.

~~

If the roles in the Chess households were clear, Leonard's ideas about managing a business were equally clear. His eye was on the company as a whole, and on how to protect its revenue, even if he blurred the lines between the accounts of the various Chess musicians and employees. Tracy was speechless during one meeting when Leonard was preparing the royalty checks. He looked at the statement with Jamal's royalties, which were considerable, and at Lewis's, which were much smaller. He went over Jamal's earnings again and then told the accountant, "That's too much money for him—give some to Ramsey."

Tracy resisted the impulse to remind Leonard that it wasn't his money he was doling out. It wouldn't have done any good anyway. Leonard played by others' rules on the external matters: union contracts, copyright licensing, taxes on the building and the like. But the internal affairs of Chess were another thing, and he operated the way he wanted to. Tracy never knew if Leonard actually followed through with royalty changes. He might have been joking. Forty years later, Jamal was certain Leonard never gave his royalties to anyone else, regardless of Tracy's memory, and Lewis said he never knew he had benefited from Leonard's unilateral largesse. Whatever transpired, it didn't affect Leonard's relationship with the two musicians.

Working with jazz musicians sometimes required Leonard to make an adjustment, however. Most had more formal education than the blues artists and were more careful in their business dealings. If a contract said a session was for three hours, then that meant three hours. Anything beyond that was overtime. "What the hell is overtime?" Leonard would ask Tracy, his heel hitting the floor. The way he saw it, you recorded until you were finished.

The length of some jazz tracks also required flexibility. They didn't always fit into the two-and-a-half to three minutes that most of the blues tunes or the beat-driven Berry and Bo Diddley numbers did. But if there was money on the line, Leonard would require them to be edited so they could be sold as a 45. Tracy marveled at how quickly Leonard swung into action after getting a call from a Philadelphia disc jockey that "Killer Joe," a track on an album by the Jazztet, one of Tracy's finds, was getting a good response. The original was too long to be issued as a single. Five minutes after Leonard hung up, Tracy was in the studio editing the song to fit the format. Twenty-four hours later it was being pressed, and in a few days it was in the distributors' hands. "Killer Joe" sold close to fifty thousand copies, which was a very large number for a jazz record and more than many of the blues discs had sold.

Leonard could be stubborn, sometimes hurting the final product. Although Tracy had grown to like the studio he felt it had its limits, particularly if one of the musicians wanted to record with a big band. Tracy lost one fight with Leonard over recording bass player Chubby Jackson with a large group. He told Leonard the studio was too small, but Leonard wouldn't yield. He didn't want to spend the money to go back to Universal, and the result was less than satisfactory to the producer and the musicians. "It was like putting a gallon of water in a quart bottle," Tracy said. "You really didn't argue with Leonard," he added. "I don't mean to say his way was the only way, but he was a strong, forceful personality."

By now Leonard had connections to every facet of the business, and he knew how to use them. He was circumspect, though, in what he shared with employees, even those with considerable authority. He gave the minimum amount of information and nothing extra. One day Leonard called Tracy into his office, handed him a demo that had just been made upstairs in the studio and asked him to drop it off at a radio station on his way home. Tracy did so, not asking any questions. On his way home from the station he tuned it in on the car radio. He hadn't been gone ten minutes when the song was on the air. Leonard obviously had talked the deejay into giving the record some play. He didn't explain any of that to Tracy, and he understood why. "It was not necessary for me to know what Leonard did to get that played. He knew it all. He told you what you needed to know."

Leonard and Phil had not paid much attention to the European market for their music, even though they knew there was potential. The trade papers ran occasional pieces about what was going on musically overseas. American pop and jazz stars had been finding audiences across the Atlantic for years, but there was much less interest in blues musicians, though Big Bill Broonzy, one of the originals, had made a fairly successful trip in 1951.

There were essentially two ways the music of Chess and the other R&B independents was getting to Britain and other European countries. The first were the arrangements between American exporters looking for overseas markets and European importers willing to gamble that various kinds of American music would sell in their home countries. The second was through licensing deals American companies like Chess made with their European counterparts. Atlantic apparently made one of the first arrangements in the fall of 1955 with Decca Limited, which had no relation to American Decca, prompting *Billboard*'s Paul Ackerman to note in his weekly column that "England is becoming rhythm and blues conscious. The sale of R&B discs in the Tight Little Isle is not large, but a beginning has been made." Mick Jagger and Keith Richards were just twelve years old when Atlantic made its overseas arrangement, but the stores these young men would later frequent were beginning to get the American R&B that turned them into the Rolling Stones.

Leonard made a similar deal with British Decca. Under the arrangement, the Chess brothers licensed their recordings to Decca Limited, and that company could do what it wanted with the music in Britain. The habit among English record companies, according to Allen Arrow, one of the brothers' attorneys, was to pick songs they liked, have a British artist make a copy, and then release that version instead of the original American record. Sometimes Decca Limited would release the original, particularly in those cases where it was so well known and hard to duplicate. Berry's "Sweet Little Sixteen" was on the best-selling pop records in Britain in May of 1958, but it was on the London label, a subsidiary of Decca Limited, and not Chess.

Muddy Waters took his first trip to England in the fall of 1958, a ten-day tour in a half-dozen cities that was coordinated in Chicago by Usher. The crowds loved him, but one critic in Manchester complained that Waters did not play enough acoustic blues. "SREAMING GUITAR AND HOWLING PIANO" was the headline on one review, which said Waters's music owed "too much to the rhythm and blues style." Underlying the criticism, how-ever, was the fact that a British audience knew his music. And he seemed to have the same effect on Englishwomen that he did on his female American fans. One was so enamored of Waters that she wrote him a passel of romantic letters. The bluesman was tickled to get the attention, but because he could barely read, Waters brought them to the studio and had Usher read them aloud.

The Chess contract with Decca Limited expired in 1959, and Arrow strongly advised that it not be renewed. "The Chess label was literally buried by its licensee," he said. Arrow put together a new deal with an upstart company, Pye, that had the same kind of scrappy, aggressive, and hungry owners as Chess. Kept out of the major distribution organization in England, the Pye men were not to be deterred. They bought several Volks-wagen vans, loaded them up with records and drove around the country delivering their product to the stores—just the kind of thing Leonard and Phil could appreciate. Pye's entry into the R&B business coincided with a growth in the European market as a whole, enough so that *Cash Box* opened four offices overseas in the fall of 1959 in London, Milan, Amster-dam, and Hanover, Germany.

The Pye deal began with arrangements to release records from the Argo subsidiary. Arrow thought the company would be most interested in Ramsey Lewis and Ahmad Jamal, but a single by "Frogman" Henry turned out to be the biggest hit. That prompted Pye to expand the deal and start releasing Berry, Bo Diddley, Waters, and Howlin' Wolf.

There were also European publishing deals handled by Arc for songs put out on the Chess labels that might be recorded by foreign companies. These deals were administered by the Goodman brothers, who were quite experienced with the European market and knew there was a chance to make money on the songs overseas. At the Goodmans' urging, Leonard made a week-long trip to England at the end of April 1958 to meet some of the British music people. The trip was supposed to last a few days longer, but Leonard couldn't wait to get home. "We struggled to leave from there," he told Marshall. "Why would anyone want to go back?" "He didn't like the whole European way of doing things—the old," Marshall said of his father. "He was one of those kinds of immigrants—new car, new buildings. He liked the new."

This didn't mean that Leonard was ignoring Europe. He wanted to get the most out of the overseas market. He just didn't want to do it himself—even if he had known then how important the company presence in England was going to be for the bedrock of Chess Records, blues. Besides, there were plenty of things to attend to at home to keep the labels and the pressing plant operating at a profit. But neither he nor his counterparts at the other independents were prepared for the tumult that would hit the business in the coming months.

twelve

PLAY
FOR PAY

Like the other record men, Leonard and Phil had long ago developed a regular procedure for dealing with disc jockeys. They weren't exactly employees on the payroll, though some got money on a regular basis. They weren't really business associates either. They were occasionally called "consultants," but they were always in a special category, a status conferred by their power: the decision to play or not to play a record. The music business was hardly a meritocracy. No matter how good the song, the independents were never sure they could get their records played. But even a gesture toward the jockeys could not guarantee a hit. The minimum hope was that the record get a chance.

By now most labels considered the deejay factor a cost of doing business. It wasn't a matter of right or wrong. It was a matter of survival. Play the game or fold. Many like Chess and Atlantic and the big companies—Columbia and RCA—paid the jockeys by check and noted the sums on their tax returns as business expenses. Unashamedly they sent nice presents on holidays or special occasions, crystal, fancy silverware, and the like.

Sometimes Leonard was miffed when he didn't get the exposure he thought was warranted by his largesse, and he wasn't shy about saying so. On one trip to New York, he went to see Alan Freed at his radio station, Phil, the Goodmans from Arc Music, and Arrow, the lawyer, in tow. Because Freed was doing his show, they had to chat while the records were playing. Leonard was growing increasingly irritated because Freed was giving repeated plays to a rival label. Finally he exploded. "You motherfucker! What the hell are you playing that guy's record for when I pay you money every week? You know I pay the mortgage up in goddamned Connecticut," a reference to Freed's house and a claim made by more than one label owner wanting help from the disc jockey.

When Freed replied that he hadn't gotten anything that week, Leonard was furious. "I don't have to give you bread every week. I gave you enough bread to last you for the rest of your life." Nonetheless, he walked over to Freed, took a wad of bills out of his pocket, peeled off a few and handed them to the disc jockey along with a stack of new 45s.

"Friends," Freed said when he went back on the air, "I've just been visited by my friends from Chicago, Leonard and Phil Chess, and in honor of their presence, this is Chess Records night."

Leonard once chewed out his friend Stan Lewis in Shreveport because he was unhappy with the number of Chess and Checker plays on a show Lewis sponsored. It was beamed up north in the evening on two stations, the local KWKH and KAAY out of Little Rock. The moment was especially annoying to Leonard because he had bet one of his distributors who was listening with him that night that he would get three Chess tunes on the playlist. One record after another came on and no Chess. Lewis thought he had worked out the lineup with the jockey that night, but there was a mixup. When the program was over, Leonard called Lewis and berated him with his usual invective. A chastened Lewis sent a four-page handwritten letter of apology.

"I have tried in every way to give you all the air plays that I possibly could. But when you called me and bawled me out, I knew you were hurt & I don't blame you," he wrote. "But at the same time I was innocent and you hurt me so bad that I cried like a baby. I wish that incident would never had happened as I never wanted you to loose trust in me. . . . If I should die before you, I want you to be one of my pallbearers. Please watch over my business & see that my family don't get *any bad deals thrown to them*."

If the financial arrangements between labels and disc jockeys constituted "payola," no one considered it illegal, and no one had ever been punished for the activity. What's more, it had been going on for nearly a century. In 1863 the composer of "Tenting Tonight on the Old Camp Ground" gave the leader of a famous singing group a share of the song's earnings to make sure the group would sing the song at well-attended concerts. By 1905 music publishers on New York City's Tin Pan Alley, a boulevard of musical creativity, were paying out five hundred thousand dollars a year to get stage stars to sing certain songs. *Variety* first used "payola" in public in a front-page editorial in 1916 condemning the "direct payment evil." By the 1920s, "song plugging" was a recognized profession made up of individuals, mostly men, whose job was to persuade a vaudeville performer or a band-leader to perform a tune.

The emergence of the phonograph record combined with commercial radio broadcasting reduced the influence of plugging songs for live per-formances. Now there was a new focus of persuasion, the disc jockey on the radio. In the beginning it wasn't so much getting a record played—it was not yet clear whether air play would boost sales—but rather broad-casting the live performances of bands at hotels and ballrooms around the country.

By the late 1940s and early 1950s, however, it was clear that radio play was important in creating a hit. Sometimes gifts would arrive at a radio sta-tion wrapped in lists of songs the bearer hoped to have played. It was also clear that money was changing hands between label and jockey. *Billboard* had chronicled the disc jockey payments in a front-page piece in January 1951. By the end of the decade, payoffs were more flagrant. WKMH in Detroit offered an "Album of the Week" deal: for $350 the station would play a record 114 times a week with a commercial before and after each play for a minimum of six weeks. Another record company executive told *Time* magazine that under a formula he figured out, it took $22,000 to make a song popular in Chicago. "There are so many people to *shmeer*," he said, creating a synonym for bribe from a Yiddish word that meant "to spread." "The singer, his manager, the station, the disc jockey."

By 1960 the competition for radio play was intense. There were some six hundred labels in existence, from the multifaceted majors to seat-of-the-pants operations; one hundred single records and one hundred LPs were released every week. Everyone was looking for an edge, and not surpris-ingly the biggest help could come in major cities where well-known jockeys had a following: New York, Philadelphia, Detroit, Cincinnati. But second-tier locales were also important. If a jockey in Buffalo or Shreveport or Atlanta promoted a record and sold a few copies, a distributor could trum-pet that success in another city. "You had a story to tell," explained distrib-utor Irv Derfler, who was still selling records fifteen years after he first met Leonard in Pittsburgh with his trunkful of Tom Archia discs on Aristocrat.

Over the years there were efforts to put a stop to payola—in 1916, when payments to artists to use a particular song outstripped publishing profits; in 1934, when ASCAP, the performance rights group, was implicated in payoffs; and then as part of the congressional drive in the early 1950s to root out alleged Communists in the entertainment industry, the investigation that led to the blacklist of film writers, directors, and producers, and in the music world, most prominently, the blacklisting of the Weavers, a popular folk act. The underlying evil of payola, critics said, was cheating the public. Songs weren't being played because they were good but because of the size of a label's billfold. That sentiment dovetailed perfectly with the investigatory atmosphere that permeated Congress in 1959 over the fraud that had been exposed on television quiz shows. In October a House subcommittee held hearings on the television scandals, but no one in the record business understood then how quickly the representatives' attention would turn to radio. What once had remained largely out of public view between the labels and the deejays was going to become very public, and this time there would be penalties to pay.

Payola was of interest to many more individuals than members of Congress. The Internal Revenue Service announced in the fall of 1959 that it was going to look more closely at business expense deductions for gifts and promotion, and in December two other federal agencies said they also wanted to take a look at the subject: the Federal Communications Commission, which licensed and regulated radio stations, and the Federal Trade Commission, which policed unfair and deceptive trade practices that might harm consumers. Payola, in the agency's view, amounted to a deceptive practice because the public didn't know that money had changed hands to play a record. It could also be considered a form of commercial bribery.

Disc jockeys were the most vulnerable, and on November 21, Freed, who was one of the most visible, was fired from his job at WABC in New York, where he had been for a year. He was let go after he refused to sign a statement essentially saying that he had never taken money or gifts to promote records and that he had no financial interest in music copyrights, music publishing, recording, or merchandising concerns. Freed told station executives he could not sign such a document without being untruthful: he was involved in music publishing, he had received gifts—cases of scotch, portable radios and such—as Christmas presents. "You do know that I have and shall continue to program records for my show solely and completely on the basis of my evaluation of the records and their appeal to my listening audience," Freed wrote in a lengthy reply to ABC. His "careful programming," he went on, was the reason he was hired, the reason he was popular and the reason he had risen "from complete obscurity to my present position." His success had been "a slow building, step by step and completely dependent upon the correct and proper choice of material (records) for my shows." To ask him to sign the station's affidavit "would violate my self respect."

Two days after losing his WABC job, Freed was fired from WNEW-TV, where he produced the rock-and-roll show *Big Beat*. His firings set off a frenzy of similar actions around the country. Over the next few days several high-profile deejays were let go, among them Joe Finan in Cleveland and Mickey Shorr and Tom Clay in Detroit. Unrepentant, Clay said payola was nothing more than "a little boy who takes an apple to his teacher."

On December 4 the FTC made its first dramatic move. Three record companies, RCA, London, and Bernard Lowe Enterprises (Cameo Records), and six independent distributors were accused of deceiving the public and restricting competition by giving money to radio and television disc jockeys. Among the distributors was the Chess representative in Philadelphia, David Rosen Incorporated, where Chess sales coordinator Max Cooperstein had worked. In Chicago, Leonard and Phil breathed a sigh of relief. They were not cited, not yet anyway. But the city was taking note of the growing investigation. When popular disc jockey Phil Lind talked about the payola issue on his WAIT show, he received threatening phone calls even though he was not espousing any position. He simply aired an interview with an unnamed label owner who detailed his trouble in getting a record played without making payoffs. "If you keep blowing the whistle, you're going to end up in an alley," one caller told him. Daddy-O Daylie, who billed himself as "Chicago's number one jazz jockey," now claimed he was only "Chicago's number 29 jazz jockey," anxious to deflect attention from himself as one of the city's more prominent deejays.

The first week in January, Chess Records came in the sights of the FTC. Leonard and Phil were served with an agency complaint ordering Chess, Checker, and Argo to "cease and desist" making payments to disc jockeys. Outwardly they were unfazed and refused to comment about the allegations—Leonard was actually in Florida on his annual vacation with Revetta and the children. As soon as he returned he huddled with Nate Notkin, his longtime lawyer, and found another attorney, A. Bradley Eben, who had good political connections in the city and a feel for dealing with federal matters. Though he was normally circumspect about company business, Leonard told a *Chicago Daily News* reporter that payola was overrated in importance. "Personal contact is much more important than payola," he said. "Payola doesn't mean anything a thousand miles away. If you don't meet the guy, he isn't going to do it for you. It's better to meet the guy personally and ask him to play a tune."

At the same time the Chess brothers were served with FTC papers, Al Benson, the veteran R&B disc jockey, opened his books to the *Chicago American*, one of the afternoon dailies. Documents showed that he took in $855 every month from nine distributors and labels, among them $100 a month from Chess. That total translated into $4,795 a month in 1999 dollars or nearly $58,000 a year.

Benson denied that his monthly stipends were pay-for-play. He said they helped defray the costs of a weekly hit survey he published and advertising in a small magazine, and he refused to be on the defensive. "I won't hide behind the Fifth Amendment," he told the newspaper. "What I'm doing is perfectly legal." But the cash reimbursements for publishing costs did not explain the red Lincoln Leonard had delivered to him a few years earlier, handing over the keys as Marshall looked on.

Atlantic's Jerry Wexler knew the Chess brothers and Benson were friends. He marveled at the way Leonard could show up at the jockey's office with a stack of records and hand them to Benson one by one to be played.

By the time the House hearings started in Washington in late January 1960, the FTC had filed complaints against thirty-seven record companies and distributors. One of them, RCA, had already signed a consent decree with the FTC in mid-December promising not to give money or gifts to anyone to promote its products without telling the listening and watching public that this was being done.

Congressional testimony before the Legislative Oversight Subcommittee showed just how prevalent the payoff practice was, and in the process it provided a glimpse of the Chess brothers' activities. This was not the kind of publicity Leonard wanted, and it could not have been a happy day to know that portions of the company's tax return and its canceled checks were spread out in the official hearing record. The disclosures came during the January 27 testimony of Anthony Mammarella. He was a producer for Dick Clark's highly successful *American Bandstand* television show. He resigned from his position rather than divest himself of interests in several music-related companies.

In response to detailed questions from the subcommittee's chief investigator, Robert Lishman, Mammarella recited the various companies that had paid him money. Among them was Chess Records, whose 1957 tax return showed that Mammarella had been paid $750 for that year. The 1958 return showed that he received $900 over a period of several months, mostly through $100 checks. Leonard's and Phil's signatures were clearly legible on the checks made part of the official record. Mammarella said he also received a punch bowl, a pen and accompanying holder, and silverware as holiday presents from the brothers. He insisted that the money and other items were gifts, expressions of thanks for consulting services. In the Chesses' case, he said, they wanted his advice on changing distributors in the Philadelphia area to improve the visibility of the labels. Never, not with Chess or the other companies or distributors, did he say, "I want money to play your records."

When Cleveland disc jockey Joe Finan appeared before the committee on February 9, he testified that he supplemented his $40,000 a year salary with $15,000 in "consultant" fees in 1958 and 1959—$84,120 in 1999 dollars. Much of it came in monthly $100 or $200 checks from various companies. From Leonard and Phil he received an interest-free loan of $2,500 in 1958. He still owed $1,700.

Finan told Lishman that he had been "very close friends" of the brothers for four years, and while he couldn't remember which one he talked to, "I picked up the phone, and I asked him for the money and he gave it to me."

"Did they ask you to air any of their labels over KYW?" Lishman asked, referring to Finan's station.

"No sir."

"Have you, as a matter of fact, aired such a record label over KYW?" Lishman continued.

"Since the first day I have been on the air with WJAL [his previous station]—they are very close friends of mine."

When Lishman asked how much interest Finan was paying, he responded that it was an interest-free loan.

"Did you give a note for this loan?" Lishman wanted to know.

"No, sir, my personal word." He added that there was no timetable for paying it back, though he had tried, unsuccessfully, to do so within six months.

While the disc jockeys claimed they didn't play records for pay, the label owners thought that's what their money was buying. When he testified, George Goldner, owner of Gone Recording Corporation and Gold Disc Records, flatly admitted buying exposure on the air.

Referring to a Philadelphia jockey, Lishman asked: "Did you pay him money for playing some of your records?"

"Yes sir," Goldner replied, adding that he paid the man $500 a month for about three months.

"Now you didn't pay him that for getting his advice, did you?"

"No sir."

After inquiring about a few other disc jockeys, Lishman asked about Al Benson. Goldner admitted paying him money, but he said he understood from Benson that the payments were not for airplay but to cover the costs of putting out Benson's regular record survey. It was a tribute to Benson's ingenuity that he had enough other enterprises to disburse record company payments into activities that were related to the music business, helped him and the labels, but couldn't strictly be called payola.

For Leonard and Phil and their counterparts at other labels there was a safety-in-numbers defense to the federal inquiry. Most of the companies were paying money to radio stations in the hope of boosting their records. There was no perceived need and certainly no impetus to step back and question whether the relationships with the jockeys were proper. The Chess brothers seemed to be somewhere in the middle of the pack. Perhaps that was why neither Leonard nor Phil was called to Washington to testify. Their loan to Finan, for example, was $2,500; Morris Levy of Roulette had loaned Freed $21,000 in addition to giving him another $10,000. Nonetheless this was an anxious and distracting time. Jack Tracy heard more "motherfuckers" out of Leonard than usual, and he knew both brothers felt bad to see Freed in such a squeeze. They considered him a friend, albeit one who needed to be paid.

Without internal company documents, it is impossible to know for certain how much money Leonard and Phil paid each month to various deejays. Some were paid every month for more than a year; others might get money in spurts. But the amount was surely considerable. The brothers knew jockeys in every major city and in most of the smaller markets as well. The information on cash payments and expensive gifts to Benson, Mammarella, Finan, and Freed represented only a part of what they were spending to make sure that Chess, Checker, and Argo records could compete.

Even if a label owner wasn't called to Washington to testify, there was the continuing concern that federal investigators might demand to go through the company books, and state authorities might try to bring their own charges, as was happening in New York. Jerry Wexler spent many hours at the office of the New York City district attorney's office answering questions about Atlantic's operations, wondering whether he was going home at the end of the day or to jail. He didn't go to prison, and neither did

Alan Freed, even though Freed was one of five disc jockeys charged by the district attorney of New York with violating the state's commercial bribery laws. More than two years after his arrest on May 19, 1960, Freed pleaded guilty to a minor charge and was sentenced to a $500 fine and a six-month suspended jail term. Though he found a few other radio jobs, he never again regained his high profile. He died five years later, a broken man physically and financially.

None of the Bihari brothers at Modern out in California was called to testify, but their books were audited. The FTC didn't find anything untoward. There were no canceled checks, no tax deductions. "We were paying cash," Joe Bihari explained.

Though RCA, Atlantic, and a handful of other record companies signed consent decrees with the FTC, Leonard refused to do so. He insisted that he and Phil had done nothing wrong. Nineteen months after the FTC filed its complaint against the Chess labels, the agency formally dropped the charges. The lengthy investigation was not without result at the federal level, however. Congress did make major changes in the laws that covered the broadcast industries to give the FCC greater regulatory authority. Among them was the requirement that radio and television stations announce at the time of broadcast whether any money, service, or other valuable consideration had been received relating to the matter broadcast. Station employees who accepted a payment or any person making one was to report the payment to the station prior to the broadcast. One record executive found the entire six-month episode bizarre and unfair—"that one American business is singled out for industrial gift giving. At the same time record people were being thrown in jail, professionals in Washington were doing the very same thing. They're called lobbyists."

thirteen

TRUST
IN ME

Distracting as it was, the payola investigation could not be allowed to interrupt business operations. Even as Congress, the FTC, and the FCC were making headlines with their findings, Leonard and Phil continued the search for new talent and new projects for those already on the Chess, Checker, and Argo rosters. They trusted their hunches now, and Leonard presided confidently over a growing enterprise. Though he was occasionally self-conscious about his lack of formal education, he had consistently met the competition and prevailed. "I never took an accounting course, but I can read a balance sheet," Leonard told Arrow at one of their first meetings. "And I never went to college, I never read books, but I can tell you what the laws are, and I can tell you what's a good play and what's a bad play."

In late November 1959 the brothers had to fill one vacancy they hadn't expected. Malcolm Chisholm decided to accept an offer from Bill Putnam to work at his new studio setup in California. Within a few weeks, Leonard found his replacement, bringing in Ron Malo, a sound engineer, from Detroit. Though Malo wasn't quite as experienced as Chisholm, "he caught on pretty quick," Tracy said, though there was a period of adjustment for producers who had gotten used to Chisholm's confident hands in the control room. Around the same time Leonard signed another new talent, the first female singer with bona fide star potential, Etta James, a rough and raw young woman of twenty-two with a big voice and plenty of bravado.

Though still young, James already had six years of experience on the road behind her and two records made at the Biharis' Modern label that registered on the R&B charts. The first was "The Wallflower," which was recorded with two friends, "the Peaches," and was originally titled "Roll with Me Henry." It was an answer to Hank Ballard's "Work with Me Annie." The other was "Good Rockin' Daddy."

James was born Jamesetta Hawkins in Los Angeles to a young woman who was only fourteen at the time; the child never knew her father, who was white. She was raised for the most part by relatives whose lives centered around the St. Paul Baptist Church. By the time Jamesetta was five, everyone knew she could sing; she was a natural for the popular church choir, Echoes of Eden, and there she found her first mentor, not one of the women but choir director Professor James Earl Hines. "I didn't know any better but to imitate a man," James recalled. "Women in the choir were cool, but it was a man who brought down the sky and shook the earth. . . . He had one of those great classical gospel voices, a go-tell-it-on-the-mountain voice of glass-shattering force and hell-to-heaven range. Man, that's how I wanted to sing."

Hines encouraged the child to use her natural ability and power; he helped her with technique. Sing from the stomach, not the throat, he told her. "Don't back off those notes, Jamesetta. Attack 'em, grab 'em, claim those suckers, sing 'em like you own 'em." In her mind she got more than a singing lesson. "Talk about confidence. Professor Hines gave me enough confidence to last a lifetime."

It showed when James and two friends, who called themselves the Creolettes, got a chance to sing for bandleader Johnny Otis after one of his performances in San Francisco, where James, now fourteen, had moved. She and the other Creolettes, Abye and Jean Mitchell, were instructed to come to Otis's hotel room in the middle of the night after his show was finished. Even though this was an extraordinary opportunity, James balked. She didn't like to sing on demand. Finally she relented but only if she could sing from the bathroom. She had a reason. "Everyone sounds good singing in the bathroom," James explained. "Tile makes for great acoustics." So she sat on the edge of the tub while Abye and Jean were in the bedroom standing near the bathroom door.

Otis liked what he heard and immediately offered the group a job touring with him. He also made a few changes. The Creolettes became the Peaches. Jamesetta Hawkins became Etta James. As important, Otis parlayed his connections into a recording deal with Modern.

Joe Bihari was less impressed with the Peaches as a whole than he was with James when they met in the studio. His brother had called him back to Los Angeles from Atlanta just before Thanksgiving in 1953 to record the group's "Roll with Me Henry." James insisted that her friends be on the record, so Bihari put them as far back from the microphone as possible. Even if they had been right there with her, this was James's song. "My personality got all over that record," she said, and it caused some jealousy between her and the Mitchell sisters. James didn't mind. She was in her element. The studio was like home, the confidence Professor Hines had instilled in her evident. "I felt strong, wasn't intimidated, and felt free to be myself."

Because the melody of the song was Ballard's and the song belonged to King Records, the Biharis had to work out an arrangement to release the disc. That accomplished, the companies found they were having trouble getting airplay because of the suggestive nature of the title. So they renamed it "The Wallflower." Once the record was played, it took off, staying on the R&B charts for nearly five months.

James's second hit, "Good Rockin' Daddy," emerged just as "The Wallflower" had run its course. At the same time James and the Peaches continued traveling with Otis, literally growing up on the road. By her own admission, James got into one scrape after another, had difficulty handling her money, and developed a serious taste for drugs. She also changed her look, bleaching her hair platinum white, painting her face with layers of makeup, and dressing in provocative "cup dresses ... those supertight things," she explained, "that came halfway up the thighs with a split up the back until you could practically see my ass."

Though she continued to record for Modern for another five years, James never had another hit even though the Biharis tried a number of things, including a stint in New Orleans to record with some of Fats Domino's people. James liked the result, but the records she made there didn't do very well. She stayed somewhat busy with performances, but it was when she changed booking agents and started to work some of the larger black theaters—the Apollo in Harlem, the Royal in Baltimore, and the Howard in Washington, D.C.—that her career was propelled toward Chess. On one of her dates she met Harvey Fuqua of the Moonglows, "my first full-fledged boyfriend." It was Harvey's fellow Moonglow Bobby Lester, however, who told her about Leonard and Phil. He knew she wanted more out of her career, so Lester gave her some advice. "If you wanna be a big star, get on Chess," he told her. "The Chess brothers are some smart Jews who know how to sell records."

Late in 1959 James finally made her way to Chicago, taking the bus on a cold winter night from St. Louis after a singing date with Jackie Wilson. James and her traveling companion, Abye Mitchell, settled into an inexpensive South Side hotel intending to stay just a few days to see if they could make anything happen. It was so cold that James and Mitchell used the windowsill like an ice box, propping the window open and setting the uneaten food there to keep until the next day. They heated it up on the radiator.

The first couple of times James went over to 2120 South Michigan she couldn't get past Carri Saunders, the receptionist, she related years later. She needed Fuqua's help, but he was on the road. She finally got to meet Leonard through another intermediary and worked out the details of leaving Modern. It wasn't difficult. The Biharis were willing to let her go. "She wasn't selling for us," Joe explained. "We weren't coming up evidently with the proper material, and she wasn't either." James said that Modern wanted $8,000 to let her out of her contract and cover what she owed against her royalties but settled for $3,000. Bihari remembered it differently. Whatever James owed, he said, "we just wrote that off."

When she finally met him, Leonard was ready to get started. He gave her $5,000 to sign, enough to pay off past debts and still have $500, and put her on the Argo label. She moved into a better hotel, this one with a kitchenette. Leonard took care of the rent and made sure she had food. By the middle of January she was in the second-floor studio for her first recording session. Somehow all the creative elements came together—material, musicians, sound, and the end result was successful. Leonard liked "triangle songs," the singer, her boyfriend, and another woman, and James would be the loser. So "All I Could Do Was Cry" was perfect. The story line was about a woman watching her onetime boyfriend marry another woman: "I was losing the man that I love, and all I could do was cry." It was written by Billy Davis, who had also written a hit for the Moonglows and one for the Flamingos, and his partner Berry Gordy.

Davis and Gordy had wanted Aretha Franklin, the immensely talented daughter of Reverend C. L. Franklin, to record "All I Could Do Was Cry." Though the she wanted to break out of gospel music—and some of her early singing recorded at church had been put on Chess—her father wouldn't let her do this one. Davis and Gordy tried to interest her sister, Erma, another fine singer. She agreed to make the demo tape, but she wouldn't record it for the Anna label. She was more interested in jazz. So

Davis sent the demo over to Chicago, and it wound up earmarked for James.

Leonard brought in Riley Hampton to write the string and horn parts for a new arrangement. He first met Hampton when the young man did some work for drummer Red Saunders and his band at the small studio at 4750 South Cottage Grove. By that time Hampton, just in his early thirties, was already a seasoned arranger in his adopted city. He was originally from Arkansas and had started arranging music when he was in high school in North Little Rock, hearing all the parts in his head and telling friends what to play. He found steady work after graduation, coming to Chicago with Fletcher Henderson's band. He was drafted into the Army during World War II, into an all-black military police battalion. But he didn't leave his music behind. He joined an informal group of musicians who had turned themselves into a band and became their arranger. The group was so good that a white colonel at one Army base scrapped his own all-white band from a concert schedule when he heard the black soldiers. Hampton returned to Chicago after he was discharged, and using the GI bill, he studied at one of the city's music schools to refine his natural talent.

Hampton didn't know who Etta James was until he went over to Michigan Avenue to work on the first session early in January 1960. He sat down with her at the piano, asked her to sing a few notes, found her key, and then went home to write the arrangements. He was moved from the first note. It made the task that much easier, deciding how the instruments—horns, violins, violas, a cello—should be framed around her sound. Hampton tried to find a mental picture to illustrate the story of the songs they were going to record, hearing James's voice in his head as the narrator. Though Tracy was in charge of Argo production overall, he was just a spectator for these sessions. But like Hampton, he, too, was impressed with the new singer. "I don't think anybody with any kind of ears could have mistaken her talent," he said. "You hear it once—oh yeah, OK . . . you had to listen."

"All I Could Do Was Cry" was released the second week of March in 1960 backed with "Boy of My Dreams," a reworking of a rhythm-and-blues hit, "Girl of My Dreams." *Billboard* took note of both in the March 14 issue, praising James's singing and the arrangements. By May, "All I Could Do Was Cry" was on the R&B and pop charts, no doubt helped by James's appearance in the middle of the month on Dick Clark's *American Bandstand*. Leonard was happy and wanted more. He brought James back in the studio right before the *Bandstand* appearance to cut several new tunes, including one with Fuqua, "If I Can't Have You." Once again Hampton did the arrangements, once again the song went on the charts, and this time James appeared on *Bandstand* with Fuqua, giving the record another boost.

By the end of the year Leonard was ready to put out an entire album for James—*At Last*. The title came from a standard—written by Harry Warren and Mack Gordon—that was recorded in an October session and became a substantial hit when it was released as a single three months later. "At Last" was one of Hampton's most lush arrangements, a cascade of four violins, two violas, and a cello surrounding James's vocals. By this time Leonard gave him free musical rein. He not only created the arrangements, he hired the musicians and directed the sessions, which were among the most integrated. The string players almost always were white; black musicians made up the rhythm and horn sections. "Whatever I asked him, Leonard would give it to me," Hampton said, one of the few who did not feel constant budgetary constraints. Sometimes Leonard even listened when Hampton suggested that instead of trying to do a set number of tunes in a given three-hour session, it would be better to concentrate on one that had strong hit potential. Make sure that one comes out well and then use the rest of the session for the others.

Hampton was shackled most by time. His good ideas had to fit into two-and-a-half to three minutes for that all-important airplay. But he learned quickly. He successfully reworked another standard, "Trust in Me," which had been a big seller in 1937 for Mildred Bailey, and which was nearly as successful for James when it was released shortly after "At Last." "Trust in me in all you do," James sings. The song is a ballad about romance, but the line and the title doubled as a resonant description of how Leonard operated. A political scientist might call it benevolent paternalism, a combination of control leavened with genuine if unexpressed concern and affection for those who worked for him. "Trust in me" was Leonard's attitude. He would take care of things, although he would take of them as *he* saw fit.

The trade papers took immediate notice of the album. *Cash Box* called it "tops in vocal entertainment" and later put the singer on the cover. Alluding to her waning days at Modern, *Billboard* said it was "a real triumph for Miss James, who has recently had a great return to the pop parade after a dry spell of several years." Along with "At Last" and "Trust in Me," two other singles from the album, "My Dearest Darling" and "Spoonful" with Fuqua, would also make the charts.

On the professional side, Leonard and Phil were delighted—James had five hits in her first year at the company. Only Chuck Berry had accomplished that for Chess, and he didn't cross over to the pop charts as often as James did in his initial recordings. For all her talent, though, James would also prove to be one of the most high-maintenance musicians on the roster. Her turbulent personal life was occasionally touched by violence. In the coming years Leonard would get her into drug treatment, which he paid for, and out of jail.

Stan Lewis was Leonard's house guest during one of the singer's clashes with the police. The phone rang at 2:00 A.M. It was James, from the Cook County jail. Could Leonard come and get her? Of course. He got up, got dressed, and went to bail her out.

"You know," he would tell her in calmer moments, "you got to get your shit together."

There were some close calls with the law right in the studio. One session resembled a Keystone Kops routine, when the music came to an abrupt halt after a telephone call from downstairs. One of the musicians went over to James, whispered something to her and then escorted her down the back stairs and out of the studio as the police, coming to enforce a bad-check warrant, came up the front stairs. The session was over for the day, and everyone had to be paid even though the afternoon was wasted. Leonard was not very happy about that, but on the other hand keeping his most successful female artist out of trouble was important. "Leonard would send a lawyer wherever I was," James said.

◀◀

Though other aspects of the Chess roster occasionally got more attention than the blues and R&B, Leonard and Phil always returned to the music that put them in business. Leonard, in particular, made sure he was around when Muddy Waters, Chuck Berry, or Bo Diddley were recording. The last few months of 1959 were busy ones on Michigan Avenue for the musicians. Each was in the studio working on new songs. Bo Diddley was out with a new album the first week of 1960, *Have Guitar Will Travel*. *Billboard* gave it an enthusiastic sendoff on January 4, putting it in the "spotlight" section and noting "Bo's irrepressible humor." The magazine called the disc "Top wax." Some of the tracks, particularly "I'm Alright," showcased his appreciation of vocal harmony, mixing his driving beat with the call and response, provided here by a spirited chorus that evoked a gospel number. Several "doowop stylings," in the words of music writer Robert Pruter, also appeared on Bo Diddley's next album, released in mid-year, *In the Spotlight*. Many of the tracks were recorded at his own studio, which was in the basement of his home in Washington, D.C., where he moved in 1958. Some additional technical work to punch up the vocals and add piano tracks by the estimable Lafayette Leake was done in Chicago before the album was released. The recording process had evolved a long way from those initial sessions in 1955, when Leonard needled Bo Diddley to "sing like a man." Now he could indulge his creative spirit and draw on the resources available at Chess.

A single with two of the tunes from *In the Spotlight* had been released late in January, "My Story" backed with "Road Runner." The latter was just the kind of musical amalgam Leonard appreciated because it drew on a current fad and might reach a new audience. Bo Diddley's distinctive beat, highlighted by the ubiquitous maracas, was still there, but now his guitar had the deep country twang of Duane Eddy, a white musician who had made a spash at Harry Finfer's Jamie Records. "Road Runner" could tap into the same audience that liked Eddy's sound, even though the song might have been one of Bo Diddley's sly jokes.

Berry's newest single, "Let It Rock" backed with "Too Pooped to Pop," was released the second week in January. "Too Pooped," one of the few Berry tracks to feature horns, was typically witty. The story was about dance fads, the hook was "too pooped to pop, too old to stroll." By now Berry was a recognized master of the genre and even considered one of its senior citizens. A January *Billboard* story noted that "old" R&B hits— from 1952 to 1957—were now selling well to a pop audience. Berry was listed along with Fats Domino, Little Richard, and the Moonglows as examples of musicians finding new audiences with old material. *Cash Box* noted "Let It Rock" briefly on its "top 50 across the nation" at the end of January. "Too Pooped to Pop" registered on the *Billboard* R&B charts for three weeks in April, Berry's first hit in nine months. It was the longest he had gone between hits in four years.

Muddy Waters also released a single at the same time, "I Feel So Good" backed with "When I Get to Thinking," both from a new LP, *Muddy Waters Sings Big Bill Broonzy*. It was a tribute to the blues singer-songwriter who had hit his stride in the late 1930s and 1940s. The album was released late in January, the result of sessions the previous July and August. There was plenty of harmonica on the records, but now James

Cotton, a gifted young player, had taken over for Little Walter. Otis Spann was still playing the piano, complementing Waters's vocals with well-placed chords and trills that added texture but never overwhelmed. Willie Smith played the drums on the August 1959 session. It was his first time working for Leonard, and he didn't like his approach. "Leonard was a stickler to please," he said. "If he told you he didn't like that, there was no argument. It was his way." Years later Smith told a Waters biographer that he now appreciated that provocative style "because it brought out the best in me."

It was a mark of Waters's significance as a blues musician and a recognition of the blues roots of so much jazz that *Down Beat* paid respectful attention to the album, devoting an entire column of one page to a rather dry, intellectual assessment of the singer and the songs. The review, while laudatory, seemed at odds with the musician's visceral style and sound.

Leonard and Phil had made an obvious commitment to the Argo line, and Lewis, Jamal, and a half dozen or so other artists were making new albums through the first half of 1960. But a February ad in *Cash Box* was a reminder of what was still the heart of Chess. Running the entire length of a column, the ad highlighted some of the latest Chess releases. Featured were the most recent singles by Bo Diddley, Berry, Waters, and Sonny Boy Williamson. In April, Leonard signed two more bluesmen, Elmore James, who had recorded for Lillian McMurry's Trumpet label a decade earlier; and Buddy Guy, a young guitar player who had earned the respect of Waters. He had met Leonard playing cards at Cobra Records, the label run by Eli Toscano where Willie Dixon sometimes worked.

Now that Max Cooperstein was the national sales representative, Leonard and Phil were on the road far less than in the early years. Even so, they made sure that at least one of them attended industry conventions, particularly the annual gatherings of the American Record Manufacturers and Distributors Association, or ARMADA, as it was known. Neither brother took a public leadership role in the organization, though Leonard was now on the group's board. The meetings were useful for talking about issues the industry faced and doing a little business at the same time. The 1960 meeting was in Atlantic City at the end of June, a propitious moment for the brothers given the success they were having with a range of artists and releases: Jamal, James, Lewis, a new sextet led by Art Farmer and Benny Golson on Argo, Waters, Berry, and Bo Diddley on Chess and Checker.

While Leonard and Phil were winding up their stay in Atlantic City, Waters was getting ready to head east for one of his more unusual engagements. He was invited to be part of a blues afternoon at the Newport Jazz Festival on July 3, a program devoted to the roots of jazz and emceed by the distinguished writer Langston Hughes. It was Jack Tracy's connections that made it happen. He knew everyone in the jazz world, and among his closest friends was Nesuhi Ertegun, who ran the jazz side of Atlantic. Whenever Nesuhi came to Chicago, he and Tracy had dinner. On one of Nesuhi's visits early in 1960, Tracy mentioned that Waters was playing at Smitty's, a well-known blues club.

"My favorite singer. Let's go," Nesuhi said.

Waters was in great form that night; Nesuhi was enthralled. Tracy understood just how much when he got a call several weeks later from George Wein, another jazz friend who was also the director of the Newport festival. Was Waters available to play? Nesuhi had been raving about how great he was.

The offer was extended, but Waters had to be convinced to accept it. He had never heard of the festival, and the money wasn't that good. Francis Clay, who was his drummer now, told him he could get exposure to an entirely new and fairly prosperous audience who might then buy his records, but that was not an immediate selling point. Waters finally relented. When he and the band got there, however, their performance almost got shelved. On Saturday night, July 2, an unruly crowd of several thousand gate crashers caused a riot that forced cancellation of the rest of the festival—except for the afternoon blues show on the third. On the bill with Waters were John Lee Hooker, pianist Sammy Price, and a duo of James "Butch" Cage on the fiddle and Willie B. Thomas on the guitar.

When Waters and his band took the stage, they saw a sea of white faces, most of them young college students dressed in shorts, T-shirts, hats, and sundresses. Some probably didn't know who Waters was, and it took them a little while to warm up to the music. But before long, Waters and his band, playing with verve and abandon, brought the crowd around. By the time he sang "Hoochie Coochie Man" and "I Got My Mojo Working," many in the crowd were on their feet, waving and clapping, a few with cameras in their hands pausing to take pictures. Waters delighted the crowd when he grabbed Cotton and swung the harmonica player around in an impromptu two-step. Then he let go and did a fast-moving solo shuffle back to the microphone.

The second week in September a single featuring one of the songs Waters performed at Newport was released, "Tiger in Your Tank," which had been recorded a few weeks before the festival. The obvious sexual allusion in the title and lyrics made Nate Notkin chuckle when he thought of the paternity suits he was handling for the singer.

The word had come back to Chicago that Muddy "broke it up at Newport." Why not lease the tape from the performance and put out an album? Tracy suggested. "Sure, why not?" Leonard replied, realizing that the investment for production would most likely be covered by the sales.

Muddy Waters at Newport was released in December and was respectfully, even enthusiastically received by the trade papers. Describing Waters as a "soulful blues chanter," *Billboard* called the compilation "a fine set of the mother blues delivered in great R&B fashion." However unintentionally, *Cash Box* gave a boost to the theory behind the blues afternoon at the festival—the roots of jazz—by spotlighting the new album as a "jazz pick of the week."

Leonard and Phil had been cautious about making long-playing records, but once they took the plunge, they did so with gusto. Bo Diddley's third album of 1960 was released in mid-December, *Bo Diddley Is a Gunslinger*. The cover fit the theme of the record. Bo Diddley was dressed in a black shirt, black pants, black hat, and a white neckerchief, brandishing a brace of toy pistols. He bought all the gear in Tulsa and hired a photographer for fifty dollars to shoot a roll of film. He gave it to Leonard for the cover and complained later that he was never reimbursed.

The Argo line was especially productive. In the last quarter of the year a half-dozen new LPs, including Etta James's *At Last* and one by the jazz sextet featuring Farmer and Golson, had been released. This was on the heels of a new LP from Ahmad Jamal, a sequel to his popular *But Not for Me*, called, appropriately, *Jamal at the Pershing Vol. 2*. It was made up of previously unreleased songs from the 1958 hotel date. Coinciding with the release, Leonard authorized a new sales gambit—buy two Argos, get one free.

Prompted by Tracy, Leonard and Phil also were on the jazz social scene, hosting parties at local clubs for Ramsey Lewis, who did a recording session at the Blue Note, and for Farmer and Golson. The routine was always the same. Tracy would suggest a press party. "What's it gonna cost?" was Leonard's first response.

"It's not going to be that much."

"Well, all right," Leonard said. "But it better work."

More often than not things did work, giving the brothers the confidence to keep expanding.

fourteen

BRANCHING OUT

Etta James had shown Leonard that he could find success with a strong female singer. He found another one when he heard a song on the small California label Veltone called "I Want to Know," by the spitfire contralto Sugar Pie DeSanto. Leonard went out West right away to sign DeSanto to Chess. Johnny Otis had discovered her in San Francisco in 1951, when she was just sixteen, and promptly nicknamed her Little Miss Sugar Pie. "DeSanto" came from a friend in the business. Her new name was much catchier and easier to say than her given name, Umpeylia Marsina Balinton. Her father was Filipino, her mother black.

DeSanto was only too happy to make the move to Chess. Compared to Veltone, Chess was like one of the majors. In Chicago, Leonard set DeSanto up at the Sutherland Hotel, a few miles south of the studio, and before long she was upstairs at 2120 South Michigan working on her first album on Checker with Riley Hampton and Billy Davis, whom Leonard called in from Detroit every six weeks or so to help produce. Some of the tracks were from DeSanto's Veltone days, and while the new ones had the same edgy vocals of "I Want to Know," the arrangements and overall sound reflected the influence of Hampton and Davis.

Though half a continent from home, DeSanto felt comfortable right away. She liked the musicians—she immediately trusted Davis's taste and instincts—and thrived on the energy in the building. There always seemed to be time and space for an impromptu get-together with whoever was around, musicians either getting ready to record or just coming in off the road. "There was no room we couldn't hang in," she said. "We would just be all over the place."

While DeSanto was just getting started with Chess, James had been turning out one good seller after another. By the end of January 1961 she had three songs that registered on *Billboard*'s hot R&B chart and pop charts, one of them another duet with Fuqua. She was the most successful artist since Berry and his string of hits in 1955 and early 1956. Clarence "Frogman" Henry also returned to the charts with "But I Do," a song that originally started out as "I Don't Know Why," but changed names to avoid confusion with another song of the same title. Leonard agreed to pay for ads in the trade papers to announce the name change, an expense he was no doubt willing to absorb because of the song's success. It eventually reached number four on the pop charts. Bobby Charles, who was still part of the Chess operation though now as a promotion man in the South, wrote the tune.

Leonard considered Henry important enough that in March he went to New Orleans for a recording session with the musician. They squeezed it in just a few days before Henry went on *American Bandstand*, the third Chess artist to get on the show in a week's time. James and Fuqua had made their second appearance together a few days earlier, right before the Vibrations, a vocal group Leonard had recently signed. They performed their newest record, "The Watusi," which was climbing the charts.

The Argo subsidiary was particularly active. In mid-May, Tracy announced that seven albums would be released, including LPs by Henry, a jazz sampler featuring Jamal, Lewis, James Moody, the Jazztet, and drummer Buddy Rich, and an album by King Fleming, a popular Chicago piano player who had his own trio.

⌁

Since their time in the junk business with their father on South State Street through their years in the liquor stores and the Macomba Lounge, Leonard and Phil had made money in and from the black community. The Macomba had led to Aristocrat and Aristocrat had turned into Chess. But music was only one facet of black entertainment, and just as he had done with Reverend Franklin's sermons, Leonard was willing to try a new venture aimed at the same market but with the potential, like some of the music, to reach a white audience: albums that featured black comedians who had been popular staples of the black theater circuit. The first deal he made was with Jackie "Moms" Mabley, a sixty-three-year-old stand-up comic whose trademark on stage was a small floppy hat, a house dress, and worn-down bedroom slippers, all graced by her toothless grin.

Behind Mabley's jovial demeanor was a sly wit honed on stage after stage in forty years of performing. Blues musicians used their songs to capture life's tribulations from the particular perspective of being black in a white-controlled world. Mabley did the same thing through comedy. Her persona was an amalgam of minstrelsy and vaudeville, fused into final form by the strictures of segregation. She wasn't the plantation "mammy" but the all-knowing granny, able to serve up advice to her "children" in the audience. She offered pointed vignettes to knowing and appreciative black patrons but was never so sharp-tongued that her white fans were uncomfortable, even when she skewered white authorities about racial injustice.

Though Mabley's routines were peppered with stories on the contemporary issues of war and peace and race, there was always a generous helping of the ribald. But it was more suggestive than graphic. Given her age, a good deal of patter focused on her interest in young men. "An old man couldn't do nothin' but bring me a message from a young man" was a staple of her stage act.

Mabley's first Chess album, *Moms Mabley on Stage*, recorded live at the Tivoli theater in Chicago, had been released at the end of 1960. Her second, *Moms Mabley at the UN*, another live performance, this time in Philadelphia, was released early in 1961 and had more topical humor. She did a comic fugue on Nikita Khrushchev, whom she called "Khrush," as really being "Mr. Clean," the bald-headed master of detergent, and her advice to Castro was never to sit in a box seat in the theater. "That's the way Lincoln got it."

Mabley came to Chess through another of Leonard's important hires. In the the fall of 1959 he had brought in Ralph Bass as a kind of floating A&R man. Bass had just ended a seven-year tenure with Syd Nathan at Federal Records, a subsidiary of King that Nathan created for him. With fifteen years in the business, Bass had a wealth of experience, a number of hit records, and deep connections to the world of black entertainment. He was credited with producing a variety of music from T-Bone Walker—his landmark "Call It Stormy Monday"—to Lena Horne to James Brown.

Bass was a distinctive figure physically because of his tousled red hair, droopy red mustache, "bulbous red nose," as one observer noted, and unconventional wardrobe. He called himself "an Italian Jew." His father was of Italian descent, his mother Jewish. They wanted him to be a doctor; he loved music. He played the violin as a child in the Bronx, classical at first, then pop tunes. But an evening at the Savoy Ballroom in Harlem changed his life. "It was the most sensuous music I'd ever heard, a sexual thing," he said. Though it took him a few years and a move from the Bronx to Los Angeles to start making records, Bass was by now an unabashed fan of black music and aspects of the lifestyle that went with it. One writer who watched him for a few days in the studio described him as a "flamboyant jive-talking hep cat" with a "penchant for colorful, slightly dated hip talk." Never modest about his accomplishments, Bass's philosophy about the music he produced mirrored his self-confidence: "I didn't give a damn if whites bought it."

Bass started his producing career at Black and White Records, a small independent company in Los Angeles, in 1945. He first garnered attention working with jazzman Jack McVea on the novelty recording "Open the Door, Richard," a sly comedy routine that was based on an old vaudeville skit. Some fifteen different versions of the song were recorded. After a falling out with the company, Bass moved to Herman Lubinsky's Savoy for three years, where he worked with Johnny Otis and Little Esther Phillips, who was only thirteen at the time. He was responsible for several very successful records that enhanced his reputation in R&B circles. His reputation was growing, and in 1951 he moved back east to work for Nathan and Federal, which was headquartered in Cincinnati. It was a productive time. In his seven years at the label, he helped put together such hits as the Dominoes' "Sixty Minute Man," and Hank Ballard and Midnighters doing "Work with Me, Annie," the song that launched James when she answered it. He crossed paths figuratively with Leonard in 1956, when both were trying to sign James Brown. Bass delighted in telling the story of how he beat Leonard to the punch, courtesy of bad weather. Leonard had already sent the young singer a contract by mail and was on his way by plane to close the deal. Fog at the airport held him up, so Bass got there first and signed Brown without even seeing him perform.

Bass and Nathan eventually had a falling out. He left King at the end of July 1959. Within a month Leonard brought him to Chess.

Though Riley Hampton had put the first Etta James session together, Bass, who knew her through his Otis connection, was assisting along with Billy Davis because she was doing one of his songs, "All I Could Do Was

Cry." Sessions were often the musical equivalent of theater—musician/ actors out in the studio, directors in the control room, each occasionally functioning as critic and author. Bass brought the same energy to his after-the-fact stories that he did to the music, and if every vignette wasn't accurate down to the last detail, he believed he was at least capturing the emotional truth in the retelling. Though Davis and James had somewhat different memories, Bass was sure that after the first take of "All I Could Do Was Cry," the band wanted to do it over. Bass said no. "Etta was crying her eyes out for real," he recalled. "I told them forget it. I mean, how much more soul could I get from a singer?"

"He was the inspiration man," James said. "He would get tears in his eyes."

The best work between Bass and James was yet to come, but from the start they spoke the same language about creating music. "I didn't give a shit about technique," he said, reflecting on his style. "To hell with bad notes. They had to feel it. *I* had to feel it." The words could have come from James. "The shit I sing is feeling," she told one producer less appreciative of her talents than Bass. "I don't need sheet music."

In addition to bringing Moms Mabley to the label, Bass had also been responsible for recruiting the Vibrations and putting "The Watusi" together. The veteran group was from Los Angeles; in 1956, as the Jay-hawks, they had had a novelty rock-and-roll hit with "Stranded in the Jungle," but they had not done much of anything since. Leonard assigned them to the Checker subsidiary where Bass and the group worked up the dance number. The song used the melody of "Let's Go, Let's Go, Let's Go," which was another tune by Ballard and the Midnighters and also produced by Bass. But with the Vibrations, Bass got rid of the cowbell he had used in the opening bars and replaced it with a walking bass line. The underlying melody, however, was unmistakable. It turned into a nice hit, staying on the *Billboard* chart for five weeks, the *Cash Box* chart for more than a month, no doubt helped by that *Bandstand* appearance in March.

Leonard didn't want anything to interfere with the success of "Watusi," and he played hardball to make sure of it. Tony Gideon, a singer with a competing tune called "Wa-Too-Si" on a small local label, witnessed Leonard's tough side firsthand.

Gideon's version was on the Miss label, which happened to use the Chess pressing plant on South Cottage Grove. Anxious to get the record out, Gideon and his boss, "Cadillac Baby," the nickname for label owner

Narval Eatman, called James Gann, who was still managing the plant, and asked to get some records. Gann told them they would get eleven and no more because that was all they could pay for. Eatman and Gideon went over to the plant just as Leonard was coming in with Hoss Allen, who had temporarily left WLAC and was now doing some promotion for the label. Leonard was not pleased about another record with the name "Watusi," even though it was spelled differently and was a different melody. He told Cadillac Baby that any distributor who received the Miss records would box them up and send them right back. Besides, Leonard said, according to Gideon's recollection of the moment, he owned all the publishing rights to the song—a bluff because the melodies were different and titles could not be copyrighted.

Leonard offered Cadillac $500 for his record—the flip side was "The Way You Move Me Baby." He also wanted to sign Gideon. Cadillac initially refused, but fearful of never making any money from the record, he finally agreed to lease the master. Gideon agreed to come to Chess for a year. "Wa-Too-Si" was renamed "Whatcha Gonna Do" so it wouldn't compete with the Vibrations. As he promised to do, Leonard released the record a few weeks later. It made the local charts in Dallas, Los Angeles, Detroit, and Birmingham.

As musicians were wont to do, the Vibrations moonlighted in California as "The Marathons," and made a record called "Peanut Butter" on the Arvee label. It turned out to be a hit, rising to number twenty on the *Billboard* pop label. When Leonard learned about it, he promptly bought the master and reissued it on Argo. To connect it with the Vibrations, he ran big ads in the trade papers for " 'Peanut Butter' by the Vibrations—Recorded as The Marathons." He was determined to get the most profit possible from his investment in the group.

The success and growth of the Argo label convinced Leonard and Phil that the concept of an A&R man was a good one, someone to concentrate on the creative aspects of the music to give it consistency and energy. Despite a previous disagreement and temporary departure for another label, Willie Dixon was still a comforting hand on the blues side. Berry and Diddley had a definite sense of what they wanted to do and who should do it with them. But the music world was changing and changing rapidly. While these men and the other blues musicians continued to record and keep busy with personal appearances, they were no longer guaranteed hits or even huge sellers. If Chess Records was going to grow, the music had to grow and change, too.

It was important to get the right individuals in place, even if it took a few months or a year to make everything click. There might be a false start or two, perhaps a bad guess on a talent, but that was to be expected. Not every song could be a hit, and if a singer missed on one release, perhaps the next one would work.

By the middle of 1961 Leonard and Phil decided that Davis, the songwriter from Detroit who had sold Chess three hits, "See Saw," "A Kiss from Your Lips," and "All I Could Do Was Cry," was the man to help them keep growing. Davis had come a long way from the ambitious teenager who sang in the harmony groups that seemed to spring up on every corner in Detroit's black neighborhoods. He could see that his real flair was for songwriting and management when he started handling the business affairs of a group his cousin joined. The young men started as the Four Ames but changed to the Four Tops because Davis liked the notion of being "tops" at what they did, and a spinning top had been one of his favorite toys as a child. The name change was his call, he told them, because he was supplying most of the songs.

Although the Tops were building a name for themselves around Detroit, Davis was anxious to get his music in wider circulation so he sent some demo tapes to different record companies, among them Chess. He was familiar with the label because the group had worked on a date with Willie Mabon, and by now anyone interested in pop music knew about Berry and Bo Diddley. A week or so later Davis got an envelope from Chicago. Inside was his original letter. At the bottom was a note scrawled from Phil: "Liked your tape, like your songs, give me a call." The phone number followed. Davis thought it was a joke. His grandmother convinced him the letter was legitimate, so he called Chicago and talked to Phil, who repeated his praise for the songs.

"What about the group?" Davis wanted to know.

"Yeah," Phil said, "the group was good, too, the group was great. We liked the group, but we got a lot of groups," and he mentioned the Moonglows and Flamingos.

"Yeah, but what about my group?" Davis replied, politely but firmly.

"Come to Chicago," Phil said. "We'll talk. We'll pay for you to come."

As soon as he received the money order for the bus fare from Detroit to Chicago, Davis bought a ticket and was on his way. When he arrived at

4750 South Cottage Grove, he wasn't sure he was at the right place. He didn't know what to expect, but he was sure that a studio couldn't be in this little storefront. When Davis introduced himself to Carri Saunders, she promptly took him back to see Leonard and Phil. They got down to business right away, offering to buy two songs for one hundred dollars—more money than Davis had ever dreamed of earning from his writing.

He said no. He wrote the songs for the Four Tops. It was a package deal, the music and the group.

How about a hundred dollars for each song and the promise to buy more? Phil asked. "You you know we have a lot of artists that we need material for, and we think you've got a great career as a writer."

Davis wouldn't budge.

After an hour of dickering, Leonard finally spoke up. "I'll tell you what we're going to do. I'm going to give you what you want, and you'll give us what I want. I'll record your group if you give me these two songs."

Davis wasn't sure what it was in Leonard's presentation—perhaps it was the dead-on look from his steely blue eyes—but Davis believed he was sincere. He accepted the deal, banking on the fact that Leonard would keep his word.

Both brothers appreciated Davis's musical ability, and they had to admire the confidence of a young man who knew what he wanted and was willing to walk away if he didn't get it. This was the kind of individual Leonard wanted in the company: talented, smart, and tough-minded.

Once the agreement was reached, Phil didn't waste a minute tying down the details. Before Davis could catch his breath, he left and returned with songwriting agreements to put the tunes in Arc Music. It was the usual arrangement: Arc would be the copyright holder; Arc and Davis would split the royalties fifty-fifty. There was one other wrinkle: they wanted to give Russ Fratto, their friend and landlord, a piece of "A Kiss from Your Lips." Davis didn't know exactly why. Fratto wasn't putting in any money as far as he could see.

"Billy," said Leonard, in his most reassuring manner. "Don't worry. You'll still get whatever you've got coming to you. Just go along with it." Once again Davis took Leonard's word. He gave away a piece of his song.

The transaction proved to be mutually beneficial. Chess got good material, Davis got his music out to a wider audience than he could have on his own, and the Four Tops made a record, "Kiss Me Baby," on a bona fide label. While Leonard won his confidence, the reverse was also true. Even though Davis went back to his writing and business ventures in Detroit,

Leonard periodically invited him to Chicago. "What are you doing?" he would ask him in a typical phone call. "Why don't you come on in, spend a few days here. We're going to be recording."

Davis almost always said yes, sensing that there was some purpose to Leonard's request. He wasn't exactly becoming a protégé, but Leonard seemed be grooming him for something. For his part it was a chance to learn the business; by the same token Leonard could draw on his musical ideas. Every now and then he chose Davis for a particularly sensitive matter. In one instance Leonard promised a disc jockey—a white man at a local television station—that he would record the man's wife, a singer whose talent was well short of her aspirations. Davis dutifully set up the session and recorded a song with the ironic title "Gimme What You Got." "We didn't get much out of it," he noted later, with just a hint of a smile.

More than once on these periodic trips Davis was called in for a Diddley or Berry session. He felt he got the best results working with Berry, who was willing to listen to suggestions. Diddley, on the other hand, was resolute about what he wanted to do. Davis mostly worked in the control room, watching for the right sound balance but coming out in the studio when he thought Berry and his sidemen were not communicating so well. "Sometimes he would have phrases that were thirteen bars as opposed to twelve or seven and a half as opposed to eight, and the musicians weren't accustomed to this. . . . You'd get discord," he said, "because they'd be looking to change to the next bars." Davis took care to be discreet, never wanting to embarrass Berry in front of the other musicians and vice versa.

Leonard seemed more appreciative of Davis's contributions than Berry. Finally he told Berry he ought to do something for Davis, perhaps record one of his songs. Reluctantly, as Davis remembered it, Berry agreed to do "Too Pooped to Pop," though later he claimed it was his song. Reissues in the late eighties credit only Berry as the writer, but the original copyright in 1959 and the renewal in 1987 list Davis as the composer of the words and music.

Leonard's confidence in Davis made him a natural when he was ready to hire a new A&R man for all nonjazz operations. Though he had made a name for himself in Detroit writing hit songs with Berry Gordy for Jackie Wilson and running Anna Records with Gwen Gordy, Davis was ready to make a change when Leonard called. He worked out agreements with Gwen to end their partnership in Anna and with Berry to end their writing-producing work, and he headed to Chicago to negotiate his new deal with Leonard and Phil.

Like their first meeting five years earlier, this one had its own back and forth. Leonard's initial offer was too low. Davis had a counterproposal: "Let me have my own publishing company."

"We'll start one together," Leonard replied, hardly missing a beat, "and everything you do from this point on we'll put into the new company."

Davis said yes, and Chevis Music, a combination of Chess and Davis, was born. The move was instructive, an illustration of Leonard's ability to make a deal that furthered his own interests. To get Davis to Chicago full-time he was willing to divert resources away from Arc Music and his partners, the Goodmans. The new agreement wouldn't affect him and Phil, but the Goodmans would lose the income generated from any new songs Davis wrote or produced that normally would have gone to the New York publishing firm. Now that revenue would go to Chevis.

Leonard and Phil sweetened the deal by starting a new subsidiary in Detroit for Davis to run, Check-mate. The plan was to have Davis produce music by Detroit artists, and while a few releases were put out, none had the success they wished for. The label closed down after a few months. Though he didn't think the auxiliary people in Chicago worked as hard as they could have to sell the Check-mate releases, Davis wasn't angry. He was confident he was on the verge of greater success in the Michigan Avenue studio. Besides, he had shown his eye for talent at Check-mate. The first release was with singer David Ruffin doing "Actions Speak Louder than Words." Though the record had only modest sales, Ruffin went on to great acclaim as one of the Temptations.

Given that he already knew the Michigan Avenue studio, it wouldn't take Davis long to hit his stride.

⋙

In the midst of all of the music activity, Leonard agreed to make some changes in the studio to improve the sound. Ron Malo, Malcolm Chisholm's successor, supervised the improvements, which included putting sound-proofing material over the north wall. Later a small vocal booth was put in the back of the room. Malo also revamped some of the equipment in the control room so that multitrack recording was possible. There was a benefit beyond making the Chess, Checker, and Argo records sound better: getting other labels that didn't have their own studios to buy time there.

Along with studio improvements came new moves on the business side. Hoss Allen and Bobby Charles were working the South, occasionally joined by Leonard or Phil. Paul Gayten, headquartered in California, was doing the same on the West Coast, and Herb Gordon, who had worked for Universal Distributing in Philadelphia and for Harry Finfer at the Jamie label, was hired early in 1961 to work the East Coast. Though the record business was growing, it was in many ways still a small world. Connections made in one capacity led to a job in another. Gordon was the latest in a chain of Leonard's recruits who included Allen and national sales coordinator Max Cooperstein. His instructions were always the same to the men in the field: Go to every radio station and record shop you see. Don't miss one.

In the middle of June 1961, just as Davis was settling in, Leonard and Phil got some disappointing news. Jack Tracy told them he was going back to Mercury to be their A&R man for jazz. Helping to build the Argo label had been a wonderful experience, he said, but he couldn't pass up the chance to work at Mercury. It was the big leagues. Leonard and Phil had everything the majors had, but just on a smaller scale. Mercury was "first class," Chess was a few notches below.

Tracy's two-year adventure at the 2120 South Michigan Avenue studio had given him a clear-eyed view of how the company operated. "You knew that the final decision had to come from Leonard," he said. But more than most he appreciated the nuanced relationship between the brothers and how that defined Chess Records. "Phil was a loyal supporter of his brother," an easygoing counterpart to Leonard's sharp edges, Tracy said. "Phil was a slap on the back laugh, and Leonard didn't have time for jollity." It was one of the reasons Phil was so valuable in dealing with the all-important disc jockeys. If there were tensions or problems in one of these relationships, Tracy added, "Phil was the smoother."

That same personality was used to good effect with the musicians, so much so that Davis considered Phil the informal head of "artists relations." He knew who needed to be taken to lunch, who needed a new car, who needed a pat on the back and a word of encouragement.

Phil was also the catalyst for promotion, keeping tabs on what records were selling and where they were selling. It would not be uncommon for him to buttonhole Dick LaPalm, when he took over album promotion, or others on the sales force, and ask, "How come Detroit ordered only five thousand? You bettter get on that." Phil's ideas weren't based on any market analysis. Those thousands of miles on the road had cemented friendships with distributors and disc jockeys and given him a feel for who could help the company and how to approach them.

Though Tracy knew the dynamic on Michigan Avenue was more complicated, he conceded that "any place you were in the record business and they talked about Chess records, they talked about Leonard." If Phil was the shaded side of the family photograph, one of the reasons lay in his distaste for the limelight. Neither brother was a publicity hound, but Phil was more than content to be in the background. When he got attention, his son Terry recalled, "he wanted to get out of the way."

The brothers knew they needed to replace Tracy, but Leonard was going to take his time. It was important to find the right person. In the meantime, he and Phil had plenty to manage in the last quarter of 1961. Moms Mabley was working on another album, this one recorded at a live performance at the Playboy club that Leonard supervised. The venue reflected Mabley's growing popularity with white audiences, which meant broader appeal and more record sales. She didn't shy away from her usual routines, even when they were about race. In one pointed vignette she talked about driving her "big white Caddy" down to Miami—"I mean THEY-ami"—and getting stopped for running a red light in South Carolina. "This big white cop" pulled her over and told her she went through a red light. She knew it, she replied.

"What did you do that for?" he asked.

"I see you folks goin' on a green light. I thought the red light was for us."

Mabley's success prompted the Chess brothers to sign up two other well-known black comics, Slappy White and Pigmeat Markham.

James released another single, "Seven Day Fool." This one uncharacteristically was not a big seller, though two she did a few months beforehand reached the charts, "Fool That I Am" and "Don't Cry Baby." Each of them scored on the pop charts as well as the R&B tallies. Bo Diddley was out with a new album, so was Ahmad Jamal, and Leonard signed a new white singer, Steve Alaimo, who was a local celebrity in the University of Miami community with his group, the Redcoats. Alaimo's first single on Checker was intended to capitalize on songs that fit contemporary dance fads, a version of "Mashed Potatoes" that didn't do very well. Neither did his first album, *Twist with Steve Alaimo*. Leonard kept him on, though, hoping for better luck in the future.

In November, Leonard picked up the distribution for another small label, Tuff, and as an indication of his growing appreciation for the European market, he signed distribution deals for France and Italy with Ricordi, a European label. He was no doubt encouraged by how well the deal with Pye was working in England. "Frogman" Henry was so successful that Louis Benjamin, the head of Pye, gave him a gold record to commemorate all of his sales. *Cash Box* put the two of them on the cover of its December 2, 1961, issue.

This good news offset very bad news about Chuck Berry. On October 28, 1961, a federal appeals court upheld his conviction earlier in the year on charges of bringing a fourteen-year-old girl from El Paso, Texas, to St. Louis for "immoral purposes." It was considered a violation of the Mann Act, a broad law aimed primarily at stopping interstate trafficking in prostitution.

Berry's troubles had started three years earlier, on the night of June 2, 1958, when he was coming back to St. Louis after performing in Topeka, Kansas. As usual he was paid in cash, and he routinely carried his earnings with him as he drove from club to club in his pink Cadillac. Concerned that he might be robbed on the road, Berry kept a loaded .25 caliber pistol hidden under the front seat. On this night he had the misfortune to get a flat tire just south of the city. He pulled off the road to change it, leaving his traveling companion, an eighteen-year-old woman who sometimes accompanied him to out-of-town dates, in the car. A policeman approached Berry, and when he made a routine check, the officer discovered the concealed weapon and arrested him.

At the magistrate's court Berry pleaded guilty to two other traffic charges—driving without a proper license and improper registration of the Cadillac. He was fined $30 in court costs. Pulling out his bankroll, he peeled off another $1,250 to make bond for himself and the eighteen-year-old.

Proceedings on the gun charge were put off, but Berry was not out of jeopardy. In December 1959 he was indicted under the Mann Act for bringing the fourteen-year-old, who was an Apache Indian, from El Paso to Missouri for immoral purposes. A month later he was indicted under the Mann Act again, this time for bringing another teenager, an eighteen-year-old girl, from St. Louis to Toledo and from St. Louis to Omaha. The gun charge from his 1958 arrest was also resurrected in the indictment.

On March 5, 1960, Berry was convicted of violating the Mann Act for bringing the fourteen-year-old from El Paso to St. Louis; he was sentenced to five years in prison and fined $5,000. Three months later he was acquitted of the second Mann Act violation involving the eighteen-year-old. Berry testified that he and this young woman were in love and that he did not intend to violate the law. Two months later a federal judge ordered an acquittal on the gun charge, ruling that the weapon was illegally seized under Missouri law.

Berry's conviction in the case of the fourteen-year-old was overturned October 28, 1960, by the federal appeals court, which castigated the presiding judge for racially prejudicial remarks during the proceeding. The judges, however, made clear their distaste for Berry's behavior, calling his treatment of the girl, who was a prostitute when Berry met her, "inexcusable." They said his testimony that he intended "to make an honest woman of her had its irritating aspects." He had promised to hire her as a hat-check girl in a club he operated.

The appeals panel ordered a new trial, and Berry was convicted again, this time with a different judge presiding. The fine was the same but the prison term was three years. After the appeals court ruling, Berry was given several weeks to get his affairs in order. He reported to a federal prison on February 19, 1962.

Leonard and Phil had been very concerned about Berry's troubles for some time. They didn't like to see one of their most bankable musicians in trouble with the law, not only because incarceration would keep him from recording, but because the publicity wouldn't be very helpful either. The public was fickle, and there was no telling what audiences might think when they found out what Berry was doing offstage. They likely were relieved that only the St. Louis papers paid attention to Berry's problems. There wasn't a word about any of it in *Billboard* or *Cash Box,* and nothing in national magazines either. Perhaps it was a manifestation of covert racism in the white-controlled press, an underlying message that such things were common among black men so it could not be news. Had Berry been white and charged in the same circumstances, there might have been more publicity. When Jerry Lee Lewis, who was white, married his thirteen-year-old cousin in 1958, the outcry derailed his career. Maybe, too, the lack of coverage about Berry reflected distaste, fueled by lack of interest in the general media for this part of American music culture. The tawdry comings and goings of rock-and-roll musicians, while titillating, were beneath mainstream reporters' notice.

After Berry's second conviction in March 1961, the Chess brothers knew the outlook was bleak for a second victory from the appeals court. Anxious to keep Berry's name in circulation even if the singer was not, Leonard got him back to Chicago in the summer to record new material. One of the songs from the session had the resonant title "Everything I Do Is Wrong." The alternate name was "Adulteen." It was never issued, though two others from the session were: "Come On" and "Trick or Treat."

Phil and Marshall remembered that the company took care of Berry's legal fees; Berry had no such memory in his rendition of events in his autobiography. He said he paid his lawyer the $20,000 it cost him for the unsuccessful defense. The Berry problem aside, the year-end trade paper tallies reflected the company's successes in 1961, particularly the emergence of Etta James. *Cash Box* rated her the "best female R&B vocalist," and three of her songs were on the top fifty R&B chart for the year, "At Last," "Don't Cry Baby," and "Trust in Me." A fourth Argo release on the list was "Frogman" Henry's "But I Do." James was also represented on the best new R&B vocal group for her duets with Fuqua. They were fourteenth out of twenty-nine. Henry was rated number seven on the list of the twenty-five "best male R&B vocalists." When *Billboard* ran its year-end tally of the top fifty R&B records, the same three James tunes were on its list.

Chess may have started as a blues label, but for several years now the company had been much more than that.

~~

Confident of his ability to spot a good record, Leonard bought a few more masters from other labels, and they bore fruit in the first month of 1962. One came out of St. Louis, where Leonard picked up a tune from the local Bobbin label featuring blues singer Little Milton Campbell with "So Mean to Me." It stayed on the charts for a month, a harbinger of the successful relationships that would grow between the Chess organization and St. Louis musicians. All the ingredients were in place on that record: Milton, his friend Oliver Sain, saxophonist and director of the band, and on the piano, a young woman named Fontella Bass, whose gifts as a singer would become apparent when she came to 2120 South Michigan to record.

Leonard guessed right with another leased master, "Let Me In," by the Philadelphia vocal group the Sensations, which he put out on the Argo label and which went to number four on the pop charts. The recently signed blues singer-guitarist Buddy Guy made the charts in late February with "Stone Crazy," and two weeks later Etta James was on the charts again with her newest single, "Something's Got a Hold on Me," an uptempo number that James and a friend adapted from an old gospel song. This was no ballad, and there were no full-bodied Riley Hampton arrangements to surround her vocals. Instead James sang it with a churchy fervor, reaching back to her roots in the St. Paul Baptist choir and the inspiration of Professor Hines.

By now she and Leonard had developed a unique working relationship, at once volatile and affectionate. Gender was no boundary to his provocation. He needled and prodded her just as he egged on Sonny Boy

Williamson and Bo Diddley. Though not a musician, Leonard sometimes came out in the studio with the band during blues sessions or watched attentively from the control room; if it was a James session, he would provoke her—once or twice he even playfully whacked her with a drumstick—to get more emotion. "Sing it mother," he would tell her. He could make her cry, make her angry, make her swear.

James wasn't always convinced she got the best result. "He didn't know anything about singing. But I think it's because he cared," she said. "We was all right—so close, like a family."

In March James's third LP, titled simply *Etta James,* was released along with Moms Mabley's fourth album, *Moms Mabley at Geneva Conference.* *Cash Box* featured the James and Mabley albums in their popular picks the week of March 17, and Leonard accorded Mabley the rare honor of buying a full-page ad in *Billboard* devoted to her. It featured her three previous albums and noted that the Playboy club and the UN album were still on *Billboard*'s chart for the best-selling monaural LPs. Each had registered for two months. She was proving not only to be a good investment but also a primer on the relationship between business and culture. Mabley's base was in the black community, the main market of Chess Records and the prime reason Leonard was willing to put out her records. He could count on a certain amount of revenue just from her loyal followers. Yet by making her comedy more available, he was creating the potential for a broader audience that was looking for new entertainment.

More success for the label came in the summer of 1962. Early in August, "Reap What You Sow" by Billy Stewart was on the charts. He had been discovered in the mid-fifties by Bo Diddley, who heard the young man fiddling around on the keyboard backstage at a Washington, D.C., theater where his band was performing. Diddley made an instrumental with Stewart in 1956, "Billy's Blues," and while it was spirited, musically the result was mediocre. Stewart was a singer at heart; his family had a gospel group, and in 1957 he recorded two songs for the Okeh label. He didn't make another record until Leonard signed him in 1962. "Reap What You Sow," recorded with Stewart's road band, was the first of several hits to come.

Just as Stewart's record was climbing the chart, James's second hit of the year was released, another of her teary-eyed triangle songs, "Stop the Wedding." The introduction set the theme, the opening notes of "Here Comes the Bride" but played with a melancholy feel. In October James would have her third hit of the year, "Next Door to the Blues." Her occasional problems—personal and legal—aside, she was worth it to Leonard and Phil. She always managed to make her studio sessions, even though Leonard often had to cajole her back to Chicago. Davis got irritated now and then when she would disappear for an hour or so in the middle of a session or would argue about needing to learn a song. But James never doubted she could pull it off, in retrospect acknowledging that she was blessed with a strong constitution to go along with her talent. "Some people can't work high. I can," she later wrote. "I don't want to boast, but I may be one of those singers who has enough power to overcome the fog and filters of drugs."

It had taken more than a year, but Leonard filled the jazz A&R position in September of 1962, bringing in Esmond Edwards from the East Coast. Edwards had run the jazz side of Prestige Records for six-and-a-half years, recording among others Gene Ammons and John Coltrane. Ralph Bass had made the first overture, catching Edwards when he was in a mood to consider making a change. When he and Leonard worked out their terms, Leonard promised him a free hand to keep up the profile of the Argo line.

The biggest adjustment for Edwards was not the studio—he thought it was plenty adequate—but the free-for-all atmosphere. He was used to the more sedate surroundings of Prestige. "It was like a little family," he said. "No one was antagonistic toward each other, whether in fun or seriously." Chess may have been like a family, too, but it was a big, noisy, brawling one. "It was a traumatic change to go from Jersey [where the Prestige offices were] to Chicago," Edwards added. He marveled at "the profound lack of respect, in a humorous manner" between Leonard and Phil and the musicians, particularly the blues players. Expletives often went flying back and forth when they were in a room together. "Most conversations," Edwards said, "were conducted at a volume and intensity that I initially assumed had led to bloodshed."

It would take Edwards a little time to find his niche in the raucousness of 2120 South Michigan, but when he did he discovered that Leonard meant what he said about not interfering with Edwards's productions.

While he gave producers and musicians a relatively free hand, Leonard continued to keep tight control over the company's public profile. If other labels wanted to issue press releases about their grosses and nets, that was fine. He didn't operate that way. There had been only two breaches of his policy, one voluntary, opening the books on Ahmad Jamal's *But Not for Me* album, and one involuntary, documents accompanying Tony Mammarella's testimony before the United States House of Representatives sub-committee. So it was still guesswork to determine the volume of the company's business.

Information released by two other companies, each of them bigger than Chess, provided some means for comparison. Dot Records, which had grown every year since Randy Wood started it in the early fifties, let *Billboard* publish its sales figures in the November 13, 1961, isssue for the five years between 1957 and 1961. They showed that sales nearly tripled, going from $6.1 million in 1957 to $8.76 million in 1959 to a projected $15 million at the end of 1961. The company listed approximately six hundred albums in its catalogue, roughly eight times as many as Chess.

Atlantic reported to *Cash Box* that its gross sales at the end of 1962 were $7 million, its best year yet. Atlantic was about half as big as Dot and perhaps twice as large as Chess, where gross sales by now were probably between two and three million dollars.

Leonard and Phil were making money and had been for some time. The big unknown was how much. The profit margins depended in large part on accounting methods. Anyone's books could be arranged to show a profit, a break-even year, or a loss. But perhaps the amount of money the Chess brothers made was less important than their ability to borrow more when they needed to, a situation that arose by the end of the year.

fifteen

VOICE OF
THE NEGRO

L eonard always appreciated the importance of radio, which he considered another facet of the record business. As far back as 1953 he had flirted with the idea of buying a station and explored the possibility in New Orleans. Nothing came of it, and Leonard put the the idea on hold for a few years. But he always kept his eye out for opportunities. When he thought he had a deal to buy a southern station, he took Nate Notkin and his father along on a trip to Atlanta to meet a prospective partner, a businesswoman. The deal didn't come to fruition, but the meeting provided a moment of insight into the difference between father and son. "I don't like to be no pahtner vit no vomens," Joe Chess said in his heavy Yiddish accent right in front of this potential associate.

"Pa," Leonard replied, chuckling to cover his momentary embarrassment, "she knows what she's doing." That was all that mattered to him. Gender was unimportant, as his partnership with Evelyn Aron at Aristocrat had shown.

Leonard finally made a radio deal in 1959, buying a small daytime AM station in Flint, Michigan, WTAC, for $260,000. WTAC had been owned since August of 1954 by the First Broadcast Corporation. The president was John Shaheen, publisher of the *New York Post*. His brother, Richard, was a media broker and most likely the one who brought the willing buyer and seller together.

Leonard and Phil formed L&P Broadcasting as a separate company to run the station. It had no assets, but Leonard took care of that in two steps. First he opened an account in the First National Bank of Chicago at the end of 1957 and deposited $100,000 in it. He didn't draw on the account for a year. Then, in essence, he leveraged the record companies against the radio station. Before buying WTAC he took out $150,000 in loans from the American National Bank and Trust Company, $60,000 each loaned to Chess and Argo, $30,000 loaned to Checker. He told American National he was going to advance that money to L&P for the WTAC purchase. Notkin handled the transaction, flying with Leonard to Detroit and then driving to Flint to do the final paperwork.

Buying WTAC wasn't a whim. Leonard was serious about making the investment profitable. He didn't know anything about running a radio station, so he hired David Croninger, a friend of several years who had been the program director at WIND, a prominent Chicago station, to do it for him. He paid Croninger $1,200 a month with the chance of a bonus if the station prospered. The purchase went through in February of 1959, but Leonard didn't keep the station very long, selling it at the end of 1960 to a group of Philadelphia investors for $555,700. Even though Leonard doubled his investment, Notkin said, "it didn't go as big as he thought. Leonard thought it would have more of the Detroit market, but it didn't."

What Leonard really wanted was a radio station in Chicago. He had already found a market for the Chess music with the city's large black community, and he was convinced that the same community would respond to a radio station geared to its interests and musical tastes. While some of the stations, notably WGES and WOPA, programmed black-oriented music, that was only one piece of their daily fare. They were also trying to appeal to Chicago's many other ethnic groups—the Italians, the Irish, the Poles. WGES, for example, had aired *The Polish Early Birds* and *The Italo-American Hour* for thirty years. Leonard's station would be different, broadcasting to the black community twenty-four hours a day. If he handled this right, advertisers would line up to buy time on a station that had the potential to reach roughly a quarter of the population, a radio audience currently underserved. Listeners would get new programming. The brothers would make money.

In the spring of 1962 Leonard started negotations with Richard W. Hoffman, a former Republican member of Congress and civic leader who operated three local triweekly newspapers and one biweekly and also owned WHFC, a small AM station. He had bought the station in 1926 and licensed it in Evanston; a short time later he moved it to Cicero. The call letters stood for a catch-phrase he liked: "where happy folks congregate." A companion FM station was WEHS, named for his mother, "Elizabeth Hoffman's Station." Although the station was licensed in Cicero, by 1962 the offices were at 3350 South Kedzie Avenue, about three miles from the

Chess studio. Compared to such powerhouses as WLAC in Nashville at 50,000 watts, WHFC was tiny, 1,000 watts during the day, only 250 watts at night. The station's eclectic programming reflected Chicago's diversity: six hours a week devoted to Italian programs, about fifteen hours devoted to the Polish community, forty-two to Spanish listeners, six hours for the Lithuanians, seven for the Czechoslovakians, and thirty-three hours for the black community. The station had been the first in the city to air the great gospel singer Mahalia Jackson from a local church, inaugurating an ambitious program of Sunday broadcasts from South Side congregations.

WHFC already had a built-in audience in the market Leonard wanted to serve. Just as important, his interest in buying and Hoffman's desire to sell came together at the right moment. Hoffman was not well, he had a sister who needed care, and he was anxious to simplify his business affairs.

By the summer, the parties made a deal. "He wanted a million dollars cash, and that's it," Phil said. While that was a lot of money for the Chess brothers, Florence Summers, Hoffman's longtime assistant, thought he could have gotten more if he hadn't been so interested in selling quickly. He essentially threw in the FM station for nothing, she said.

Final approval of the sale was required from the Federal Communications Commission, and this was proving to be difficult. It was a particularly stressful time for Hoffman because he had no other offer on the table, and he periodically worried aloud to Summers that he didn't know what he would do if the FCC nixed the deal. The agency was taking its time for a number of reasons. Leonard was seeking to buy the station on the heels of the payola scandal, and there was great sensitivity in Washington about letting a record company own a radio station. The concern was obvious: that the label owner would monopolize the public airwaves with his own product. On top of that were questions about Leonard's background and his ability to meet the purchase price. He was the owner of a small record company on the South Side of Chicago, and he was expected to come up with $1 million. Was there going to be anything in the deal that could come back to haunt the FCC?

Although Notkin drew up the papers and handled other routine legal matters relating to the transaction, he was out of his element in dealing with the agency. He told Leonard he needed to hire a lawyer who specialized in FCC work.

Leonard had already designated a program director for the station, Frank Ward, who had held the same job for the Rounseville Radio Group, a consortium of seven radio stations in the country, six of them devoted to black programming. Ward had gotten to know Vincent Pepper, a Washington, D.C., lawyer who was a communications expert and had also been an executive in the Rounseville organization. Ward told Leonard that Pepper was the man to steer him through the FCC.

They met over the phone, and Leonard hired him. Pepper liked Leonard from the start. He could feel a sense of purpose in their first conversation. "Leonard was driven, driven to succeed, and he didn't like to waste a lot of time in the process of doing it," Pepper said. If he got results for Leonard, Pepper was sure he would have a good steady client for the future and probably a loyal friend.

In his five years of practice Pepper had established a good relationship with Rosel Hyde, the FCC chairman. It was critical to have Hyde on his side to make the case that Leonard and Phil had a right to own the station, even if they had to negotiate some conditions on the sale. One other thing was important—that Leonard get through the agency's routine background check. Part of that included checking with the Federal Bureau of Investigation to see if a prospective owner had been in any serious legal trouble. All that came back on Leonard was an FBI report from 1952 about allegations made against him concerning inappropriate use of a copyrighted song. The allegations had warranted no federal action.

After a series of negotiations between Pepper and the commission, the agency offered a deal: Leonard could buy the station as long as Chess, Checker, or Argo releases were no more than 10 percent of the playlist. When Pepper presented the offer to Leonard, he laughed. "If I have two records on the top one hundred in *Billboard* at one time . . ." and his voice trailed off. Limiting him to 10 percent of the playlist would be no problem. In fact, he would be delighted if he could get 10 percent of anybody's playlist. He authorized Pepper to accept the proposal, but even then the final tally couldn't have been closer. The commission approved the sale the third week in December by a 4–3 vote. Leonard was so grateful for Pepper's work that he gave him a bonus when he sent in a check for the fee.

Leonard didn't keep a million dollars on hand, so he got another loan. By now he was a good credit risk. Bobby Charles happened to be in town the day the deal was finalized. He chuckled as he watched Leonard slowly sign the check to Hoffman. It seemed as though it took him ten minutes to form the twelve letters of his name. "It killed him to let go of that much money at one time—on a bet—cause that's what it was," Charles said. "It was a gamble."

"I hope I never have to write another one that big," Leonard said, as he finished the final *s*.

When Leonard and Hoffman had their final meeting, they took pictures. Leonard insisted that one be taken of the seven-figure check. When Notkin admired an American flag that was standing in his office, Hoffman gave it to him, noting that it was one that had been flown over the Capitol in Washington, albeit briefly.

The first thing Leonard did after acquiring the station was announce new call letters: the FM station, which would carry the same programming as the AM one, would change from WEHS to WHFC, a link with the past. But the AM station would become WVON—Voice of the Negro. It was understandable given the music and the market that had put him and Phil in business and in a sense made that million dollar check possible. Listeners who tuned in to 1450 on their AM dial on April 1, 1963, heard the first WVON broadcast. To spread the word beforehand Leonard took out a two-page ad in the *Chicago Defender* proclaiming the arrival of his new station to his target audience. The message was as direct as the venue: "WVON," it said in six-inch high letters. "Your 24-hour-a-day radio station."

Summers, who stayed on through the transition, knew immediately that things were going to be different. It wasn't just the programming; Hoffman and Leonard had few things in common. Hoffman was well educated and urbane; Leonard, in Summers's view, was the "the charming rogue" with little appreciation for high culture. There used to be live musical broadcasts from the Kedzie offices, and in the studio was a beautiful handcrafted Steinway piano. To Leonard it was just another instrument that wasn't going to get much use at VON. He had it carted over to 2120 for sessions and rehearsals. Summers was heartbroken when she saw it a few years later, still functioning but no longer the beautiful instrument she had known.

∿

Leonard attacked his newest radio venture with the same gusto he put into the record business. In hiring Ward to run the station he had selected an experienced radio man. Even though the manager was only thirty-two he had worked as a deejay and on the business side at stations in Miami, Cincinnati, and Buffalo, each of them with large R&B audiences. Working with Ward, Leonard set about building a staff who knew Chicago and knew the music that would appeal to the city's black community, which had grown to nearly 900,000 and was still growing. It would exceed one million within two years. Given all the radio stations he'd visited and all the programs he listened to, Leonard knew what he wanted in a disc jockey.

Cyrla Czyz and her children.
Left to right: Lejzor, Fiszel, and
Malka Fejgel in Motele, Poland,
circa 1925. *Courtesy of*
Mae Silverbrand

Joseph Chess (born Yasef Czyz)
in Chicago, circa 1925.
Courtesy of Mae Silverbrand

Fiszel, Malka, Cyrla, and Lejzor Czyz at the grave of Malka Czyz, the mother of Yasef Czyz, in 1928 before Cyrla and her children left for the United States. *Courtesy of Mae Silverbrand*

The passport picture of Cyrla, Malka, Fiszel, and Lejzor Czyz. *Courtesy of Mae Silverbrand*

on List	(This column for use of Government officials only)	Family name	Given name	Yrs.	Mos.	Sex	Married or single	or occupation	Read	Read what language [or, if exemption claimed, on what ground]	Write	(Country of which citizen or subject)
1		Pulik	Chazia	29	-	f	m	Wife	yes	Polish	yes	Poland
2	UNDER 16	Pulik	Sora	8	-	f	s	Student	yes	Polish	yes	Poland
3	UNDER 16	Pulik	Michla	6	-	f	s	Child	-	-	-	Poland
4		Rubin	Abram	57	-	m	m	Shoemaker	no	going to son	no	Poland
5		Rubin	Cyrla	56	-	f	m	None	no	going to son	no	Poland
6		Sieluncsyk	Icek	51	-	m	m	None	yes	Jewish	yes	Poland
7		Sieluncsyk	Eta	53	-	f	m	None	no	going to daughter	no	Poland
8		Nebozuk	Tekla	34	-	f	m	Wife	yes	Polish	yes	Poland
9		Nebozuk	Anna	16	-	f	s	Farmeratte	yes	Polish	yes	Poland
10	UNDER 16	Nebozuk	Marja	15	-	f	s	Farmeratte	yes	Polish	yes	Poland
11		Czyz	Cyrla	37	-	f	m	Wife	yes	Jewish	yes	Poland
12	UNDER 16	Czyz	Malka-Fejgel	13	-	f	s	None	yes	Jewish	yes	Poland
13	UNDER 16	Czyz	Lejzor	9	-	m	s	None	yes	Jewish	yes	Poland
14	UNDER 16	Czyz	Fiszel	6	-	m	s	Child	-	-	-	Poland
15		Jackier	Lea	54	-	f	m	None	yes	Jewish	yes	Poland

The page from the manifest of the *Mauritania* showing the Czyz family, lines 11 through 14, and Cyrla's sister-in-law, Chazia Pulik, and her two daughters, at the top of the page, lines 1 through 3. The women's husbands had immigrated to the United States in 1922 and settled in Chicago. *National Archives*

BELOW LEFT: Leonard Chess circa 1931, when he was fourteen. *Courtesy of Mae Silverbrand*

BELOW RIGHT: Phil Chess's graduation picture from Chicago's Marshall High School in 1939. *Courtesy of Mae Silverbrand*

Leonard and his wife, Revetta, circa 1945, with Revetta's brother Bert Sloan and a friend. *Courtesy of Marshall Chess*

ABOVE: Phil and his wife, Sheva, in 1946, after he returned from the Army. *Courtesy of Pam and Terry Chess*

RIGHT: Tom Archia, mainstay at the Macomba Lounge, the brothers' nightclub at 3905 South Cottage Grove in Chicago. *Chess files at MCA/Universal Group*

ABOVE LEFT: Andrew Tibbs, whose singing at the Macomba prompted Leonard to get into the record business. *Courtesy of Joseph Grayson*

ABOVE RIGHT: An ad for the Macomba from the June 22, 1947, *Chicago Bee*, the only known ad Leonard took out for the club.

BELOW: One popular grouping at the Macomba: Claude McLin, saxophone; Leroy Jackson, bass; Clarence "Sleepy" Anderson, piano; Wesley Landers, drums. *Courtesy of Charles Walton*

Evelyn and Charles Aron, the founders of Aristocrat Records. Leonard joined the company in October 1947. *Courtesy of Stephen Aron*

The first ad for Aristocrat Records, which ran in the May 1947 issues of *Billboard* and *Cash Box*.

RIGHT: Buster Williams, circa 1952, music distributor and pressing plant owner and the one who told Leonard to change the name of his label from Aristocrat to Chess. *Courtesy of the Williams Family*

BELOW: The first ad for Chess Records, which was in the July 15, 1950, issue of *Cash Box.*

BELOW: The first Chess catalogue, which was a flyer, printed on pink paper that was folded in thirds. Pictures of a few Chess musicians were on the cover. *The John Tefteller Collection*

CHESS RELEASES

REC. NO.	TITLE	ARTIST
1425	My Foolish Heart / Bless You	Gene Ammons
1426	Walkin' Blues / Rollin' Stone	Muddy Waters
1427	Me and My Baby / If You Believe In Me	Jimmy Bell
1428	Good Bye / Do You Really Mean It	Gene Ammons
1429	Chabootie / Full Moon	Gene Ammons
1430	You Can't Win / Achin' Heart	Andrew Tibbs
1431	Pennies From Heaven / Last Mile	Gene Ammons
1432	Mona Lisa / Benny's Bounce	Claude McLin
1433	Jug Head Ramble / Can Any One Explain	Gene Ammons
1434	Sad Letter / You're Gonna Need My Help	Muddy Waters
1435	That's All Right / Ludella	Jimmy Rogers
1436	You Got To Get It / Pretty Eyes	Dozier Boys
1437	I'm Going Through / Thank You Jesus	Rev. Gatemouth Moore
1438	Slow Drag / Nothin' From Nothin'	Lucky Thompson
1439	Blue Moods / Saturday Night Boogie	Floyd Simth
1440	No Home Blues / Send For The Doctor	Doc Pomus
1441	Louisiana Blues / Evans Shuffle	Muddy Waters

REC. NO.	TITLE	ARTIST
1442	Going Away Baby / Today, Today Blues	Jimmy Rogers
1443	Joliet Blues / So Glad I Found You	Shoe Shine Johnny
1444	All Of My Life / People Will Talk About You	Calvin Bostick
1445	Boppin' With Santa / Talk Of The Town	Gene Ammons & Tom Archia
1446	Tennessee Waltz / Pop Goes The Weasle	Claude McLin
1447	My Head Can't Rest Anymore / Take A Little Walk With Me	Baby Face Leroy
1448	Mean And Evil Daddy / Blues At Twilight	Tom Archia
1449	My Baby Told Me / Korea Blues	J. B. & His Bayou Boys
1450	Prelude To A Kiss / Don't Do Me Wrong	Gene Ammons
1451	I'm In Love With You (And I Hope You Are In Love With Me) / Fleetwood Blues	Calvin Bostick
1452	Long Distance Call / Too Young To Know	Muddy Waters
1453	The World's In A Tangle / She's In Love With Another Man	Jimmy Rogers

AL HIBBLER'S RELEASES

REC. NO.	TITLE	ARTIST
1455	What Will I Tell My Heart / It Don't Mean A Thing	Al Hibbler
1456	"Trees" / Lover Come Back To Me	Al Hibbler
1457	"Solitude" / Feather Roll Blues	Al Hibbler

1425 _____	1441 _____
1426 _____	1442 _____
1427 _____	1443 _____
1428 _____	1444 _____
1429 _____	1445 _____
1430 _____	1446 _____
1431 _____	1447 _____
1432 _____	1448 _____
1433 _____	1449 _____
1434 _____	1450 _____
1435 _____	1451 _____
1436 _____	1452 _____
1437 _____	1453 _____
1438 _____	1455 _____
1439 _____	1456 _____
1440 _____	1457 _____

Mark quantity in space at side of record Number

Drop in the mail box

THE CASH BOX

LUME XIV.   NOVEMBER 15, 1952   NUMBER

One of the biggest disks in the Rhythm 'N Blues field is currently "Juke" by Little Walter put out on the Checker label. Above Al Benson (left), leading R & B disk jockey on WGES in Chicago, interviews Little Walter (center) as Leonard Chess (right), prexy of Checker Records, looks on. "Juke," which has gone into the smash category, is the first record which Little Walter has cut for the label.

Disc jockey Al Benson, Little Walter, and Leonard on the first *Cash Box* cover to feature the record company, here celebrating the success of "Juke" on the Checker subsidiary. *Used by permission of Edna Albert*

Leonard, Little Walter, and disc jockey McKie Fitzhugh in a South Side Chicago record shop to promote "Juke." *Courtesy of Marshall Chess*

From 1951–54, the Chess office was at 4858 South Cottage Grove. "Juke" got a test run with passersby when it was played on a record player set up near the doorway. *Chicago Historical Society*

ABOVE: Phil with Harvey Fuqua, *far right and holding a carton,* and Pete Walton, of the Moonglows, during a 1956 recording session at Universal Studios. *Don Bronstein*

RIGHT: A family portrait for Marshall's bar mitzvah, April 17, 1955. *Clockwise from top:* Leonard, Revetta, Elaine, Susie, and Marshall. *Courtesy of Marshall Chess*

It was not unusual for Leonard and Revetta to hold a racially integrated social event, even though this was 1955, a time of segregation written into law. The Chess family's cleaning lady, Virginia Jones, and her husband, Curtis, were guests at the bar mitzvah dinner at the Morrison Hotel. To their left were Marty and Millie Witzel, who introduced Leonard and Revetta to each other. *Courtesy of Marshall Chess*

Disc jockey Sam Evans, *far right,* at a table that included Atlantic Records executive Jerry Wexler, next to the woman at Evans's left; Wexler's partner, Ahmet Ertegun, *center,* with dark-framed glasses; and next to Ertegun, Zenas Sears, the Atlanta disc jockey. *Courtesy of Marshall Chess*

The Chess building at 2120 South Michigan Avenue, the company's most famous studio and its headquarters from 1957 through the fall of 1966. *Cash Box/Used by permission of Edna Albert*

ABOVE LEFT: Leonard, Buddy Rich, and Jack Tracy, the head of jazz production, in the fall of 1960. One of the unusual features of the studio was the height of the control room (visible through the window behind the men). The vocal booth at the right was later moved to the other end of the room. *Don Bronstein*

ABOVE RIGHT: The menu from Batts Restaurant, the unofficial Chess commissary. Written on the back of this menu was the sequencing for a Muddy Waters album. *Chess files at MCA/Universal Music Group*

ABOVE LEFT: Etta James, the company's major female star, and producer Ralph Bass, during an October 29, 1969, session in Los Angeles. This was the first session after Leonard had died in Chicago. *Ray Avery*

ABOVE RIGHT: Billy Davis, the head of all non-jazz production from 1962 to the spring of 1968, in the studio with Fontella Bass, who had a hit with "Rescue Me," circa 1964. *Don Bronstein*

Ahmad Jamal at the Pershing Hotel, 1958. His album, *Live at the Pershing—But Not for Me*, was the first big jazz seller on the Argo label. Jamal was one of the label's most successful artists. *Don Bronstein*

ABOVE: Muddy Waters, the premier Chess blues artist, Chicago 1963. *Raeburn Flerlage*

LEFT: The union pay sheet for Koko Taylor's "Wang Dang Doodle" session. As leader of the band, Willie Dixon was paid double. *Chess Files, MCA/Universal Music Group*

A page from the Chess artist ledger showing royalty payments for tax purposes. *Courtesy of Terry Chess*

From Artist Ledger}

Sidney Barnes - 1916 E. 82nd St - Chicago, Ill.
c/o Tskiee music Publishing (Producers toy)
Chuck Berry — Berry Park, Wentzville, Mo. — 7754.25
Carl Bonafede 2123 N. Seminary - Chgo, ILL. — 1200.00
Clea Bradford ✓ 3106 Lawton Pl. St Louis, mo. 63103 — 1127.21
Ray Bryant ✓ 139 W. 82nd St Apt 7-C N.Y., N.Y. — 7209.00
Chester Burnett ✓ 829 E. 88th St. Chgo, Ill. — 1675.82
Milton Campbell ✓ 3128 Market St. East St. Louis Ill. 99 — 72.89
Wayne Cochran c/o The LAKH-1501 70½ St-Causeway — 5107.30
Dave Crawford 1925 Austin Rd S.W. - Atlanta Ga 30331 — 750.00
Norman Dayron 5319 S. Kimbark, Chgo, Ill. — 1000.00
The Dells ✓ 8000 S. Harvard Ave, Chgo, Ill. — 25,111.97
Willie Dixon 7636 S. Troop Ave - Chgo, Ill. — 4203.00
Maurice Dellison (Fred. Y Writer) Chgo Ill 60621 — 4000.00
Frank D'Rone ✓ 4930 Johnson - Hollywood, Florida — 964.83
Richard Evans 8516 So. Dorchester Ave, Chgo, Ill. — 22,783.32
Billy (Willie) Foster (Artist 4340.30 - Writer 3449.47) — 7789.77
Ernest Franklin ✓ 5228 S. Drexel - Chgo Ill 60615 — 791.10
Graham Paper Press 1160 Willow - Green Bay, Wisc. — 900.00
Etta James Los Angeles Calif (and F.G. #1097) — 3442.72
Ellington Jordan 4818 Tacoma St. Apt. 27 Los Angeles, Calif. — 2177.52
Ramsey Lewis ✓ 30 N. LaSalle Suite 800 Chgo, Ill 60602 — 57,000.24
Isaac Holt 134 N. LaSalle, Chgo, Ill 60602 — 2596.60
Eldee Young 134 N. LaSalle, Chgo Ill 60602 — 2596.60
Dewey Ramsdat Markham ✓ Bronx, N.Y. — 30,787.54
Robert Miller ✓ 2901 So. Michigan Apt #315 Chgo, Ill 60616 — 14,875.00
McKinley Morganfield 4339 S. Lake Park Ave, Chgo, Ill 60653 — 2649.37
Radiants ✓ 6030 So. Green, Chgo, Ill. — 3084.51

BELOW LEFT: Leonard, *right,* with Harry Goodman, his partner in Arc Music, on a fishing trip in Canada in the mid-sixties. *Courtesy of Marshall Chess*

BELOW RIGHT: *From left,* Stan Lewis, the Chess brothers' friend and a record shop owner from Shreveport, Louisiana, Leonard, and Gene Goodman, Harry's brother and also a partner in Arc Music, in Miami in 1966. *Courtesy of Marshall Chess*

Leonard in the studio at 320 East 21st Street with Ben Branch. *Courtesy of Dick LaPalm*

Leonard with James Gann, who ran the pressing plant at 320 East 21st Street. Gann had also built a small pressing plant at 4750 South Cottage Grove. *Courtesy of Marshall Chess*

Leonard with Lucky Cordell, one of the disc jockeys at WVON, the Chess brothers AM station, in June 1968 when Cordell was promoted to a management position. *Courtesy of Lucky Cordell*

Three of the WVON disc jockeys, known as the "good guys," during a fund-raising event. *From left,* Franklin McCarthy, E. Rodney Jones, and Bill "Doc" Lee. *Courtesy of Lucky Cordell*

In 1965 WSDM, the Chess FM station, developed a jazz format and featured female disc jockeys, known as "Den Pals." Their on-air signature was "WSDM— the station with the girls and all that jazz." *Clockwise from the top:* "Halavah," Merle Nadlin; "Hush Puppy," Linda Smith, later well known as Linda Ellerbee; and "Beep Beep," Karen Beckman. *Courtesy of Burt Burdeen*

A WSDM bumper sticker circa 1966. *Courtesy of Burt Burdeen*

Leonard, Marshall, and Phil in May 1969, in the executive office at 320 East 21st Street. *Chicago Tribune*

Marshall and Phil in 1996 at the old Chess studio at 2120 South Michigan Avenue. *Courtesy of Charles Walton*

One function of the *Defender* ad was to introduce the audience to the station's personnel.

The first page of the two-page spread was a clock, and set at intervals on the dial were pictures of the disc jockeys and personalities who would be on the air. Several were names familiar to many in the black community: Leonard's old friend and sometime associate Al Benson; disc jockeys Stan "Ric" Ricardo, coming over from what had been WGES but was now WYN-R; Pervis Spann, known as "the blues man," who came over from WOPA, the station where Marshall used to deliver the latest Chess blues to Big Bill Hill; Reverend Bud Riley, who came from WTAQ in LaGrange; and Herb Kent, a holdover from WHFC.

Since arriving at HFC from WBEE, another small local station, Kent had built a name for himself in radio circles. He was known as the "cool gent," a nickname he created after a friend told him he should find a rhyme as a catch phrase. It started out as an ad ploy, when he told listeners to go out and buy something. "Tell them you were sent by Herb Kent, the cool gent." One of Kent's specialties was "dusty records" time, when he played popular records from previous eras. He was so popular with teenagers because of the record hops he sponsored on weekends that the *Defender* dubbed his young listeners the "pied-piper following." Leonard had a particular soft spot for Kent because he set up the initial lunch between Hoffman and Leonard to discuss the possible purchase of the radio station.

Leonard also brought in Bernadine Washington, a fashion coordinator at a large South Side department store and fashion commentator on WCFL, another of the city's stations. Active in civic organizations and South Side politics, Washington was well known among black Chicagoans. In addition to community work on behalf of the station, she would get regular time on the air for *On the Scene with Bernadine,* a combination of advice and fashion tips for the women listeners.

Leonard's selection of E. Rodney Jones to be the program director blended his instincts about disc jockeys and his determination to make a deal. He had known Jones for nearly a decade, first meeting him when Jones hosted a show in Kansas City on KUDL. Leonard followed his career when Jones went to St. Louis for eight years and then came to Chicago for a short and unhappy stay at WYN-R. His departure from that station coincided with the final stages of Leonard's purchase of WVON. When Jones said he was thinking about leaving town, Leonard urged him to stay. Just come on over to the record company until the FCC gives the final approval, he told him. Leonard found a place for Jones working the phones with Max

Cooperstein's promotion staff. When the HFC deal was finally in place, Jones, too, was ready to start building a format he and Leonard hoped would be successful.

Though Leonard had brought in black disc jockeys and personalities of note, the upper management of VON was still all-white and would remain so for several years. Ward stayed barely a year. He was replaced by another experienced radio man, Lloyd Webb. As program director, Jones was the only black individual with a degree of authority, and he intended to use it. "The people hired by Leonard to run the operation, they were of the white race. But hell, they didn't know nothin' about what the hell was goin' on in the South Side or the West Side," Jones said. "They were from the North Side. They had to rely on the blacks that were working there."

The racial dichotomy rankled some, particularly for a station that thought of itself as the "Voice of the Negro." But the way Leonard operated VON, like the way he operated the record company, reflected the times and the overarching importance of money and power. Leonard knew there was a profit to be made from an untapped market, and to make it he had to create a station that served the black community better than it had been. If he could demonstrate VON's popularity, he could bring in the ad revenue. Just as he hired A&R men at Chess to produce the music that worked, he wanted people on the air who could deliver, and he left them alone. It would have been a grand and important gesture to have a black general manager running the "Voice of the Negro," but Leonard's gut instinct told him that a white man going out to sell VON to potential advertisers, most of them white-owned companies, would fare better in the early sixties than a black man, no matter how talented he was. With a million dollars at stake, he was not willing to take any chances. Besides, the people who represented the station to the public—the deejays and other on-air personalities—were black, and to the general public it was a black station, so much so that crossover artists such as Nat King Cole, Sammy Davis, and Lena Horne were considered too "pop" to be played. Few listeners knew that Leonard or Webb existed. On top of that there were only a handful of stations in the country owned by black individuals or with blacks in key management positions.

◆◆

WYN-R, Jones's former employer, was Leonard's major competition. When Texas broadcaster Gordon McClendon bought the station in 1962

and changed WGES to the new call letters—"winner" was its nickname—
he also brought in new faces with new voices. The *Defender* called them
"non-accented Negroes," who were more polished than Benson and
Ricardo. McClendon forced the two out because they didn't fit in. Benson
dismissed his replacements as "funny niggers." McClendon not only
switched the call letters but also scrapped broadcasts to all the other various ethnic audiences. McClendon's lieutenants said the station was aiming
for the black community by playing rock and roll and beefing up the news
operation.

Leonard's challenge was to beat them at their own game. That meant the
programming had to fit the audience. It was a delicate matter. The black
audience was not monolithic. Some listeners liked jazz, others gospel, still
others R&B or rock and roll, though some segments of the community still
cast a dubious eye on the latter, finding it too raw and unsophisticated. And
even within the R&B–rock-and-roll genre there were gradations based on
the subjective elements of one's taste.

WYN-R had jumped off to a fast start with an advertising deluge and
sales promotions, the most elaborate a $4,000 "treasure hunt" with the
promise of free gifts. "Just how long it'll last no one knows for sure," wrote
Defender radio reporter Bob Hunter, who chronicled the radio station
"war for the Negro market."

Leonard was banking more on smart management, good programming,
and experienced disc jockeys to make his station successful. The station had
its own promotional giveaways and contests, but they were much less frequent than WYN-R's initial efforts. At least one had some substance: a
$14.50 reward—an amount that reflected the station's place on the dial—
for the news tip of the week.

Though Ward, the first general manager, had brought a format concept
with him from his previous job in Florida, Leonard made sure it was flexible enough to let his disc jockeys project their personalities on the air. "I
want you all to talk shit" was how Leonard put it, letting the jockeys know
that they should not feel constrained by any formula. Another crucial element was developing a news operation. Jones felt strongly about this. A station that held itself out as the "Voice of the Negro" had to have a staff that
could report news "pertinent to the community you are serving." Though
the *Defender* was an important outlet, Jones knew that the radio station
could have a larger impact because it was easier to listen than to read.
Moreover, many blacks in the city worked in jobs where radios were accessible: domestics, cab drivers, janitors, and garage workers.

It didn't take long for Leonard to see his million-dollar gamble pay off. By the end of September, WVON had overtaken WYN-R as the most popular station among black Chicagoans. Reporting the results of a late summer survey among black listeners, the *Defender* pronounced it "the new star in Chicago's radio galaxy." Franklin McCarthy and Ricardo provided the morning chitchat; Jones came on in the afternoon until early evening, followed by Kent. Spann hosted an overnight blues show just as he had on WOPA.

While all of the station's jockeys were given credit for VON's popularity, Jones was singled out for special praise. "I've brought a little soul back to town, baby," he told the paper. "And he has, too," wrote Hunter, the radio reporter. "He offers a refreshing change from the boring rock-a-billy sound that some of the other stations feature." The turnaround was particularly sweet for Jones given his brief and unhappy tenure at WYN-R. "The same person they got rid of," he said years later, "I kicked their ass in three months, but I didn't know what the hell I was doing supposedly."

To fight back, WYN-R made some changes. But they only served to undermine the station even more. It had started out with a combination R&B–rock-and-roll format but, apparently to differentiate itself from VON, gradually played less R&B and increased the amount of pop music. By the end of 1963, it had become indistinguishable in the minds of many listeners from the Top 40 powerhouse WLS, and it was losing listeners week by week. "WVON literally gulped up the city's Negro audience," *Billboard* wrote in 1964, noting that in the evenings, according to a just-completed survey, the station was "almost unbelievably" in second place behind WLS. It was no lower than sixth during other periods in a twenty-four-hour cycle. "The Pulse," a national company that surveyed local radio stations, reported that by May 1964 VON captured 44 percent of the area's black audience between six A.M. and noon and 48 percent between noon and 6 P.M. WYN-R was a distant second with 14 and 17 percent respectively.

Leonard wasted no time using the results. A glossy brochure was put together for potential advertisers with a pointed message: There is a large black consumer market in Chicago and WVON can help you reach it. With words and pictures, the brochure described the station's varied community service activities and provided an hour-by-hour breakdown of on-air programming. As important, it included a wealth of data collected by an independent research firm about black Chicago's spending potential. Two key facts were highlighted: "for the first time in history Negro families' median income is over $5,260"—some 289,000 households—and that meant "$1,244,471,000 effective buying income."

"A spot on VON," the brochure promised, will "result in more sales with greater profit to you in the Chicagoland Negro market."

Suddenly it became important for labels to get their records on VON's playlist. If you didn't, the stores might not stock your records. And if you were in the VON mix, it could be a springboard to breaking a record in other major markets: New York, Boston, Cleveland.

Leonard had made his share of mistakes and released plenty of records that lost money to keep him humble. But the immediate success of WVON had to be considered a triumph. Few could argue with his ability to bring together the individuals who created the right mix and the right feel to make VON work. McClendon, the YN-R owner, hadn't fully appreciated the dynamics of Chicago's black community. Leonard came closer than most whites did, the result of a lifetime of personal and professional associations that were more than just superficial. "He hung out with blacks," said Charles Walton, the chronicler of the South Side music scene who had watched Leonard since he ran the Macomba. It was as succinct an explanation as any for his success.

The rise of VON was all the more vivid when matched against the fortunes of YN-R. Fifteen months after Leonard's station debuted, YN-R gave up music altogether and became an all-news station, WNUS. One of the disc jockeys who defected to VON was Lucky Cordell, whose career Leonard had watched and nurtured for almost a decade. Cordell had been one of Benson's protégés at WGES, though the two had gotten off to a rocky start because of Benson's penchant for control. Cordell was chafing to get on the air; Benson kept telling him he wasn't ready yet and only gave him brief spots. Not only that, he ended up getting fired from the station, and it took three months to find another job. It was Leonard, whom he had gotten to know when he went to the Chess office to pick up records for Benson, who told him about an opening at at WGRY in Gary.

Leonard had actually done more than find work for the aspiring disc jockey. Leonard thought he knew the young man well enough so that he could tell when something was wrong. During one visit in 1953, he persisted in questioning Cordell until he admitted that he had missed three car payments.

How much did he owe? Leonard asked.

About $75, Cordell said.

No, Leonard said. What he meant was the total owed on the car.

About $1,500, Cordell told him.

Leonard pressed his intercom and told the secretary to make out a check for $1,500.

"Well hold it," Cordell said, worried about when he could pay it back and what Leonard wanted in return.

Leonard waved him off. "I'm betting you'll make it. If you make it, you'll pay me back. If you don't, you don't owe me."

"Now tell me that's not a big encouragement to a guy," Cordell said, recalling the moment decades later.

Leonard's instincts were right again. Cordell was an immediate success in Gary, climbing to the top of the ratings in a very short time. He paid Leonard back in monthly installments of about $100 each. Within a year or so, he had enough to pay the balance of what he owed. Proud and appreciative, he went over to Leonard's office and handed him the money. It felt particularly good because it was just before Christmas. Leonard smiled, but instead of pocketing the cash, he reached for a scrap of paper, wrote a note and then pushed back the money: "To Barbara and the girls, Merry Christmas. Debt paid in full, and for you, fuck you."

By 1961 Cordell was back in Chicago. WGES was only too glad to have him on the air now in a far more substantial role. He was never certain why Leonard didn't immediately recruit him for VON, but he knew it was only a matter of time before he came over to the station. When he did early in 1964, Leonard promised him he would prosper. Cordell had no reason to doubt him. On the air he was dubbed "the Baron of Bounce." Eventually he became the station's first black general manager.

In the meantime VON turned into exactly what Leonard had hoped—an integral part of the black community. Though it ignored three out of every four people in the metropolitan area, "it reaches out for that fourth person and says 'Friend, this is for you'," said an admiring *Chicago Daily News* writer. General manager Webb could brag to the paper that by the end of 1965, when the station was not yet three years old, it got half of the black radio audience. Numbers like that continued to make the station attractive to the advertisers.

Reflecting the relationship between station and audience, the main disc jockeys, Cordell, Spann, and Kent, were known as the "good guys," a term also used by deejays in New York and Los Angeles. Webb, the general manager, liked to emphasize the public service aspect of the station. It embraced sponsorship of community events, editorials that focused on local and national issues, and local news broadcasts about issues of interest to black Chicagoans and the black community in general. Every Saturday morning, Bertel Daigre, a political adviser to Congressman William L. Dawson, who represented the South Side, hosted a meeting with constituents that was aired live over the station.

One of VON's favorite fund-raising gambits was the "sleepless sit-in." Spann, Cordell, Kent, and Jones would set up a trailer at one of the shopping areas on the South or West Sides for their broadcasts, and listeners would bet which deejay would be the first to fall asleep. Barrels to collect dollar bills and coins were outside the trailer for contributions in support of one or another jockey. During one sit-in $19,000 was raised for civil rights projects in Mississippi. On another occasion the station donated twenty-four hours of time to the NAACP. As a result the organization raised $21,000 in membership fees. Other groups that benefited from VON events were the Urban League, the Congress of Racial Equality, and Operation Breadbasket, an offshoot of the Southern Christian Leadership Conference run by Jesse Jackson, who was just emerging in the mid-sixties as a civil rights leader.

Combining a community program with a nod to the station's ownership, VON sponsored Easter egg record hunts in parks on the South and West Sides. Dyed Easter eggs were stuck into the holes of the 45s—no doubt Chess returns—and hidden in the greenery for the children to find.

"We get down with the people," Leonard explained to a *Billboard* reporter. "We report on the neighborhood church's annual picnic, and we're just as close to the community's musical tastes. We survey outlets constantly but never identify ourselves."

Webb, the general manager, and Jones, the news director, each had a favorite story to illustrate how well this community connection worked. "One morning a man saw a gas station being held up. The attendant and the robber killed each other," Webb said. "The witness ran to the phone. He didn't call the police, he called us." For Jones it was the story about a listener who called the station before calling the police to report a missing child.

Another pivotal element was the evening talk show hosted by Wesley South, who had done a similar kind of program at HFC. On VON, he quickly turned into an institution as moderator of the first talk-radio show geared to black Chicago. South had an ideal background for the job. He had written for *Ebony* and *Jet* magazines covering some of the earliest civil rights activities in the Deep South, and then had written a column for the *Chicago American,* "South's Sidelights." His rich baritone and precise delivery commanded attention as soon as he said "good evening." Medgar Evers had been on his show three days before he was shot to death outside of his Jackson, Mississippi, home. The night he died, so many calls poured into the station that the lines were jammed, disrupting phone service in parts of the city. Another show a few days earlier, when federal civil rights legislation was being discussed in Congress, was so popular that 2,400 callers got the busy signal in the hour South was on the air. Illinois Bell told South that in the two-week period surrounding Evers's murder, more than 16,100 callers were unable to get through to express their opinions on his show. Yet another indication of the station's power to influence came during a dispute with the city over crowded conditions in the black schools. When South used the airwaves to help organize a one-day student boycott to protest, 95 percent of the students stayed home on the designated day.

His guest list was eclectic but tended toward the political. Comedian and activist Dick Gregory called in regular reports from Mississippi and Alabama, Thurgood Marshall came on to talk about his activites for the NAACP legal defense fund, the Reverend Martin Luther King, Jr., was on several times, so was Malcolm X, Elijah Muhammad, Jackie Robinson, and a young Charles Percy, a white politician who came to realize the importance of this forum for reaching a significant part of the black community, who could be helpful to him in his approaching campaign for the United States Senate.

One story South loved to tell involved an abbreviated on-air conversation with Alabama governor George Wallace, who invited South to "come down here and see we're nice people."

"Well, I don't know if I would be accepted. I'm a Negro," South replied.

"Say that again . . ."

South repeated that he was a Negro. The next sound he heard was a click as Wallace hung up.

South had his own political aspirations. When he ran for Congress—unsuccessfully—Leonard gave him $7,500 in cash and $7,500 in VON advertising. He also kept South on full salary for eight weeks when he was part of a cultural exchange to Czechoslovakia. Leonard had him call in with regular reports. "I genuinely had an affection for him," South said years later, though it never ceased to bother him that the "Voice of the Negro" was operated at the highest levels by white men and that Leonard paid the minimum union scale to the jockeys when South thought he could have "shared the wealth." On the other hand, if VON had to be owned by a white person, Leonard was better than most. "You could talk to him," South said. "He would listen, he would ask you questions."

Leonard loved the radio station, but he knew it was the profits at 2120 South Michigan that had made the VON enterprise possible. The goal now was to make sure the record business continued to flourish.

sixteen

THE SOUL OF
A MAN

Before he even made the suggestion, Billy Davis knew what Leonard would say when he told him he wanted a house band—musicians who would get a salary whether they played or not: "What are you going to be paying those guys for?"

"I want a group of musicians I can depend on," he explained, good enough to play contemporary music. "If I put them on the payroll, they become exclusive to Chess Records. They won't be running the streets, openly anyway, to Vee Jay or other companies." Davis had to convince Leonard that in the long run the setup would save the company money and make the music better. It was something other studios were doing to good effect—Motown in Detroit, Stax in Memphis, and King in Cincinnati.

He won his argument. The core of the group was Maurice White on drums, Gerald Sims on guitar, Louis Satterfield on bass, and Leonard Caston on the piano and organ, though other musicians would occasionally cycle in. White, Satterfield, and Sims were in jazz groups together, and the three had played on a Betty Everett record, "You're No Good," that won them appreciative notices. They were trained musicians and prided themselves on the ability to play any kind of music, so when an opportunity came to audition for some Chess sessions they took it. It wasn't only Davis who listened to their music. Leonard was in the control room, too, interested in hearing what these young men sounded like if he was going to pay them every week regardless of what they turned out. While he could agree to that concept, though, he wanted to impose some kind of structure, and he thought a time clock was a way to monitor their work. The musicians could punch in at noon and then punch out around six when their sessions were over.

"Can you imagine that?" said an incredulous White. "We can't do that." He and Satterfield told Leonard the punch cards would have to go or they would. "We are creative people. We can't work on the clock, man."

A sheepish Leonard relented. It didn't take long for both brothers to appreciate that these musicians could help make a song into a hit. The blues would always be a cornerstone, but the brothers kept reminding themselves they had to adjust to new sounds. Now it was soul, the fusion of rhythm and blues with gospel. The beats were a little different and the frequent addition of horns made for a more sophisticated melding of singer and band. It was music Davis understood and felt confident he could produce. His imprint was audible on Billy Stewart's "Strange Feeling," a ballad released in the fall of 1963 with lush vocal backup harmonies that surrounded Stewart's trademark rapid-fire style of repeating lyrics. Friends called him "motormouth." The record only stayed on the charts for a couple of weeks, but it was a harbinger of the success Davis would find with Stewart and other artists.

Getting Stewart into this new groove and away from his road band in recording sessions took some doing. The road musicians did whatever the singer wanted, and "that was the same thing over and over again," Davis said. He didn't mind that Stewart came to sessions without every song completed, but if he wanted to work out the arrangements in the studio, Davis insisted that his people finish the job. "Billy was a little skeptical," Sims remembered, wondering whether he and the other musicians Stewart had never met knew what they were doing. But it didn't take long for the singer to realize that the rhythm section Davis had brought together could make him sound good. "Then we clicked," said Sims, the guitar player.

Results also made Stewart receptive to Davis's suggestions. Helping the A&R man was the fact that Davis had Leonard's support and confidence. He trusted his judgment. So there was no argument when Davis wanted to keep working with Mitty Collier, a young singer whom Leonard had signed at the end of 1960 but whose first couple of releases hadn't clicked. "Lackluster" was the way one critic described them. With the continued backing of Davis and the Chess musicians, however, her fortunes changed. She got on the charts in 1963 with an "answer" song to Little Johnny Taylor's "Part Time Love," now titled "I'm Your Part Time Love." The production was a prototype of what Davis could do. Its bluesy feel was underscored by the incisive guitar of Sims and the strong bass from Satterfield. The addition of horns as a counterpoint to Collier's penetrating vocals turned what could have been an ordinary blues tune into something more. Davis didn't throw around superlatives, but he felt there was something special about Collier—"a great singer. She had the heart and soul," even if she didn't have the onstage dynamism of an Etta James or Sugar Pie DeSanto.

Like the other women, Collier loved the atmosphere around the studio, particularly working with Davis. "He just inspired me," she said. "We grew up together. It was really a family thing. . . . We just hung around the studio every day." No place was off limits, including Leonard and Phil's offices. If she wanted to talk to either Chess, she walked right in.

If Leonard had had any doubts about the wisdom of hiring Davis full-time and hiring house musicians, Davis was making them disappear rapidly.

Leonard still made the final decisions on whether an artist stayed or was let go, however, and still kept his eye out for records from other labels that hadn't done well but might be rescued by Chess. Though Steve Alaimo's first releases on Checker were disappointing, Leonard kept him on. Alaimo finally found success early in 1963 with "Everyday I Have to Cry Some," a song about an old girlfriend that he recorded on his own in Miami. The song went to number forty-six on the *Billboard* pop chart, placed in the *Cash Box* survey of the top fifty R&B songs, and the magazine profiled Alaimo in its February 9 issue.

As "Everyday I Have to Cry" was peaking, Leonard picked up a disc from the tiny Formal label featuring Jan Bradley, another Mississippi transplant to Chicago who had formed a musical partnership with the talented and versatile Curtis Mayfield. He had written and produced "Mama Didn't Lie," a song whose upbeat tempo obscured its biting lyrics about men whose "greatest pastime . . . is playing tricks with every young girl."

The song was barely noticed when Formal released it in November 1962, but when Chess put it out a month later and gave it some promotion, the record got much more attention, showing up on the R&B charts by early February and rising to number fourteen on *Billboard*'s pop charts by March 9. In a way, Bradley was the reverse of Alaimo. His first songs didn't do much. Then he clicked with "Everyday I Have to Cry." Bradley stayed with Chess for a few more years, and while he made several other records, none of them did nearly as well.

◂▸

In the fall of 1963, Leonard decided to bring his old friend Dick LaPalm into the company on a full-time basis. Since their first meeting in 1956 over a Paul Gayten song, LaPalm had been working steadily as a consultant to promote the entire Chess roster on Top 40 radio. He was still working primarily with Nat King Cole, now in New York, where Cole was running his own label. Almost from the beginning LaPalm wasn't happy, so in the summer of 1963 he called Leonard. "I think it's time to come home," he told him. They made a tentative plan that LaPalm would be back by the end of September. September turned into October and LaPalm still wasn't back. Leonard was getting anxious, telling him in one phone call, "We got so much stuff coming out we really need you to start work right away." Maybe, Leonard suggested, he could start from his New York office.

LaPalm agreed, even though he and Leonard had never discussed salary. LaPalm's official title was vice president in charge of album sales, and immediately LPs started arriving in New York for him to promote. A few weeks into the arrangement an envelope arrived from Chicago with a check from Leonard and the notation that it was for two weeks' work. "I should have spoken to Leonard about a salary," LaPalm said to himself, half irritated, half amused at the paltry sum. Rather than call Leonard up and have an argument over the phone, he simply mailed the check back uncashed to his home in Glencoe.

A few days later the phone rang. "Hey, motherfucker. I sent you a check, you sent it back."

"Well," LaPalm replied, "it's not enough money."

"You must have done pretty well with Nat Cole."

"Yes I did," LaPalm replied.

Leonard asked him how much he wanted; he gave him a five-figure number, and Leonard agreed to it, throwing in an extra fifty dollars for good measure.

LaPalm's instincts told him the deal would work out all right. Difficult as Leonard could be about money, he trusted him. The man had come through when he needed a $1,500 loan, providing the money with no questions asked when LaPalm showed up at the house to get the cash. All Leonard wanted to do was play gin rummy, beating LaPalm as he always did.

The financial dynamic between Leonard and the blues musicians hadn't changed since Waters's first success with "I Can't Be Satisfied." What they were paid was based more on what they asked for than what they might be owed under a contract. Davis witnessed the arrangement firsthand, watching an encounter between Leonard and Sonny Boy Williamson, who was back on the charts for a few weeks in the spring of 1963 with "Help Me." A talented but often difficult man, he treated the company like his personal bank, much as he had Lillian McMurry's Trumpet Records years earlier down in Jackson. Davis was in the office when Williamson came in one day asking for money. After swearing at each other in their usual good-natured fashion, Leonard gave him some. How such transactions occurred intrigued Davis. There was rarely a direct payment of cash. Instead, Leonard or Phil would authorize a company check for the specified amount, and then the musician could cash it with the in-house accountant. The individual got his or her money, but the brothers also had a record of the payment.

"I love Sonny Boy," Leonard told Davis after Williamson left. "If I gave him $100,000 today, he'd be broke tomorrow. He doesn't have to worry about anything 'cause I'll make sure that he lives and his rent is paid and so forth. But I'm not going to give him a lot of money 'cause it's gonna be gone, and he'd still be back here looking for money."

Davis didn't know what to think. Leonard gave Williamson what he felt like giving him. That didn't seem right. But Davis couldn't argue with the fact that Leonard was probably correct in his assessment of where the money would go. "At the time I didn't translate that into 'boy, he's stealing their royalties and not paying them,' " Davis said, reflecting on the scene years later, "because I witnessed in some cases what he was talking about. Was it paternalistic? Right, but that's the way Leonard was, right or wrong. I never witnessed him totally refusing those guys anything," he added, "and at the same time I do realize that perhaps they were not paid all their royalties at one time. That's just the way it was. I often thought to myself, 'I wonder if I'm getting paid all my royalties?' then I realized hey, whatever is missing I don't miss. If I'm not getting paid all of it," Davis went on, "I'm getting paid as much as I would expect to get paid and probably more than I would from other people. Plus you know, I've asked thousands and thousands of dollars from Chess for different things and never once was refused for anything, you know. So there was times when I was ahead of the game, I'm sure, as far as I'm concerned."

Some days the first-floor hallway at 2120 looked like the line at a bank teller's window. "Leonard would go sneak out the back door so many people were standing there looking for money," said Etta James, who had more than one bill paid by the Chess brothers. "But if you didn't catch Leonard, you'd catch Phil."

⌒

Chicago had a reputation as a gangland city, symbolized by the notorious Al Capone. It was generally assumed that anyone in the entertainment business or even near it had to be "mobbed up," the general description for paying protection or giving kickbacks for one thing or another. There were occasional raised eyebrows and a sidelong snicker or two about the brothers' close friendship with Russ Fratto, a man of Italian heritage, but there is no evidence from FBI, Chicago, or Illinois state law enforcement files suggesting that Leonard was involved in activities related to organized crime. Phil denied any such connections; Marshall said he never saw any evidence of it. But that didn't mean the Chess brothers were immune to the problems inherent in a business made up of combustible parts: talented but idiosyncratic individuals, liquor, drugs, odd hours, a tradition of dealing in cash, and finally, a commodity, records, easily bootlegged for black-market profit. Allen Arrow, the brothers' New York lawyer, never forgot the scene outside 2120 South Michigan on his first trip to Chicago: Leonard and Phil, baseball bat in his hand, running down the avenue chasing a young man with an armful of records.

Phil had lost more than records from the building. When a set of golf clubs was stolen from his car, he thought they were gone for good until one of the employees brought in what he said was a new set of clubs. He had gotten a great deal through a friend, he explained. The clubs were Phil's. Whoever had stolen the clubs sold them to a fence, and the Chess employee subsequently bought the set. No one was ever sure whether the entire deal had been an inside job.

Every now and then a musician, having had too much to drink, came into the studio brandishing a gun, but no one was ever hurt. Billy Stewart caused a momentary ruckus when he was impatient to be buzzed into the office and took out his pistol to shoot the doorknob off. All was forgiven later on when he passed around the Maryland crabs he had brought, packed in dry ice, from his home in Washington, D.C.

It was fortunate for Stewart that Leonard and Phil maintained a good working relationship with the Chicago police. One night Marshall forwarded a message to his father from a detective he knew. Stewart was in custody for shooting his driver in some kind of disagreement, the officer told them on the phone. What did they want him to do? Exactly what kind of gesture was made is murky now, but no charges were filed, the driver was not seriously hurt, and Stewart's career was not interrupted by the incident.

There was always the possibility of burglary at the studio, so Leonard was not suprised when he got a call on a Sunday morning in the fall of 1963 about a break-in. He got there as quickly as he could. But the call was a hoax. When Leonard got out of his car, he was accosted by thugs who beat and robbed him. The assailants had been tipped off that he carried large amounts of cash—often as much as $500. The attack stopped only when passersby startled the robbers, who fled. No one was ever arrested for the crime; Leonard was hospitalized for several days with a badly swollen face and some other minor injuries.

Marshall was going to school in California when this happened. He learned about it in a phone call to his mother, and it crystallized his thinking about his life and his future. His heart was in the record business—"I was raised to be in it. It's in my blood," he would tell friends—and now his family needed him. He was going to quit school. Though it bothered his mother more than his father, he didn't care what his parents thought about his decision. To stay in school was "living in bullshit. I know what I want to do. I want to be a record man."

In fact, Marshall already was one, if on a small scale. It had started with the Gene Ammons session in 1950, when he fell asleep in the corner of Universal Studios. He graduated to sweeping the floor, getting coffee and rolls and taking money to the bank on Cottage Grove Avenue, to packing records at 2120 South Michigan, working at the small pressing plant in the early morning shift before nine A.M., and then finally riding around Chicago with Howard Bedno, who worked for the distributor Paul Glass. Marshall watched how the pitch was made to the jockey or the store owner, learning the steps of an introduction, a favor, a budding friendship, a deal. By the time he graduated from New Trier High School in the spring of 1960, he had sampled every phase of the business.

In the fall Marshall had headed off to the University of Denver. The city was small: it had a radio station and record shops but no Chess distributor. So Marshall was ready to try out what he learned on his own. His first stop was KTLN, where Joe Finan, who had been implicated in the payola scandal, was now working. He had known Leonard and Phil from his days in Cleveland, and Phil told his nephew to stop by the station and try to get a few Chess records on the playlist. Marshall was so nervous about making the first overture—even to a family aquaintance—that he had to go around the block three times to work up his courage to go in. But he did, and he warmed to the task. He remembered the drill: take Finan out for a nice steak dinner, pay for a bottle of wine, make him a friend, and get his confidence that the information you're passing on is good: a record is breaking in Chicago, it might be good to give it play in Denver. "You might even get somebody a girl, if you have to," Marshall added. But he never paid anybody cash and never bought them drugs.

When he transferred to the University of Southern California in the middle of 1962, Marshall picked up in Los Angeles where he left off in Denver. Now he had the benefit of a bona fide Chess office, run by Paul Gayten, and he spent as much time helping with distribution as he did with his class work. Side deals in the record business took priority over the library and term papers. His curriculum really amounted to an apprenticeship for coming home to the record company. He had already taken accounting courses. Now he added one in radio and television to learn how to edit tape and took a science course about plastics. On top of that he was a budding entrepreneur. Working with Gayten and two area disc jockeys, Marshall was operating his own version of the Macomba Lounge, albeit only one night a week. The four made a deal with the owners of the California Club, a popular nightclub in the heart of Watts, the black neighborhood of Los Angeles, to host local live acts on the night the club was closed. Running the program were two popular disc jockeys, a white man known as "Ted Q," and Margie Williams, a black woman who was the on-air companion of Hunter Hancock, the city's influential R&B deejay, who also was white. Marshall had gotten to know Williams on the weekly trips he and Gayten made to KCFJ, Hancock's station, to deliver the latest from Chess. "Ted Q," Margie, Gayten, and Marshall split the door receipts from their weekly event; the club owners kept the bar sales.

Instead of staying in California during his summer break in 1963, Marshall came back to Chicago to work at the studio. Max Cooperstein, the national sales coordinator, thought a live Bo Diddley album would do well, so he huddled with the guitar player to pick a date from his schedule that would work for a remote recording. They settled on a club in Myrtle Beach, South Carolina, "the Redneck Riviera," Marshall called it. Leonard let him go down with the band to run the operation. They set everything up for July 5 and 6 at the Beach Club, a venue frequented mostly by whites anxious to hear more lively fare than their hometown radio stations farther inland generally played.

The first evening went fine. By the second night things were rolling, band and audience in high-energy sync. Suddenly Jerome Green jumped off the stage, still keeping the beat with his maracas. The young white women crowded around him to dance. In a flash the police, all of them white, rushed forward and pulled the plug, literally and figuratively. Racial decorum had been violated. This kind of mingling with its obvious sexual overtones had to be stopped. "Jew nigger lover," one of the policeman yelled at Marshall when he asked what was going on. "We're gonna lock you up and it will take them weeks to find you."

This is unbelievable, Marshall thought to himself, absorbing the double hit of anti-Semitism and racism hurled his way.

No one was arrested because the band complied with police orders. Marshall shuddered at the thought of what might have happened had tempers flared even more. One of Diddley's road men kept a pistol in a paper bag he carried around.

Even though the remote session was cut short, the band did manage to get enough on tape to get an album out. *Bo Diddley's Beach Party* was released in the fall.

The summer had been an exhilarating one for Marshall. He went back to school in California with mixed emotions. His heart was really at 2120 South Michigan Avenue, and halfway through the semester, after his father was beaten up, he called it quits. "School was a joke," he said. "Graduating was never my focus. I was educating myself for Chess Records." He was back in Chicago by the late fall, in time to share one of the nation's wrenching tragedies with other members of the Chess Records family, the assassination of John F. Kennedy. He was up in the studio with Ron Malo and a few musicians when they got the news. Everything shut down, the radios were turned up, and in the midst of shock and tears, Malo had the presence of mind to turn on the tape machine to record the broadcast as events unfolded.

Settling back in the city, Marshall got his own car and an apartment a few miles from the studio. It was just the basics as he defined them: bed and stereo, with a few accessories from his mother. Leonard put him on the weekly payroll, $200 gross, about $175 net. He didn't discuss the subject with his son; he just asked him what he needed to live on and then made his own decision.

The major question was what Marshall would do now that he was back in Chicago. In the beginning, at Leonard's request, he was his father's shadow. He chauffeured him everywhere, from home to the studio, to the VON office on Kedzie in the latest model black Cadillac Leonard now owned. One of the rituals was the daily car wash at a gas station one block away on Indiana Avenue, just a few doors down from Batts.

This went on for a month, two months, nearly three months, and

Marshall still didn't know his role beyond watching his father as he went from meeting to meeting, deal to deal. He was desperate for specifics: where should he sit, what should he do? Finally he couldn't keep silent any longer. During one of their drives, he finally asked the question: "What's my job?"

"You stupid motherfucker," his father told him. "Your job is watching me—driving me and watching me. And when you're ready you can do it."

"That was it," Marshall said, marveling years later at the chilly simplicity of his father's plan.

One day late in the winter of 1964, Leonard decided Marshall was ready. He told him to go to Europe with Harry Goodman, their partner from Arc Music, to learn what he could and then come back to set up a Chess operation in Europe. Though the Vietnam War was escalating and the draft an ever-present possibility for young men Marshall's age, he failed his physical because of a slight deformity on his left thumb. He would be called only in an emergency. So he and Goodman took off for London, where Arc had a small publishing office. Marshall met Louis Benjamin of Pye Records, who was handling the Chess products under a licensing deal, and then they went to Paris, Cologne, and Milan. Goodman introduced Marshall to his contacts in all the cities.

In a few months Marshall would go back on his own to negotiate contracts to increase Chess Records' international presence. In the meantime there was plenty happening on the music front in Chicago to keep everyone busy.

◆◆

Chuck Berry had been released from prison on October 18, 1963, ten days shy of his thirty-seventh birthday. The company kept his name before the industry, taking out periodic ads, one of them a full-page spread in both *Billboard* and *Cash Box*, to promote an album with his songs that other musicians had recorded. A 15 percent discount was offered on already released LPs. *Berry on Stage* didn't do very well. Perhaps listeners were put off by dubbed-in applause to simulate an audience.

If the thought ever entered their minds that Berry's career was in jeopardy, neither Leonard nor Phil ever expressed it. They intended for him to pick up where he left off, even if the rock and roll that made Berry famous was changing. They could see in their own studio that the music was different now. That's what made Davis and the newer artists they were working to bring in so important, and why it was also important to have Esmond

Edwards turning out jazz discs on Argo. The brothers still believed in Berry, though, and if he had songs, they would make records. In fact he had come to record on August 1 on a work furlough two months before his final release. Only three songs were recorded, and only one of the three was released, "No Details." A remake of "Brown-Eyed Handsome Man" with horns and a calypso beat was put on the shelf.

Berry had not let his songwriting talents languish in prison. He kept composing, and within two months of his release he returned to the studio in Chicago. Not only that, Leonard succeeded in getting Berry's parole arrangements transferred to the city so he would have more freedom to move about. Both men were anxious to have him start making money again. As soon as Berry got to Chicago full-time early in 1964, Marshall took him shopping, courtesy of Leonard. It wasn't merely for an upcoming road tour, but "just to be sharp every day," Marshall explained. Time away had made Berry two years out of style, and he wanted to look good driving his Cadillac. Part of the arrangement in these first weeks back was to have Marshall act as Berry's road manager. They had an ambitious itinerary: stops in Flint and Saginaw, Michigan, where Berry played with the rhythm section from Motown Records, the company started by Billy Davis's former partner, Berry Gordy; and then they went out to San Francisco's Cow Palace, where Berry was part of a big rock-and-roll show sponsored by two prominent disc jockeys, Tom Donahue and Bob Mitchell. Then it was on to San Diego to perform at a gathering for hundreds of sailors.

Cadillacs aside, Berry had a reputation for being cheap. It always irritated Etta James when she sang backup on some of his 1960 sessions that he would never buy lunch for the musicians. All they got were packaged crackers with peanut butter. Traveling with Marshall on the road, Berry never wanted to stop to eat at restaurants, even when Marshall complained that he was hungry. Berry never seemed to be, but then Marshall learned why. One night he saw him heating up a can of food on a hot plate he carried in his suitcase—"too cheap to buy a meal," Marshall grumbled.

By March 7, Berry's first post-prison song made the charts, "Nadine." It was a first cousin to "Maybellene," with the same peppy beat and witty lyrics that talked about a woman and a car. Maybellene's Coupe de Ville became Nadine's "coffee-colored Cadillac." Leonard and Phil gave it a good send-off, buying a full-page ad in *Cash Box* to declare "Back Again with another 'Chart Buster'—Chuck Berry—'Nadine.' " The song stayed on the charts for more than two months.

By the end of May, "No Particular Place to Go," another of Berry's tunes that was written in prison, was also on the charts. While the words were new, however, the melody was the same as "School Day," a hit seven years earlier, and the subject was a favorite, cars. "Ridin' around in my automobile" was how the song began. At the same time Berry came up with new words for another old tune, "Wabash Cannonball." This one became "Promised Land," and the story line was about a journey from Norfolk, Virginia, to the promised land of California. Berry wanted to be sure of the details in the song's itinerary, but prison officials balked at giving him an atlas, he explained in his autobiography, "for fear of providing the route for an escape." "Promised Land" went on the charts by the end of the year along with two other tunes, "You Never Can Tell," and "Little Marie."

Cash Box had put Berry on the cover of its June 6 issue—though it used a 1956 picture—noting in the caption that he was "back in action." In its typical fashion of not talking about scandal, there was not a word about where he had come back from. Not only was Berry getting publicity for his new records, his older ones were catching on with other performers. Johnny Rivers and Lonnie Mack recorded "Memphis"; the Beatles, a new English group taking America by storm, released "Roll Over Beethoven"; the Beach Boys updated "Sweet Little Sixteen" and turned it into "Surfin U.S.A."; and Dion Di Mucci—he did not use his last name—recorded "Johnny B. Goode."

All in all it was a productive and welcoming return not only for Berry but for Chess and Arc, the publishing company with the copyright to the songs. There were no more Alan Freeds or Russ Frattos listed as cowriters, but it still rankled Berry that Arc made money every time someone bought a record with one of his songs or the song was played on the radio, on television, or during a live performance.

〜

Etta James continued to be the studio's major female star. Ralph Bass longed to produce a record that could capture more completely the energy and emotion he heard every time she sang but that never fully made it onto vinyl. It wasn't her fault. It was simply the raw immediacy that got lost in the process of transferring a moment in time into a moment for history. The solution, Bass thought, was a live album put together in a setting they both liked, before an audience that would take what James had to offer and give something back. By now Leonard had learned that it generally paid off to give his producers a free hand, even if he was sometimes disappointed when the record failed to sell. He gave the okay for this project.

Bass and James went down to Nashville, and she picked The New Era club, in the heart of the city's black community and a favorite of the local R&B stars, for the live recording. Though known as the center of country music, Nashville had deep roots in blues and R&B, as the trio of disc jockeys on WLAC had shown fifteen years earlier. On Friday evening, September 27, 1963, the place was packed, abuzz with expectations of a good show and the knowledge among audience members that they, too, were being recorded. James was more than a little anxious. This was her first live album. She was used to a studio, with a control room and engineers and several takes if necessary. Here a recorder was sitting in the middle of the room, and there was one chance to get it right. "It's just a gig," she told herself.

"Ladies and gentlemen," the announcer said, to ascending chords from the band. "Ladies and gentlemen, the star of our show, and how about a big round of applause for Miss Etta James."

"Whoa, sometimes I get a feeling," she growled, prompting hoots from crowd members who immediately recognized the opening of "Something's Got a Hold on Me." "And I got a feeling like I never never had before."

"Yeah," the audience roared back, and James was off. Watching from the side of the bandstand, Bass felt the explosion of sound. The song built phrase after raucous phrase for nine minutes—an eternity in R&B music— singer and audience feeding off one another. "I forgot everything technical," Bass said. "My only thought was 'were the engineers capturing all of this on tape?' "

The challenge was to find the same hot mix the next night. He and James had chosen some new songs, but Bass wanted only the barest of rehearsals beforehand, just enough to get James's key and make sure the band knew the chord changes. He wanted everything to be fresh and spontaneous. By the time she sang the very last note, no one was disappointed.

The album that resulted was appropriately named *Etta Rocks the House* and included a sensual "Baby What You Want Me to Do," the Jimmy Reed song; Barrett Strong's "Money"; "Something's Got a Hold on Me"; and a handful of others. Bass dashed off the liner notes by hand on the back of Argo sales forms. The only changes for the actual album reflected the cuts made to shorten a couple of tunes.

"Baby What You Want Me to Do" was released as a single at the end of

1963, and was on the charts early in 1964, where it stayed for a month. The album did even better, staying on *Billboard*'s "top LP's" chart for more than two months.

Leonard's good eye for obtaining masters paid off again when he purchased the effervescent novelty song "Hi Heeled Sneakers" by Tommy Tucker, whose real name was Robert Higginbotham. It was really a twelve-bar blues tune but the tone was witty, not melancholy, and the story was about getting ready for a date—wear a red dress, those "high-heeled sneakers" and a "wig hat on your head"—not the usual blues theme of bad woman/bad man. One amusing piece of advice was to wear some boxing gloves "in case some fool might want to fight." The song was a hit. More important, it inspired Higginbotham to write an answer for his own song, "Slip-in Mules." He took the idea to Davis, who loved the play on shoes, and they both heard Sugar Pie DeSanto's voice in their heads as they put the finishing touches on the tune. It was written one day, recorded the next, and on the charts a few weeks after it was released.

"Baby my red dress in the cleaner, but my shift will steal the show," DeSanto sang, with the same wit and spirit as the original. "Can't wear my high-heel sneakers cause they hurt my toes so bad," she tells her boyfriend. So wear some spats and shoes "to match my low-heeled slip-in mules."

~~

Over the years Leonard and Phil looked to disc jockeys not only for record play but for tips on talent. Nothing had changed on that two-way street except now the deejay might be one of their own. In the spring of 1964 Bill Doc Lee, who had a gospel show on VON, was taken with a young singer who had won a talent contest at the Trianon Ballroom, a popular South Side spot on Cottage Grove Avenue and Sixty-second Street. Her name was Jackie Ross, and she was only eighteen years old, but she had already made a record at the behest of Sam Cooke, a family friend. Lee thought she had a future as a singer, so he took her down to the Michigan Avenue studio to introduce her to Leonard and Phil and Billy Davis. They listened to her sing and liked what they heard. By now Davis had two writers working for him, Carl Smith and Flash McKinley, and the three thought they had a tune that was perfect for Ross, "Selfish One." It had the full-bodied sound with a beat—accentuated here by propulsive piano chords—that was becoming a trademark of the arrangements Davis liked, pop inflected but still soulful. "Oh selfish one why keep your love to yourself," Ross sang. "It's like a souvenir that just sits on the shelf." By August the song was on the charts, and it stayed on *Billboard*'s tally for nearly three months. Davis not only could feel good about the effort, he stood to make some extra money. Because this was his production, the song belonged to Chevis Music, and the mechanical royalties and any performance fees were split between him and Leonard and Phil.

For her part, Ross was disappointed in the amount she received in royalties on the sales of the record. "I walked into Leonard's office," she remembered, "hands on my hips and said, 'I want to know where the rest of my money is.' " She was expecting more for a record that went to number eleven on the *Billboard* R&B chart and made it onto the pop charts, although near the bottom. "I was not satisfied with what I was told," she added. She disagreed with the notion that she shouldn't concern herself with sales royalties because the record was really a means to better and more performing dates. "They sounded like I should be grateful because they put my name out there so I could work."

Told later of Ross's criticism, Davis was perplexed. He said she never complained to him at the time. He believed she got a good count from the Chess business office because it was the same count used to give him his publisher's royalties from the song, and he was satisfied.

Ross's bad feeling festered over the next two years, even though she made several more records—none as successful as "Selfish One"—and toured with other Chess artists around the Midwest. She would leave the label in 1966.

In the spring of 1964, Davis had a chance to help Mitty Collier find her way back onto the charts. It was one of those collaborations that grew out of being in the studio every day with the same people. There was an intuitive musical understanding among them. Caston, the keyboard player, also played the piano for a church and often had gospel albums with him to learn new songs. One day in May he was noodling around on a song written by James Cleveland, "I Had a Talk with My God Last Night." "What is that?" Davis asked, struck by the melody and the words. He asked Caston to play it a few more times, and then after changing some words—"God" became "man"—he wanted Collier to come into the studio and try it out. With a little more fiddling, it turned into a ballad, still prayerful, but now about a man and a woman: "I had a talk with my man last night. He reassured me that everything was still all right. As the night grew light, my news got bright. He made me know I was the star of the show."

The song was released in the summer, and it took off. There was a brief tiff with Cleveland, who contended that Davis and Caston had taken his song. Davis retorted that the melody was an old gospel tune and that Cleveland was not the writer. He was given the credit in later reissues, however.

"I Had a Talk" gave Collier a new, higher profile and steady work. But she felt that neither she nor Jackie Ross nor Sugar Pie DeSanto got as much attention as they deserved. "Etta James was like the sacred cow, so to speak, Etta was the shining star," Collier said. It caused some private resentment among the other women who felt they had to wait in line for studio time and didn't get the same push for their records with the promotion men and the disc jockeys that James did.

The one time Collier saw an all-out effort on her behalf was when Max Cooperstein heard a song while he was in the Florida, "Sharing You," that he thought was perfect for Collier. "Mitty needs this song," he told Davis, and early one morning she was awakened by a phone call and told to get to the studio. "I didn't know anything," she said, "but the band was there, they laid down the track, I read the words off the paper, and they had a dub of it on VON before I got on the expressway and got home."

"Sharing You" was Collier's most successful single.

Leonard had come to accept advertising as a necessary part of the business. It was something like the joke about chicken soup for a bad cold: it might not help, but it couldn't hurt. LaPalm thought there were ways to make it help more, by making the ads more interesting. He took charge of the content, and by the spring of 1964, six months after his arrival, there was a noticeable difference in what appeared on behalf of the company in the two major trades, *Billboard* and *Cash Box*. Instead of the basic black box with the necessary information—artist, song title, record number—there were conversations between two records or cartoon figures exchanging comments about the latest releases, better graphics, and fancier displays of album covers. Whether they contributed to sales, though, was hard to gauge.

Finding new ways to make money from old music was never far from Leonard's mind. The quality of the underlying recording was certainly important, but the success of any venture also depended on larger and more evanescent cultural matters—trends that emerged for one reason or another and captured the public's attention. The trick was to find music that could ride the current wave. One of the challenges was to get mileage out of the blues music even as its popularity was on the wane. The black audience was diminishing, having moved on to embrace sounds with different beats and different story lines. But there was a feeling on Michigan Avenue that Muddy Waters, Howlin' Wolf, Sonny Boy Williams, and the like could be repackaged to take advantage of the popularity of folk music among white listeners. A case could easily be made that blues was a part of the folk heritage. So the company set about planning a "folk blues" series that would package material by the main bluesmen. The musicians in turn got booked at folk festivals in the United States and in Europe. Waters was particularly busy in October 1963, playing four dates in Germany as part of the "American Folk Blues Festival."

Three months earlier, on July 26, he had gathered with other Chess bluesmen at the Copa Cabana, "a rude, cavernous second floor hall-turned-nightclub," in the words of music writer Pete Welding, on the West Side of Chicago. On that sweltering summer evening Willie Dixon directed a live recording featuring Waters, Howlin' Wolf, Otis Spann and Lafayette Leake, two of the premier blues keyboard men, Fred Below on drums, and Buddy Guy, the spirited young guitar player who was something of a Waters protégé. Most of the audience was black, but a number of whites were also there, many of them folk music fans from universities in the area. If the music was not the traditional sort of folk fare, it was nonetheless irresistible. Before the the first number was half over, the dance floor was packed.

Even though Waters and Wolf were established blues stars, everybody got paid the same—$112 for the session, according to union rules, except that Dixon, as the leader, got double.

Leonard got extra mileage out of the effort, with a little musical sleight of hand thrown in as well. The album was released on Chess as *Blues from Big Bill's Copa Cabana* and it featured one of Waters's classics, "Got My Mojo Working," and an exciting performance by Guy doing "Worried Blues." On Argo those same songs were packaged into *Folk Festival of the Blues*. Sonny Boy Williamson wasn't at the club that night, but one of his tracks was put on the record with applause added to simulate a live recording.

In theory, it made sense to cast the bluesmen in the folk idiom, but that was only one element of the larger picture. Not factored in was the popularity of blues, and particularly the blues of the Chess stars, with young English groups. The Beatles made no secret of their affection for the music that had come out of 2120 South Michigan Avenue. On their first trip to the United States, they said they wanted to meet Muddy Waters and Bo

Diddley. When a white reporter covering their tour asked "Muddy Waters—where's that?" Paul McCartney was appalled. "Don't you know who your own famous people are here?"

Another group that followed in the Beatles' footsteps paid similar homage, the Rolling Stones, who had named themselves after Waters's 1950 song. "When we started the Rolling Stones," said guitarist Keith Richards, "our aim was to turn other people on to Muddy Waters." One of the ways they did that, aside from the name of the band, was to record a song he had done ten years earlier in their own saucy style, Dixon's "I Just Want to Make Love to You." It was one of their first hits in England.

The band's success with such tunes had multiple benefits beyond introducing the music to a much wider audience. It also produced revenue for the writer from the mechanical royalty for each sale of a Stones record and additional royalties from radio play and various performances. Songs that had very little commercial value when they were written were now worth much much more, a fact that was critically important in disputes that would arise in later years over who should profit from the material.

The Rolling Stones made their first trip to the United States in June 1964. Five hundred fans met them at the John F. Kennedy Airport in New York, where they were to join a tour that included Bobby Vee and the Chiffons. Though the Stones and the Beatles were both English groups, the Beatles had a more clean-cut, gentlemanly appearance, even with their "mop-top" hair. The Stones had even longer hair, and while they may have worn neckties and dress shirts, they behaved with an insouciance that implied rebellion. When the band finally got to their hotel after doing radio and television interviews that were beamed across the country, they were trapped inside because of the crush of fans out on the street. Some of the young women were brandishing scissors, hoping to get close enough to one or another of the musicians to cut off a lock of his hair.

After a stop in San Antonio, Texas, the group went to Chicago, to the home of their musical heroes, 2120 South Michigan. It was Marshall who had taken a call early in the spring from Andrew Oldham, the band's twenty-year-old manager, asking how he could arrange a visit and do a session. Marshall gave them the basics, and two days, June 10 and 11, were set aside for them to come to the studio.

Marshall was the group's informal tour guide. He escorted them to the back offices to meet his father and Phil. Neither was overly impressed with the Stones, though Phil was the more talkative of the two. "My father said two words," Marshall recalled. The group's appearance made more of an impression than their music and what it might mean for the business if these white rock-and-rollers found an audience for the Chess music. It was one of the few times Leonard's business instincts failed him. He hadn't appreciated the Beatles either. Neither brother could get over the long hair. *Freaks,* they thought, a sentiment shared by some who didn't know their music and couldn't comprehend their personal style. When Marshall gave Brian Jones, one of the guitar players, a ride home later in the day in his new red Porsche, the top down, they heard shouts of "homo" when passersby saw Jones's long hair. Those taunts aside, the band did have a multitude of fans in Chicago. When their recording session was finished, they tried to hold a news conference on Michigan Avenue and nearly got arrested. The crowd was blocking the street, and a city police officer, unimpressed by the musicians, bellowed an ultimatum: "Get out of here or I'll arrest the bunch of you."

Thirty-five years after the Stones' first visit to the Chess studio, the moment retains a *Rashomon*-like quality. Participants and observers remember it differently—who was there, who said what to whom, what happened and on what visit something might have taken place. The Stones came to the Michigan Avenue studio two more times between June 1964 and May 1965. Dick LaPalm said the main bluesmen weren't even there when the band first came. Jones made a pest of himself asking over and over, "Is Willie Dixon here?" In the beginning, LaPalm insisted, "none of the artists were very impressed. None of the people at Chess gave a damn who they were."

Keith Richards is responsible for one of the most widely circulated myths about the Chess operation. In a well-publicized interview he claimed that when he came into the building and went upstairs to the studio, he passed a man in coveralls on a ladder painting the ceiling. Someone said, "Oh, by the way, this is Muddy Waters." "He wasn't selling records at the time," Richards said, "and this is the way he got treated."

Pungent, colorful, the story was politically salable to those who see the Chess brothers as little more than racist exploiters. But it didn't happen. "That's a lie. I can't even imagine it," said Billy Davis, who was at the studio every day, all day. "I never saw Muddy painting or nailing or scrubbing or any of that bullshit . . . If he went up on a ladder Leonard would be the first one to say 'get your ass down. You know, I don't want you fallin' off those damn ladders.'"

In more erudite terms Edwards, the jazz A&R man, who, like Davis, was at the studio every day, echoed the sentiment. "Leonard had too much respect for Muddy. I never saw it," he said. "I'm no friend of the Chess family, but fair is fair." LaPalm was sure Waters wasn't even in the building that June day: "Muddy was never on a ladder painting a wall at Chess records. That's a fabrication."

Waters never spoke about his alleged painting in the interviews he gave about the Rolling Stones and Chess.

Not in dispute about this June visit are the songs that were recorded in those two days, among them: Waters's "I Can't Be Satisfied," and "2120 South Michigan" an instrumental written in honor of the building. "2120" and five other songs from those sessions were included on the band's second album, *12x5*. Also clear was the benefit the bluesmen derived from the band's continuing interest and homage to them. They insisted that Howlin' Wolf perform with them when they did the television show *Shindig* on a second trip to the United States. Even more important and even more than the Beatles, the Stones were the catalyst for other white groups to take the music that came out of 2120 South Michigan and record it anew.

"When that happened, I thinks to myself how these white kids was sitting down and thinking and playing the blues that my black kids was bypassing," Waters told music writer Robert Palmer years later, reflecting on the Stones' visits and their aftermath. "That was a hell of a thing, man, to think about."

Waters's observation alluded to the continuing challenge of the record business: understanding the audience and finding the right music to capture a piece of the market. Leonard and Phil were fortunate to have the right elements in place to keep on top of the business. The chemistry between in-house talent and out-of-town musicians would give them another boost just when they needed it.

seventeen

DON'T MESS UP
A GOOD THING

L ike Billy Stewart, Little Milton was used to working with his road band. It was that elusive sense of comfort seasoned with loyalty. These musicians had helped him make his name, and he felt he was in good hands working with Oliver Sain, who not only wrote songs and arranged them but also played the piano and the saxophone. Their work together on the Bobbin label produced good music; so did their first releases on Chess. Billy Davis liked the group, too, but he thought he could do something more, setting Campbell's husky but inviting voice to some new material with punchy arrangements. It wasn't that he wanted Milton to give up singing the blues, but he wanted to take those well-known changes and give them a twist, a flatted chord here or there, a different beat, horns as a counterpoint to the vocals.

The second floor on South Michigan resembled a laboratory now, musicians, arranger, producer adding and subtracting ingredients to get the best compound. With blessings from Leonard and Phil, Davis was the master chemist, shuttling between studio and control booth to confer with the musicians when he had an idea or to argue with Ron Malo, the engineer, about the sound he wanted. Malo aimed for balance among the instruments. Davis wanted a particular feel. Bring up the drums, bring up the bass, he would tell the resistant Malo. Out in the studio Davis tested the dynamics with the other instruments and the singer. Sometimes he moved the musicians around for a better mix, readjusted the microphones, or suggested the guitar player try something different to accent a lyric. He would sing the part if that helped get his point across. Maurice White considered the sessions a tutorial. "He taught me how to break down a song and build it back up again," he explained. "He allowed the musicians to be free enough to make a contribution."

Like Leonard, Davis knew the importance of making the music accessible for radio play. He had a feel for lyrics and surrounded himself with writers who could not only embellish his ideas but come up with their own hooks as well. Carl Smith and Raynard Miner were his mainstays now. He had brought the two young men together because he thought they would collaborate well. Miner, the younger of the two, was appreciative of the mix. "Chemistry was happening," he said. If something clicked, they all stood to gain financially with each record sale. There was extra incentive for Davis because everything he wrote or produced went into Chevis Music, his partnership with Leonard and Phil.

Smith and Miner's first collaboration for Little Milton was "We're Gonna Make It," an optimistic take on romantic partnership: "We may not have a cent to pay the rent, but we're gonna make it" is the first line, but it is introduced by a brass flourish and then a dramatic pause before Milton sings. The horns were originally in the middle of the song, but Davis thought they worked better at the beginning, a clarion call to pay attention.

The combination of his instincts and ideas and Milton's ability to pull it all together paid off. "We're Gonna Make It" went on the charts in March of 1965, rose to number one on *Billboard*'s R&B tally, to number twenty-seven on the pop listing, and to number eighteen on the *Cash Box* Top One Hundred. It stayed on *Billboard*'s chart nearly four months. With this kind of result Milton didn't mind giving up his road band in the studio. Like most other recruits he appreciated the "very warm, intimate type feeling" on Michigan Avenue. "It felt good to know that we had somebody in charge that was interested in helping you express your personal contribution in recording," he said of Davis. He also noticed that neither Leonard nor Phil interfered with the music. Busy now with the details of running a multipronged operation, they might stop in on a session now and then but they pretty much left Davis and Edwards alone. One of the keys to their success was knowing when to get out of the way.

There was more to the St. Louis connection than Sain and Milton. Fontella Bass, a young singer-piano player, had come to their attention when they heard her in a music revue and were drawn to her penetrating voice. It was a bonus that she was adept at the keyboard, though it should not have surprised anyone who knew her background. Her mother, Martha, was a member of the Clara Ward singers, and as a child, Bass not only played the piano and sang in her church, she also went on the road with her mother. By the time Sain and Milton recruited her to play the key-board on the Bobbin releases, Bass was at home on the stage.

When Milton went out on his own in 1963, Bass and another young man, Bobby McClure, became featured singers in the Oliver Sain revue. But within a few months, Bass left the revue after a disagreement with Sain and headed to Chicago, where she had relatives. John Burton, the brothers' longtime associate who handled some of the legal matters involving Chess musicians, got to know Bass and persuaded her to sign with the company.

Bass's first recording reunited her with McClure and Sain for "Don't Mess Up a Good Thing." Sain wrote the song while he was commuting between St. Louis and Chicago. One of his bandmates drove the car while he composed. In the studio, Sain willingly put his song in Davis's hands. The musicians were playing the right notes, and Bass and McClure were singing the right words, but something was wrong. The song just felt dead.

"Can I make a suggestion?" Davis asked.

Sure, Sain replied.

"Do you all do the Uncle Willie?" Davis asked, referring to an upbeat dance popular with black teenagers in Chicago. "Let's put it there."

Adding that beat made all the difference in the world, transforming a lackluster effort into a "lively warm-hearted rhythmic pop-blueser," in the words of *Cash Box*. The vocal tradeoffs between Bass and McClure—her gentle accusation, "you been cheatin' on me," his aw-shucks confession, "now I mighta cheated just a little bit, baby"—were particularly effective.

"Don't Mess Up a Good Thing" made the *Cash Box* Top One Hundred listing and the *Billboard* charts right after it was released at the end of January 1965 and remained on the tallies for fifteen weeks. While the song proved to be the high point for McClure's career, it was just the beginning of bigger things for Bass and an entree into the company for her mother. Martha Bass would make four gospel albums under the supervision of Ralph Bass (no relation).

~

Though Billy Stewart still argued about using his road band in the studio, disagreements with Davis were getting shorter and less frequent, particularly when the singer needed money. Then he was only too ready to sit down and listen. Davis had brought in Phil Wright, an arranger with a strong jazz background, to enhance the music Satterfield, White, and Sims were creating around the singer. Wright was one of the side benefits coming out of the Jackie Ross sessions the previous year. She had been playing clubs around Chicago and was booked to perform at the Sutherland Hotel with the band in residence. When she came in for a rehearsal, she had the list of songs she wanted to sing but no music. The bandleader told her she needed to get arrangements, and he suggested she talk to Wright, who played the piano and arranged. Ross gave him the material, he sat down with her at the piano to listen to her sing, and then went home to write the parts that were later performed. Ross didn't have the money to pay him; he would have to see Davis at the Chess studio. By the time Wright went over to Michigan Avenue, word of his talents preceded him. Davis paid him for the Ross work and asked him to stay on.

Wright was amused at how lax the Chess operation could be for a company that from the outside appeared to be a well-honed music machine. He had no idea that in addition to writing arrangements he would also make some extra money writing lead sheets—the basic melody and lyrics—for songs that needed to be registered for copyright protection. Some of the songs had been recorded and out on the market for months, if not a year or two. Wright's arrival meant the chance to catch up on the backlog of work. He took care of some Chuck Berry tunes but frequently had to argue with him about getting paid. "He was haggling over two dollars," the astonished Wright said. "He paid me, but you had to bargain with him."

Every now and then the lax paperwork caught up with the company from the opposite direction. Songs written by outside writers were recorded by Chess singers but the necessary licenses had not been obtained from their publishers ahead of time. There was a stern exchange of letters from Barrett Strong's company after Etta James recorded his song "Money" without first getting the requisite permission. The matter, like other similar problems, was resolved once the proper filings were made.

Wright rarely saw Leonard or Phil in the studio, though he knew they kept abreast of all the operations. When Jackie Ross went out on the road, Leonard asked Wright to go out with her for a month to rehearse the band and act as road manager.

One of Wright's first assignments at Chess had been writing those punchy horn parts on Milton's "We're Gonna Make It." Davis hoped he would have the same success with Stewart. Wright could see the singer's talent. Stewart knew what he wanted, and when he couldn't find the words to explain it, he sang the parts. Wright's challenge was to find ways to complement Stewart's trademark rapid-repeat vocals without getting in the way. Too much from any of the instruments would muddy the overall effect.

Out of their early 1965 session with Caston on piano, Sims on guitar, Satterfield on the bass, and White on drums came two hits: Stewart's own "I Do Love You" and "Sitting in the Park." His album, also titled *I Do Love You,* spent three months on *Billboard*'s top R&B album chart. Even more success was to come from this collaboration in the coming year. In the meantime Wright's work with another Chess artist, writer-singer Tony Clarke, helped make "The Entertainer" a hit. It was Clarke's take on the old adage "the show must go on," broken heart or not.

⩘

Although the Chess operation had grown considerably in the last few years, the atmosphere at 2120 South Michigan still seemed like a bustling and busy family, if a larger one. Leonard and Phil, Max Cooperstein, the national sales manager, Dick LaPalm, and Marshall all had offices, but there were few formalities. Doors were open, phones rang, salesmen, disc jockeys, and musicians still came in and out, and upstairs, the addition of the rehearsal studio in back of the main room provided another place to gather and create. There was always the feeling that something good might happen if the right people were in the same room, instruments at the ready, to toss musical ideas back and forth. It might start with a few bars of melody, a lyric, or even just a beat. To increase that likelihood—and because the operation was running out of space at 2120—Leonard and Phil bought a small storefront across the street that had been the Chicago office/studio for the Cincinnati-based King Records.

Smith and Miner, the writers, often took over the space as their private domain. It didn't have much in it—a couple of chairs, a piano, a beat-up tambourine. When they got together they didn't have a set way of working, but Miner generally came up with hooks like "we're gonna make it," and Smith found the story of the song to flesh out the lyrics.

Though Miner was blind, he moved around the studio and the world with the pace and grit of someone who could see. Barely twenty, he had been writing songs and getting them recorded since he was twelve. He managed and wrote for a "girl group" that was first called the Lovettes and then the Gems, and with Davis's help he convinced Leonard and Phil to put out a couple of their tunes on the Chess label in 1963.

In the summer of 1965 Miner was fooling around with a song that he temporarily called "Take Me with You." He liked it well enough that he called Smith and told him to meet him at the new office space across from the studio. When they had the basic elements in place, they couldn't wait to play it for Davis. He liked what he heard, but he had a few suggestions. The title wasn't quite right; call it "Rescue Me," he said. He gathered Satterfield and White and a few other musicians in the rehearsal studio at 2120 to listen to the basic elements and then come up with their parts. Phil Wright made a demo tape and took it home to write the horn parts to go over the top. Davis thought the package would be perfect for Fontella Bass, who was in town for a recording session.

As Miner and Davis remembered it, the two writers took a tape over to Bass's hotel and played it for her. Bass said she didn't think much of the song. Davis reassured the writers she would come around.

Bass's recording session was set for September 2. There were a number of songs scheduled; "Rescue Me" was at the very end, and the plan was just to get the basic rhythm tracks and her vocals down. The backup vocals and horns would come later. Satterfield started in with the bass line: "Ja ja ja ja JUM jum jum JUM ja ja jum"; White followed with a drum flourish and then came Bass's soaring vocals: "Rescue me, take me in your arms. Rescue me, I want your tender charms." Rather than take his customary seat in the control booth, Davis stayed in the studio. As the song was winding down, he had an idea—let the instruments drop off one by one until it is just Satterfield repeating the bass line and then, finally, just Bass. One by one he tapped each musician on the shoulder to stop until only Bass was singing.

When they were finished, there was dead silence that seemed to Miner to last an eternity. Everybody knew they had a hit. All that needed to be done was to add the backup singers and the horn parts. Satterfield would reprise his bass line on the trombone, which had been his first instrument when he played in the Red Saunders band several years earlier. Gene Barge, whom Phil had brought back as a producer to help Davis, would play the sax. The Gems, Miner's friends, would do the vocals.

That "Rescue Me" turned out to be one of the company's biggest hits was not in dispute, but memories differ on how it reached the public. Miner, Pete Cosey—the erudite, versatile guitar player who had replaced Sims in the rhythm section—and VON deejay Herb Kent remembered that Leonard did not want to release the song. Kent was sure that he was the one who convinced Leonard he had a big seller after Miner brought him a dub. But Davis, who was in charge of the production, said it didn't happen that way at all. He recalled taking the finished product to Leonard's office, where he played it for Leonard, Phil, and Max Cooperstein, and that all three had the same reaction—this was a hit. Leonard was on the phone to

VON right away, he said, to tell them a dub was on the way over and to get it on the air. Miner may have talked to Herb Kent about "Rescue Me," Davis added, but he said there was never a moment when Leonard balked at putting the record out—"maybe just not as fast as Raynard wanted it."

"Rescue Me" rose to number one on *Billboard*'s R&B chart and to number four on its Hot One Hundred. It stayed on the magazine's charts for nineteen weeks. The *Cash Box* tallies put the record at number two on the journal's R&B listing and number three on its Top One Hundred. Bass's career got a terrific boost. By the end of the year she tied with Barbara Mason for first place on the *Cash Box* R&B listing for best female newcomer and placed number four in the general category of women singers behind Petula Clark, Shirley Ellis, and Marianne Faithfull. Her album, *The New Look*, released a few months later, was number ninety-three on *Billboard*'s Top LPs (the magazine listed 150) and stayed on the chart for two months.

Three decades after recording "Rescue Me," Bass had markedly different memories of its creation from Davis and some of the musicians. "I just literally wrote the song," she said. "You know anybody can do rhythm takes. You have to put the melody over the top of them. . . . I was tricked out of the publishing," she insisted, referring to the fact that because she was not listed as the writer—Smith and Miner got the credit—she received none of the mechanical royalties from the sale of every "Rescue Me" record and none of the performance royalties that went to Chevis Music, the song's publisher. When Leonard handed her an $11,000 royalty check as her artist royalties, she was sure the amount was far below what she should have earned. In fact, she argued often with Leonard about the money she was making, marching into his office to demand, "Leonard, what is this?" When he told her she didn't trust anyone, "you don't even trust your mother," Bass didn't flinch.

"You're right Leonard, 'cause I know if I got some money in my purse my mother gonna take it."

Some of the musicians on "Rescue Me" were perplexed by Bass's anger over the tune. Satterfield, the bass player, insisted that "she didn't do nothin' but sing the song," implying that the words and music made the hit, not the voice that gave them life. Like Miner, Davis said Bass "had nothing to do with the writing." Cosey, who played guitar, took the middle ground. When everyone went in the studio, "there was a definite song. It was more than a skeleton. There was a body," he said, "but Fontella embellished quite a bit, especially the ending."

Davis believed that Bass was paid proper royalties on the sale of the record. As a partner in Chevis Records he was paid publishing fees on the same count that determined Bass's royalty. He believed the count was fair. "The record ended up selling over a million copies, or over seven hundred thousand, which was like a million for us," he said. But Bass's insistence that she was underpaid could have reflected another aspect of the Chess operation—that the company's royalty rate was a percentage point or two below the industry standard. So even if the singer was paid on an accurate sales count, her royalties would still have been less than she wanted—a reflection of Leonard's insistence on doing business his way.

Because of the vagaries of deadlines for list making, though, "Rescue Me" failed to make the top one hundred list of singles for 1965, a surprise for a record that rose so high on the trade paper charts and stayed on the *Billboard* tally nearly five months.

The matter of sales figures was a constant issue. Million sellers now were certified by the Record Industry Association of America, but in order to get that certification, a company was required to open its books so that sales could be verified. Leonard refused. He didn't think it was anybody's business how much the company was selling. LaPalm always thought that Leonard was motivated in large part by the wish to keep artists from nagging him for more money, and no doubt there was something to that. But he had always held internal business matters close to the vest, even when the company was small. Only once, at the urging of Dave Usher for an Ahmad Jamal record, had he let an outsider see sales figures and then publish them.

~~

The jazz operation was humming along smoothly under the direction of Esmond Edwards. He had more than a passing interest in successful records. After he had finished his first year as Argo's A&R man, Leonard called him in and told him he would have to take a one-third salary cut. Things hadn't gone as well as he and Phil had hoped. Edwards had no way of challenging Leonard's figures. On top of that he had gotten married two months earlier and felt he had no choice but to accede to Leonard's wishes. He liked the work, particularly the musical freedom to do as he wished, and he promised himself to remember Leonard's pledge that if things improved on the jazz line, he would get his salary reinstated.

Most of Edwards's sessions with the various jazz musicians were done in the studio in Chicago, but he liked recording in clubs, where the immediacy of the live audience added something extra. "It's like the home team advantage," Edwards explained. "You have your rooters there. It's an inspiration to the performers." Ahmad Jamal and Ramsey Lewis were especially suited for these kinds of projects because they played so many live dates. Neither musician nor producer knew how a night would go; there couldn't be retake after retake like the studio work. But it was worth taking a chance when everything clicked.

With a large black population and plenty of small venues for live music, Washington, D.C., was a good city for jazz. The atmosphere in the Bohemian Caverns, a popular night spot not far from the White House, matched its name: dark, cozy, and a little avant-garde. Lewis and his trio— still Eldee Young on bass and Red Holt on the drums—thought the club was the perfect place for a live recording. Edwards flew east to supervise the production. He hired a freelance engineer whose speciality was remote work handled from a custom-built van set up outside. The electrical lines were run into the microphones in the club, and even though the equipment was rudimentary compared to what was in the Chicago studio, it was sufficient to get a good sound.

Edwards and the trio scheduled three nights at the Caverns, May 13, 14, and 15, 1965. Their plan was to get enough good tracks that Edwards could edit into an album and maybe release one or two tunes as a single. By the time the trio started into their version of the popular song "In-Crowd," the audience was already revved up. First came a few fast-paced bass notes from Young, then Holt came in on the drums, and then Lewis played the familiar opening notes of the melody. The audience clapped to the beat, patrons shouted encouragement as the song built. Then they quieted down for a delicate solo from Lewis. When the trio finished, nearly six minutes after they started, Edwards understood how Ralph Bass must have felt standing by the stage at the New Era club in Nashville when Etta James delivered her knock-out performance.

Back in Chicago, Edwards shaped the three nights of material into an album, *The In-Crowd*. The challenge was to trim the selected tunes down to manageable size—two-and-a-half to three minute bites—for an appropriate length and then select a couple of tracks to be put out as singles. "In-Crowd" was a natural. It was released early in August, and neither he nor the trio had to wait very long to see what the public thought. Within two weeks it was on the trade paper charts. It climbed to number four on the *Cash Box* Top One Hundred and to number five on *Billboard*'s Hot One Hundred. The album did just as well. It rose to number four on *Billboard*'s top LP tally, and stayed on the chart for nearly three months.

But that was just the beginning. Over the next several months, the trio released three other singles, two of them their version of pop tunes "Hard Day's Night" and "Hang On Sloopy." The third was "Wade in the Water." It was Lewis's personal take on the well-known gospel song done in a studio production that featured brass parts arranged and conducted by another talented Chess associate, Richard Evans. All three sold well enough to make the charts and stay there for several weeks. A "best of" album and another LP built around "Hang On Sloopy," *Hang On, Ramsey* also made the album charts. On top of that, when the Grammy awards were handed out in March of 1966 for the previous year, the single of "In-Crowd" brought Lewis and the company their first honor. Leonard was understandably happy when he and Lewis came to terms in the fall of 1965 on a long-term contract with Argo. Three hits in a row from an instrumental group was unheard of. *Cash Box* put the trio on the cover of its October 2, 1965, issue and designated the group the best instrumentalists of the year in its final polling. Lewis won a similar designation from *Record World* in its year-end edition.

A previous *Cash Box* cover, the one for May 15, should have disabused anyone who thought Chess was only a blues label. The cover featured several of its big-selling artists, including Lewis, Ahmad Jamal, Tony Clarke, Billy Stewart, Little Milton, Fontella Bass, Bobby McClure, and the Radiants, a popular vocal group that had two songs back-to-back on the *Billboard* R&B charts. The only representative from the earlier era was Chuck Berry.

Proud and happy that the music he produced had been so well received, Edwards went to Leonard at the end of 1965 and told him it was only fair to have his salary reinstated. Not only that, Edwards wanted his own publishing company so that he could make some money from the original songs his musicians brought in for him to produce.

Leonard rarely did anything without a negotiation, and this was no different. He restored Edwards's salary, though he declined to give him a bonus even in the face of Argo's unmistakable successes. But he had to deal on the publishing. His counteroffer: Leonard and Phil and Edwards would split the proceeds. Rather than have a partnership like Chevis with Billy Davis, Edwards would have his own company outright, but they would divvy up any new tunes that came in so that if a musician had four original songs, two would go to Arc, the other two would go to Discus, the name Edwards picked for his company.

It was naïveté, Edwards said years later, that contributed to his not getting a better deal for himself, though there was no guarantee that Leonard would have agreed to producer royalties for the Argo hits. "That wasn't the day of benevolent management," he noted.

~~

Leonard and Phil had done a lot of business based on a handshake and an understanding, including such large matters as selecting the name of one of their labels. They had never taken the formal steps to protect "Argo." They knew that British Decca had a spoken-word label of the same name, but Decca had not put anything out in the United States. Besides, the understanding was that the spoken word and music were two different things, so there was nothing to worry about. Everything had worked without a hitch for a dozen years, but right in the midst of Argo's hottest period, British Decca changed its mind. The company wanted to start releasing discs in the United States, and, they said, there couldn't be two Argos.

Marshall tried to negotiate a deal with his British counterparts so that the Chess operation could continue to build on Argo's strong base of Lewis, Jamal, and James. But by September 1965, Leonard decided it wasn't worth any more haggling. They decided to give up the name voluntarily and come up with a new one. Leonard assigned the task to Dick LaPalm, the jazz enthusiast and promoter and the creative hand behind the company's ad campaigns. Find something with another *A,* he instructed. So LaPalm came up with "Apogee," unusual to be sure, but in vogue because of interest in the space program. "Wow," he thought to himself, "that's a great word . . . The astronauts are now in apogee," the point, the television broadcasters explained, when they were the farthest from the earth in their orbit.

"How do you spell it?" Leonard wanted to know when LaPalm made the suggestion. "It's hard to say, and my distributors will have a bad time saying it. What does it mean?"

LaPalm told him, but Leonard was unconvinced. He picked up the phone, called a friend who had a distributing company called Cadet and asked if he could rename his subsidiary "Cadet." Sure, was the reply, so he told LaPalm to change Argo to Cadet.

"It doesn't start with an *A,*" LaPalm said.

"Well, the second letter is an *A.* It's close enough."

On October 4, the company announced it was "voluntarily" relinquishing the Argo name and that all future music that had been on the Argo line would now be on Cadet. The *Billboard* story announcing Cadet noted the irony of the name change coming at a time when the subsidiary had just tallied the largest volume of sales for a six-month period in the company's history.

As the one in charge of advertising, it was up to LaPalm to put the best face on the Argo/Cadet name change. So he came up with a mini-essay that ran as a full-page ad in *Billboard, Cash Box*, and *Down Beat*, among other publications. Across the top was Chess-Checker-Argo, only Argo was crossed out and Cadet was written above it.

"A name is easy to change; a reputation isn't," the ad began. "We've been known as Argo records for ten years and during that time we've built and enjoyed a reputation for producing phonograph records of unsurpassed excellence. But names are not unique, and if an organization finds that they alone no longer answer to and for the record of their name, and that their individuality is at stake, a new identity must be established. *Our name was Argo. Our new name is Cadet*. The name and *only* the name has changed." Underneath was the new Chess logo, the head of a chessman's horse instead of the old chess piece, and the statement "There's a World of Excitement on Cadet."

By now Leonard trusted LaPalm's advertising ideas. He didn't even flinch when LaPalm told him he wanted to contract with *Cash Box* to run a one-column company ad every week on the magazine's "radio active" page. This was a survey of radio stations in selected markets that showed what releases the stations were adding to their playlists each week, and it was the first page the jockeys and program directors turned to. The space was expensive, but LaPalm wanted to get the company's name in front of them on a regular basis. He varied the copy, sometimes highlighting a mix of singles that were coming out on the three labels, sometimes filling the column with pictures of album covers, and sometimes combining a song title or LP cover with copy. He considered it a coup to have sewed up the spot; other record companies were waiting in line for it.

Typical of the entrepreneurial spirit at Chess was the deal LaPalm made with Bob Hope in mid-October to put out an album created from Hope's 1964 Christmas show for American soldiers serving in Vietnam. The two had been on the same plane to Los Angeles, and after LaPalm reintroduced himself—they had met when he worked for Nat King Cole—he asked Hope why he had never done a comedy album. Nobody ever asked, he replied. LaPalm told him he thought he could make one work, even though it was far afield from anything Chess had done. They had put out comedy albums, but the crowd that knew Bob Hope didn't know much about Moms Mabley, Pigmeat Markham, or Slappy White, mainstays of the black comedy circuit, even though they had some crossover appeal.

A deal was finally hammered out with Hope's people, and the comedian suggested that instead of just having a series of comedy bits, it would be better to have some narrative that set the scene. LaPalm agreed, and he hired Alex Dreier, a well-known commentator, to put together the explanatory material between the segments, which featured Hope, comedian Jerry Colonna, the actress Jill St. John, and singers Anita Bryant and Janis Paige. Chicago *Sun-Times* columnist Irv Kupcinet wrote the liner notes. He offered a taste of Hope's genial humor. "We're so close to the enemy that when you send out your laundry, it comes back with a fortune cookie," the comedian joked at a stop in Korea. Other parts of Kupcinet's commentary showed their age thirty years later. "Bob has another knack, which the GIs appreciate," he wrote. "He has the good taste to include some livin' dolls in his troupe. . . . If there's anything a GI stationed in a distant outpost likes, next to Bob Hope, it's a luscious doll to gaze at. There's nothing like a dame to bring out the tiger in our Yanks."

When the Hope project was finished in the early fall of 1965, it was set to come out on the Argo imprint. But LaPalm had an idea: why not kick off the Cadet line with this unusual offering, even if it would mean doing the jackets all over again? Leonard thought about it for a few minutes, and then told LaPalm, "Go ahead." *Bob Hope: The Road to Vietnam* sold very well, and LaPalm was always amused when people stopped him to say, "I didn't know Bob Hope was part of Chess Records."

◀◀

One of the few things that did not turn out the way Leonard wanted was the effort he and Phil made to buy a radio station in Camden, New Jersey, WCAM. It had been owned by the city for thirty-nine years, and since the early sixties, rock-and-roll music was banned in favor of programming geared to families and public service. The city was anxious to sell its holdings and reap the financial benefit. Local officials and the Chess brothers agreed on a purchase price—$1.4 million paid out over three years—and Leonard and Phil planned to change the format to resemble WVON, broadcasting to the area's black communities, particularly the large market of nearby Philadelphia. The sale was announced in the newspapers early in January 1966 pending FCC approval.

When he learned of the Chess brothers' plans, Max Leon, the owner of WDAS in Philadelphia, was more than unhappy. Like Leonard and Phil, Leon was a white man who pitched his station to the city's black audience.

He filed a petition with the FCC in opposition to the sale contending that he would suffer "direct, substantial, and drastically increased economic injury" if the sale went through. He argued that the commission should not approve the sale without first holding a hearing on the L&P Broadcasting application. On July 29, 1966, the commission agreed with Leon and ordered a hearing to be held on several issues. Under the terms of the contract, the city of Camden had the right to terminate the deal with Leonard and Phil if the sale could not be completed in a timely manner. They exercised that option shortly after the commission's decision. It was a major disappointment for the brothers.

Back in Chicago, VON was running smoothly, even though the FCC had thrown a wrench into operations. Early in 1965 the agency issued new regulations essentially barring an AM station from simulcasting all of its programming on its FM affiliate. That meant that L&P Broadcasting would have to come up with a new format for WHFC. First the call letters were changed to WSDM—"smack dab in the middle"—where the station was on the spectrum, at 97.9. Then Leonard and Phil recruited their old friend, Mickey Shorr, the former Detroit disc jockey to revamp the FM operation. Leonard told Shorr he had a man in mind to handle the music programming, Burt Burdeen, who hosted a jazz show on another station and had also done liner notes on some Argo albums and production work on a few others.

One spring morning in 1965 Burdeen was awakened by a phone call about 7:30. "Why are you still sleeping, you SOB?" Leonard growled. He told Burdeen he wanted to meet with him later in the day and took him over to meet Shorr. Leonard didn't tell Shorr he had to hire Burdeen, but he wanted him to consider the young man. Burdeen got the job after he made a demo tape that showed what he could do.

Shorr had some intriguing ideas about how to make WSDM stand out. He volunteered them to a young reporter, Linda Smith, who was interviewing station operators about the impact of the FCC ruling for *Sales and Marketing,* a small magazine known as "SAM."

When Smith asked the obvious, "What are you going to do?" Shorr said the programming would be "pop-oriented jazz or jazz-oriented pop." The music would be pitched to "reach everyone too old for the Rolling Stones and too young for Lawrence Welk." That was only half of it. "We're going to use female voices," Shorr explained. Hugh Hefner had made thousands and thousands of dollars exploiting women's bodies, he told her. WSDM was going to use their voices. They wouldn't use their real names; they would be given on-air nicknames, easy to say and seductive. WHER in Memphis had used all female announcers since 1955, and it had worked to good effect.

By the way, Shorr wondered, had anyone told Smith her voice sounded like "someone who walked barefoot through a gravel pit." Before Smith could answer, not knowing if it was a compliment or a criticism, Shorr offered her a job.

"How much are you paying?" she asked.

"Sixty-four dollars and fifty cents a week." It was more than Smith was making at SAM, so she accepted. Once the programming got up and running, Smith debuted on the air as "Hush Puppy," giving the station's new salute as breathlessly as barefoot-in-gravel would allow: "WSDM, Chicago—the station with the girls and all that jazz."

Shorr named his female jockeys and announcers "Den Pals." It was his takeoff on Hefner's playmates. They were white and black women; all were under twenty-four years of age, Shorr's arbitrary cutoff. It didn't take long for the local newspapers to pick up on his gambit. Six weeks after WSDM debuted, the *Chicago American* noted in a feature with four pictures that "Curvey, cute 'Den Pals' (not disc jockeys) give new station an off-beat format." By the end of 1965 the station was generating its own ad revenue, and within a year it had risen high enough in the ratings that Leonard gave serious consideration to syndicating the format. The idea never panned out although the station had developed a following in neighboring cities in Illinois, Indiana, and Wisconsin.

WVON and WSDM shared the same quarters on South Kedzie, and although they were separate operations aimed at different audiences, the "Den Pals" came to understand what an important part of the black community WVON had become. Chicago was a city with its share of racial tensions, and when violence erupted after one racially charged incident, friends cautioned Smith, who was white, against going to work because she would have to travel through the black South Side. She waved off their concerns, announcing that this was her job and she intended to go. Smith was convinced that she and other white colleagues would be all right because they worked for VON. "Purely because they [black Chicagoans] knew we worked there, we were given sort of a free pass," she said.

Smith stayed at SDM for nearly three years, one of many young women who got their first chance to learn about broadcasting—running a sound board, editing copy, managing a program—through the station. Some of them parlayed that experience into great success. Smith became well known to millions across the country as Linda Ellerbee, the award-winning television reporter and producer.

"Leonard in essence through Mickey gave me my first job in broadcasting," she said many years later. "I might have never thought about broadcasting without Leonard and Phil Chess." Were the women exploited? Maybe, Ellerbee conceded. After all, Shorr frankly told her, "women will work very cheap." "But at least they hired women," Ellerbee said, "which was more than other stations did. I will never forget that." Nor would she forget the time she became pregnant, and not knowing where else to turn, asked Leonard for $600 to pay for an abortion. He gave her the money, though he tore into her for behavior he thought was reckless. She left his office feeling ashamed and in tears, but she reminded herself that he had provided the money without hesitation and he didn't fire her.

Leonard learned about the radio business the same way he had learned about publishing, relying in the beginning on experienced associates and then coupling their knowledge with his common sense. Phil was his private sounding board. Arc and Chevis were constant sources of income now, so both brothers were receptive to a proposal Allen Arrow, their lawyer in New York, made to them and the Goodmans about how to structure a $200,000 loan that Vee Jay Records had asked for. The company was struggling through much of 1965, tangled in litigation over its efforts to put out Beatles records in the United States. A move to California and an effort to diversify its music had not worked out as well as executives hoped. The company returned to Chicago in the fall hoping to recoup. In the meantime the principals knew they needed some extra cash and asked Leonard and Phil for the money. In consultation with Arrow, they came up with a deal to give Vee Jay the loan with Conrad, its publishing company, as collateral. The loan was actually made in the name of Arc Music. Neither the Chess brothers nor the Goodmans thought Vee Jay was going to survive, and their prediction proved to be accurate. When the company defaulted on the loan, Conrad Music and two affiliated subsidiaries became a part of Arc. Among the songs were several written by the estimable bluesmen Jimmy Reed and John Lee Hooker, and the soul singer Jerry Butler.

It seemed at the end of 1965 that nothing could go wrong. On the music front Cash Box's top fifty R&B listing showed five company records. Financially, it was the best year in the corporation's history. LaPalm and Cooperstein had little trouble convincing Leonard and Phil to host a meeting for Chess, Checker, and Cadet distributors in Puerto Rico, January 14–16. In the plush surroundings of the Americana Hotel, the meeting was intended as an opportunity to take orders for the new year's merchandise, boost morale, and give the company another dose of publicity. When the three-day session was over, Leonard announced that one million dollars worth of orders for albums were placed, the most ever. Not mentioned, however, was the right of distributors to return most of their unsold merchandise. So while one million dollars' worth of orders was a good benchmark, there was no guarantee the orders would result in one million dollars' worth of revenue. Still, the announcement generated coverage in the most important outlets, *Billboard* and *Cash Box*, and it was successful enough that the event would be repeated the next year, this time with a custommade brochure, "Sand, Sun & Sales," that included a promotional pitch from LaPalm, glossy descriptions of the new records, and various discount options for the distributors.

Though it had yet to reach its full potential, the Chess international operation was beginning to bear fruit, and some of the distributors who came to Puerto Rico had traveled from Europe to attend. Their presence was in large part the result of Marshall's efforts. He had found his niche: building up the Chess presence in Europe and even Japan through contacts he had made on his first trip with Harry Goodman. (He was also getting experience on the editorial front, writing the liner notes as "Marshall Paul" on two new Chuck Berry albums.) Whatever money came in from overseas sales was gravy; Leonard and Phil hadn't put much effort into exploiting the potential. The opportunity was a perfect fit for Marshall. He loved to travel. He had gone to Cuba when he was sixteen, and he loved European culture—sipping espresso on the Left Bank in Paris, buying clothes at fashionable London stores, sharing the company of European women. He also wanted to show his father he could make money. Though it wasn't the singular motivating factor for developing the European market, he was determined to get Leonard's approval, even if he might never hear the words "good job." Both would know he had succeeded when the sales receipts came in, and he could show his father the bottom line. This was language Leonard understood, and acknowledged by his father or not, the son would know he had passed a test.

Marshall's first endeavor did not go well. He had to negotiate a new deal with Louis Benjamin, the head of Pye Records, for the release of Chess material under the Chess imprint but still through Pye. The day after the papers were signed Marshall realized he had made a bad deal. The terms he negotiated left almost no profit for Chess, Checker, or Cadet after the artists were paid their royalties. "I figured wrong," he told himself. Even though Benjamin offered to redo the deal out of respect for Leonard and affection for his son, Marshall refused. He would live with the terms for the life of the contract as a reminder never to make the same mistake again.

In honor of the company's expanded presence in England, Benjamin threw a party for Marshall and the musicians he brought with him: A&R director Davis, Jackie Ross, Buddy Guy, and Johnny Nash, another singer on the label, each of whom had popular records out.

The deal in England was just the beginning. Over the next several months, Marshall returned to Europe to set up special distribution arrangements with companies in France, Holland, Germany, Italy, and a company called Sonet that covered Scandinavia. When Harry Goodman introduced Marshall to Sonet in the spring of 1964, he had already done his homework and had suggested to his father and uncle that they handle the company lines. He even had brought a tape of Berry's "Nadine" as a musical hors d'oeuvre for what would follow. The owners were so excited that they rushed right into their recording studio to listen.

The German deal with Deutsche Grammophon was a natural. The company already had shown an interest in blues, sponsoring the American folk festivals on the continent that had featured some of the Chess and Checker men. Marshall was convinced they would do better for the label than a company Arrow had selected whose sales had been below expectations. Marshall attributed the meager revenue to the lack of the Chess product in the stores and little airplay on important radio stations. After all, records had to be seen and heard to sell.

The deals with the European affiliates followed a basic scenario: master tapes were shipped to the various companies; they pressed the records, and then film and negatives were sent for covers and label copy, with the logo of the overseas affiliate stripped into the final copies. The deals also allowed for repackaging material released in the United States to appeal to the foreign markets. In some cases prices were slashed to make a Chess purchase more attractive to a new teenage market not yet familiar with the music. There were also a few export arrangements that involved sending the original Chess products overseas to be sold.

Marshall's climb up the learning curve was most evident when he went to Japan with Arrow for introductions into that country's music industry. Arrow had already negotiated one licensing agreement, but it was time to review the contract, which was with a subsidiary of Victor called Cosdel. Marshall thought it was a good strategy to let Cosdel know he was looking for other possibilities, so he solicited an offer from a company called Nippon Columbia. His Japanese counterparts thought they had reached an agreement and came to Marshall's hotel room to seal the deal before going to dinner. Marshall told them he needed to think about it, throwing a wrench into the negotiations and local custom. According to Japanese tradition, Arrow told him, there is no dinner unless the deal is completed. When the Japanese businessmen realized the agreement wasn't firm, they canceled dinner and the deal. Marshall went back to lock things in with Cosdel, as he had originally planned, but with slightly better terms because of his brief flirtation with the other company.

With the labels' increased presence in Europe, it was important to get the artists overseas while their records were popular. Marshall took Fontella Bass to England to promote "Rescue Me," where she appeared on the popular television show *Ready, Steady, Go*. On a subsequent trip he pushed the Ramsey Lewis trio, hoping to capitalize on their popularity in America. On these trips, which Marshall took every three or four months, he was decidedly not his father's son—or his uncle's—when it came to picking accommodations. "Why didn't you stay at the YMCA?" was Phil's reaction when Esmond Edwards had presented him with a modest hotel bill for an out-of-town session. Marshall would have none of that. He liked to travel in style, and he stayed at the best: the Intercontinental in London, the very posh George V in Paris. The decision was made easier by the fact that the American dollar was so strong and made prices seem modest.

Within a year Marshall saw the results of his efforts. Revenues from the foreign sales were $150,000 ($790,000 in 1999 dollars), many times more than any previous year. He kept separate books for the foreign accounts, not only to keep a tally for himself but to make a case for a bonus. "It was my way of saying 'I want a piece of it,' " he explained. "It was how I played my father. The last thing he would do," Marshall added, "was say 'You did a great job.' "

∿

Shifting musical tastes continued to mean a decline in blues sales despite the repackaging of Muddy Waters, Howlin' Wolf, and others on the roster as folk musicians and an intensive advertising effort by LaPalm. In addition to the regular ads in the trade magazines, he also sent out one-page fact sheets to distributors with peppy descriptions of the products and attractive displays of the album covers. Their liner notes aimed for authenticity. Several were signed by Willie Dixon, and though the content reflected his views on the subject, the actual prose was likely penned by a ghostwriter. Ralph

Bass lent his hand to a few. It was a testament either to working lunches or to the continued informal way of doing business—perhaps both—that the sequence of songs for the Waters *Real Folk Blues* album was sketched out on the back of a Batts menu.

The blues series were not blockbuster sellers but found a steady audience, enough so that a few more albums would be put together under the rubric of "more real folk blues." Regardless of the bottom line, however, blues music was always going to be a part of Chess as long as Leonard and Phil were around. Dixon was keeping busy as an independent producer for the company with a free hand to do what he wanted. There was still plenty of good and exciting blues in the clubs around town, some of it coming from unknown talents who were just having a good time in the evening after work. Cora Taylor—known to friends as Koko—had been in Chicago since 1953, coming north from Memphis with the man who would soon be her husband, Robert "Pops" Taylor. During the day she cleaned houses in the affluent neighborhoods on the city's North Side; at night she and her husband visited the clubs, where Taylor sometimes sat in with the city's legends: Waters, Howlin' Wolf, Jimmy Reed. Her big voice never failed to impress, and finally Big Bill Hill, the deejay at WOPA, introduced her to Dixon. He signed her to a management and production contract, and her first record under Dixon's tutelage came out in 1962 on a small label, the result of an informal jam in Dixon's basement.

The record was a surprise to Taylor, who hadn't known her mentor was even going to issue it. She learned about it when he gave her a $25 royalty check. "Not only was I young, but I was very inexperienced," she said. "I had never recorded for anyone else before." She put herself in Dixon's hands: "Willie Dixon negotiated how the songs would go, arranged the music, and selected musicans. My job was to sing, and that's what I did, no more no less."

Dixon took Taylor to the Chess studio in the summer of 1964 and then again in January 1965. She made two records—and an impression on Leonard. He complimented Taylor on her big voice, and although he didn't say much more, that was enough. She was happy to be in the building. "When they agreed to record me," she remembered years later, "they made me feel like I was sittin' on this pedestal."

Dixon called another session for December 7, 1965. Three songs were scheduled, "Blues Heaven," "I Got All You Need," and "Wang Dang Doodle," a song Dixon had written a few years earlier and given to Howlin' Wolf. It was an adaptation of an old lesbian song, "The Bull Daggers Ball," which was a humorous catalogue of the raffish characters who frequented the event.

Even though Dixon cleaned up some of the language in "Wang Dang Doodle"—"Fast Fuckin' Fannie" became "Fast Talkin' Fannie"—his list of who's "gonna pitch a wang dang doodle" was plenty colorful in its own right: "Tell Automatic Slim, tell Razor Totin' Jim, tell Butcher Knife Totin' Nanny, tell Fast Talkin' Fannie, we're gonna pitch a ball, down to that union hall. . . ."

Dixon surrounded Taylor with the veteran blues musicians on the Chess roster: Fred Below on drums, Buddy Guy on guitar, Lafayette Leake on the keybord, and added Gene Barge and Donald Hankins on the saxophone and Jack Myers on the bass. (Each of them made the union scale of $61 for the two-hour-and-fifty-minute session; Dixon pocketed $122 for running it.) The musicians spent most of the time on "Blues Heaven" and "I Got All You Need." Guy thought "Wang Dang Doodle" was almost a throwaway. They put it together in a couple of takes, but a few weeks after it was released in the spring of 1966, "Wang Dang Doodle" was on the *Billboard* and *Cash Box* R&B charts, ending a two-month dry spell for the company, whose last chart hit had been Ramsey Lewis's "Hard Day's Night."

"Wang Dang Doodle" became Taylor's signature song, still a crowd pleaser three decades after it was released. Taylor didn't know how many copies of "Wang Dang Doodle" sold; she accepted what payout Leonard and Phil gave her and professed to be satisfied. "I did not make a million dollars. I did not make fifty million, I did not make twenty-five million," she said. "But I got a hit record, and that title's been carrying me over the road all of these years."

Taylor's major disagreement with the Chess brothers was not over money but over aesthetics. When they released her first album two and a half years later, she was upset that the cover was a mottled graphic of her face, not a photograph like most album covers were. Leonard Diamond, Leonard's nephew (and called "Lennie") who now worked for the company, swung between shock and stifled laughter as he listened to Taylor and his uncle battle over the art department's concept for the cover. "Why isn't my picture on this?" Taylor demanded.

"Are you trying to kill your career?" Leonard shot back, partially in jest, a reference to Taylor's down-home appearance. Despite her disappointment, he refused to yield. The album came out the way Leonard wanted.

Billy Davis loved the collaborative process—writer, musician, arranger, and singer contributing together to make the whole. Billy Stewart was at ease with the studio setup now, and Phil Wright, the arranger, felt he had a special understanding with the singer. Maurice White, the drummer, got a kick out of the times Stewart would stand in the middle of a circle of musicians, directing them as though he were the conductor. Nobody seemed to mind because they all respected his talent.

Stewart liked to adapt the standards to his own stutter-style vocals, and Wright was more than happy to work up arrangements for such tunes as "Over the Rainbow," "Foggy Day," and "Summertime." What Stewart had in mind for the latter was a far cry from the haunting, elegant presentation of Leontyne Price. This would be a full-bodied, up-tempo treatment of the Gershwin classic with Stewart backed by seventeen musicians. By this time, Leonard scarcely flinched to see a small orchestra in the studio.

Wright wrote the horn parts, hired the extra musicians and ran the rehearsals. Davis stitched the final production together. The song, which was part of Stewart's *Unbelievable* album, took off immediately when it was released in the summer as a single. By September 3, 1966 the record had risen to number eight on the *Cash Box* Top One Hundred and to number ten on the *Billboard* tally. The disk was doing so well that the company decided to retitle the album, itself a bestseller, *Summertime* and repackage the LP to emphasize the hit.

The free-for-all collaborative spirit was evident on another song that had been recorded in April, the result of Davis's intuition to pair the energetic contraltos Etta James and Sugar Pie DeSanto. They had known each other since they were teenagers in California, and their voices and styles were similar. Davis got them together in the small rehearsal studio on the second floor with Miner and Smith and a few musicians "to get something that's down and raunchy." Out of the on-the-spot collaboration came "In the Basement," a high-spirited romp about having an impromptu party where "there's no cover charge or fee and the food and drink are free." "The music sort of took over—and the energy," Davis said. The record made the charts for a few weeks after it was released early in the summer, though the "down and raunchy" that Davis wanted made it more popular with R&B listeners than the audience used to more mainstream music.

The eighteen months between the beginning of 1965 and the summer of 1966 had been an unbelievable ride for the Chess enterprise. Every division was performing well, and so was the radio station. But Leonard was restless. He told Phil it was time to think about expanding, time to take another gamble in the hope of a big payoff.

eighteen

320 EAST 21ST STREET

Record company, radio station, pressing plant, writers, producers, a house band, ad men, salesmen, promotion men—Leonard and Phil had all of it now. Twenty-one-twenty South Michigan was bursting at the seams by the spring of 1966. It was time to move and time, in Leonard's mind, to do it in a big way. Why not have everything in one place and make Chess a one-stop operation: write the music, record it, press the record, pack it, and ship it out of the same building?

The brothers' old friend from Memphis, Buster Williams, first owned jukeboxes, then became a distributor, and then pressed the records he distributed. Leonard and Phil would go Williams at least one better—musical concept to shipping carton under one roof. The more Leonard talked it over with Phil and Marshall the more he liked the idea.

The key thing was finding the right space. Enlisting the services of the Arthur Rubloff Company, they found an eight-story building at 320 East Twenty-first Street that was for sale. It was owned by the 3M company but had an interesting history. The building was constructed between 1920 and 1921 for Columbian Colortype Company, which made banknotes, stock certificates, and the like. The upper floors were rented to a variety of printing and publishing companies. Revere Tape Recorder eventually took over the building, and by the sixties it was owned by 3M, which had bought out Revere.

Leonard thought the price for 172,000 square feet—$425,000—made it a great buy. It would be more than seven times the size of the 24,000 total square feet at 2120 South Michigan, and just a few blocks east, it would still be close enough to Michigan Avenue and close enough to the old studio to be part of the Record Row ambiance. In the early days, after Leonard bought out Evelyn Aron, Aristocrat Records was just the two brothers, Sonny Woods, and Carri Saunders. Now there were two hundred people involved in the Chess operation.

Space and location were only two of the attributes of the new building. It was well kept up, had a loading dock, plenty of parking, and enough power lines coming in to handle the demands of Leonard's plan. There was one unusual extra: previous owners had outfitted the penthouse with a barber-shop, sauna, and facilities for massages and showers. The major expense would be building the recording studios with state-of-the-art equipment and building the pressing plant. James Gann was still running that operation, which had grown considerably. In 1962 Leonard had moved it out of 4750 South Cottage Grove to much larger quarters on Wentworth Avenue. The ownership structure was also revamped—Gann had stock now, so did the Chesses' friend Russ Fratto. He sold some of his shares to Stan Lewis, whose record business in Shreveport was thriving. The company was now called Midwest Pressing, and it had a branch in Nashville, Midsouth Pressing. Gann would oversee the installation of equipment in the new building.

The Chess brothers' purchase was announced in July 1966; the first part of the move took place in September. *Chess* in sedate silver letters, brought over from 2120 South Michigan, ran vertically on the left side of the door. A big sign for WVON was put on the top of the building, affixed to a thin metal frame not visible from the ground. When the sign, which also had lit-tle musical notes on it, was lit up, it appeared to be floating in the air.

Leonard envisioned the "recording center of the Midwest" on Twenty-first Street, and he was willing to pay a hefty price—$1.5 million—to make it happen. Almost half of the amount, $600,000, was for the pressing plant. The budget for the main studio and three smaller ones was $150,000. The sound mixer, at $35,000, was coming from Germany. Leonard and Phil even recruited engineers from the Illinois Institute of Technology to help them with the design.

After the initial move in September, everyone shuttled between the two places while the construction was completed about nine months later, in the late spring of 1967.

Leonard, Phil, Marshall, Max Cooperstein, Dick LaPalm, and Richie Salvador, a rising sales-promotion man who was another recruit from David Rosen's distributorship in Philadelphia, were on the first floor. The warehouse and stockroom were on the second floor. The pressing plant and attendant machinery took up the third, fourth, and fifth floors. On the sixth and seventh floors were the studios and the offices for the music production staff. Billy Davis and Esmond Edwards had their own wood-paneled offices and shared a private secretary. Their writers and arrangers also had their own offices. The eighth floor was the commissary, with coffee and soft drink machines and packaged foods that could be heated up. The barbershop-sauna that came with the building remained in the penthouse, though there was no staff to run it.

Gone was the bustling immediacy of Michigan Avenue. Nobody knew what kind of personality the company would have in these more chic surroundings. Chess may have been a corporation for many years, but it was never "corporate." The separation of executives from the creative end, however, was bound to work a change. So was the dynamic in the new studio. It was at least twice as large as the space at 2120 South Michigan. For anyone doing a session with strings, horns, singers and such, the extra room was a boon. Edwards loved it. But Davis worried about something being lost in the transition—that ephemeral energy that came from everyone working together in such close quarters. Davis was glad to have a new office, glad the company was prospering, but he didn't feel at home the first time he walked into the new studio, and he never got used to it. "It had a totally different sound," Davis said. The much larger open area required different placement of musicians and the use of "baffles"—essentially movable soundproofing walls—for a better blend of the instruments.

Davis was among the first to recognize a major problem with the all-in-one concept. During one of the first sessions he detected a mysterious low rumbling sound. He couldn't figure out what it was or where it was coming from. The drummer wasn't playing. There was no construction on the street seven floors below. There was no train line that ran by the building. Then he realized the problem: the noise from the hydraulic system for the pressing plant was traveling right up the elevator shaft into the studio. Even the best soundproofing couldn't keep it out.

There was no good solution to the problem. Gann told Leonard a stark truth: "We made a big mistake. We should never have moved in there." The answer was not to record while the presses were running. The dilemma required rescheduling both operations to get the music made and the product out the door.

Pressing was an important economic element of the new building. At peak capacity, twenty-four singles presses could churn out 125,000 singles in an eight-hour shift. If the presses could run around the clock, the number would triple. Sixteen LP presses could produce 16,000 albums a day. The plant wasn't only for Chess products. They accounted for about 40 percent of the operation, and the company still had some products pressed at plants in other parts of the country. The rest of the business on East Twenty-first Street came from other labels.

The glitch with the pressing plant noise did not obscure the overall success of the move, however. It was not only a statement about the company's growth but also a factor, like the radio enterprise, that kept Leonard engaged in the business. He loved the competition almost for its own sake. When Lennie Diamond, his nephew, visited Leonard in the hospital after one of his episodes of heart trouble, Diamond wondered why his uncle kept pushing himself. "You know this is going to kill you. Why don't you just retire?" Diamond asked. "You probably have got more money than you could spend."

"You don't understand," Leonard replied. "It's not the money. It's the game."

Vince Pepper, the brothers' radio station lawyer, saw Leonard's competitive streak firsthand in a most unlikely setting, on vacation in the Bahamas. He and Leonard and Phil and their wives had gone into a jewelry store conveniently located next to the casino so that winners didn't have to go far to spend their earnings on a fancy bauble or two. Phil saw a watch he liked, and the shop owner told him a price. Phil was ready to pay when Leonard stepped in. No, no, no, he told him. You have to bargain. I'll show you. Leonard started by telling the owner he would pay cash. How much lower would that make the price? Told the new amount, Leonard made a new offer. Let's assume that in addition to the watch we want that ring, and he motioned to one that Pepper's wife liked—a profusion of small diamonds, emeralds, and rubies, just short of garish but perfect for the casino life. After hearing the revised amount, Leonard still wasn't finished. He decided to throw in a pin for his wife and then one or two other pieces. He ended up getting the watch for half the original amount, but he spent more than a thousand dollars doing it. "He could have just paid a hundred bucks for the watch and saved another thousand," Pepper recalled, but he knew that Leonard didn't see it that way. "In his mind, he won." The shopkeeper was so ecstatic that after the Chess party left, he closed the store and took the rest of the day off.

Leonard's competitive streak extended to card games, even when he was playing with his young nephew. Phil's son Terry occasionally accompanied

Leonard on business trips for the radio stations. Leonard loved to play gin rummy regardless of the hour. On one late-night plane flight back to Chicago, Terry only wanted to sleep but Leonard kept poking him in the arm. "Let's play," he said. When Terry protested that Leonard would win, he insisted anyway.

"You know you really stink at gin," Leonard said after winning the third or fourth hand.

⋙

Despite the continuing success of the Chess operation, there were always cautionary tales in the industry to remind an executive that things could get worse. There were likewise examples of somebody who was doing better. As the renovation of 320 East Twenty-first Street was under way, Leonard and Phil witnessed the final, sobering collapse of their onetime competitor Vee Jay. On February 24, 1967, five thousand Vee Jay master tapes were auctioned off before a federal district court official as part of the company's bankruptcy proceedings. The Chess brothers could take heart from the fact that they had managed their own expansion and diversification more profitably. But their friends the Ertegun brothers and Jerry Wexler over at Atlantic were demonstrating that a small independent company could become even larger and more successful than Chess. In June of 1967, when the move into the new Chess studio was nearly completed, Atlantic set a record with the number of singles it placed on the *Billboard* Hot One Hundred—eighteen, including numbers one and two, Aretha Franklin singing "Respect" followed by the Young Rascals and "Groovin'."

Atlantic had diverse artists—soul singers Franklin, Wilson Pickett, and Percy Sledge, pop groups like Sonny and Cher and the Bee Gees—and diverse places to record. Some sessions were in Memphis, using the studio and personnel at the Stax label; some were in Muscle Shoals, Alabama, a hamlet in the northwest corner of the state where Franklin had been particularly successful. The Fame studio, under the direction of Rick Hall, was building a reputation for an innovative, popular sound with musicians Wexler described as "Alabama white boys who took a left turn at the blues."

"I was hot and happening," Hall said. "Leonard was terribly envious of my relationship with the 'New York Jews,' as he called them"—a reference to Wexler.

It was a combination of conversations with Leonard by phone and Max Cooperstein in person, when he traveled through Alabama on his road trips, that got the ball rolling. The deal wasn't jelling long-distance, so Cooperstein told Hall he should come to Chicago to meet with Leonard and Phil and some of the staff. At a later meeting among the brothers, Marshall, Cooperstein, and Billy Davis, they reached an agreement: Hall would get $100 an hour for studio time and producing the music, and then 4 percent of 100 percent of the retail price on any records sold from the Muscle Shoals sessions. It marked a significant change in the way the studio had done business in the last five years. Instead of finding talent and bringing the artists to record under Billy Davis or Esmond Edwards, now they were going to send Chess performers to Alabama to record.

It wasn't as though the studio was in a barren period—Little Milton, Bo Diddley, Billy Stewart, and Etta James all had songs on the charts. But there was the feeling that a jolt of creative energy was needed, even though the annual winter meeting, again in Puerto Rico, produced $2 million worth of orders. On the other hand Chuck Berry left the label for Mercury and a deal he couldn't pass up. He told *Rolling Stone* the label had given him $150,000 on a three-year contract. Leonard didn't put up a fight, but he was sure Berry would be back. "Go, and I'll see you in three years," he told him. (Berry did return as soon as his contract expired.)

Davis wasn't very keen on the Muscle Shoals idea. It cut into his domain, but he couldn't deny that the studio was successful. He didn't feel great about the new plan, he told Leonard, but he understood.

One of the first Chess artists to go down to Muscle Shoals was Laura Lee, who had just signed with the label. Like so many other singers, Lee's roots were in the church and gospel music, but in 1965 she switched to the secular, recording for the Ric-Tic label in Detroit, her hometown. When she came to Chicago, she first worked with Davis and Leonard Caston. Bobby Miller, one of Davis's producers, had even written a song for her, "Dirty Man," about the troubles she was having with her boyfriend. But Lee and the Chess team couldn't get the song to click. Hall didn't think much of the song either and told Leonard. But he was insistent so Hall and the musicians gave it a try.

It made all the difference. Even though they used the same musical elements that Davis did—guitar, bass, drums, organ, and horns—Hall put them together in a spare but effective way that brought out the best in Lee's dark vocals: In a deliberate cadence she sings about a "dirty dirty man" with a dirty mind, who cheated on her. But he forgot one thing: she's a good housekeeper who will "sweep all of the dirt, yessir, out in the street."

"Dirty Man" gave the company its first taste of success with the Muscle Shoals studio, rising high on the *Billboard* and *Cash Box* charts. A second Muscle Shoals production, "Uptight Good Man," also made the charts at the end of the year, though it didn't do quite as well as "Dirty Man."

At the same time the company signed Irma Thomas from New Orleans, another soul singer with a deep, smokey voice and an engaging stage presence. Three of her songs from the Alabama sessions were released, though only one, "Good to Me," was a major success despite her appealing vocals and the solid arrangements behind her.

What Leonard really wanted was to team the Muscle Shoals men with his favorite female singer, James. He cared enough that he flew down to Alabama with her to record on August 23 and 24, 1967. Their arrival was quite a sight—James, her boyfriend, a trunk full of furs and fancy dresses not at all appropriate for the 100 degree weather, and two French poodles. "You never saw such an entourage of crap," Hall joked. "We had a big time."

James's recordings were among the best she had done in the last few years. The first release paired two classics—"Tell Mama" backed with "I'd Rather Go Blind," a song she cowrote with Ellington Jordan, a friend who was serving time in prison. But because James was having tax problems, she put her boyfriend's name down as the writer along with Jordan. The song, with its dramatic wish to go blind rather than "see you walk away," became a staple of James's live performances for years to come. James remembered that it moved Leonard to tears the first time he heard it.

"Tell Mama" featured snappy horns that propelled the melody forward and complemented James's lusty vocals, inviting a former boyfriend to come back and "tell mama" and "I'll make everything all right." It was the song Leonard wanted her to do, and it was a big hit—number ten on *Billboard*'s R&B chart, number twenty-three on the pop chart, a similarly good rating in *Cash Box*. It was also the title track of another album, which turned out to be her most popular to date. A third notable song came out of James's December 6, 1967, session, her version of Otis Redding's "Security." It outsold the original. The Chess–Muscle Shoals relationship would eventually wind to an amicable halt, but no one could deny that the experiment had been worth it.

For his part, Hall learned a valuable lesson from Leonard about what a producer should do. When he told Leonard that he didn't have any songs he was excited about for another Chess act, Leonard chided him. "I thought that's what a producer's job was, finding the songs." "No one had ever put it to me that way," Hall said later. "I thought he was right. Leonard talked like that: 'Get off your ass and find the damn song.' "

※

The top personnel at the record company had been stable for some time, but it was inevitable that there would be changes. After five years running the jazz side, Esmond Edwards left in late August 1967 to join Verve Records. He was replaced quickly by one of his favorite arrangers on the staff, Richard Evans, who had done work for Ramsey Lewis and filled in on Ahmad Jamal sessions after Edwards and Jamal had a testy disagreement in the early sixties. Most important, Evans had put the musical flesh on the bare bones of an intriguing Edwards concept, "soulful strings"—cellos combined with flutes, oboes, vibraphones, conga drums, and a conventional rhythm section to record R&B music, pop standards, and original material.

Edwards wanted to break away from the traditional use of violins. He had nothing against the instrument, though he occasionally found the sound of violin arrangements "high and tinny." The sound that came from a cello, "low pitched and earthy," would be much more interesting, the string version of a saxophone. Edwards was confident Evans could write the parts that would bring his ideas to life. One of the things he liked about working with the arranger was Evans's willingness to stick to the original concept and not substitute his own. Not much had changed since Riley Hampton had brought in strings seven years earlier for Etta James: they were white; the rhythm section was black.

Edwards was momentarily taken aback at Leonard's initial reaction to the Soulful Strings' first album, *Paint It Black,* which included a version of the Rolling Stones song of the same title with cellos and conga drums. It didn't sound anything like Mick Jagger. "What is this shit?" Leonard asked, his customary expression for music he didn't understand, at least at first blush. The irritation at what might be a waste of money on a foolish exercise was obvious. But he released the album, and then shared in the good times when it went on the *Billboard* charts for nearly four months, albeit near the bottom. Edwards didn't worry about Leonard's grumbling. He had groused before at some of Edwards's ideas, but he had never vetoed anything his jazz A&R man wanted to do.

Paint It Black sold well enough for Leonard to approve a second album,

Groovin' with the Soulful Strings. According to *Billboard*'s tally, *Groovin' with the Soulful Strings* proved to be one of the most successful albums on the Chess roster. It registered on the top LP listing for thirty-four weeks, from November 1967 through the summer of 1968, rising to number fifty-nine out of two hundred. Only Ahmad Jamal's first album on Argo, *But Not for Me*, and two Ramsey Lewis albums had done better.

Paint It Black included what turned out to be a hit single, an Evans composition called "Burning Spear" that was written in honor of Kenyan independence. It scored well on both the *Billboard* and *Cash Box* charts, showing up on their listings for more than a month early in 1968. It amused Evans that a song to mark an important event in an African country was being recorded almost exclusively by white musicians because the bass player who was black, didn't show up. A versatile white guitar player had to fill in.

Evans did not expect to succeed Edwards as the Cadet A&R man, but he got a call late in August asking him to come to Twenty-first Street to meet with Leonard and Phil. Joe Segal, who was still active in the city's jazz circles, told Evans he thought he would be offered the A&R job. If he didn't want it, Segal told him, he did.

When Evans walked into the meeting room, the senior people were sitting around the table: Leonard, Phil, Marshall, Cooperstein, and LaPalm. Evans decided ahead of time that he would insist on a good salary if he was going to take the job, and it would have to be better than the $16,000 he had made the previous year arranging.

"How's $35,000?" Leonard asked. Evans accepted on the spot, barely able to believe what he heard.

Over the next two years Evans produced and arranged three other Soulful Strings albums that made the charts and an album with Woody Herman that earned a Grammy nomination.

◂▸

Like most self-made men, Leonard had a very personal relationship with his money. He had made it through hard work, tough decisions, and more good choices than bad based on his competitive instincts. He would spend it as he saw fit, and that included the salaries he paid, the bonuses he doled out, the deals he made with artists, and now, because of enough financial success, his own style of philanthropy. He divided most of his energies and money between two arenas: Jewish and black organizations.

Leonard was a member of the Jewish service group B'nai B'rith, and raised money for Israel Bonds and the Combined Jewish Appeal, two organizations that sent privately raised aid to Israel. One fund-raising effort for Israel bonds honored Leonard and Phil's parents, Joe and Celia Chess, at a testimonial dinner at the Sheraton-Chicago hotel. The brothers were on such good terms with *Cash Box* that the magazine wrote about the event.

Leonard's greater involvement, though, seemed to be with the black organizations. He was a member of the Chicago Urban League and the NAACP and a regular contributor to local black churches. In May of 1963, during the civil rights demonstrations in Birmingham, Alabama, Leonard was so upset by the footage of children being knocked down by fire hoses and marched off to jail that he asked Bishop Chester Bailey of the Hyde Park Bible Church, who was a friend of Dr. King's, to come to VON to talk about what he could do to help. When Bailey arrived for their mid-morning meeting, Leonard told him he had hardly slept the night before. He had a $2,000 check for King, he said, but he didn't know how to get it down to him in Birmingham. Bailey told him he would take it, and by 2:00 P.M., Leonard had arranged for Bailey to fly down to Alabama. He told the bishop to tell King there was more money if he needed it.

But while Leonard may have worried about the social justice implications of the protests in Birmingham, the promotion and sales people worried that the unrest would hurt sales. By coincidence Bobby Charles was in Birmingham calling on radio stations there and in surrounding counties that catered to the black community. Aghast at what he saw, he was also afraid for his safety. A white man in a car with Illinois plates at a black radio station, he had already been stopped by the police, who were randomly checking anyone with out-of-state plates. Charles didn't think his Louisiana drawl and his Louisiana driver's license made much difference to Alabama lawmen hostile to outsiders. On the other hand, he was not thrown in jail or otherwise harmed. But he was anxious. He called Chicago—it was probably Cooperstein he spoke to—and told him he was leaving town.

"Work the records," he was told.

"No thank you," Charles said. "You come do it if you want."

Since WVON's first year of operation, the disc jockeys—the self-styled "good guys"—had raised money for Christmas food baskets that were distributed to the city's needy. The funds came from sales of year-end albums of the jockeys' favorite R&B songs from previous years. They drew from

Chess and Checker recordings and those of other participating labels including Roulette and Old Town. By 1967 they raised enough money to cover four thousand food baskets.

In part to honor him, in part to keep raising money for the organization around him, the Chicago Urban League named Leonard its Man of the Year at a February 1967 awards dinner. He was cited for his involvement in the organization's activities and the cash he brought into the League's coffers from his network of friends and associates. His well-thumbed address book—it had a black leather cover but only a handmade plastic name tag glued to the front—was a who's who of the R&B-blues world: artists, lawyers, label owners, distributors. Most had been neatly typed by one of the secretaries but Leonard had made additions and changes in his own bold scrawl to reflect a new connection or a new address for an old acquaintance.

The closest Leonard came to discussing his views about race in public came in a June 1967 article in the *Chicago Daily News*: "Leonard Chess: The Voice Behind WVON." His comments were blunt and to the point. He did not tread lightly. "I made my money on the Negro, and I want to spend it on him," he told reporter Dean Gysel.

"Those who turn to 1450 on the radio will hear a rhythm and blues barrage that is unintelligible to the Mantovani and John Gary fan," Gysel wrote. Leonard agreed. "We program for the lower-to-middle class Negro." He said he was sure that all blacks listened to R&B "although not all will admit it. He likes jazz with the windows open but blues when the windows are closed. I'm a Jew, but I don't like some of the Jewish music my father listened to," he went on. "Some of it I like. It's the same with the Negro. . . . We want a Top 40 format with Negro music, not the Uncle Tom. . . . Stepin Fetchit."

On political matters concerning race, Leonard was a moderate. He supported Dr. King's civil rights activities but he was uneasy about King's growing outspokenness on the escalating war in Vietnam. He did not like Adam Clayton Powell, the fiery congressman from New York, and he had no use for Stokely Carmichael, whose style was much more provocative and abrasive than King's. Each man was mentioned on VON only in straight-ahead newscasts. "Carmichael's a phoney and putting him on the air gives him dignity," Leonard told Gysel. And Powell? "We don't make an editorial judgment of him."

He supported open housing laws, but believed economics was part of the equation: "I'm for it if the Negro can afford it. What happens is that if he can't afford the house, he subdivides it."

The last word in Gysel's article came from an unnamed black newspaperman: "Chess does have many Negroes in his businesses and in positions of authority. He tries to be a nice guy and make money. One thing you can say about him is he's got great business horse sense."

A few weeks after the *Daily News* story was published, the Chess brothers were featured as part of a *Billboard* package on blues music that also profiled the Ertegun brothers and Jerry Wexler at Atlantic and Berry Gordy at Motown. The basics of the story on Leonard and Phil—two Polish immigrant boys grow up to build a successful record company—were accurate, but the story left out important information and some of the key facts were wrong.

The *Billboard* piece may have been the first to foster the misimpression about the Macomba Lounge as a place that drew Ella Fitzgerald and Louis Armstrong. Perhaps Leonard was engaging in some mythmaking about the tiny after-hours club. Aristocrat Records was discussed, but no mention was made of Evelyn Aron, who founded it, or of the fact that Leonard came to work for her on that first Andrew Tibbs record and then was an Aristocrat salesman before becoming her partner and eventually buying her out. The first office of Aristocrat was given as Seventy-first and Phillips, actually the home of the B&H Liquor & Delicatessen, which was run by Leonard's brothers-in-law: Bert Sloan, his wife Revetta's brother, and Harry Silverbrand, his sister Mae's husband. Leonard may have worked there, but if he did, he was making pastrami sandwiches, not records. The first address for Aristocrat was 7508 South Phillips, the painting shop run by Charles Aron, Evelyn's husband.

Perhaps it was the *Billboard* writer who embellished Leonard's story about dangling a microphone in the studio washroom to create an echo chamber: "That was the first echo chamber effect ever used on a record." Most engineers credit the men at Universal Studios with the first such sound effect, done for the Harmonicats a good five or six years before Leonard produced a record.

The misinformation in the *Billboard* story has had a long afterlife. This was one of the few pieces of any length to appear about the Chess brothers and their operation, and the fact that it was in a magazine well regarded among music enthusiasts gave it even greater credibility. The errors that were in the piece were picked up and on occasion embellished in later accounts of the company, creating myths at odds with the facts. The article, like a shorter story on the company in an October 1964 *Record World*, performed a disservice by ignoring the important role of Evelyn Aron and fostering the misimpression that Leonard and Phil started Aristocrat Records.

♦♦

Marshall had come a long way since chauffeuring his father around Chicago and standing a few paces away while he watched how Leonard operated. The European deals Marshall set up were a continuing source of profit, but now he wanted to insert himself more directly into the music. He felt it was an appropriate time. Although Chess, Checker, and Cadet singles and LPs had registered on the charts during 1967, only one single, Little Milton's "Feel So Bad," and one album, Ramsey Lewis's *The Movie Album*, did well enough to register on *Billboard*'s year-end charts. None made it onto the end-of-the-year *Cash Box* tallies.

In December 1967 Marshall announced that he was launching a new label, Cadet Concept, which would use some in-house production along with music created by outside producers. Along with the new label would be a new group, Rotary Connection. Marshall described it to the music press as seven voices that are "a concept rather than a group" and backed on its first LP by a twenty-piece orchestra and some new electronic engineering techniques. At the same time Ralph Bass, working under the Checker line, was expanding what he called the "Gos-Pop sound" to give more exposure to such vocal groups on the roster as the Soul Stirrers and the Violinaires.

When Marshall told a *Billboard* reporter that he intended to take the Rotary Connection on tour and to use "psychedelic effects and even smells" at their concerts, it marked a new phase for the company that was beyond anything Leonard and Phil could have imagined twenty years earlier. This was a time of transition, though no one knew then how big the transition would be.

nineteen

FINAL
TRACKS

The promising start of 1968 held no clue to what the end of the year would bring. Etta James and Laura Lee were still on the *Billboard* and *Cash Box* charts with the records produced in Muscle Shoals. Billy Stewart had another modest hit at the end of January with "Cross My Heart," but the surprise development was the resurgence of the Dells, a vocal group that had found only modest success in the early sixties when the five singers, all friends from Thornton Township High School in Harvey, Illinois, cut some records on Argo.

After a sojourn at Vee Jay, they re-signed on the Cadet label in the summer of 1966. Nothing really clicked under Billy Davis's tutelage, so in the middle of 1967 the Dells started working with Bobby Miller, another producer in the company who was also a prolific songwriter, and Charles Stepney, a new arranger who brought classical training to his R&B duties. Davis had hired him to write lead sheets, but when he got to know the young man, he could see that Stepney had good ideas, enthusiasm, and an interest in arranging. He decided to give him a chance.

Things began to change for the better. Talents bloomed in new combinations. Stepney seemed to know just the right chords to complement Miller's melody and lyrics, and both seemed able to communicate easily with the singers. On top of that Miller relished the opportunity to work with the Dells, and his enthusiasm for the collaboration was contagious. The first song he offered them, the dramatic ballad "O-O I Love You," was released in the fall of 1967 and got some attention in *Billboard*. But it was the flip side that really took off, the uptempo "There Is," written by Miller and

Raynard Miner. The opening bars and the opening lyrics set the pace and spirit, repeating the phrase "there is" before each important element—the place, the girl, the face, and finally "the love I need so much."

When the group played it for Harvey Fuqua on a visit to Detroit, he told them they had a hit. "There Is" reached the *Billboard* and *Cash Box* pop charts by mid-February 1968, climbing to number twenty in *Billboard* and to number twenty-four in *Cash Box*. But this was just the beginning. By mid-May the group had another bestseller, "Wear It on Our Face," and in June the Dells had their biggest hit to date, "Stay in My Corner." The song was a remake of their Vee Jay effort, but this time lush strings, well-timed horns, and vocal backup to supplement the group's own harmonies propelled the song to number one on *Billboard*'s R&B chart and to number ten on the Top One Hundred; it registered equally impressive numbers in *Cash Box*.

Anxious to make the most out of the group's popularity, the company put out an album, *There Is,* early in May, and by the summer it had climbed high on the best-selling album charts, the first of four LPs over sixteen months to garner national attention for the group. In the fall of 1968 the Dells had another big seller with "Always Together." Although it wasn't as successful as the previous three singles, this new team of writer, arranger, and singers was still working well together.

➤➤

Marshall kept abreast of everything that was going on at the studio, but he was immersed in Cadet Concept. "Rotary Connection"—a name that Rollin Binzer, one of the company's advertising consultants, had come up with—was absorbing much of his time now. He envisioned the Connection as "soft psychedelic" music made with a biracial group of musicians and a sound that would reflect the culture of his generation. Experimenting with drugs was certainly part of it; so was new technology applied to old forms to bend the notes and transform the musical ideas, all to give the audience, whether at home in front of speakers or in a theater, a multidimensional listening experience.

A college student in Los Angeles in the early sixties, Marshall had seen the frontier of the psychedelic era in the unlikely venue of Cantor's Delicatessen on Fairfax Boulevard. During the day Cantor's served up corned beef sandwiches, blintzes, and chicken soup to the local clientele. After midnight it became a hangout of the avant-garde. It was not unusual to see patrons, blissful looks in their eyes, coming in for a snack dressed like Peter Pan or some other fairy-tale figure.

In Chicago Marshall heard Timothy Leary speak, growing wide-eyed as Leary came onstage in a flowing white robe after Bob Dylan warmed up the audience. Marshall smoked his share of marijuana in the office after hours, and whenever the night watchman smelled the odor during his rounds, he would report to Leonard the next day. Unhappy with his son's recreational habit, he didn't lecture him, though a look or a gesture conveyed his displeasure. The same went for Marshall's evolving wardrobe. Gone were the suits and ties; now he wore jeans and longer hair and grew a mustache. But it was Phil, rather than Leonard, who addressed the matter. "You looked so much sharper before you started doing this hippie shit," he told him.

Fitting the music to the culture was only part of the Rotary Connection idea. Marshall was sure the moment was right for this kind of music to find an audience. FM stations willing to play unusual albums were emerging; disc jockeys would listen to the LP as soon as a promotion man brought it in and if they liked it, play the music right away. All Marshall needed to do was put the pieces together. He was confident he could, and joked to himself that he had the most important ingredient: the keys to the studio.

The commissary on the eighth floor played a crucial role in the project. One day in the fall of 1967, Marshall and Charles Stepney happened to be getting lunch at the same time. When Marshall sat down at a table with Stepney, he noticed Stepney was carrying a big portfolio stuffed with papers. He had seen Stepney carrying around books on Beethoven and Bach, and he asked what all the papers were. It was a symphony that he was writing, Stepney replied, part of his course work in college.

Intrigued, Marshall told him about his ideas for Rotary Connection and his own growing appreciation for classical music. He had just gotten married, and his wife, Diane, played a lot of Beethoven. He heard a connection to psychedelic rock. "It flipped me out with those gigantic climactic things—Da Da Da *Dah*," he said, mimicking the opening of the Fifth Symphony. Marshall sensed in Stepney a willing and interested listener and asked him to help. "I wallow in concepts and ideas," he said. "I need someone to translate that into music." Stepney seemed equally intrigued with Marshall, and the two started to meet regularly. That Stepney was respected by the house musicians Marshall planned to use at the core of Rotary Connection made him even more confident the project could work. Louis Satterfield and Phil Upchurch were still there, but Gerald Sims and Maurice White had left. Pete Cosey and Bryce Roberson were playing guitar, and Morris Jennings was the drummer.

Marshall recruited six singers—two women and four men. Minnie Riperton, who had sung with the Gems behind Fontella Bass on "Rescue Me," recorded solo as "Andrea Davis," and had also worked as a receptionist at the studio, had an extraordinary three-octave range. Judy Hauff, a white woman, worked for the Catholic diocese in Chicago. Marshall thought her "beautiful, clear church voice" was a perfect complement to Riperton. They were joined by Sidney Barnes, a black writer-singer, and three other white musicians who came from a local band, Bobby Simms, Mitch Aliotta, and Kenny Venegas.

Added to all of this was a string section from the Chicago Symphony. Stepney wrote all the arrangements, and at the first session, he was so nervous about working with the new musicians that he broke into a sweat. Marshall had to calm him down before they could start.

Once the sessions were finished in the fall of 1967, he and Stepney spent a couple of months working on the tapes, trying to get the proper mix. In the meantime, Binzer came up with an unusual album jacket. On the front Riperton and Hauff were each shown four times, lying on their backs, wearing flowered halos and wings and revealing bare shoulders and bare, crossed legs. Giant open hymnals covered the rest of them. The repeated pictures of each woman were arranged in a circle, their toes meeting in the center like a scene from a Busby Berkeley movie.

The back cover was no less unusual. Set into a giant hymnal was a picture of the group lying in a circle, with Riperton passing a marijuana cigarette to her fellow singers and Marshall and Stepney. On the bottom of the open pages were four stones and four beetles, Marshall's nod to the Rolling Stones and the Beatles. Over in the left-hand corner was a small pile of marijuana. When Sears, which was a popular record outlet in Chicago, realized there was a picture of drugs on the jacket, the company refused to put the album on its record racks.

As soon as he heard what was happening, Marshall called Binzer. We have to do something, he said. Sears sales were too important to lose. Binzer found the answer. A tiny picture of a hippie—a mop of black hair, thick mustache, wire-rimmed glasses whose lenses were the front cover picture—was slapped over the pile of marijuana and a whole new set of jackets was printed. "This was a pot-smoking album," Marshall explained, "but we didn't want any problem."

Rotary Connection opened with "Amen." The first sounds were some unusual guitar notes, an organ in the background, then came a single, distant voice before the group burst forth with a full-throttle "A-men." The rhythm picked up and the sound got louder, but the song retained a churchy, even reverential feel, although it was hardly the "Amen" of the local Methodist or Episcopal church down the block. The group's versions of the Rolling Stones' "Lady Jane" and "Ruby Tuesday," and their take on Dylan's "Like a Rolling Stone," and Sam and Dave's "Soul Man," were equally inventive. Riperton's operatic trilling on "Lady Jane" astonished most listeners. In between some of the songs were brief instrumental interludes, each under a minute, with unusual titles: "Pink Noise," "Sursam Mentes," and "Black Noise."

Rotary Connection was an immediate hit in Chicago when it was released early in 1968. "A psychedelic soul group" said one writer, that could sing "intricate vocal harmonies against a backdrop of electric sounds." Powerful WLS played it over and over. The pressing plant couldn't make the albums fast enough. The LP started selling in the Midwest, and by March it was on the *Billboard* and *Cash Box* best-selling album charts. Rotary Connection stayed on the *Billboard* chart for thirty-four weeks and almost as long on the *Cash Box* tally. Only Ahmad Jamal, Ramsey Lewis, and the second Soulful Strings had sold better.

For all its success, though, *Rotary Connection* showed the company's limits. "It sold big but we couldn't spread it nationwide," Marshall said. "It was big where it was big, but we weren't strong enough in white radio promotion to bring up the numbers." Nor did they have enough clout to get a single off the album into a bestseller position. But it was an auspicious start for Cadet Concept with the promise of more success to come.

~~

Though Leonard was still running the company and still approved everything that went out the door, it was clear how much he was enjoying the radio stations. Now he spent 60 percent of his time on South Kedzie at VON and SDM and 40 percent at 320 East Twenty-first Street. He and Phil had gotten over their disappointment at losing the Camden, New Jersey, radio station and had turned their attention to other possibilities. Leonard found a good deal in Milwaukee, just one hundred miles due north. It was a city with a substantial black population that he believed would be receptive to VON-style programming. He made a deal to buy WFOX-AM for $260,000 from the Fox Broadcasting Company. A marketing survey Leonard commissioned noted that of Milwaukee's seven AM stations, ten

FM outlets, and six television stations, none had a contemporary music format, and "only a single station—not licensed in Milwaukee but putting a signal over the area—was endeavoring to place any emphasis on the special needs of minorities." On April 1, L&P Broadcasting formally took over WFOX, renamed it WNOV and brought in individuals to duplicate the format that had been so successful in Chicago.

The good news about the purchase was offset by a significant change at the studio. Billy Davis told Leonard he was accepting an offer with McCann-Erickson, a major advertising firm, to be its music director. One of the company's big accounts was Coca-Cola, and Davis had produced radio commercials for Coke using Fontella Bass, who was still with Chess despite her complaints about money, and Little Milton. McCann-Erickson executives were so pleased with Davis's work that they asked him to leave Chess and produce commercials for them. Although he said no, the company renewed its offer month after month. Davis finally told Leonard what was going on. He couldn't figure out why McCann-Erickson wanted him so badly when there must be a thousand producers available. On top of that, he didn't know anything about advertising.

The agency must really want him, Leonard said, and he should think about expanding his career, just as he and Phil had diversified their business interests. They would be sorry to lose him, and he certainly wasn't pushing him out the door, but why didn't Davis consider accepting the offer? "Make 'em pay you a lot of money," Leonard added. "And tell them to give you a one-year contract. If you don't like it, you come back home."

That helped Davis make up his mind. Another important factor was the realization that Leonard was spending more time at the radio station and less time on Twenty-first Street. Davis got along well enough with Cooperstein, who was the general manager, and Marshall, but it was not the same as when Leonard was focused 100 percent on the music business. Because he had been an important and unifying creative element, Davis's departure left a significant void.

"If it wasn't for Leonard Chess I might not have made that move," Davis said years later, reflecting on how well his decision turned out. He eventually became one of the agency's senior vice presidents and its worldwide music director.

Davis's leaving meant a seismic shift for Chess. Tremors of another sort rocked the entire city after the April 4 murder of Martin Luther King, who was gunned down on the balcony of his hotel in Memphis, where he had gone to support striking sanitation workers. Angry black citizens rioted around the country; in Chicago some two hundred businesses would be destroyed before the rioting was contained. One of the people Mayor Richard Daley called after the violence erupted was Leonard, asking him to use VON to help spread a message of nonviolence. As soon as he finished talking to Daley, Leonard called Binzer, the advertising man, and asked him to put together an ad that could run in the *Chicago Tribune* urging calm.

Binzer was young—roughly Marshall's age—but Leonard trusted him. He personally had taught him the ways of Chicago's South Side. Three years earlier a mutual friend had brought Binzer and his two partners to see Leonard to discuss print ads for the radio station. "We were an agency with an attitude," Binzer admitted. They didn't offer clients options. They came in with their pitch and said, "This is it." For VON, Binzer had come up with pictures of black cats and "artsy fartsy" photographs of jazz instruments embellished with some copy about the radio station. Leonard hated the ads on sight.

The meeting was at the South Michigan Avenue studio, and right after looking at the presentation, Leonard, poster in hand, went out in the back, grabbed a young man pushing a dolly full of records and asked him, "What do you think of this piece of shit?"

Binzer protested. It wasn't fair for the boss to ask an employee for his opinion, especially when the question was so loaded.

"You, big mouth," Leonard said, motioning to Binzer. "You come with me. If you want to run these fuckin' ads in the morning, we'll run them."

By this time it was around 7:00 P.M. and nearly dark. Leonard took Binzer out to his car, and for the rest of the night and into the early morning, he drove him around the South Side of the city, to bars, lounges, and taverns Binzer had never seen. He met Muddy Waters at one place, saw a man get stabbed at another. Binzer watched at a third as Leonard gave the poster to one patron who went straight to the back door, which opened onto the alley, set the paper on the ground, propped a chair in the doorway and then, for maximum effect, stood on the chair to urinate on the poster. Binzer was getting the message: he didn't understand black music. It had also dawned on him that he and Leonard were the only white people he saw in all the clubs. But Binzer wasn't afraid. Being with Leonard was like being with a star. Wherever they went, people knew who he was and welcomed him. By the time Leonard dropped Binzer off at his office, the young man was shell-shocked, taught an indelible lesson in an unforgettable manner.

So when Leonard called him on that tense and sad day in April 1968, he was sure Binzer would find the right touch for the newspaper ad. Binzer remembered a picture of King standing in front of an American flag that had been taken by a professional photographer who was a dear friend and who had done work with the agency. Fortunately his office was just a few blocks away. He raced over and got the picture and came up with some copy. MARTIN LUTHER KING LIVES was stripped across the top. On the bottom in smaller letters the message continued: "In every one of us. In the work he started. In the goals he achieved. In the goals we *must* carry on. The Staff and Management of *WVON* join its community in sorrow for our nation's loss and in tribute to the memory of a great American."

Binzer sprinted over to the *Tribune* so the ad could get in the Sunday paper, April 7. Thousands of copies were reprinted to be passed out.

Over at VON an excerpt from one of King's speeches preaching nonviolence was aired every half-hour. Deejays suggested that motorists drive with their headlights on to honor King's memory, and in the weekend after his death programming was switched to gospel, spiritual, and inspirational music.

As soon as Max Cooperstein heard the news, he thought it would be a good idea to put together a record honoring King, whom he had met. He called Gene Barge, who was a member of the Southern Christian Leadership Conference, King's organization, and a member of the "Operation Breadbasket" band, a group of musicians whose live performances every Saturday morning were broadcast over WVON under the auspices of Jesse Jackson's civil rights organization. Barge called Ben Branch, a saxophone player who ran the band, and several of the Chess house musicians to pull the album together. In a short time *The Last Request* with King's picture on the cover was recorded and ready for sale. The selections included an instrumental, "Precious Lord Take My Hand," "Motherless Child," "We Shall Overcome," sung by a choir led by Jackson, and "The Battle Hymn of the Republic." Royalties from album sales were to be given to the SCLC.

Chess was one of several music companies that responded with fundraising recordings. Atlantic gave $5,000 to King's family out of advance royalties from a new record by Solomon Burke, one of its stars, and $5,000 to the SCLC from an advance on the Hudson Chorale's record "I Have a Dream." Twentieth Century–Fox donated royalties from its *I Have a Dream* album, which was made up of clips from Movietone News Tapes.

Epic Records planned to donate royalties from a single by the East Harlem Children's Chorus singing "You've Got to Be Taught" from the musical *South Pacific*. Unart, United Artists' economy line, reissued an address King made in 1964, and royalties from the album were to be given to the SCLC.

⋙

With Billy Davis gone, Marshall got more involved in the music operation. He moved his office to the eighth floor, taking over a spacious room that had been the president's during the 3M tenure. By the summer he made some changes in the staff, believing the company needed a creative jolt. Among the writers he fired was Raynard Miner, who was hurt, angry, and dumbfounded. Miner's track record was well known, however, and he was hired right away to write for Motown. Smith, Miner's writing partner, had already left, and within a few months the rest of the original rhythm section Davis had put together would also be gone.

Satterfield, the bass player, would leave to join his friend Maurice White, the drummer, as part of Earth, Wind and Fire. He wanted to expand the kind of music he was playing and he wanted to make more money. He didn't think that would happen under Leonard and Phil. "I didn't think they were sharing the money properly with the people who were making it," he said. "You got a bigger building, a bigger place, you're pressing records, but you haven't given me another dime. That was kind of a hard blow," he said, recalling the moment years later. "You got this great big old building. I know we had something to do with that."

Ironically, Satterfield's friend Gerald Sims, the guitar player, decided to come back just as he was leaving. But Sims was coming back more as a producer than as a session musician. Right away he could see things were different, "more chaotic," he thought. Producing duties were shared among Barge, Ralph Bass, Richard Evans, and Marshall, though Marshall was concentrating most on Cadet Concept. He wanted to bring more of his own ideas, musical and business, to fruition, and hoped to build on the success of Rotary Connection.

One of the arrangements Marshall had negotiated with Pye's Louis Benjamin at the beginning of the European deals was the right to sift through the company's masters that had not already been licensed to someone else—songs that were not a hit or that had been a hit in England but were not released in the United States. On one of his overseas trips early in 1968 to check on the international operations, Marshall went to the Pye offices, set himself up in a vacant room, and started going through the masters. He came across a record called "Pictures of Matchstick Men" by a group called the Status Quo. As soon as he heard the unusual sound effects and offbeat lyrics, he knew it would be a hit in the United States and knew it was perfect for Cadet Concept. He paid Pye $300—their agreed-upon price for any master—and put out the record on his label early in May. Within a week it was on the *Billboard* and *Cash Box* Top One Hundred. It rose to number twelve in *Billboard*, number fifteen in *Cash Box*. "Pictures" stayed on the charts for four months, one of the company's most successful singles. But neither blues, nor R&B, nor rock and roll, it didn't register on the trade paper R&B tallies, where Chess had made its name.

Once again the limits of the company in the pop arena were exposed. Marshall wanted to capitalize on the Status Quo's single with an album, *Message from the Status Quo.* The LP was released, but "we blew it," he said. "We just didn't have it—we didn't have the distribution power like Columbia or RCA. I was looking forward to a half-a-million seller, and it was a stiff. It probably sold fifty or eighty thousand."

But even though the album was a financial disappointment, the success of "Pictures of Matchstick Men" enhanced Marshall's reputation. In the space of four months he had had a hit album and a hit single.

Now he wanted to turn his ideas to the blues world, bringing Muddy Waters and Howlin' Wolf, the men whose music was the foundation of the company, into his musical vision. "What I'm trying to do with blues is put a modern thing to it," he explained to one writer, adding that his musicians wanted to do the same.

In May of 1968 he brought Waters into the studio to work with a new band on new arrangements of old songs and an improbable version of the Rolling Stones' "Let's Spend the Night Together." In place of the Waters regulars were Stepney, Barge, Satterfield, Phil Upchurch, a new session musician, Pete Cosey, Morris Jennings, and Roland Faulkner. Cosey, Upchurch, and Jennings, all black, joked about calling the group "The Electric Niggers." Marshall liked it; Leonard put his foot down and said no.

Though he was no longer part of the house band, Cosey was glad to come back for the project. He had been made to feel comfortable at Chess from his first sessions three years earlier in the Michigan Avenue studio, and he knew that Leonard liked him. He called him, "rabbi," most likely, Cosey thought, because of Cosey's professional look and demeanor—

trimmed beard, glasses, elegant speaking style. "Hello rabbi, how are you today?" was Leonard's usual greeting when he saw him.

Cosey was flattered to be playing with Waters, whom he had long admired. He thought he had been called in for a traditional blues session and was surprised to see a lot of electronic equipment in the studio. To help get the psychedelic sounds he wanted, Marshall had a new amplifier brought into the studio, and Ken Minhan, who delivered it, stayed around for a few minutes to watch part of the session. He remembered Waters grousing, "I don't like that damn wah-wah thing," but Marshall was determined to follow through.

The resulting *Electric Mud* was released in October. Publicity shots for the album included a picture of Muddy wrapped in a white robe, his black pompadour teased exceptionally high, a quizzical look on his face.

The critics hated the album. It was an insult to Waters, a disservice to his music, misconceived from beginning to end. Some of the harshest words came from the highly regarded Pete Welding in *Rolling Stone*. The entire production, he wrote, "evinces absolutely no understanding of either contempary rock or Waters's music. All the character and power of the latter is totally defaced by the excessive guitar work, overbusy drumming and bass playing, inept horn parts (which are often out of tune in the bargain) and by—most important—the utter irrelevance of the arrangements and their too thick textures to the music. . . . The album, sadly, is nothing more than a parody of both Waters' music and contemporary instrumental practices, the use of the latter, amounting to little more than an ugly patchwork of effects."

Waters later agreed with one interviewer who called the album "dogshit."

The critics and Waters may have hated *Electric Mud*—though Marshall insisted that in the beginning Waters liked the project—but the public bought it. The LP was the first Waters album that made the *Billboard* and *Cash Box* charts, registering in both trades for two months. Cosey believed the criticism was misplaced. From a musician's perspective he thought the ideas were good ones and that Stepney's arrangements were "brilliant—took the music in a totally different direction." He would "bet the ranch," he added, that none of the critics could play the parts that had been written to back up Waters.

Thirty years after what he called "an experiment," Marshall admitted he was stung by the criticism. He said the album was misunderstood by blues purists who thought he was trying to change the direction of Waters's music. "I wasn't at all," he insisted. "He was the vocalist in a concept—that was just a concept." Marshall added that he now realized that using Waters this way "was a big mistake" because he was far too central a figure in blues to be put in another musical context.

A subsequent album with Howlin' Wolf and the same personnel got the same rough critical treatment. Wolf made no bones about his distaste for the project, so much so that the LP was given this unwieldly title: *This is Howlin' Wolf's New Album. He doesn't like it. He didn't like his first electric guitar either.*

At the same time, two more Rotary Connection albums were released. The second one, *Aladdin*, had the same feel as the first but featured all original music. While the LP made the album charts, it was not nearly as successful as its predecessor. A third album, *Peace*, was released right after *Aladdin*, just in time for Christmas. Binzer came up with a provocative ad to publicize the LP. He was still reeling from the violence that had marred the Democratic Party's convention in Chicago in the summer. He had been among the thousands of protesters gathered in Lincoln Park on the city's near north side protesting the war in Vietnam and challenging Mayor Daley and the police as they tried to keep order. Outrage at the rough treatment of demonstrators still burned inside, and Binzer was determined to have some of that sentiment revealed in the ad campaign. He hit upon a dramatic metaphor: Santa Claus, wounded and lying on a stretcher in the very same Lincoln Park, his bag of gifts torn open, a gun nearby.

The full-page color ad ran in the December 7 *Billboard*. Underneath the wounded Santa was a small picture of the Rotary Connection and the simple word *Peace* in old-fashioned lettering.

The response was immediate and angry. Leonard was aghast. Original or not, it was hurting business. Some stores threw their records out, linking the ad and the album to sacrilege. So many readers called *Billboard* to protest that the magazine wrote an editorial, "Peace on Earth?" in the December 21 issue. "In this holiday season of December, 1968, love lies bleeding. 'Peace on Earth . . . good will to men' is an illusion. Our cities are wracked with civil disorder. Crimes of violence are at an all time high." Overseas the situation was equally grim—"war, starvation and assassination define the human condition. In view of these unassailable facts, some are questioning the traditional symbols of our society. . . . The Cadet ad was not drawn up in a moment of frivolity," the magazine said. "It represents concern over the state of humanity. It tells it like it is. To regard Santa today as smiling and happy is at once a cruel and deceptive mockery. To those who have protested the Cadet ad," the editorial concluded, "we urge: Search thyself. The truth will bring strength and make possible a healing process."

Leonard made it clear that there would be no more provocative ads like this one. He didn't fire Binzer and his colleagues, though he needled them in his own way where they felt it the most, over money. Sometimes he would require an in-person meeting before paying their bill. Then he would complain about overcharging, taking kickbacks from the printer "and doing every scurrilous thing," Binzer said. Leonard took particular glee in jabbing at Tom Hurvis, who handled the agency's books. During one of these haggling sessions, Leonard was particularly aggressive, refusing for the moment to pay a $12,000 bill, which the men were desperate to have to cover their expenses.

"Okay, Hurvis, I'll double it or nothing," Leonard said. "Do you have the balls to do that?" Hurvis knew he had to say yes. Leonard pulled out a coin, flipped it, and Hurvis called "heads." Leonard looked at the coin but never showed it. Then he reached down to pull a check out of his drawer already made out—for $24,000. "Get the fuck out of my office," he told them, his ritual completed.

᭞

Leonard liked attention for the company, but not controversy. This was even more important now, as 1968 was drawing to a close, because he and Phil had made a critical decision. They were ready to sell Chess Records. Leonard wanted to spend more time and energy on the radio stations. He loved the enterprise and thought there was room for growth. He even thought about branching out with Phil into television—they would sell VON to raise the capital. It sounded fine to Phil. TV was something new and exciting, and it didn't have the rough grind of the record business. Leonard was willing to live with the federal and state regulations that governed the industry. He would hire experienced people to help him through the maze; the strategy had worked before, and it would again. He and Phil confided only in Allen Arrow, the lawyer in New York who handled much of the legal business for the record company and Arc Music.

By coincidence, Arrow also represented a tape company headquartered in Sunnyvale, California, just south of San Francisco, called GRT—General Recorded Tape. Under the leadership of Alan Bayley, GRT, which was publicly held, was trying to expand its enterprise from simply making tape cartridges of other companies' music, among them Chess. Bayley hired Arrow to do some work, impressed by the way he handled the licensing arrangements for the Chess material. During one of their routine conversations in the fall of 1968, Bayley told Arrow that the only way for GRT to survive was "to acquire our own artists." He was convinced that before long record companies would make their own tapes, crimping GRT's growth.

On the same day, Leonard happened to call Arrow and said he wanted to talk about the future. He and Phil had been discussing what to do with the company—neither man was going to work forever or live forever, he said, and in fact, they had a proposal from ABC Records to buy Chess. Leonard said he didn't feel that was the right move. He was concerned about what would happen to Marshall in such a big operation. He wanted to know what Arrow thought.

Amazed at the coincidence, Arrow told Leonard about the conversation he had just had with Bayley, whom Leonard knew because of the tape licensing arrangement. Leonard told Arrow that ABC had given him a deadline to make a decision, though Arrow was not sure whether that was true or whether it was just a ploy to get Bayley to sit down quickly to negotiate. "See if you can get Bayley out here," Leonard told Arrow.

He immediately called Bayley's office, tracked him down at a California airport, and Bayley agreed to change his plans and fly to Chicago to meet Leonard and Phil. Arrow flew out to Chicago from New York, and the four men met the next day to work out the broad strokes of a deal. Arrow had a conflict, however. He had represented both companies, and, he told the men, now that he had brought them together, he needed to step back so they could hire new lawyers. Leonard would have none of it. He was going to have Nate Notkin, his longtime personal lawyer, handle some of the arrangements, but he told Bayley that if Arrow could not represent Chess along with Notkin, then there would be no deal. Bayley agreed, and GRT got its own counsel.

Nothing was made public yet, but the basics of the deal were set: the purchase price for all the Chess entities, including the labels and the pressing plants but not Arc Music, was $6.5 million and twenty thousand shares of GRT stock. Bayley was more interested in the Chess catalogue and the artists than he was in the building at 320 East Twenty-first Street, which he knew was expensive to maintain, and the pressing plants. "But those were hard assets that Leonard and Phil wanted to be paid for," and he agreed to include them in the package. Bayley also wanted to know more about Leonard, and he had instructed one of his lawyers, Leonard Ware, to compile a "dossier" on him to see if there was anything in his background that could sully the deal. The report contained nothing to change Bayley's mind.

Marshall didn't think there was anything unusual when he got a call from his father on Leonard's mobile phone. He had been one of the first to get a car phone because he couldn't stand the thought of wasting time when he could be doing business on his many trips between his house in Glencoe, Twenty-first Street, and the radio stations on South Kedzie. The phone was a somewhat clumsy device that required dialing a mobile operator who then connected the person in the car with the other party.

"Phil and I talked," he told his son. "We decided to sell the company to GRT."

Marshall was stunned. He didn't know what to say. He never dreamed that there would not be a Chess Records that he would eventually run. "This is for you," he had heard over and over through the years. He considered the record company his birthright. "It was always going to be mine." Years later Marshall could not remember what he said to his father on the phone, only the feeling of disbelief that washed over him.

Leonard must have sensed it on the other end of the line; he told his son they would talk when he got to the studio. Once they sat down Leonard explained the terms of the sale. He assured Marshall that he could expect a million dollars, enough to start his own label all over again if he wanted. You can make it, his father added. You're going to be all right.

"That pacified me," Marshall remembered.

He also got a deeper understanding of the reasons his father wanted to sell the company. It was not only his growing enjoyment of the radio business and the possibilities of television, or even a purchase price above what he had hoped. He told Marshall that it was getting more and more difficult for white people to own a company geared to black consumers. Jesse Jackson was pressuring Chess, just as he was pressuring other companies that did business in the black community, to hire more blacks in senior positions. Marshall had been at one meeting with Jackson and other civil rights activists where Jackson made his concerns more than plain. Not long afterward Marshall brought in a black man as an art director, but their association was not successful and didn't last very long.

The news of the sale leaked out at the end of October. The front page of the November 2, 1968, *Billboard* announced "Chess to Be Sold to GRT," though no details were included in the story. The coming weeks were filled with days and days of tedious negotiations between Arrow and Notkin on one side and the GRT lawyers on the other, all spread around a long table in Leonard and Phil's office. Most of the haggling came from the GRT side, "about every comma and every semicolon," Notkin remembered. Sometimes the principal GRT lawyer would insist on a change from something that was written, "and sometimes what he wanted was worse for him than what we had," Notkin said. It was more than likely the longest negotiation either Arrow or Notkin had on behalf of the Chess brothers. They didn't do business that way. They made a decision, made a deal, gave a handshake, maybe put a few things in writing, and moved forward.

By the end of the year the details were nailed down, including separate employment contracts for Leonard, Phil, and Marshall. The deals for each of the entities—there were ten separate corporations—required individual black-covered binders filled with legal-size sheets spelling out the terms of the agreement. Although the purchase price was $6.5 million plus GRT stock, the company only had to come up with $4.7 million in cash. Leonard in effect lent GRT $1.79 million at 7 percent interest by agreeing to hold eight separate notes that had staggered due dates. The first was due January 2, 1970, the last January 2, 1973. To have a seller take back notes as part of the purchase prices was not unusual in commercial transactions. In this case it was evidence of how much Leonard wanted the deal to go through. There was one more round of meetings in California the first week in January 1969 to sign the final papers for the sale.

The last session proved to be as difficult as the earlier negotiations. The night before Leonard learned that the GRT people found some things that made them uneasy. They wanted to lower the purchase price, but they wouldn't give the specifics. The next day Arrow demanded that Bayley and his lawyers tell them what they were concerned about; Leonard and Phil guessed that they determined that the amount of Chess annual sales had been overstated. *Billboard* and *Record World* had reported that Chess sales for the previous twelve months were $2.2 million with pretax earnings expected to be $850,000.

The two sides were at a standoff for several hours, but they finally reached an agreement: the closing would go forward with some minor adjustments, with further adjustments to come within the following two months. The deal closed in an atmosphere "of substantial mistrust" between the parties, Arrow said. Leonard and Phil grumbled about "dealing with a gentile mentality." "I'm sure," Arrow added, "the GRT people thought they were dealing with Jewish greed."

~~

It didn't take long to feel the changes on East Twenty-first Street. When Arrow flew out to Chicago six weeks or so after the closing, he walked in the front door toward the executive offices, and instead of the usual activity, he saw men in white shirts, their sleeves rolled up, pencils in hand, sitting at desks poring over books.

"What is all this?" he asked Leonard. These were the accountants and bookkeepers for GRT, he was told. "They're all the bank people," Leonard added, "and they can figure out within ten cents how much money we lost and where it was lost. Phil and I used to sit around and never could understand how we were making so much money or why," he added, only slightly tongue in cheek.

Marshall was uneasy from the beginning of the transition. He felt like someone was always watching over his shoulder, "and we weren't used to that . . . They were changing the organic nature of the company without knowing it, trying to make it more businesslike because they were a public corporation. They bought a family company that was making black music, and they tried to turn it into a suits and tie corporation."

To the outside world, the transition was going smoothly enough; GRT had big plans. The trade papers carried intermittent stories about the company's continuing efforts to diversify not only in the United States but also in Europe. At the same time, the company sought to show that it was moving quickly to broaden the reach of Chess, putting out new radio commercials for its products, concentrating more on college sales, and adding to the promotion staff.

There was still plenty of music that had been in the pipeline, principally more records from the Dells. Between January and August 1969, four songs made the charts, including a remake of "Oh, What a Night," which rose to number one on the *Billboard* R&B tally. Little Milton returned to the charts at the end of January with "Grits Ain't Groceries," and then "Let's Get Together" in July.

At the same time Marshall was trying to pursue his creative vision, still basking in the success of the Rotary Connection and his astute decision to release "Pictures of Matchstick Men." When the top one hundred songs of

1968 were listed in the trade papers, "Pictures" was number fifty-five on *Billboard*'s list and number eighty-eight on the *Cash Box* tally, the only Chess record to register.

Marshall had hired a publicity man, Loren Coleman, though his father only reluctantly agreed with the decision. The evidence was in Coleman's modest accommodations—a small office in the unused penthouse barbershop, with a table, a barber's chair, and a typewriter. But he got results. Stories about Chess musicians and their records were showing up in papers around Chicago and in other parts of the country. Coleman recycled the information but offered each paper fresh pictures. Leonard became a believer when the Dells stormed into his office, livid about their exclusion from a long story on the record company in the *Chicago Tribune*.

"Can you get me off the hook?" Leonard asked.

Coleman called his contact at the *Daily News*, and within weeks there was a feature on the Dells.

Though the "electric" blues albums he produced were savaged by the critics, Marshall was intrigued by another blues idea that one of his old high school friends, Mike Bloomfield, and Bloomfield's friend Norman Dayron suggested. Why not do an album with Waters backed by the younger musicians, like Bloomfield and the harmonica player Paul Butterfield, who were inspired by him? Marshall loved the concept and suggested they add other musicians from other labels. He would take care of the details of their releases to Chess. Bloomfield would come courtesy of Columbia, Butterfield from Electra, and he recruited Donald "Duck" Dunn from Stax and Buddy Miles from Mercury. Sam Lay, who had been playing drums behind Waters, would join the band along with Otis Spann, his favorite on the keyboard. Spann willingly left a New York nightclub engagement to do the recording. They would call the album *Fathers and Sons*.

Bloomfield and Butterfield were coming to Chicago for a charity concert on April 24, so Marshall and Dayron planned the recording sessions around that event. Beforehand Dayron spent three weeks going through the Chess vault to select the right Waters tunes, and Marshall hunted for some 1950 vintage amplifiers to bring into the studio. "We set a mood," he explained. "There was lots of booze—champagne for Muddy and beer for the younger guys." Sonny Woods, now in his twenty-first year with Leonard and Phil, kept the supplies flowing.

A couple of the sessions lasted five hours, the music interspersed with periods of discussion among the musicians. Some blues fans were allowed to watch—extra room was one of the benefits of being in the much larger facility at Twenty-first Street. "It was just a totally cooperative effort," Marshall said.

The live concert segment was equally successful. "The sound of five thousand kids singing 'I've Got My Mojo Working' is the most powerful thing I've ever heard," Marshall recalled, referring to the Waters classic, which was the final track on the two-record album.

The critics who hated *Electric Mud* loved *Fathers and Sons*. In addition to the psychic boost of good reviews, the album had the added benefit of giving Waters a new, higher profile with white fans. Though Dayron was given the producing credit, Marshall had acted as the executive producer, sharpening the overall concept and making sure the pieces came together. After the album was released in mid-August, the company put together the largest promotional effort for any of its albums. Marshall went on a thirteen-day, seven-city tour in the East to talk up the LP; Dayron went to the major cities in California, and Richie Salvador went to the mid-Atlantic states while three other promotion men, new additions in the GRT regime, headed south and to Texas and Colorado.

Fathers and Sons was a high point, but instead of being an omen of the good things to come under GRT's stewardship, the album would prove to be one of the last bright spots Leonard would see from Chess.

~

The public position at East Twenty-first Street was that things were growing, changing, and expanding. New people were coming in even as one senior executive was leaving. Max Cooperstein left in the summer of 1969 for MGM. He had expected to have more authority under the GRT regime, and when things moved in a direction he didn't like, he decided to leave. In July, the company had announced a "total expansion" with most changes coming in the sales and promotion departments. Marshall was vice president of the producing corporation, Salvador was general manager, and both were operating in the shadow of GRT executives.

Leonard and Phil were still part of the company in name, but now Leonard was devoting even more time to the radio stations. It was much more than going over to Kedzie and looking after the operation. VON had grown and part of its growth came from the ability to attract national advertisers. That meant trips to New York to meet with sponsors. Every now and then Leonard would take his nephew Terry, Phil's son, who was now helping run WSDM, the FM station. They made one of those quick trips the week of October 9.

Leonard still came to the studio every day, and there was nothing unusual about his early morning arrival on October 16, a Thursday. Near lunch time he was ready to leave and head over to the radio station. He had just talked to Marshall, who was in California on a business trip and was heading home later that day. As Leonard was walking down the hallway on the first floor toward the door, he saw his nephew-in-law, Lennie Diamond and a salesman for Columbia Records, and stopped to talk with them. Lennie told his uncle he had just come from a meeting with the accountant GRT had installed at the studio. Columbia, which was doing some custom record pressing for Chess, was putting the Chess account on hold because of unpaid bills over the last few months.

"What do you mean?" Leonard asked, astonished at the news. "We've got lots of money." He walked straight into the accounting office and asked what was going on. The accountant explained that he couldn't pay the pressing bill because he didn't have the money. GRT had been pulling cash out of Chicago for other operations.

"Listen, motherfucker," Leonard yelled, "this company has my name on it. You call them up and tell them to pay the bill now."

Lennie Diamond told his uncle thanks and wanted to talk a little more, but Leonard brushed him off. "I'm late for lunch with Bernadine." Bernadine Washington was now a vice president at VON and frequently joined Leonard for lunch. She often drove with him between the studio and the station. He walked toward the door to leave; Lennie headed out to get something to eat.

Leonard never made it to VON. Two blocks from the station, he slumped over the steering wheel, stricken with a heart attack. Washington tried to control the car, but it crashed into two parked vehicles. Leonard was dead, fifty-two years old.

"I couldn't find his pills, I couldn't find his pills," Washington sobbed over and over again to Lucky Cordell when she got to the station. He tried to console her. There was no chance Leonard could have survived even if she had given him his heart medication, Cordell told her. The other station employees were in shock.

Cynthia Strohacker—"Maybe" was her on-air name—was the "Den Pal" scheduled to handle the afternoon segment on SDM. But the regular format was scrapped; instead, Burt Burdeen put the station on automatic programming.

Phil took the call from South Kedzie with the grim news. He raced over to Lennie Diamond's office. "Leonard's dead! Leonard's dead!" he screamed. "Get over to my parents' house." Diamond left immediately to tell Joe and Celia Chess and Mae Silverbrand, Leonard's sister, what had happened.

Dick LaPalm was in Los Angeles for a friend's wedding; his wife was to join him later. She called him at his hotel and told him the news. He canceled his plans and headed to the airport to fly home. Meeting with GRT people in Los Angeles, Richie Salvador was summoned to the phone. It was his secretary, Esther Bacith. "You better come back here," she told him. "Leonard died."

By this time Marshall was already on an airplane heading home. When he landed, his wife was at the gate to meet him, a look on her face he had never seen before. "Your father died," she said, giving him the news unadorned by sentiment.

Marshall didn't say a word. He was too stunned even to cry. His wife drove him straight to his parents' house in Glencoe. Revetta was sobbing. Phil was in the kitchen, doubled over in tears, the first time his children had ever seen him cry. He was the one who had gone to identify the body earlier in the day. When he got back to Oakridge Drive, he walked in the house carrying a small paper bag. Inside were the few things Leonard had kept in his pockets. "This is all that is left of a wonderful man," he said, throwing the bag on the floor and overcome with grief. When Salvador got to the house later in the evening, Phil wept all over again. "What am I gonna do, Richie? Why is this happening to me? He was my life."

Jewish tradition is to bury the dead as quickly as possible. In this case, it would have meant burying Leonard on Friday before sundown, the start of the Jewish Sabbath, which extends through Saturday at sundown. But because his death was so unexpected, it would take time to make arrangements for the funeral, and many friends in the business would want to come from all parts of the country. So the funeral was held on Monday, October 20.

Weinstein and Sons Chapel on Peterson Avenue was packed. A line of those hoping to get in extended well down the block. There were as many black mourners as white, Chess musicians, business associates, and clergymen. Leonard's friends from the record business came—Gene and Harry Goodman from Arc Music and Arrow, the lawyer; Jerry Wexler and the Erteguns; Stan Lewis from Shreveport; Hoss Allen, the Nashville disc jockey; Buster Williams from Memphis; Vince Pepper, the lawyer for the radio stations, among them. After the service, most of the mourners joined the caravan out to the Westlawn Cemetery for the burial—so many, Lennie Diamond remembered, that some of them were still trying to get in the gates by the time the interment was over.

Muddy Waters was heartbroken. "It's all over, Leonard," he said in tears at the gravesite, a devastated LaPalm looking on. "It's just all over. There ain't no more record company. No more nothin', Leonard."

Dozens of friends accompanied the family back to the house in Glencoe. According to Jewish tradition, there was a large bowl of water outside the front door so all who entered could wash their hands first. The meaning of the ritual is to avoid bringing death from the cemetery into the home of the living.

The mood inside lightened. For a few hours the shock of Leonard's death gave way to memories of his vigor in life. Most everyone had a story to tell about when they first met him or how they argued with him or what he taught them. Binzer relived all over again those hours on the South Side of Chicago when Leonard took "this Jew from Indiana" who thought he knew the world and showed him what he had missed.

The first record to bear the Chess label nineteen years earlier had been Gene Ammons playing his saxophone on "My Foolish Heart." So it seemed fitting that a few plaintive notes from a saxophone introduced the comments that VON news director Roy Wood read over the air not long after Leonard died. "Leonard Chess will be remembered as long as phonograph records and musical tapes are played," Wood said. "As long as people listen to and enjoy radio entertainment Leonard Chess will be well remembered. . . . Leonard Chess was a Jew, but he was too universal to notice it," Wood added. But he drew on this signal element of Leonard's life as he closed his tribute. "What do you say to a friend when he leaves your presence bound for Home?" he asked, as "My Precious Lord" crescendoed in the background.

"Shalom."

EPILOGUE: LAWSUITS
AND LEGACIES

The shock and sadness over Leonard's death was compounded for his family by the fact that Leonard died without a will. Nate Notkin had given him three drafts, but Leonard, whose superstitions were well known, always resisted signing the document. Everyone knew the consequences of dying intestate: the government would get a substantial share of his estate. Revetta, his widow, would get most of the rest. Marshall realized immediately that he would lose the money he was expecting to start a new label independent of GRT. In a tense meeting with Phil and Notkin, he had to restrain himself from grabbing the most recent draft of the will and writing Leonard's name at the bottom. Only years later, after untangling what he called "this ball of pain inside" and descending into heavy drug use, would he fully understand his despair as the reality set in. "I lost what I thought was my birthright," he said, "and then I lost the money I was supposed to get through losing that birthright."

Day by day in the weeks and months after Leonard's death, he saw his dreams dissipate and the company his father and uncle built come apart piece by piece. "It was like cancer from the moment GRT arrived, eating away at Chess Records," Marshall said. "That's the way I would describe it."

Alan Bayley, the president of GRT, tried to say all the right things to a grieving staff when he came to East Twenty-first Street a few days after Leonard's funeral. He wanted to reassure everyone that Chess Records would continue to operate smoothly and turn out good music. Privately, Bayley had tapped Richie Salvador to be the new president of the company. "I did not look on Marshall as being equipped to replace Leonard," he said.

"In fact I felt he never would have that capability." When Marshall learned of the decision, he told Bayley he would have no part of it. In a late-night confrontation at Bayley's hotel in Chicago, Marshall told him either he came to work the next day as the president of Chess or he was leaving.

Bayley capitulated and gave Marshall the title. He had to tell Salvador things had changed, but Salvador was nonetheless given considerable authority: executive vice president in charge of all daily operations, in effect the mandate to run the company. Phil was designated "staff vice president"—a title with not much responsibility. For all practical purposes he was no longer a part of the company. It was clear to Marshall that the GRT men neither appreciated nor understood Phil's role in building Chess Records—the symbiotic relationship, in Marshall's mind, "where the sum was greater than the individual parts." Leonard had been the leader, the aggressive one out in front, but Phil had been with him every step of the way, broadening the company's reach through his own contacts and operating with the unspoken trust most often found between siblings raised in a close family. The new owners were likewise unable to understand the institutional history that Phil could give them—simply put, how the business worked. Put off by an unpolished exterior, they failed to recognize the business acumen that would bring him handsome profit in later ventures. To Bayley, Phil was "the valued gofer for Leonard. That's about it for Phil."

Just how much was changing under GRT's ownership became apparent to Marshall when he was sent to a seminar run by the American Management Institute. They wanted him to learn how to be an executive, how to manage, how to prepare budgets. Every few weeks they called him out to California for a meeting. "What can you project?" they asked him.

"I don't know what to project. That's not how we run our business," he told them. "We try to make hits, and I cannot tell you how many hits we're going to have this year." Who would have thought that the well-received *Fathers and Sons* would fail to sell? When Peter Guralnick, a perceptive and prolific music writer, went to the Chess offices early in 1970, he was greeted in the warehouse by a grumbling stock man taking back boxes of unopened albums. "Who put out this fucking stiff?" he wanted to know.

Marshall was growing increasingly discontent, and when he made a trip to San Francisco in the early spring of 1970, he decided that when he got back he would quit. His decision was triggered by an evening at a Bay Area club where he heard a young musician named Boz Scaggs. Marshall was taken with his music—"Soulful," he thought, "like a white man who was black." Right then Marshall knew he would resign and do whatever it took to start up his own label. Scaggs would be his first act. They talked about their plans when Scaggs drove him to the San Francisco airport for the flight back to Chicago. They made a handshake deal on their new venture.

When Marshall delivered the news to Bayley, he tried to talk him out of it. GRT needed a Chess around, he said, and Bayley suggested they work something out. Perhaps Marshall could have his own label but distribute it through GRT. The idea was appealing, so he negotiated a contract that included all the terms he wanted and waited to sign the papers. In the interim, however, GRT changed the management structure. In mid-April 1970, Len Levy, who had been president of Metromedia Records and before that a vice president at Epic Records, was named the head of GRT Records, a new entity that had just been formed to embrace Chess and three other record labels the company was trying to manage. Levy looked at Marshall's proposed agreement and decided it was too generous. The deal was off.

Marshall quit. He negotiated a year's salary, his car, a 1967 Ferrari, and the furniture from his eighth-floor office on East Twenty-first Street. The only thing he really cared about was the Oriental rug. He told Scaggs he couldn't start a new label. He was too depressed.

Within a week or so after his GRT deal soured, Marshall got a phone call from a friend in the record business, Bob Krasnow, who was running Blue Thumb Records, another GRT entity. Krasnow told him the Rolling Stones' contract with London Decca would expire soon and they were also looking to get a new manager. Krasnow suggested that he and Marshall make a joint pitch to the group. Marshall thought about it for a few days and then called Krasnow back. Their egos were too big to work together, he said, but would Krasnow mind if he called Mick Jagger? He knew Jagger from the sessions at 2120 South Michigan, and he had spent time with him on a few trips to England. Krasnow gave him Jagger's home number. Marshall reached him right away, and Jagger was interested. He asked Marshall to fly to London so they could talk some more, and after a few more meetings, Marshall was headed to Europe to start a new career in the record business.

The last Chess had left Chess Records.

In the meantime, Phil completed the sale of WVON to Globetrotter Communications. Selling the lucrative entity had been part of Leonard's plan to reinvest the money in a television station. Globetrotter paid $9 million, though not all of that money was paid out at the closing. The sale price represented a ninefold profit over the original purchase price. By the summer of 1971 Revetta sold her share of L&P Broadcasting, which she got after Leonard's death, to Phil for $450,000. On January 2, 1973, Phil sold WNOV, the station in Milwaukee, to Courier Communications for $385,000. While the sale price was $125,000 over the 1968 purchase price, Vince Pepper, who handled much of the legal work for the radio stations, was sure that if Leonard had not died eighteen months after NOV was bought, he would have made the station even more profitable. Three weeks after the NOV sale, on January 27, Phil, his wife, Sheva, and their youngest child, Kevin, moved to Tucson, Arizona.

Phil turned his attention to other business pursuits, principally real estate, but he held on to WSDM, the FM station, which Terry was managing. Terry eventually turned it into a progressive music format and in March 1977 changed the call letters to WLUP. In December 1978, Phil and Terry decided to sell the station to Heftel Communications, which was operated by Cecil Heftel, a Democratic member of Congress from Hawaii. The purchase price was $5.25 million.

ᴧᴧ

One unpleasant matter that had been hanging over Leonard and Phil since 1962 was a lawsuit filed against them and the Checker subsidiary by Don Robey, who ran Peacock Records. Robey claimed that the Chess brothers had illegally signed the Five Blind Boys of Alabama, a vocal group, to Checker while they were still under contract to his label. Leonard and Phil claimed that when they signed the group, they were told the singers were free to contract with another label. Charges and countercharges of perjury and double-dealing abounded. The FBI was asked to investigate.

At a 1963 trial in a Chicago federal court, Judge J. Samuel Perry found in favor of Robey, awarding him $150,000 in damages. While the case was on appeal, Leonard and Phil filed a motion to vacate the judgment because some of the singers were now saying they gave perjured testimony. One key piece of evidence was a document purporting to show a contract with one date and markings showing that the date had been altered to make the contract appear to have been in force earlier. In 1966, a federal appeals court ordered a new trial, chastising Perry for "a failure to exercise sound legal discretion" in considering the evidence the Chess brothers had presented. The second trial took place in 1969, and once again Perry found in favor of Robey and the Peacock label. He awarded Robey $350,000 in damages. The Chess brothers appealed once more. In a decision handed down August

6, 1970, the appeals court threw out the judgment a second time, renewing its harsh criticism of Perry.

Neither Phil nor Leonard's estate ever paid Robey a penny, but the years of litigation, Phil and Marshall said, had been a headache and cost them thousands of dollars in lawyers' fees.

♦♦

Though the press releases and stories in the trade papers tried to suggest the opposite, Chess Records was coming undone. In April 1970, GRT closed the pressing plant in Chicago; a few months later the executive offices were moved to New York, though the studio remained in operation on East Twenty-first Street and the warehouse there still stored records. Within a year, GRT's record division was almost bankrupt. Company officials had to renegotiate the notes Leonard agreed to when Chess was sold to get a lower interest rate and to extend the payment period another three years. Marvin Schlacter, who ran Janus Records, was brought in to replace Levy.

When he took over in March of 1971, Schlacter reorganized the record division once again. While he brought some stability to the operation, financial problems persisted. "GRT had never been in direct control of artists, in the development and promotion of artists," said Alan Bayley, reflecting on the situation years later. While GRT knew how to market and distribute tapes that others had made, the record company venture, he conceded, was new territory. Not only did they have problems developing new material for the artists, they didn't do well with the catalogue—the records that had been made in the two decades of Chess operation. "We had quite some plans and hopes, I should say, more than anything else, of deriving quite a bit of value out of the old Chess catalogue," Bayley said, "and we hadn't done a good job with it at all, of mining that old Chess catalogue for value."

Bayley had never wanted the building at 320 East Twenty-first Street, so he was anxious to sell it when the opportunity arose. But he had to go to court in the spring of 1973 to get permission to remove a lien on the building—the result of the company's financial difficulties—before the sale could go through. The new owner promptly cleaned house. Hundreds of records were sold for next to nothing, but thousands remained. A crew of day laborers with power saws came in and destroyed whatever had been left in the storeroom and carted them away.

GRT's declining fortunes became apparent again when Leonard's estate was finally settled in 1974. It was valued at $4,009,000, but more than half that amount, $2,160,000, had been paid in taxes. Revetta received one-third of the assets and the remaining two-thirds was divided among the three children. Only a portion of what the four received was in liquid assets. The rest was tied up in stocks, including GRT. In that final accounting, the GRT stock was valued at $3.41 per share. By the time Marshall could sell his portion the price per share had dropped to $1.78.

With the record division in New York now closed and essential personnel in California, Bayley was ready to sell off more assets. In August 1975, he concluded a deal with Joe and Sylvia Robinson, the owners of All Platinum Records in Englewood, New Jersey, to sell the Chess, Checker, and Cadet master tapes for a reported $950,000. The new owners intended to keep operating the label as an ongoing concern, but they had to release one of their premier acts—the Dells. They couldn't afford them. Six years after Chess records was sold, barely a skeleton of what Leonard and Phil had built remained.

◀◀

As they were making records in the studio and out on the road doing club dates and concerts, some of the Chess recording artists, particularly the blues artists, grumbled from time to time about how little they were getting paid from the company. By the seventies, when more and more whites had discovered blues and the artists who made the original music, the artists' allegations of exploitation intensified. So did their ability to make their voices heard, through fans, some of them lawyers and agents, eager to help them right what they believed to be past wrongs. Bo Diddley lodged some of the loudest complaints. "Bo Diddley ain't got shit," he told *Rolling Stone* in 1987. "My records are sold all over the world, and I ain't got a fuckin' dime. If Chess Records gave me in all the time that I dealt with them, if they gave me $75,000 in royalty checks, I'll eat my hat. Boil it and eat it . . . When I left Chess Records [under GRT's ownership], they said I owed them $125,000."

When he asked Gene Goodman about his song publishing royalties, "Gene told me to go dig up Leonard," Diddley said a few years later. Time after time, he added, he was told his deal was "in the contract. That's what it is, CON-tract." In 1969, just after Chess was sold, Diddley had spoken more benignly about Leonard and Phil to the magazine *Blues Unlimited*. "I feel that we were like a family. This is the way I felt. I felt I was for them and they was for me and we were for each other."

Without documents—Bo Diddley's contracts, the sales figures for his records, the costs to make the records, and the advances he may have received—the accuracy of Diddley's allegations were difficult to judge. But his anger reflected the view among some musicians that they were cheated, an allegation steadfastly denied by Phil and Marshall. "What's missing from Bo's version of events," Marshall insisted, "is all the gimmes. Bo was one of the biggest takers." In those early years, he said, "it was a constant refrain of 'I need, I want'—five hundred dollars at a clip that could add up to thousands by the end of a year."

The money was advanced against expected royalties. In the early 1950s the rate was about two cents a record, the industry standard. Royalties were not yet based on a percentage of the record's selling price, which came to be the practice in later years. "When the statement comes and they don't get a lot of money, right away you beat 'em out of it. . . . They forgot what they did," Phil said. He rarely talked about work at home, but every now and then his children would hear him refer to this musician or that who got in trouble in some far-off city and needed bail money. "Who do you think took care of that?" Phil asked.

Even if advances and sales figures were documented, Diddley mistrusted those statements. "How am I gonna get the right count on his stationery?" he asked, referring to Leonard during a 1984 interview. "He ain't Jesus. How's he gonna give me the right count?"

The bitterness Bo Diddley displayed toward the Chess brothers in later years came as a surprise to Phil. "He always seemed to me like he was happy." Diddley's later anger also surprised Etta James. "When I was there with Leonard," she said, "God, Leonard treated Bo like some kind of royalty."

Diddley himself gave a different cast to his Chess years when he spoke at a gathering October 24, 1999, at the old Chess studio on Michigan Avenue. Had it not been for the company, he said, "no tellin' where I'd be, probably maybe in jail or dead, something like that. I'm just tellin' you the honest to God's truth because I had no direction. I got direction out of here."

In 1955 Chuck Berry had had to share the writing credit and thus the writer royalties on "Maybellene" with Alan Freed, the disc jockey, and Russ Fratto, Leonard and Phil's good friend. Beyond that he was unhappy with the payments he was receiving through Arc Music for all of his other songs. He claimed that during the time he was in prison, he received none of his writers' royalties. When the original copyrights expired, Berry enlisted the help of William Krasilovsky, a highly regarded New York entertainment lawyer, to get many of his songs out of Arc Music and into his own publishing company, Isalee. The agreement with Arc also provided that the publishing rights on some other songs would be split between the two.

In 1974 Howlin' Wolf filed a lawsuit against Arc Music asking for $2.5 million in damages for unpaid royalties from his songs. He claimed that the Goodmans and the Chess brothers defrauded him of the copyrights and therefore the profits he could earn from his music. The complaint alleged that not only was Wolf not given money from domestic sales but the foreign royalties were also deliberately and illegally kept from him. To get Wolf to sign various publishing agreements, the complaint added, Gene Goodman "resorted to guile, and cunning and made false statements and representations" to Wolf and concealed important information. Goodman denied the allegations in a formal answer filed with the federal court. The two sides reached an undisclosed monetary settlement after Wolf's death in 1976. Arc retained the publishing rights to his songs.

In 1976 Muddy Waters and Willie Dixon filed identical lawsuits against the publishing company, alleging fraud and conspiracy and asking to be paid money damages and to have their publishing contracts voided. The essence of the claims was that Arc Music failed to pay appropriate royalties to the writers through several methods of undercounting. Among them was the claim that because Chess did not pay the mechanical royalty to Arc Music for any song put out by a Chess artist-writer on the Chess labels, Arc did not in turn pay half of that mechanical rate to the songwriter as was the standard practice. Marshall insisted that Chess paid the songwriters their portion of the mechanical royalty directly. Documents filed in the Howlin' Wolf suit appeared to support his point. Among the exhibits proposed by Howlin' Wolf's lawyer for his litigation were royalty checks from Chess to Wolf "insofar as they apply to Burnett [Wolf's real last name] as a songwriter." Whether the amounts were all they should have been was a matter in dispute, but the checks suggested that Chess was paying Wolf royalties as a songwriter.

Another charge was that amounts due Waters and Dixon were as a matter of course "substantially understated" and that royalties due from foreign sales were not reported at all so that the income could remain in Arc

Music instead of being disbursed to the songwriter. Though the complaints acknowledged that Waters and Dixon as songwriters received periodic payments, these payments, the lawsuits alleged, were gross understatements of what was owed.

Phil and the Goodman brothers denied the allegations. However, no discovery—the process of gathering evidence and deposing witnesses under oath—to determine the facts ensued. The Waters and Dixon suits were settled within weeks of their filing. The terms of the settlement were confidential. However, as copyright renewals came up, Arc returned the songs to the writers.

"Nobody wanted to deprive these people of the right to their songs. If they wanted to have the rights, back they were going to get it," said Peter Herbert, a New York entertainment lawyer, who was one of the Arc attorneys. "Nobody wanted to fight these guys. We just saw this as an effort on the part of an agent to renegotiate a better publishing deal with somebody else. But the scurrilous charges that were being made—we didn't believe them. We never did." Herbert added that "as a point of reality" it was customary for songwriters to sign over the rights to their songs to a publisher "to exploit them in print and for cover records," with the proceeds being split between publisher and writer.

Reflecting on her time at Chess, Mitty Collier remembered getting a 1967 Pontiac Bonneville from Leonard, which was worth around $4,000. "Well, that's a lot of money, but you have to pay them back," she said. "They bought it and then would take the payments out of the royalty." If she had wanted money instead of the car, Collier said, Leonard would have given her that, but the cash, too, would have been paid back out of her royalties. "We never paid it back," she added, referring to herself and others on the Chess roster. Everyone was "always in the red. You never saw any evidence that you were paying it back. We got a fraction of a cent out of every record. The biggest money I earned was from my personal engagements."

Part employer, part banker, part protector, Leonard and Phil weren't doing anything different from any of the other independent label owners, and they were more generous than many. But the brothers never thought they were running a charitable institution, and they expected to get back at least some of the money they advanced. Disagreements remained over how much was advanced and how much was earned against those advances—information in the control of the record company and all the more powerful because so many of the recording artists, particularly in the early days, had little formal education and grew up in poverty. None of the critical documents from the fifties and early sixties survived into the nineties. The Chess Records sale in 1969 to GRT and then again in 1975 to All Platinum meant a loss of important paperwork—production costs, sales figures, royalty payments to the artists, amounts advanced to an artist on the royalties. Lennie Diamond, Leonard's nephew, was convinced that "a lot of people got off the hook" when Leonard died because he could no longer collect on debts written down on the scraps of paper he stored in his safe.

But one thing still rankled the artists: if Chess was growing and prospering, it was doing so because of the musicians who made the music the public was buying. If the recording artists themselves weren't prospering in equal degree, then there was only one conclusion to draw: they were being cheated and their profits stolen. Phil and Marshall rejected that notion. Neither apologized about the past. "My father was tough. He was no angel," Marshall said. "But he wasn't a thief, and he wasn't a crook." In his mind the fact that so many musicians stayed so long with the company was evidence that Chess was a good place to be. Of the major Chess artists— Waters, Wolf, Walter, Berry, Diddley, James, Jamal, and Lewis—only Berry left before Leonard sold the company, and he came back when his contract with Mercury expired. Jamal described his long tenure as "a very happy marriage. I was good to them. They were good to me."

The relationship between Etta James and Leonard was complicated, volatile, loving, and frustrating, sometimes all at once for both of them. It was also illuminating, just like the encounter Billy Davis had witnessed between Leonard and Sonny Boy Williamson over Williamson's request for money. Leonard's concern about James's drug problems and her overall well-being was genuine. When she bought a house in California, Leonard put it in his name. He made the mortgage payments and charged them against her royalties. James's friends told her she was crazy to trust him. They were sure she would never see the deed again.

A week after Leonard died, James was at her house when she heard a knock at the door. "A white man in a plain blue suit and gray tie was standing there," she recalled in her autobiography. "He looked like an accountant or banker. 'I'm a friend of Leonard Chess,' he said. 'Leonard told me that if anything ever happened to him, I was to give you this.' " He handed James an envelope. Inside was the deed written out in her name.

"I know in my heart," James wrote, "that if Leonard hadn't snatched the deed from me years before, I would have lost the house. . . ."

⌒⌒

Through the late seventies and into the 1980s, the Chess masters fared no better at All Platinum and its later incarnation, Sugar Hill, than they had at GRT. The Robinsons dropped the idea of operating the label as an ongoing concern and were unable to come up with any sustained program for reissuing the music; by 1985 they were in serious financial trouble. The much larger MCA Records, which had been distributing All Platinum, acquired the entire Chess catalogue that year, and by 1986, an organized and increasingly ambitious reissue program began. The first elements were simple reproductions of originals. But in 1987, when Andy McKaie took over as the A&R director of MCA's special markets divison, he started a much broader program. He began to issue compilations that brought together in separate packages blues material, jazz, rhythm and blues, rock and roll, and later soul music. He also repackaged the music of individual artists, gathering their records in boxed sets with extensive liner notes and pictures. The boxed sets received three Grammy nominations, and the one devoted to Chuck Berry won the 1989 Historical Album Grammy.

McKaie had some eight thousand master tapes at his disposal. They were stored in rough chronological order in a specially built vault at Universal, the entertainment complex headquartered in Los Angeles and the parent company of MCA. The Chess masters were stacked side by side in various-sized boxes with handwritten labels on shelves eighteen feet high, Muddy Waters mixed with Billy Stewart, Bo Diddley, Little Walter, the young Four Tops, Chuck Berry, Etta James, Fontella Bass, and the dozens of other musicians who came through the Chess studio.

In 1997, the fiftieth anniversary of Leonard's entry into the business on the Aristocrat label, McKaie put out a special anniversary series with a distinctive gold and black design to mark the occasion.

At the same time Chess music was becoming more visible, so was the old studio at 2120 South Michigan Avenue. When the record company moved from South Michigan to 320 East Twenty-first Street, Joe Chess continued to own the old building. Ralph Bass, the producer, kept watch on the property, and for a time, his wife ran a dance school upstairs, refurbishing the studio with mirrors and a barre for the dancers. In 1979, Gerald Sims, the original guitar player in the house rhythm section, bought the building from Chess for about $50,000. He turned it back into a studio and recorded off and on over the next several years.

In 1989 the Chicago City Landmarks Commission recommended that

2120 South Michigan Avenue be designated a landmark, protecting it from demolition or substantial change. The lion's share of the work to protect the building was done by Tim Samuelson, an architectural historian at the commission and a longtime blues aficionado. The city council made the designation official six months later, in May of 1990. In 1993, Marie Dixon, the widow of Willie Dixon, who had died in 1992, bought the South Michigan Avenue building from Sims for the Blues Heaven Foundation, which Dixon had created a few years earlier. She and her family continued to raise money to refurbish 2120 for a museum. The building formally reopened in September 1997 and began to offer tours for visitors a few months later.

In October 1999 the Chess studio was given a special landmark status as part of the Clinton Administration's "Save America's Treasures" program. One of the unfortunate by-products of the blues mythology was the claim, repeated by Shirli Dixon Nelson, Dixon's daughter, and some tour guides, that black artists, from Muddy Waters and Chuck Berry to unknown session musicians, were not permitted to come in the front door but were required to use the back entrance. Musicians sometimes used the back door at 2120 South Michigan, often to bring their instruments up to the studio because it was more convenient. But there was no truth to the claim that they were barred from coming in the front door. "That's bullshit, absolute bullshit," said Billy Davis, echoing the view of many musicians. Some could not recall ever using the back door in countless trips to the studio.

Just how far myth had traveled from reality was apparent one day in 1995 when Samuelson was giving a group of visitors a tour of the building, which was still being restored. He talked about its history, how the studio was built, and how Leonard and Phil had gone from running a nightclub to running a successful record label. Afterward a young black man told Samuelson he didn't much care for his tour: "Too much about those old Jews," he said. Lost in the interpretive buzz of the blues culture was the fact that "those old Jews" were Chess Records.

After Leonard died, his share of Arc Music should have reverted to the other three partners, Phil and Gene and Harry Goodman. But Phil asked that his brother's share be given to Revetta, and the Goodmans agreed. Until her death in 1983, she received one-quarter of the profits from the publishing company. When Revetta died, Marshall became the fourth partner in Arc. He was the last surviving member of his immediate family. His sister Susie had died of a drug overdose in 1973. Elaine died in 1976 from complications following surgery.

After leaving GRT, Marshall had stayed with the Rolling Stones for five years, developing Rolling Stones Records with its distinctive logo of red lips. The Stones chapter behind him, Marshall successfully fought his drug habit and involved himself in various independent record projects. In 1992, after the death of his brother Harry, Gene Goodman told Marshall he wanted to sell the publishing company. Marshall instead suggested that *he* run it. Goodman and Phil, who was still living in Arizona, accepted Marshall's proposal. In 1994 he brought in his cousin Kevin, Phil's youngest son, to help him run Arc.

But Marshall never gave up on the idea of starting his own label. In 1998 he brought together three musicians he wanted to work with—a white guitar player and singer, Murali Coryell, and two sidemen who were black, Bill Foster and Rod Gross. The album they made was a mix of blues and R&B called *2120* on a label Marshall called CZYZ, the original family name in Poland.

On March 11, 1999, Marshall was ready to put his signature on the final papers for the project. The pen was in his hand when he realized what day it was. He decided to wait twenty-four hours, until March 12, 1999. It was his father's birthday. Had he lived, Leonard would have been eighty-two years old. When the first compact disc was ready for production, Marshall made sure that the last three digits of the industry registration number read 312—the numeric equivalent of March 12. It was the same kind of talisman his father and uncle had used on the first record for the Chess label, Chess 1425—the address on South Karlov in Chicago, their first home in America.

Leonard and Phil set out to make a living in the 1940s, not to make music. But the one had become the other. A half-century later the music played on.

DISCOGRAPHY

This discography begins with Chapter 4, Leonard's entry into the record business, and lists selected songs that are relevant to the specific chapter. Not included are Chapters 12, *Play for Pay,* about payola, and Chapter 15, *Voice of the Negro,* about the Chess-owned radio station in Chicago, WVON.*

4. IMMIGRANT TO ARISTOCRAT

Fishin' Pole. Tom Archia. Originally Aristocrat 601 - MCA CHD2-9387
Ice Man Blues. Tom Archia. Originally Aristocrat 602 - MCA CHD2-9387
Bilbo is Dead. Andrew Tibbs. Originally Aristocrat 1101 - MCA CHD2-9387
Boogie Woogie Blues. Clarence Samuels. Originally Aristocrat 1001- MCA CHD2-9387
Johnson Machine Gun. Sunnyland Slim. Originally Aristocrat 1301- MCA CHD2 9387
Gypsy Woman. Muddy Waters. Originally Aristocrat 1302 - MCA CHD2 9387
I Can't Be Satisfied. Muddy Waters. Originally Aristocrat 1305 - MCA CHD2 9387
I Feel Like Going Home. Muddy Waters. Originally Aristocrat 1305 - MCA CHD2
9387

5. MEMPHIS CONNECTIONS

My Foolish Heart. Gene Ammons. Originally Chess 1425 - MCA GRD 2-812
Rollin' Stone. Muddy Waters. Originally Chess 1426 - MCA CHD/C4-9340
Rocket 88. Jackie Brenston & His Delta Cats. Originally Chess 1458 - MCA CHC/D4-9352
Moanin at Midnight. Howlin' Wolf. Originally Chess 1479 - MCA CHD/C4-9340

*Many but not all of the selections can be found on three basic MCA compilations of Chess material: *Chess Blues* (MCA CHD/C 4-9340), *Chess Rhythm and Roll* (MCA CHC/D4 -9352), and *Chess Soul* (MCA CHD2-9388). For more jazz selections, consult *the history of chess jazz* (MCA GRD2-812). For the Aristocrat years, see *The Aristocrat of Blues* (MCA CHD2-9387).

6. CHECKERS, CHARTS, AND COPYRIGHTS

I Don't Know. Willie Mabon. Originally Parrot 1050/Chess 1531 - MCA CHD2-9385
Juke. Little Walter. Originally Checker 758 - MCA CHD/C4-9340

7. BLUES WITH A FEELING

Hoochie Coochie Man. Parrot 1050/Originally Chess 1560 - MCA CHD/C4-9340
Reconsider Baby. Originally Checker 804 - MCA CHD/C4-9340
Sincerely. Originally Chess 1581 - MCA CHD/C4-9352

8. THE BEAT HAS GOT TO MOVE

Bo Diddley. Originally Checker 814 - CHC/D4-9352
Maybellene. Originally Chess 1604 - CHC/D4-9352

9. MONEY IN THE SONG

See You Later Alligator. Bobby Charles. Originally Chess 1609 - CHC/D4-9352
I'll Be Home. The Flamingos. Originally Checker 830 - CHC/D4-9352
Ain't Got No Home. Clarence "Frogman" Henry. Originally Argo 5259 - CHC/D4-9352

10. 2120 SOUTH MICHIGAN

School Day. Chuck Berry. Originally Chess 1653 - MCA CHD3-80001
Rock 'n Roll Music. Chuck Berry. Originally Chess 1671 - MCA CHD3-80001
Little Village. Sonny Boy Williamson. Originally from Chess LP 1536 - MCA CHD2-9343

11. ALL THAT JAZZ

Poinciana. Ahmad Jamal. Originally from Argo LP 628 - MCA GRD2-812
Killer Joe. The Jazztet. Originally from Cadet LP 664 - MCA GRD2-812

13. TRUST IN ME

All I Could Do Was Cry. Etta James. Originally Argo 5359 - MCA CHD 9367
At Last. Etta James. Originally Argo 5380 - MCA CHD 9367
Trust In Me. Etta James. Originally Argo 5385 - MCA CHD-9367
Road Runner. Bo Diddley. Originally Checker 942- MCA CHD2 19502

14. BRANCHING OUT

I Want to Know. Sugar Pie DeSanto. Originally Veltone 103 - MCA CHC/D4-9352
Something's Got a Hold on Me. Etta James. Originally Argo 5409 - MCA CHD 9367
and MCA CHD 9184 (live performance)
Reap What You Sow. Billy Stewart. Originally Chess 1820 - MCA CHC/D4-9352

16. THE SOUL OF A MAN

Mama Didn't Lie. Jan Bradley. Originally Formal 1044/Chess 1845 - MCA CHD2-9388
High Heeled Sneakers. Tommy Tucker. Originally Checker 1067 - MCA CHC/D4-9352
Slip-in Mules. Sugar Pie DeSanto. Originally Checker 1073 - MCA CHD 9257
Selfish One. Jackie Ross. Originally Chess 1903 - MCA CHD2-9388
I Had a Talk with My Man. Mitty Collier. Originally Chess 1907 - MCA CHD2-9388

17. DON'T MESS UP A GOOD THING

We're Gonna Make It. Little Milton. Originally Checker 1105 - MCA CHD/C-9340
Don't Mess Up a Good Thing. Fontella Bass and Bobby McClure. Originally Checker 1097 - MCA CHD2-9388
I Do Love You. Billy Stewart. Originally Chess 1922 - MCA CHD/C-9388
Rescue Me. Fontella Bass. Originally Checker 1120 - MCA CHD/C-9388
In-Crowd. Ramsey Lewis Trio. Originally from Cadet LP 757 - MCA GRD2-412
Wang Dang Doodle. Koko Taylor. Originally Checker 1135 - MCA CHD/C-9340

18. 320 EAST 21ST STREET

Dirty Man. Laura Lee. Originally Chess 2013 - MCA CHD 2-9388
Tell Mama. Etta James. Originally Cadet 5578 - MCA CHD 9367
I'd Rather Go Blind. Etta James. Originally Cadet 5578 - MCA CHD 9367

19. FINAL TRACKS

O-O I Love You. The Dells. Originally Cadet 5574 - MCA CHC/D4-9352
There Is. The Dells. Originally Cadet 5574 - MCA CHD-9333
Amen. The Rotary Connection. Originally from Cadet Concept LP 312 - MCA CHD 9365
Soul Man. The Rotary Connection. Originally from Cadet Concept LP 312 - MCA CHD 9365
Let's Spend the Night Together. Muddy Waters. Originally from Cadet Concept LP 314 - MCA CHD 9364
Got My MoJo Working, Parts I and II. Muddy Waters. Orignally from Chess 2LPS 127 - MCA CHD 92522

NOTES

1. THE MEN ON THE CHESS BOARD

2: "A Jew": James, *The Immigrant Jew in America*, p. 125.

3: "If you": Richie Salvador interview, July 1, 1999.

2. COMING TO CHICAGO

5: Motele: Cutler, *The Jews of Chicago*, pp. 40–43; Rose, *Chaim Weizmann: A Biography*, p. 7.

6: sing songs: Mae Chess Silverbrand interviews, August 22, November 19, 1997.

7: beets, carrots: Interviews with Silverbrand, Phil Chess, October 23, 1997; Sadel Pulik Cohen, October 29, 1997; Marshall Chess, October 8, 1997.

7: Halsted and Maxwell streets: Silverbrand interviews; Chicago city phone books, 1928, 1929; Cutler, pp. 40, 58; Wirth, *The Ghetto*, pp. 192–93.

7: "Anything": Cutler, p. 66; Wirth, pp. 232–33.

7: Others . . . headed south: Harry Pulik interview, December 10, 1997; Joseph Pulik naturalization papers.

8: "Motelers": Norman Schwartz interviews, July 28, 1997, November 17, 1997; History of Anshe Motele provided by Schwartz.

8: medical advice: Silverbrand interview, August 22, 1997.

9: "*Schlim! schlim!*": Silverbrand, Chess, Cohen interviews.

9: "*Des es*": Silverbrand, Chess interviews.

10: Lawndale: Silverbrand, Cohen interviews; Cutler, pp. 209–12; *Local Community Fact Book, Chicago Metropolitan Area*, p. 107.

11: hot dog: Phil Chess interview, October 23, 1997.

12: Franklin Park: Phil Chess, Silverbrand interviews.

12: Shirley Adams: Phil Chess, Silverbrand interviews; Millie Witzel interview, December 8, 1997; Adrian Silverbrand Mallin interview, November 6, 1997.

13: "Ragsoline": Cohen interview, December 7, 1997; Irving Cutler interview,

December 7, 1997.

13: Old bottles: Phil Chess, Silverbrand, Cohen interviews.

13: Revetta Sloan: Witzel interview, Marshall Chess interview, December 12, 1997.

14: Chess and Sons: Phil Chess interviews; Chicago City Yellow Pages, 1942–1948.

14: "hand clappers": Phil Chess interviews.

14: Cut-Rate Liquor: Witzel, Marshall Chess interviews; Phil Chess interview, January 30, 1998.

15: 708 Liquor Store: Silverbrand interviews, Charles Parham interview, December 23, 1997; *Chicago Defender*, October 14, 1944, p. 6; Chicago City Yellow and White Pages, 1944–46; *Chicago Defender* entertainment ad pages, January 1944–December 1946; liquor licenses for 5060 S. State Street and 708 E. 47th from the Illinois Liquor Control Commission.

16: "a small string": Rowe, *Chicago Blues*, p. 63; Palmer, *Deep Blues,* p. 157.

16: twenty-five dollars: Liquor license for Macomba Lounge from the Illinois Liquor Control Comission.

16: deli: Liquor license for B&H Delicatessen from the Illinois Liquor Control Commission, Chicago City White Pages, 1946, 1947.

17: "HALF A MILLION": Drake and Cayton, *Black Metropolis*, pp.60–61.

17: bombed: Drake and Cayton, p. 79.

17: soldiers: Harry Pulik interview, December 10, 1997.

17: Savoy Ballroom: Drake and Cayton, pp. 78–79; Palmer, *Deep Blues*, p. 139.

18: Coconut Grove: Travis, *Autobiography of Black Jazz*, pp. 41–43, 83–84.

18: South Cottage Grove: Interviews with Charles Davis, November 13, December 24, 1997; Charles Walton, September 30, October 20, November 21, December 4, 1997.

19: "Chicago's Finest": *Chicago Defender* national edition, January 23, 1944, p. 9; September 1, 1945, p. 6; *Chicago Defender*, city edition, January 6, 1944, p. 10, Aug. 12, 1944, p. 11.

19: population increased: Statistics from Hirsch, *Making of the Second Ghetto*, pp. 24, 26, 29; see also Lemann, *The Promised Land,* for an extensive discussion of this subject.

20: inflate rents: Hirsch, pp. 24, 26, 29; Drake and Cayton, p. 576.

20: "two main features": Rowe, p. 26.

21: "meeting place": Rowe, p. 47.

3. THE MACOMBA LOUNGE

22: Drexel Boulevard: Information on the area around the Macomba Lounge comes from Chicago City Transit Authority pictures and Chicago city phone books, 1940–47.

23: "Everybody": Pomus, "About Andrew Tibbs," *Living Blues*, January/February 1992, p. 40.

23: "pimps and whores": Phil Chess interviews; Phil Chess interview with Charles Walton, 1983.

23: "nothing illegal": Walton interviews, February 26, 1998, March 13, 1998.

23: the bar curved: Interviews with Phil, Sheva, and Marshall Chess.

24: Tom Archia: Tom Archia information from website created by Robert Campbell, http://hubcap.clemson.edu/~campber/aristocrat.html.

25: the "regulars": Interviews with Walton, Charles Parham, Cozy Eggleston, Silas Butler, Vernel Fournier, Phil Chess.

26: take in the scene: Walton interviews.

26: Ella Fitzgerald: Chicago Bee, July 2, 1946, p. 15; May 4, 1947, p. 14; interviews with Phil Chess; Rowe, p. 62.

27: "continuous entertainment": Chicago Bee, June 8, 1947, p. 11; June 15, 1947, p. 15; June 22, 1947, p. 18; June 29, 1947, p. 15; Marshall Chess interview.

27: pint of whiskey: Eggleston interview, February 16, March 4, 1998.

28: X's: Phil Chess interview.

29: "Is you black": Interviews with Phil, Sheva, and Marshall Chess.

29: the only whites: Alyne Salstone interview, February 11, 1998.

30: "heavy traffic": From Gloria J. Coleman, "The DuSable Hotel Locale: Descriptive Analysis of an Era and an Area Circa 1940–50," April 1980 master's thesis for Northeastern Illinois University, pp. 21–22; Fournier interview, November 11, 1997.

30: prostitution: Dave Young interview with Charles Walton, date unkown.

31: chrome-plated: Marshall Chess interview, October 8, 1997.

31: go fishing: Marshall Chess interview, March 26, 1998.

32: so tired: Witzel interview.

32: "I had to wait": Sheva Chess interview, October 23, 1997.

4. IMMIGRANT TO ARISTOCRAT

33: Evelyn Aron: Interviews with Stephen Aron, March 18–19, 1998; Julie Marx, March 17, 1998; Ilene Kline, February 24, 1998; Alyne Salstone, John Salstone, February 10, 1998; Ruth Friedman, September 12, 1997; Marshall Chess.

34: Billboard's top ten lists: Billboard, Sept. 13, 1947, p. 27.

36: ten distributors: Billboard, July 5, 1947, p. 37; information from Aristocrat Record website and from Robert Campbell, producer of the web site.

37: Andrew Tibbs: Andrew Tibbs interview with Charles Walton, date unknown; Jim O'Neal interview with Sammy Goldberg, November 3, 1982, O'Neal private papers.

37: "in charge": Billboard Encyclopedia, 1947–48, 9th edition, p. 424.

38: "Bilbo Is Dead": Tibbs interview with Charles Walton, date unknown; Tibbs obituary, Living Blues, January/February 1992, p. 38.

38: time left over: Dave Young interview with Charles Walton, date unknown; Clarence Samuels interview, April 20, 1998; Tibbs obituary, Living Blues, January/February 1992, p. 38.

38: Teamsters: Peter Guralnick, Feel Like Going Home, p. 184; Marshall Chess interview, March 30, 1998; Norman Leftwich interview, March 18, 1998; Gwen Kesler interview, May 4, 1998; Henry Stone interview, May 18, 1999; Joe Bihari interviews, June 18, July 13, 1998.

39: Buick: Irv Derfler interview, June 3, 1998.

40: black Cadillac: Marshall Chess interview, October 8, 1997.

41: a rawer sound: Palmer, pp. 155–57; Rowe, pp. 67–69; Tooze, *The Mojo Man*, pp. 75–80.

41: Lonnie Johnson: O'Neal and O'Neal, Muddy Waters interview, *Living Blues*, March/April 1985, p. 26.

41: venetian blinds: O'Neal and O'Neal, p. 34.

42: "my kind of stuff": O'Neal and O'Neal, p. 32.

42: the Jackson distributor: *Billboard*, July 5, 1947, p. 37; January 24, 1948, p. 107; June 19, 1948, p. 21; *Cash Box,* December 25, 1948.

43: $10,000: Nate Notkin interviews, March 27, May 21, 1998; Stephen Aron interview, March 18, 1998.

43: "She dug me": Welding, "Muddy Waters," *Rolling Stone*, November 9, 1968, p. 11; O'Neal and O'Neal, p. 34; Jonathan Benjamin interview, June 3, 1998; Ernie Leaner interview with Charles Walton, date unknown.

44: beauty salons: O'Neal and O'Neal, p. 35; Rowe, pp. 70–71; Tooze, p. 82.

44: "my buddy": O'Neal and O'Neal, p. 35.

45: "my very ambition:" Transcript of program on black radio written by Charles Walton.

46: "poor recording": *Billboard*, July 10, 1948, p. 104; September 18, September 25, 1948, p. 29.

46: "no help": Reverend Dwight Gatemouth Moore interview, April 15, 1998.

46: "financial difficulties": Art Sheridan interview, September 10, 1997.

48: number twenty-six: *Billboard,* July 30, 1949, pp. 96–97, 104.

48: Dozier Boys: *Cash Box,* October 1, 1949, p. 14.

49: a long, dark Chrysler: Stan Lewis interview, February 17, 1998.

50: Blues Rockers: *Cash Box*, January 14, 1950, p. 7; Aristocrat website.

5. MEMPHIS CONNECTIONS

51: Fire trucks: Bobby Blevins interview, July 14, 1998; Marshall Chess interview, April 26, 1998; Phil Chess interview, October 23, 1997.

52: Waters . . . chafing: Palmer, p. 163; Tooze, pp. 94–96; Welding, *Rolling Stone*, November 9, 1968, p. 11.

52: sign a will: Notkin interview, May 21, 1998.

53: Waters's drummer: Palmer, p. 164; Tooze, p. 100.

53: "this could tell you": Phil Chess from *Sweet Home Chicago*, 1993 MCA video.

53: backbeat: Eddie Johnson interviews, June 11, 1998, November 10, 1997.

54: Buster Williams: Ed Newell interview, June 25, 1998; Robert Williams interview, June 26, August 27, 1998; Gordon, *It Came from Memphis*, p. 28; *Fortune*, November 1956; *Commercial Appeal*, March 23, 1950, March 20, 1957.

55: the rate varied between: Receipts from Plastic Products in the files of Lillian McMurry/Trumpet Records, University of Mississippi Blues Archive, Oxford, Mississippi.

55: Baskin's: Marshall Chess interview, April 26, 1998.

56: touting the label: *Cash Box,* January 21, 1950, p. 15 is an example.

56: They didn't fraternize: Johnson interview, June 11, 1998; Blevins interview, July 14, 1998.

57: "slight diskery": *Billboard*, August 5, 1950, p. 13.

57: first catalogue: Chess catalogue, courtesy of St. George Records.

58: "Rocket 88": Sam Phillips interview, July 22, 1998; Bihari interview, July 13, 1998; Palmer, pp. 222–23; Escott, *Good Rockin' Tonight*, pp. 21–25; Williams interview, July 6, 1998; Newell interview, July 6, 1998.

59: ad campaign: *Cash Box*, April 28, 1951, p. 12.

60: a firm grip: Marshall Chess interview, April 26, 1998.

61: WLAC: Hoss Allen interview, July 12, 1996; Beverly Keel, "A Hoss of a Different Color: Rock and Roll Radio Before Alan Freed," from Keel, a professor at Middle Tennessee State University.

61: "They started banging": Kesler interviews, May 4, 1998, July 8, 1998; Stone interview, July 8, 1998.

61: "thank you": Bihari interview, July 13, 1998.

63: tiny fingers: Marshall Chess interview, April 26, 1998; Notkin, May 21, 1998.

63: "This is for me": Palmer, pp. 231–33; Escott and Hawkins, pp. 29–32; Rowe, pp. 134–38; Phillips interview, July 22, 1998.

64: "wonderfully": Malcolm Chisholm interview, June 25, 1998.

64: signed Wolf: *Cash Box*, September 22, 1951, p. 9.

65: bittersweet joke: Phillips interview, July 22, 1998.

65: disputes: Bihari interview, June 18, 1998; Ike Turner interview, July 25, 1998.

6: CHECKERS, CHARTS, AND COPYRIGHTS

67: incorporate: Chess and Checker incorporation papers from the Office of the Illinois Secretary of State.

67: Walter: Little Walter background, Palmer, pp. 200–03, Tooze, pp. 72–73; Rooney, *Bossmen: Bill Monroe and Muddy Waters*, pp. 112–13; Jimmy Rogers interview, *Living Blues*, Autumn 1973, pp. 14–16.

69: "When you start": Session tapes from MCA/Universal Music Group vault. Tape includes the preproduction sheet from Universal Studio of Chicago.

69: dancing joyfully: Marshall Chess interview, October 8, 1997.

70: first five hundred: Rowe, pp. 88–89; *Cash Box*, August 2, 1952, p. 15.

70: Walter's success: O'Neal and O'Neal *Living Blues,* March/April 1985, p. 33; Jimmy Rogers interview, *Living Blues*, September/October 1997, p. 25.

70: dropped some coins: Rowe, p. 89.

71: Willie Mabon: Rowe, p. 132; liner notes for *Chess Blues Piano Greats*; Evans interview, February 1998; John Brim interview, July 7, 1998.

71: in Harlem: Hymie Weiss interview, October 30, 1997.

72: "platinum returns": Bihari interview, July 13, 1998.

73: shoot them both: Brim interview, July 7, 1998; Buddy Guy interview, July 7, 1999; Beatrice Burnette Mabon interviews, December 17, 1998, August 12, 1999.

73: Marshall never heard: Marshall and Phil Chess interviews.

74: Talent scouts: *Cash Box*, December 20, 1952, p. 17; January 3, 1953, p. 14.

74: sending letters: *Cash Box*, February 28, 1953, p. 9.

75: unreleased material: Rogers interview, *Living Blues*, Autumn 1973, p. 16; Brisbin, "Jimmy Rogers: I'm Havin' Fun Right Today," *Living Blues,* September/October 1997, p. 25; see Fancourt, *A Discography of the Blues Artists on the Chess Labels, 1947–75* and Ruppli, *The Chess Labels: A Discography,* for Rogers and Waters records.

75: spent the night: *Cash Box*, December 20, 1952, p. 17; Stan Lewis interview, May 1, 1998.

76: allowed to drive: Marshall Chess interviews, October 8, 1997, April 26, 1998; Bihari interview, July 13, 1998.

76: she picked songs: *Cash Box*, February 21, 1953, p. 10.

78: The writing credit: Copyright information from the copyright files and applications at the Library of Congress; Noel Silverman interviews; Gary Roth interviews, spring 1998.

78: John Henry Burton: Phil Chess interview, August 17, 1998.

78: "fifty percent of something": Marshall Chess interview, August 4, 1998.

7. BLUES WITH A FEELING

81: Willie Dixon: Dixon with Snowden, *I Am the Blues*, pp. 23–82, esp., 54–55; liner notes by Don Snowden for MCA Records *Willie Dixon* boxed CD set; Dixon interview with Charles Walton at the Wise Fool lounge in Chicago, early 1980s; DeCurtis, "Willie Dixon and the Wisdom of the Blues," *Rolling Stone*, March 23, 1989, p. 109.

83: Santa Claus: Marshall Chess interview, September 23, 1998; Dixon, p. 113.

84: Picking the tunes: *Billboard*, May 23, 1953, on percent of industry; February 28, 1953, on disc jockey Alan Freed, Art Sheridan interview, September 10, 1997; Phil Chess interviews.

86: Sam Griggs: Jackson, *Big Beat Heat*, pp. 61, 105.

87: free publicity: Marty Ostrow interview, January 18, 1999; Irv Howard interview, January 11, 1999; Irv Lichtman interview, January 11, 1999.

87: Otis Spann: Tooze, pp. 108–9; Rooney, p. 124.

88: WMRY: *Cash Box*, December 19, 1953, p. 26.

89: Deutsch's: Chicago city phone books; Chicago city directories; Phil Chess interviews, Oct. 1997, October 19, 1998; Marshall Chess interview, October 8, 1997.

91: "no charts": Dave Myers interviews, November 13, 1997, June 12, 1998.

92: "Hoochie Coochie Man": Dixon, pp. 83–84; Dixon interview, *Living Blues*, September/October 1988, pp. 20–22; Rooney, pp. 124–26; Palmer, p. 167.

93: terrific network: Marshall Chess interview, September 23, 1998.

94: paternity suits: Nate Notkin interview, May 21, 1998; Joseph Notkin interview, October 13, 1998.

94: who should pay: Lillian McMurry interview, August 28, 1998.

95: "take $100 out": Ryan, *Trumpet Records: An Illustrated History with Discography*, pp. 19–20; McMurry interview.

95: $672.01 in arrears: Trumpet Record papers, University of Mississippi Blues Archive, Oxford, Mississippi.

96: "your children": Walton interview with Phil Chess, 1983.

97: Jack Ford: Jack Ford royalty statement, Stan Lewis private papers.

97: "Reconsider Baby": Notes from *Chess Blues* boxed CD set, p. 36; Stan Lewis interviews.

98: "Moondog": Jackson, *Big Beat Heat*, pp. 63–67; *Cash Box*, January 16, 1954.

98: Moonglows: Jackson, p. 42; Propes, "The Moonglows: The Commandments of Doo-Wop," *Goldmine*, February 8, 1991, p. 11; Pruter, *Doo-Wop: The Chicago Scene*, pp. 59–61.

99: By coincidence: Phil Chess interview, Oct. 19, 1998.

99: Freed had taken a writing credit: U.S. Copyright EU 375537; EP 85776; Jackson, p. 105.

100: "cat music": Cash Box, July 3, 1954, p. 56.

8. THE BEAT HAS GOT TO MOVE

101: Ellas McDaniel (Bo Diddley): White, *Living Legend: Bo Diddley*, pp. 18–35; Loder, "Bo Diddley, The Rolling Stone Interview," *Rolling Stone*, February 12, 1987, p. 76; Billy Boy Arnold interview, October 21, 1997; Dwyer, "Bo Diddley," *Blues Unlimited* 71 (April 1970), pp. 4–6; Lydon, *Boogie Lightning*, pp. 51–78.

103: Leonard listened intently: Arnold interview; Phil Chess interview, November 23, 1998.

103: other versions: White, p. 56; Shaw, *Honkers and Shouters*, pp. 307–8.

104: "sing like a man": Arnold interview; Chess-Checker session tapes of Bo Diddley; White, pp. 57–58.

105: Bo Diddley beat: Braunstein, "Bo Diddley, Bo Diddley, Where Have You Been?" *Chicago Tribune* magazine, January 6, 1980, pp. 19–20; Hannusch, "Bo Diddley Is a Guitar Slinger," *Guitar Player* 174 (June 1984), p. 62; Rowe, "I Was Really Dedicated: An Interview with Billy Boy Arnold, *Blues Unlimited* 126 (September/October 1977), pp. 4–7; 127 (November–December 1977), pp. 10–12; Fancourt, *A Discography of the Rhythm and Blues Artists on the Chess Labels*.

105: the kind of plug: Alan Freed air check, WINS, April 1955; *Billboard*, May 7, 1955, p. 28.

106: "rock and roll": Jackson, p. 83; Palmer, p. 223; *Variety*, March 23, 1955.

107: bar mitzvah: Marshall Chess interviews, Marshall Chess private papers.

109: "nothing derogatory": Arnold interview.

109: "around black people": Broven interview with Paul Gayten, "I Knew Leonard at the Macomba," *Blues Unlimited* 130 (May–August 1978), pp. 8–10.

109: greater distance: Jerry Wexler interview, November 28, 1998.

110: blacks and Jews: Lincoln, *Coming Through the Fire: Surviving Race and Place in America*, p. 85.

110: "gold mine": Clark, "Candor About Negro-Jewish Relations," *Bridges and Boundaries: African Americans and American Jews*, p. 91.

110: "own everything": White, p. 31, citing a 1975 Diddley interview with Cliff White.

110: "a little Jewish boy": Little Richard, from *Hail Hail Rock and Roll*, Universal Pictures, MCA Home Video, Inc., 1988.

110: Miami Beach: Marshall Chess interview, December 7, 1998.

111: headed to New Orleans: Marshall Chess interview, December 10, 1998.

112: The magazine's poll: *Cash Box*, June 18, 1955, p. 35.

113: Berry . . . Chuck: Berry, *The Autobiography*, see especially pp. 1–3, 25, 86, 88–89, 93; Wheeler, "Chuck Berry, The Story," *Guitar Player*, March 1988, pp. 51–52; *Hail Hail Rock and Roll*; Lydon, *Rock Folk*, pp. 9–15.

115: "a go-getter": *Hail Hail Rock and Roll.*
115: outdo Johnson: Berry, p. 93.
116: mascara box: Johnnie Johnson interview, December 22, 1998.
117: Eagle River: Phil Chess interviews; Terry Chess interview, April 14, 1999.
118: with Berry as coauthor: U.S. Copyright records at the Library of Congress; Lance Freed interview, January 10, 1999.
118: Freed on the payroll: Wexler interview, November 28, 1998.
119: three thousand records: *Cash Box*, December 25, 1954, p. 35.
119: "Look darling": James, *Rage to Survive*, p. 95.
120: McMurry's twenty-year battle: Lillian McMurry papers; McMurry interview, August 28, 1998.

9. MONEY IN THE SONG

123: "See you later": Bobby Charles interview, January 5, 1999.
124: "thefting my music": *Billboard*, March 5, 1955, pp. 13, 18; see generally, Krasilovsky, *This Business of Music.*
125: label-publisher was pushing: *Billboard*, February 4, 1956, p. 55.
125: Phil's jaw dropped: Charles, Phil Chess interviews.
126: Dale Hawkins: "The Hawk Rocks Again: Interview with Dale Hawkins," *Rock and Blues News,* May–June 1999, p. 5.
126: a stormy start: Dick LaPalm interviews.
127: "my pains": Charles interview.
127: The Flamingos: Zeke Carey interview, February 15, 1999; McGarvey, "I Only Have Eyes for You: The Flamingos' Story," *Now Dig This* 97 (April 1991).
128: Their liturgy: Zeke Carey interview, Phil Chess interview, February 18, 1999; Flamingos background information from Pruter, *Doowop: The Chicago Scene*, pp. 22–33, 50–52, 56–58.
128: "Fats" Washington: Contract between Ferdinand Washington and Stan Lewis, from Lewis private papers.
129: "too clean": Jones, "Nate Nelson of the Flamingos," *Goldmine*, March 1978; McGarvey, *Now Dig This* 97 (April 1991).
129: the bare bones: *Now Dig This* 97 (April 1991), p. 29.
130: "A Kiss": Zeke Carey interview; Tancredi, "The Flamingos—The Early Years," *Bim Bam Boom* 4 (February–March 1972), pp. 4–7; Billy Davis interview, February 23, 1999.
131: "Marterry": *Billboard*, February 4, 1956, p. 15; March 3, 1956, p. 76; *Cash Box*, March 17, 1956, p. 34.
133: poll of R&B disc jockeys: *Cash Box*, July 14, 1956.
134: "Country": Gene Barge interview, January 28, 1999; Phil Chess interview, January 29, 1999; Birnbaum, "Daddy G," *Chicago Reader,* June 24, 1984, pp. 8–19; Pruter, "A Talk with Daddy G," *Goldmine*, March 1982, p. 24–25.
134: Freed provided . . . a bonus: *Billboard*, November 17, 1956, p. 16.
135: sermons: Phil and Marshall Chess interviews; Chess files at MCA/Universal Music Group.

10. 2120 SOUTH MICHIGAN

136: 2120 South Michigan: Chicago city phone books and city directory for 1957; *Cash Box*, February 23, 1957; interviews with Tim Samuelson of the Landmarks Commission, later the Chicago Historical Society.

136: commercial tenants: Report of the Chicago City Landmarks Commission on 2120 South Michigan Avenue.

137: heart attack: Marshall Chess interviews; Chisholm interviews, June 25, October 8, 1998, February 26, March 23, July 26, 1999; *Cash Box*, March 9, 1957, p. 38; March 23, 1957, p. 42, March 30, 1957, p. 42, April 6, 1957, p. 36.

138: the chance to build a studio: Jack Wiener interviews, September 15, 17, 1997, October 1, 1998, February 12, 22, March 18, March 24, 1999; Samuelson interview, February 23, 1999; *DownBeat*, "A Young Man's Fancy," September 19, 1957.

140: redwood trim: *Cash Box*, May 11, 1957; Landmarks Commission report.

140: first sessions: Dixon, pp. 101–4; *Cash Box,* June 27, 1957, p. 36.

141: parking fee: Wiener interviews.

141: it was efficient: Marshall Chess interview, March 1, 1999; Terry Chess interview, April 14, 1999.

142: sitting in folding chairs: Marshall Chess interviews.

142: outselling 78s: *Billboard*, April 14, 1956, pp. 30, 94.

143: long-playing records: *Billboard*, October 13, 1956, p. 17.

143: 26 percent: *Billboard*, February 16, 1957, p. 23.

143: It was the flip side: *Billboard*, March 9, 1957, p. 61; *Cash Box*, March 2, 1957, p. 38.

145: "white youngsters": *Memphis Press Scimitar*, April 29, 1959, p. 1 of Metro section.

145: *Billboard* gave it a boost: *Billboard*, August 7, 1954, p. 39.

146: RCA . . . full-page ad: *Billboard*, December 3, 1954, p. 59; December 24, 1955, p. 17 ; Guralnick, *Last Train to Memphis,* see pp. 195–233.

146: four songs after his name: *Billboard,* January 26, 1957, p. 44.

146: "something of a trend": *Billboard*, January 26, 1957, p. 48.

148: Harry Finfer: Harold Lipsius interview, March 3, 1999.

149: "a small town": From recording of "Little Village."

150: pseudo–talent scouts: *Cash Box*, October 19, 1957, p. 44; Marshall Chess interview, March 18, 1999.

150: summoned to Chicago: Max Cooperstein interview, February 11, 1999; *Cash Box*, September 28,1999.

11. ALL THAT JAZZ

151: Dave Usher: Dave Usher interviews, February 24, 25, March 12, 1999; Wiener interviews, Joe Segal: *Chicago Tribune*, April 12, 1992, p. 12 of Arts section.

153: Four Strings: Charles Walton interview, April 1, 1999.

153: live album: Ahmad Jamal interview, April 26, 1999; Ahmad Jamal's notes for *But Not for Me* in Chess files, Universal Music Group; Howard Bedno interview, March 24, 1999.

154: "cocktail" music: *Down Beat*, Jazz and Record Reviews, vol. III, p. 106.

154: number-one jazz bestseller: *Down Beat*, December 11, 1958, p. 35.

154: cumbersome process: Marshall Chess interview, March 18, 1999.

155: 107 weeks: Whitburn, *Top LPs 1945–72*.

155: West Side Cleffs: Ramsey Lewis interview, February 26, 1999; Phil Chess interview, March 24, 1999; Red Holt interview, April 1, 1999.

156: nice plug: *Billboard*, March 30, 1957, p. 60.

156: "hit the heights": *Down Beat*, April 18, 1957, p. 15.

156: three cents: Information comes from files on the Jazz Exponents album, *Jazz Exponents* Argo 622, in Chess files, Universal Music Group.

156: distinctive spine: Usher interviews; *Billboard*, July 7, 1958, p. 36.

157: "I'm gonna die": Chisholm interview, October 8, 1998.

157: the promotion he got: *Cash Box*, September 20, 1958, p. 52.

157: "Kangaroo Split Pack": Usher interviews, *Cash Box*, November 1, 1955, p. 44.

158: London House: Usher interviews; Chisholm interview, March 23, 1999.

158: $6,500: *Billboard*, September 28, 1959, p. 26.

160: his own plant: James Gann interview, October 27, 1998.

160: Father Salistine: Gann, Wiener interviews.

161: aspiring drummer: Terry Chess interview, April 14, 1999.

162: these distribution deals: *Billboard*, June 23, 1958, p. 3.

162: "thirty thousand": Chisholm interview, October 8, 1998.

162: Big Bill Hill: Marshall Chess interview, March 18, 1999.

164: hot pink Cadillac: Usher interview, March 23, 1999.

164: a telegram: *Cash Box*, October 3, 1959, p. 6.

165: compilations of . . . singles: Information on the albums from Victor Pearlin.

165: piece of cardboard: Ramsey Lewis interview, February 26, 1999; Red Holt interview, April 1, 1999.

166: "What do you think . . . ?" Usher interview, February 25, 1999.

166: Tracy accepted the offer: Jack Tracy interviews, February 17, March 20, April 6, April 20, 1999; *Cash Box*, August 15, 1959, p. 28.

166: "goddammit": Tracy interviews.

167: swimming pool: Interviews with Marshall, Pam, Phil, Terry and Sheva Chess.

170: preparing the royalty checks: Tracy, Jamal, Ramsey Lewis interviews.

174: "Killer Joe": Liner notes, *The History of Jazz*, MCA Records; Tracy interview, March 20, 1999.

171: "He knew it all": Tracy interviews.

172: "SCREAMING GUITAR": Tooze, citing *Manchester Evening News*, October 27, 1958, p. 2.

172: had Usher read them aloud: Usher interview, March 23, 1999.

172: Volkswagen vans: Allen Arrow interview, March 23, 1999.

172: four offices overseas: *Cash Box*, October 3, 1959, p. 6.

173: "We struggled": Marshall Chess interview, March 18, 1999.

12. PLAY FOR PAY

174: a rival label: Arrow interview, June 28, 1998.

175: three Chess tunes: Stan Lewis interviews, February 17, 1998, April 20, 1999; Lewis private papers.

175: "payola": Eliot, *Rockonomics*, pp. 69–71; Jackson, *Big Beat Heat*, p. 244; Paul Ackerman testimony before the House Interstate and Foreign Commerce Committee's Legislative Oversight Subcommittee, April 26, 1960, esp. pp. 902–3; *Time*, November 23, 1959, p. 64.

176: "a story to tell": Irv Derfler interview, March 3, 1999.

177: "careful programming": House subcommittee hearing record, pp. 1374–75.

178: Freed was fired: Jackson, pp. 247–49, citing Freed testimony from closed session before the House subcommittee; *New York Times*, November 22, 1959, p. 1, November 24, p. 31.

178: set off a frenzy: Jackson, p. 252; *New York Times*, November 29, 1959, p. 66.

178: the FTC: *New York Times*, December 5, 1959, p. 1; *Billboard*, December 7, 1959, p. 2.

178: threatening phone calls: *Billboard*, September 28, 1959, p. 3; November 16, 1959, p.3.

178: "number 29": *Billboard*, November 16, 1959, p. 3; January 18, 1960, p. 8.

178: "Personal contact": *Chicago Daily News*, January 11, 1960.

179: red Lincoln: *Billboard*, January 11, 1960, pp. 2, 4; Notkin interview, March 28, 1999; Wexler interview, December 19, 1999; Marshall Chess interviews.

179: *American Bandstand*: Anthony Mammarella testimony before the House subcommittee, pp. 741, 761–63.

180: Joe Finan: House subcommittee hearings, pp. 244–45.

180: George Goldner: House subcommittee hearings, pp. 1095–1100.

181: Atlantic's operations: Wexler interview, April 15, 1999.

182: a broken man: *New York Times*, May 20, 1960, p. 1; Jackson, pp. 313–315.

182: no canceled checks: Bihari interview, April 8, 1999.

182: dropped the charges: *Billboard*, September 18, 1961, p. 4.

182: major changes: *Congressional Quarterly Almanac*, 1960, pp. 356–57.

182: "singled out": Eliot, p. 79.

13. TRUST IN ME

183: "read a balance sheet": Arrow interview, June 29, 1998.

183: Ron Malo: *Billboard*, November 16, 1959; Tracy interviews.

184: her first mentor: James, pp. 18–19; see also Grendysa, liner notes for *Etta James: Her Best*.

185: "My personality": James, pp. 48–49; Bihari interview, June 18, 1998.

185: "supertight things": James, p. 74.

185: "some smart Jews": James, pp. 77–79.

186: settled for $3,000: James, pp. 92–94; Bihari interview, April 8, 1999.

186: took care of the rent: James interview, June 14, 1999.

186: Aretha Franklin: Davis interview, April 28, 1999.

187: string and horn parts: Riley Hampton interview, April 13, 1999.

187: a mental picture: Hampton interview, April 8, 1999; Tracy interview, April 6, 1999; James, pp. 96, 101.

188: appeared on *Bandstand*: *Cash Box*, May 14, 1960, p. 26; May 28, 1960, p. 29.

188: on the cover: *Cash Box*, March 11, 1961.

189: "You know": James interview.

189: Keystone Kops: Phil Wright interviews, June 11, 16, 1999; James interview, June 14, 1999; Stan Lewis interview, May 1, 1998; James, pp. 126–28.

190: his own studio: See Pruter, *Doo-Wop: The Chicago Scene*, pp. 74–75.

190: "old" R&B hits: *Billboard*, January 11, 1960, p. 4.

191: "a stickler": Tooze, p. 170.

191: respectful attention: *Down Beat* compilation of reviews, 1962, p. 251.

192: Newport Jazz Festival: Tracy interview, April 20, 1999; Tracy liner notes, *Muddy Waters at Newport*.

192: unruly crowd: *New York Times*, July 4, 1960, p. 1; Tooze, pp. 171–74.

193: "a fine set": *Billboard*, December 19, 1960, p. 23; *Cash Box*, December 24, 1960, p. 29; *Down Beat,* 1962 compilation of reviews, p. 251.

193: never reimbursed: Bo Diddley conversation with Andy McKaie, reproduced in MCA Records' *Bo Diddley* boxed CD set.

193: "it better work": See *Cash Box*, "Record Ramblings" for March and April 1960; Tracy interview, April 21, 1999.

14. BRANCHING OUT

194: Sugar Pie DeSanto: Sugar Pie DeSanto interview, May 19, 1999.

195: They squeezed it in: *Cash Box*, March 25, 1961, p. 44.

196: jovial demeanor: See Williams, *The Humor of Jackie Moms Mabley*.

197: "I didn't give a damn": Ralph Bass unpublished papers; Fleming, "A Life Recording," *Chicago Reader*, March 7, 1980, p. 1, 28–32; *Cash Box*, August 15, 1959, p. 23; *Billboard*, September 4, 1959, p. 39; Guralnick, *Feel Like Going Home*, p. 199.

198: "forget it": Rock and Roll Hall of Fame Sixth Annual Induction dinner program, 1981, p. 29; James interview, June 14, 1999; Lydon, *Boogie Lightning,* pp. 81–98.

198: "Watusi": *Cash Box*, May 20, 1961, p. 6; Gann interview, August 28, 1999; Robert Pruter interview, May 3, 1999; Pruter, *Doo-Wop: The Chicago Scene*, p. 79; *Chicago Soul*, p. 194.

200: "Liked your tape": Davis interviews, February 23, April 28, May 27, July 14, July 22, 1999.

202: "You'd get discord": Davis interview, June 1, 1999.

203: Check-mate: *Cash Box,* November 4, 1961, p. 16; Davis interview, May 4, 1999.

203: supervised the improvements: *Cash Box*, February 4, 1961, p. 18; Tim Samuelson provided information on studio changes.

204: every radio station: Charles interview, May 5, 1999.

204: back to Mercury: Tracy interviews; *Billboard*, June 26, 1961, p. 16.

205: "Mashed Potatoes": *Cash Box*, September 2, 1961, p. 12; *Billboard*, February 17, 1962, p. 42, *Guinness Encyclopedia of Music*, vol. 1, p. 56.

205: Ricordi: *Cash Box*, November 25, 1961, p. 37; December 23, 1961, p. 30.

206: Berry's troubles: Berry, pp. 207–9; 212; newspaper articles from the *St. Louis Post-Dispatch* and *Globe Democrat* from the Mercantile Library of St. Louis.

209: "he cared": Booth, "Etta James: Twenty Years On," *Soul and Jazz,* April 1976, pp. 46–48; Esmond Edwards interview; James interview.

210: strong constitution: James, p. 154.

210: "led to bloodshed": Edwards interview, April 8, 1999.

15. VOICE OF THE NEGRO

212: "Pa": Notkin interviews, May 21, 1998, May 5, 1999.

212: WTAC: L&P Broadcasting application to the Federal Communications Commission for the purchase of WTAC, Flint, Michigan; *Broadcasting Yearbook*, 1958; Vincent Pepper interview, May 12, 1999; Phil Chess interviews; Notkin interview, May 10, 1999.

214: eclectic programming: *Broadcasting Yearbook*, 1961–62.

214: "a million dollars cash": Phil Chess interview, May 18, 1999; Florence Summers interview, May 26, 1999.

215: "Leonard was driven": Pepper interview, April 7, 1999.

215: background check: FBI report on Leonard Chess obtained under the Freedom of Information Act; referral to Federal Communications Commission August 9, 1962, noted on investigation papers.

215: 10 percent of the playlist: Pepper interview.

215: "on a bet": Charles interview, May 5, 1999.

216: Summers was heartbroken: Summers interview, May 26, 1999.

217: "cool gent": Herb Kent interviews, May 24, May 26, 1999.

217: urged him to stay: E. Rodney Jones interview, May 25, 1999; *Chicago Defender*, September 21, 1963.

218: "rely on the blacks": Jones interview, May 26, 1999.

219: "funny niggers": Walton interview, May 24, 1999; *Chicago Sun-Times*, November 2, 1962.

219: "war for the Negro market": *Chicago Defender*, January 12–18, 1963, March 30, 1963.

219: $14.50 reward: *Chicago Defender*, September 21, 1963, p. 28; Jones interviews; *Chicago Defender*, Jan. 12–18, 1963.

220: special praise: *Chicago Defender*, September 21, 1963, p. 28; Jones interview.

220: 44 percent: The Pulse, Incorporated, from the private papers of Marshall Chess.

222: "a big encouragement": Lucky Cordell interview, April 14, 1999.

223: $19,000: WVON advertising brochure from Burt Burdeen private collection.

223: "We get down": *Billboard*, August 20, 1966, p. 34, *Chicago Daily News,* December 4, 1965; Jones interview, May 26, 1999.

223: evening talk show: Wesley South interview, May 26, 1999; June 18, 1963, Illinois Bell Telephone Company letter to Wesley South, from Wesley South private papers.

224: George Wallace: South interview, May 26, 1999; *Chicago Daily News*, December 4, 1965.

16. THE SOUL OF A MAN

225: house band: Davis interviews, February 23, May 27, 1999.

225: time clock: Louis Satterfield interviews, June 23, 1999; Maurice White interview, June 29, 1999.

226: new groove: Gerald Sims interview, July 14, 1999; Davis interviews; Pruter, *Chicago Soul*, pp. 116–17; Pruter, "Billy Stewart: The Fat Boy Lives On . . . ," *It Will Stand* 17/18 (1981), pp. 18–20.

227: "He just inspired me": Mitty Collier interview, July 15, 1999.
227: Jan Bradley: *Guinness Encyclopedia of Musicians,* vol. I, pp. 56, 312; Pruter, "Jan Bradley," *Soul Survivor,* Winter 1987–88, pp. 18–20; Pruter, *Chicago Soul*, pp. 154–57.
228: "come home": Dick LaPalm interview, January 22, 1999.
229: "Was it paternalistic?": Davis interview, February 23, 1999.
230: baseball bat: Arrow interview, June 28, 1998.
230: forwarded a message: Marshall Chess interview, June 4, 1999.
233: *This is unbelievable:* Marshall Chess interview, June 11, 1999.
235: calypso beat: DeWitt, *Chuck Berry: Rock and Roll Music*, p. 99.
235: Berry's road manager: Marshall Chess interview, May 10, 1999; Berry autobiography, pp. 219–21.
235: "too cheap": Marshall Chess interview, May 10, 1999; Topping, "Marshall Chess Shoots the Breeze," *Blues Unlimited* 142 (Summer 1982), p. 14.
236: an atlas: Berry, pp. 216–17.
236: Johnny Rivers: *Cash Box,* August 29, 1964, p. 6.
237: liner notes: *Etta Rocks the House* paperwork, Chess files, MCA/Universal Music Group.
238: "Selfish One": Jackie Ross interview, July 29, 1999; Davis interviews, June 16, July 30, 1999.
239: "I Had a Talk": Collier interview, July 15, 1999; Pruter, "The Mitty Collier Story," *Goldmine*, December 1981, p. 25.
241: paid the same: Chess Producing Corporation pay sheet for July 26, 1963, session, Chess files, Universal Music Group.
242: "where's that?" Cook, *Listen to the Blues*, p. 181.
242: trapped inside: Miles, *The Rolling Stones: History, Chronology*, pp. 18–19.
243: "Get out of here": *Chicago Daily News*, June 11, 1963, p. 56; Miles, p. 19.
243: on a ladder: Richards, "Muddy, Wolf and Me," *Guitar Player*, September 1998, p. 88; Davis interview, May 27, 1999; Edwards interview, June 1, 1999; LaPalm interview, May 25, 1999.
244: "these white kids": Palmer, "Muddy Waters: The Delta Sun Never Sets," *Rolling Stone*, October 5, 1978, p. 56.

17. DON'T MESS UP A GOOD THING

245: a tutorial: White interview, June 29, 1999.
246: "very warm": Milton Campbell interview, June 2, 1999; see Keil, *Urban Blues*, pp. 88–90, for a discussion of the "We're Gonna Make It" session.
247: "Don't Mess Up": Greensmith, "The Fontella Bass Interview," *Blues Unlimited* 147 (Spring 1986), p. 21; Oliver Sain interview, February 10, 1999; Greensmith, "The Bobby McLure Interview," *Blues Unlimited* 147 (Spring 1986), p. 25; *Cash Box*, January 23, 1965, p. 20.
248: lead sheets: Phil Wright interview, June 11, 1999; Paul Serrano interview, June 23, 1999; Pruter, "Jackie Ross," *It Will Stand* 20 (1983), pp. 6–8; Chess file on *Etta Rocks the House.*
249: Smith and Miner: Raynard Miner interview, July 2, 1999; *Chicago Defender*, February 29, 1964.

250: "Rescue Me": Interviews with Fontella Bass, June 16, 1999; Pete Cosey, September 3, 1999; Marshall Chess, Davis, Wright, Miner, Satterfield, White; Greensmith, *Blues Unlimited* 147 (Spring 1986), p. 22.

251: "wrote the song": Bass, Satterfield, Cosey, Davis,Wright interviews.

252: salary cut: Edwards interview, April 8, 1999.

253: "In-Crowd": *Cash Box*, September 18, 1965, p. 40, December 25, 1965, p. 20; *Record World*, December 25, 1965, pp. 6–7.

254: salary reinstated: Edwards interview, June 28, 1999.

255: Cadet: LaPalm interview, January 22, 1999.

256: Bob Hope: LaPalm interview, June 23, 1999; *Cash Box*, October 30, 1965, p. 36.

257: WCAM: Federal Communications Commission ruling, July 29, 1966, FCC66-701; Pepper interviews.

258: "you SOB": Burt Burdeen interview, July 17, 1999.

259: "Hush Puppy": Linda Ellerbee interview, July 15, 1999.

259: "Curvey": "THE GIRLS Do ALL the Talking," *Chicago American*, April 21, 1965, Section 2, p. 17; "Smack Dab-in-the-middle's on Top," *Chicago's Daily News*, April 9, 1966; "The Sultry Sound of WSDM/FM", *Omnibus Chicagoland* January 1968.

260: $200,000 loan: Arrow interviews, June 29, 1998; May 28, 1999; *Billboard*, December 4, 1965, ad announcing Conrad is part of Arc Music.

260: Puerto Rico: *Cash Box*, January 29, 1966, p. 6; *Billboard*, January 6, 1966, p. 6.

261: custom-made brochure: Marshall Chess private papers.

263: Japanese tradition: Arrow interview, May 28, 1999.

263: foreign sales: Marshall Chess interviews; *Cash Box*, December 11, 1965, p. 56.

264: sequence of songs: Album files from Chess files at MCA/Universal Music Group.

264: "My job": Koko Taylor interview, January 22, 1998; notes from "Koko Taylor: What It Takes," MCA Records.

265: union scale of $61: Session papers, Chess files, MCA/Universal Music Group, Taylor interview, January 22, 1998; Rowe, p. 172; Guy interview, July 7, 1999.

265: "a hit record": Taylor interview; Leonard Diamond interview, September 29, 1997.

266: retitle the album: *Cash Box*, September 10, 1966, p. 28.

266: "In the Basement": Davis interview, May 27, 1999; Sugar Pie DeSanto interview, May 19, 1999; James interview, June 14, 1999.

18. 320 EAST 21ST STREET

267: in one place: Marshall Chess interview, July 9, 1999; Phil Chess interviews, July 5, 1999, November 16, 1998; *Cash Box*, September 3, 1966, p. 28; March 18, 1967, p. 7; *Chicago Daily News*, July 8, 1966; files of Tim Samuelson of the Chicago Landmarks Commission and the Chicago Historical Society.

268: floating in the air: Tim Samuelson interview, July 18, 1999.

268: recruited engineers: Phil Chess interview, November 16, 1998.

269: "totally different sound": Davis interview, July 14, 1998; Edwards interviews.

269: "a big mistake": Gann interview, October 27, 1998; Cash Box, March 18, 1967, p. 42.

270: "going to kill you": Leonard Diamond interview, September 29, 1997.

270: "he won": Pepper interview, April 7, 1999.

271: gin rummy: Terry Chess interview, April 14, 1999.

271: "Alabama white boys": Wexler, Rhythm and the Blues, p. 207.

272: Mercury and a deal: Marcus, "Roll Over Chuck Berry," Rolling Stone, June 14, 1969, p. 17; Salvo, "A Conversation with Chuck Berry," Rolling Stone, November 23, 1972, pp. 35–42; Berry, The Autobiography, p. 226.

272: Muscle Shoals: Davis interview, July 14, 1999; Marshall Chess interview, July 22, 1999; Max Cooperstein interview, July 22, 1999; Rick Hall interview, January 18, 2000; Pruter, Chicago Soul, pp. 126–27; Billboard, February 18, 1967, p. 3; Cash Box, February 18, 1967, p. 7; see also Guralnick, Sweet Soul Music, p. 375.

272: Laura Lee: Wright and Pack, "Laura Lee," Soul Survivor, Summer 1986, p. 4.

273: team the Muscle Shoals men: Hall interview; James, Rage to Survive, pp. 171–74; Pruter, pp. 127–28; Billboard and Cash Box, September–December 1967; James interview, June 14, 1999.

274: "soulful strings": Edwards interview, April 8, July 15, 1999; Richard Evans interviews, March 25, 1999, July 17, 1999; Cosey interview.

275: "Burning Spear": Richard Evans interview, March 25, 1999.

276: $2,000 check: Bishop Chester M. Bailey remarks on VON tribute to Leonard.

276: "Work the records": Charles interview, May 15, 1999.

279: Billboard's year-end charts: Billboard, December 30, 1967, pp. 42–43; Cash Box, December 12, 1967, pp. 16–20.

279: "psychedelic effects": Billboard, December 9, 1967, pp. 1, 10.

19. FINAL TRACKS

280: the Dells: Bob Pruter interview with Mickey McGill, October 8, 1991; Pruter, Chicago Soul, pp. 109–13; Billboard, July 20, 1968, p. 26.

281: Cantor's Delicatessen: Marshall Chess interview, July 22, 1999.

282: Rotary Connection idea: Marshall Chess interview, July 22, 1999; Bob Pruter interview with Marshall Chess, August 21, 1996; Lind, "Minnie Riperton: Rotary Connection's Angel," Illinois Entertainer, January 1980, p. 6; Peterson, "The Chicago Sound," Chicago Tribune Magazine, May 11, 1969, pp. 51–62.

285: WNOV: Exhibit D of L&P Broadcasting Federal Communication Commission application to buy WFOX in Milwaukee, Wisconsin; 1970 Broadcasting Yearbook, p. B-225.

285: McCann-Erickson: Cash Box, April 6, 1968, p. 10; Davis interview, February 23, 1999.

286: "You, big mouth": Rollin Binzer interview, July 27, 1999.

287: with their headlights on: Billboard, April 20, 1968, p. 74.

287: The Last Request: Max Cooperstein interviews; Barge interview, August 5, 1999.

287: fund-raising recordings: *Billboard*, April 20, 1968, p. 1.

288: creative jolt: Marshall Chess interview, July 22, 1999; Raynard Miner interview, July 2, 1999; *Cash Box*, August 10, 1968, p. 32.

288: "sharing the money": Louis Satterfield interview, June 22, 1999.

290: *Electric Mud:* Welding, *Rolling Stone*, p. 11; Peterson, *Chicago Tribune Magaine*, May 11, 1969, p. 62; Cosey interview, September 29, 1999.

291: unwieldly title: Peterson, *Chicago Tribune Magazine*, May 11, 1969, pp. 60, 62.

292: a $12,000 bill: Binzer interview.

292: GRT: Notkin interview, May 21, 1998; Arrow interviews; Alan Bayley interview, September 2, 1999.

295: $4.7 million: March 12, 1970 document file in Cook County, Ill. probate court in the estate of Leonard Chess, No. 69-9515, Notkin interview December 3, 1999.

296: "a gentile mentality": Arrow interview, May 28, 1999.

296: "a family company": Arrow interview, May 28, 1999; Marshall Chess interview, July 22, 1999.

297: publicity man: Loren Coleman interview, August 3, 1999.

297: *Fathers and Sons*: Marshall Chess interview, July 22, 1999; *Billboard*, August 16, 1999; Tooze, pp. 224–25.

299: slumped over: Interviews with Marshall Chess, Lucky Cordell, Richie Salvador, Dick LaPalm, Cynthia Fendel, Burt Burdeen, Leonard Diamond, Terry Chess, Phil Chess.

301: the burial: Diamond interviews; Marshall Chess interview, July 22, 1999.

301: "It's all over": Dick LaPalm interview, July 8, 1999.

EPILOGUE: LAWSUITS AND LEGACIES

302: "I lost": Marshall Chess interviews, April 26, 1998, July 22, 1999.

303: Bayley capitulated: Marshall Chess interview, July 22, 1999; *Billboard*, November 8, 1969; *Billboard*, April 18, 1970, March 13, 1971; Baker, "Marshall Chess Comes Full Circle," *Goldmine* 78 (November 1982), pp. 14–16.

303: "We try to make hits": Marshall Chess interview, July 22, 1999; Guralnick, *Feel Like Going Home*, p. 201.

304: sale of WVON: *Broadcasting Magazine* yearbooks, 1971–1979; Notkin interviews, April 27, May 10, August 9, 1999; *Broadcasting Magazine*, January 29, 1973, p. 75; Pepper interviews.

305: Five Blind Boys: See *Peacock Records, Inc. v. Checker Records, Inc.*, 430F2d 85, August 6, 1970; Phil and Marshall Chess interviews; Notkin interview, April 27, 1999; FBI information from file 74–2186 obtained under the Freedom of Information Act.

306: renegotiate: June 14, 1973 documents filed with the Cook County, Ill. probate court in the estate of Leonard Chess.

306: Marvin Schlacter: *Billboard*, March 13, 1971, p. 3; *Cash Box*, March 13, 1971, p. 7; *Record World*, March 13, 1971, p. 3; Tom Bonetti interview, August 4, 1999; Alan Bayley interview, September 2, 1999.

306: power saws: Bob Sladek interview, August 5, 1999.

307: valued at $4,009,000: March 20, 1974 documents filed in the estate of Leonard Chess.

307: "ain't got shit": Loder, *Rolling Stone*, February 12, 1987, pp. 76, 98; Marshall Chess interviews.

307: "CON-tract": Bo Diddley interview, May 28, 1999.

308: "a family": Dwyer, *Blues Unlimited*, April 1970, p. 6.

308: "gimmes": Marshall Chess interviews.

308: bail money: Terry Chess interview, April 14, 1999.

308: "the right count": Bo Diddley interview with Phil Kuntz, 1984, Phil Kuntz private papers.

308: came as a surprise: Phil Chess interview, November 16, 1998; Marshall Chess interviews; James interview, June 14, 1999.

309: Wolf filed a lawsuit: Complaint and supporting documents in *Chester Burnett, known professionally as Howlin' Wolf vs. Gene Goodman and Arc Music*, 74CIV. 1959.

309: money damages: *Willie James Dixon v. Arc Music Corp., Gene Goodman, Philip Chess and Harry Goodman*, 76CIV.5764; *McKinley Morganfield v. Arc Music Corp., Gene Goodman, Philip Chess and Harry Goodman*, 76CIV.5763; Peter Herbert interview, July 29, 1999.

310: Pontiac Bonneville: Mitty Collier interview, August 5, 1999.

311: "marriage": Ahmad Jamal interview, April 24, 1999.

311: "I know in my heart": James, pp. 188–89; James interview, June 14, 1999.

312: $50,000: Sims interview, July 14, 1999.

313: back entrance: *Blues Access,* Winter 1999, p. 12; Spring 1999, p. 8; Interviews with Barge, Campbell, Marshall Chess, Phil Chess, Chisholm, Collier, Davis, DeSanto, Edwards, Evans, James, Johnson, LaPalm, Jimmy Lee Robinson, Ross, Sain, Satterfield, Sims, Tracy, White, Wiener, Wright.

313: "those old Jews": Samuelson interviews, October 1997; August 6, 1999.

BIBLIOGRAPHY

BOOKS

Bellow, Saul. *The Adventures of Augie March*. New York: Penguin Books, 1996.

Berry, Chuck. *The Autobiography*. New York: Harmony Books, 1987.

Brabec, Jeffrey and Todd, *Music, Money and Success*. New York: Schirmer Books, 1994.

Broadcast Music Inc. staff. *BMI 50th Anniversary*. Nashville: The Country Music Foundation, 1990.

Broadcasting Yearbooks. Washington, D.C.: Broadcasting Publications, 1958–73.

Chicago Fact Book Consortium: *Local Community Fact Book, Chicago Metropolitan Area, 1990*. Chicago: The University of Illinois at Chicago, 1995.

Cook, Bruce. *Listen to the Blues*. New York: Charles Scribner's Sons, 1973.

Cotten, Lee. *Shake, Rattle, and Roll: The Golden Age of American Rock n' Roll*, vol. 1, 1952–55. Ann Arbor, Mich.: Pierian Press, 1989.

Cutler, Irving. *The Jews of Chicago*. Urbana: The University of Illinois Press, 1996.

Danner, Frederic. *Hit Men: Power Brokers and Fast Money Inside the Music Business*. New York: Vintage Books, 1991.

DeWitt, Howard A. *Chuck Berry: Rock and Roll Music*. Ann Arbor, Mich.: Pierian Press, 1985.

Dixon, Willie, with Don Snowden. *I Am the Blues*. New York: DaCapo Press, Inc., 1989.

Drake, St. Clair, and Horace A. Clayton. *Black Metropolis*. Chicago: University of Chicago Press, 1993.

Eliot, Marc. *Rockonomics: The Money Behind the Music*. New York: Franklin Watts, 1989.

Escott, Colin, with Martin Hawkins. *Good Rockin' Tonight: Sun Records and the Birth of Rock and Roll*. New York: St. Martin's Press, 1991.

Fancourt, Les. *A Discography of the Blues Artists on the Chess Labels, 1947–57*. Faversham, Kent, England: L. Fancourt, 1989.

——. *A Discography of the Rhythm and Blues Artists on the Chess Labels, 1947–75.* Faversham, Kent. England: L. Fancourt, 1991.

Frazier, E. Franklin. *The Negro Family in Chicago.* Chicago: University of Chicago Press, 1932.

Gabler, Neal. *An Empire of Their Own: How the Jews Created Hollywood.* New York: Anchor Books, 1989.

Gart, Galen, ed. *First Pressings: The History of Rhythm and Blues,* 8 vols. Milford, N.H.: Big Nickel Publications, 1995.

Gillett, Charlie. *Making Tracks: Atlantic Records and the Growth of a Multi-Billion-Dollar Industry.* London: W. H. Allen, 1975.

Gordon, Robert. *It Came from Memphis.* Boston: Faber and Faber, 1995.

Guralnick, Peter. *Feel Like Going Home: Portraits in Blues and Rock'n'Roll.* New York: Outerbridge & Dienstfrey, 1971, reissued by Back Bay Books, 1999.

——. *Last Train to Memphis: The Rise of Elvis Presley.* New York: Little, Brown and Company, 1994.

——. *Sweet Soul Music.* Boston: Back Bay Books, 1999.

Hinton, Milt, and David G. Berger. *Bass Line: The Stories and Photographs of Milt Hinton.* Philadephia: Temple University Press, 1988.

Hirsch, Arnold R. *The Making of the Second Ghetto.* Cambridge: Cambridge University Press, 1984.

Jackson, John A. *Big Beat Heat: Alan Freed and the Early Days of Rock & Roll.* New York: Schirmer Books, 1991.

James, Edmund J., et al. *The Immigrant Jew in America.* New York: B. F. Buck &Company, 1906.

James, Etta. *Rage to Survive: The Etta James Story.* New York: Villard Books, 1995.

Keil, Charles. *Urban Blues.* Chicago: The University of Chicago Press, 1966.

Krasilovsky, M. William, and Sidney Shemel. *This Business of Music,* 7th ed. New York: Billboard Books, 1995.

Leadbitter, Mike, ed. *Nothing but the Blues.* London: Hanover Books, 1971.

Larkin, Colin, ed. *Guinness Encyclopedia of Music.* Chester, Conn.: New England Publishing Associates, 1994.

Lemann, Nicholas. *The Promised Land.* New York: Vintage, 1992.

Lincoln, C. Eric. *Coming Through the Fire: Suriving Race and Place in America.* Durham, N.C.: Duke University Press, 1996.

Lydon, Michael. *Boogie Lightning: How Music Became Electric.* New York: DaCapo Press, 1980.

——. *Rock Folk.* New York: Citadel Underground, 1990.

Miles. *The Rolling Stones: A Visual Documentary.* London: Omnibus Press, 1994.

Neff, Robert, and Anthony Connor. *Blues.* Boston: David R. Godine, 1975.

Palmer, Robert. *Deep Blues.* New York: Penguin Books, 1982.

Pruter, Robert. *Chicago Soul.* Urbana: University of Illinois Press, 1992.

——. *Doowop: The Chicago Scene.* Urbana: University of Illinois Press, 1996.

Redd, Lawrence N. *Rock Is Rhythm and Blues (The Impact of Mass Media).* Lansing: Michigan State Press, 1974.

Rooney, James. *Bossmen: Bill Monroe and Muddy Waters.* New York: The Dial Press, 1971.

Rose, Norman. *Chaim Weizmann: A Biography.* New York: Viking Press, 1986.

Rowe, Mike. *Chicago Blues*. New York: DaCapo, 1981.

Ruppli, Michel. *The Chess Labels: A Discography*. Westport, Conn.: Greenwood Press, 1983.

Ryan, John. *The Production of Culture in the Music Industry: The ASCAP-BMI Controversy*. Lanham, Md.: University Press of America, 1985.

Ryan, Marc. *Trumpet Records: An Illustrated History with Discography*. Milford, N.H.: Big Nickel Publications, 1992.

Salzman, Jack, ed., with Adina Back and Gretchen Sullivan Sorin. *Bridges and Boundaries: African Americans and American Jews*. New York: George Braziller in association with the Jewish Museum of New York, 1992.

Sanjek, Russell. *From Print to Plastic: Publishing and Promoting America's Popular Music (1900–1980)*. Brooklyn, N.Y.: Institute for Studies in American Music, Conservatory of Music, Brooklyn College, 1983.

———. *Pennies from Heaven: The American Popular Music Business in the Twentieth Century*, updated by David Sanjek. New York: DaCapo Press, 1996.

Schulberg, Budd. *What Makes Sammy Run*. New York: Vintage, 1990.

Shaw, Arnold. *Honkers and Shouters: The Golden Years of Rhythm and Blues*. New York: MacMillan, 1978.

Tooze, Sandra. *Muddy Waters: The Mojo Man*. Toronto: ECW Press, 1997.

Travis, Dempsey. *An Autobiography of Black Chicago*. Chicago: The Urban Research Institute, 1981.

———. *The Autobiography of Black Jazz*. Chicago: The Urban Research Institute, 1991.

Wexler, Jerry. *Rhythm and the Blues*. New York: St. Martin's Press, 1993.

Whitburn, Joel. *Joel Whitburn's Top LPs, 1945–72*. Menomonee Falls, Wis.: Record Research Inc., 1973.

———. *Joel Whitburn's Top R&B Singles, 1942–95*. Menomonee Falls, Wis.: Record Research Inc., 1996.

White, George. *Living Legend: Bo Diddley*. Chessington, Surrey, England: Castle Communications plc, 1995.

Wirth, Louis. *The Ghetto*. Chicago: University of Chicago Press, 1928.

ARTICLES

Baker, Cary. "Marshall Chess Comes Full Circle." *Goldmine*, November 1982.

Birnbaum, Larry. "Daddy G." *Chicago Reader*, June 24, 1989.

Booth, David. "Etta James: Twenty Years On." *Soul and Jazz*, April 1976.

Braunstein, Bill. "Bo Diddley, Bo Diddley, Where Have You Been?" *Chicago Tribune Magazine*, January 6, 1980.

Brisbin, John Anthony. "Jimmy Rogers: I'm Havin' Fun Right Today." *Living Blues*, September/October 1997.

Broven, John. "I Knew Leonard at the Macomba—an Interview with Paul Gayten." *Blues Unlimited* 130 (May/August 1978).

Cotten, Lee. "The Hawk Rocks Again: Interview with Dale Hawkins." *Rock and Blues News*, May–June 1999.

Dahl, Bill. "Ralph Bass." *Living Blues*, July/August 1997.

DeCurtis, Anthony. "Willie Dixon and the Wisdom of the Blues," *Rolling Stone*, March 23, 1989.

Dwyer, Bill. "Bo Diddley." *Blues Unlimited* 71 (April 1970).

Fleming, John. "A Life Recording." *Chicago Reader*, March 7, 1980.

Greensmith, Bill. "The Fontella Bass Interview." *Blues Unlimited* 147 (Spring 1986).

———. "The Bobby McClure Interview." *Blues Unlimited* 147 (Spring 1986).

Hannusch, Jeff. "Bo Diddley Is a Guitar Slinger," *Guitar Player* 174 (June 1984).

Jones, Wayne. "Nate Nelson of the Flamingos." *Goldmine*, March 1978.

Lind, Jim. "Minnie Riperton: Rotary Connection's Angel." *Illinois Entertainer*, January 1980.

Lisheron, Mark. "Rhythm and Jews." *CommonQuest*, Summer 1997.

Loder, Kurt. "Bo Diddley, The Rolling Stone Interview." *Rolling Stone*, February 12, 1987.

Marcus, Greil. "Roll Over Chuck Berry." *Rolling Stone*, June 14, 1969.

McGarvey, Seamus. "I Only Have Eyes for You: The Flamingos' Story—Zeke Carey Interviewed." *Now Dig This*, 97 (April 1991).

Moon, D. Thomas. "Strange Voodoo: Inside the Vaults of Chess Studios." *Blues Access*, Winter 1999.

O'Neal, Jim. "Andrew 'Andy' Tibbs." *Living Blues*, January/February 1992.

O'Neal, Jim and Amy. "Muddy Waters Interview." *Living Blues*, March/April 1985.

Peterson, Clarence. "The Chicago Sound." *Chicago Tribune Magazine*, May 11, 1969.

Pomus, Doc. "About Andrew Tibbs." *Living Blues*, January/February 1992.

Propes, Steve. "The Moonglows: The Commandments of Doo-Wop." *Goldmine*, February 8, 1991.

Pruter, Robert. "Billy Stewart: The Fat Boy Lives On . . ." *It Will Stand*, 17/18 (1981).

———. "The Mitty Collier Story." *Goldmine*, December 1981.

———. "A Talk with Daddy G." *Goldmine*, March 1982.

———. "Jackie Ross." *It Will Stand* 20 (1983).

———. "Jan Bradley." *Soul Survivor*, Winter/1987–88.

Rowe, Mike. "I Was Really Dedicated—An Interview with Billy Boy Arnold." *Blues Unlimited* 126 (September/October) 127 (November/December 1977).

Salvo, Patrick William. "A Converation with Chuck Berry." *Rolling Stone*, November 23, 1972.

Tancredi, Carl. "The Flamingos—The Early Years." *Bim Bam Boom* 4 (February–March 1972).

Topping, Ray. "Marshall Chess Shoots the Breeze." *Blues Unlimited* 142 (Summer 1982).

Welding, Pete. "Muddy Waters." *Rolling Stone*, November 9, 1968.

Wheeler, Tom. "Chuck Berry, The Story." *Guitar Player*, March 1988.

Wolfson, Cary. "Rooster Pickin's: Back Door Blues." *Blues Access*, Spring 1999.

Wright, Doug, and Richard Pack. "Laura Lee." *Soul Survivor*, Summer 1986.

PERIODICALS

Billboard. 1947–1970, including the *Billboard Encyclopedia*, 1947–48, 9th edition.

Cashbox, 1947–1970.

Chicago Defender, 1946–49, selected issues thereafter.

Down Beat, 1957–1963, including *Down Beat Jazz Record Reviews*, vols. I–IV, Chicago: Maher Publications.
Record World, 1963–69.
Tri-State Defender, 1955.
Variety, 1955.

PRIVATE PAPERS

Burt Burdeen
Marshall Chess
Terry Chess
Cynthia Fendel
Phil Kuntz
Dick LaPalm
Stan Lewis
Lillian McMurry
Robert Pruter
Tim Samuelson
Charles Walton

UNPUBLISHED MANUSCRIPTS

Bass, Ralph. "I Didn't Give a Damn if Whites Bought It: The Story of Ralph Bass."
Coleman, Gloria. "The Dusable Hotel Locale: Descriptive Analysis of an Era and an Area Circa 1940–50." April 1980 master's thesis for Northeastern Illinois University.
Keel, Beverly. "A Hoss of a Different Color: Rock and Roll Radio Before Alan Freed."

MISCELLANEOUS

Chess Records files, including selected tapes from recording sessions, MCA/Universal Music Group, Universal City, California.
Chicago city phone books, 1922–65.
Chuck Berry clip file from the *St. Louis Post-Dispatch* and *Globe Democrat* courtesy of the Mercantile Library of St. Louis.
Hail Hail Rock and Roll, Universal Pictures, MCA Home Video, Inc., 1988.
Record Row: Cradle of Rhythm and Blues. The Chicago Production Center, WTTW, Window to the World Communications, Inc., 1997.
Records of the Illinois State Liquor Commission and the Office of the Secretary of State.
Sweet Home Chicago, MCA Records—Initial Film and Television, Chicago, Vanguard Films, 1993.

ACKNOWLEDGMENTS

Many individuals provided help, humor, insights, constructive criticism, and more than a few tapes and CDs for this project. Several deserve special mention.

I began this book and signed the contract with St. Martin's before I met or talked to any of the Chess family. The intent was to write the book from available documents and resources but with the hope that Marshall, Leonard's son, and Phil, Leonard's brother, would agree to talk to me when they understood the focus of the book—how the Chess brothers built their company. Once I was introduced to Marshall—and my great thanks to Peter Herbert for making the introduction—he granted me many hours of interviews. No question was off-limits, none was answered "no comment." I appreciate his candor and the fact that neither Marshall nor Phil, or any family member, asked to see any part of the manuscript before publication. Phil made himself available whenever I asked, and the challenge was always to find the right question that might prompt a good story about the record business. My thanks also to Sheva, Phil's wife, and their children, Terry, Pam, and Kevin. Through her stories and wonderful photographs, Mae Chess Silverbrand, Leonard and Phil's older sister, allowed me to glean some understanding of the family's life in Poland before they came to the United States, and she remembered with great clarity important moments of the family's early years in Chicago. My thanks, too, to Joyce and Leonard Diamond and Adrian Mallin.

Ron Elving and Phil Kuntz became editors-in-progress. They read every word of the manuscript, some of them twice or three times, and if I tried their patience, they were gracious enough not to grumble. Ron's ear for language and acute appreciation for tone kept me on track in the very beginning when I might have veered off in the wrong direction. He could see when the words I had chosen failed to live up to the story. Phil's insistence on the telling detail, his willingness to help me find obscure information and individuals who hadn't been heard from in years, and his good-natured, if occasionally sharp prodding made me strive to fill in the blanks. I am indebted to both of them. They bear no responsibility for the final product but deserve credit for making me tell the best story I could.

Joe Davis was my technical wizard, getting me out of jams when the computer refused to cooperate.

The serendipity of research led me to Charlie McGovern, Smithsonian historian and curator, who had a full set of Galen Gart's valuable *First Pressings*, a ten-volume compilation of the history of rhythm and blues. Charlie became a third informal editor, and because of his wide-ranging knowledge of music, he caught mistakes and helped sharpen my thinking at important points. Ed Sedarbaum, the first copyeditor I ever worked with, inspires me still.

In Chicago, Norman Schwartz, a founder of the Chicago Jewish Historical Society, answered questions, found documents, and took pictures that helped me understand Chicago's large Jewish community and where the Chess family fit. Tim Samuelson, whose dogged work in the early nineties led to the preservation of the Chess studio at 2120 South Michigan Avenue, allowed me to use his voluminous files on the building. When he moved to the Chicago Historical Society, he gave me valuable research assistance—locating documents, nailing down addresses and phones numbers, and providing insights about the city and its history.

Charles Walton, musician and historian, was a bridge to the past. I am forever grateful for his generosity in allowing me to listen to tapes of his own interviews and review documents he had collected. He opened many doors for me in the long research process. And I particularly appreciate his willingness to read the manuscript as it unfolded. Concerned that I had not caputured the atmosphere in one of the early chapters, he told me, "You write like a white person." I had to plead guilty to the charge, but he prompted me to take another and, I hope, more successful crack at the material.

Robert Pruter was a great help in two respects. His two books, *Chicago Soul* and *Doowop: The Chicago Scene,* are full of valuable information and a fine contribution to the literature of this musical genre. Bob went more than the extra mile, giving me copies of the many stories he had written about Chess musicians and several of his interviews. His read of the manuscript prompted several improvements, and most important, allowed me to correct errors.

Catalina Soto, the administrative assistant to the director of the Illinois Liquor Control Commission, was both patient and efficient in getting me the information that provided details of Leonard's early business ventures.

Great thanks also to Peter Guralnick, who took time to read the manuscript. His astute observations and suggestions, delivered in the most gracious manner, made the final product better. And thanks to Mary Eva Candon and her colleagues at Berliner, Candon & Jimison, my landlords, who made me feel so welcome.

Andy McKaie of the Universal Music Group allowed me to roam through what remains of the Chess archive. He and his assistant, Jo Ann Frederick, never raised an eyebrow as I wandered through the files and wandered into their office with intermittent questions. The chance to go through the boxes of material was an immeasurable help, as was the hour I spent in the Universal vault amid the eight thousand tapes that represent the life of the Chess Producing Corporation.

At the Library of Congress, reference librarians and their assisants in the Performing Arts Reading Room and the Recorded Sound Reference Center were helpful, patient, and persevering. They made me feel at home when they knew what I wanted as soon as I walked in the door. My thanks to Charles Sens, for his persistence in answering the pesky questions, and to Marcus Hanes, Sam Perryman, Carl Cephas, and Bill Harvey. Thanks to Wynn Matthias, Jan McKee, and Bryan Cornell in the Recorded Sound division. And thanks, also, to Jim Snyder in microforms for finding all the Chicago city phone books I needed from the 1920s through the early 1950s.

Several individuals helped me understand the intricacies of music publishing. Thanks to Allen Arrow; at BMI, thanks to Gary Roth in the legal department, Lara Meshel in research, Peg Farthing in Nashville, and David Sanjak. Additional thanks to Noel Silverman and William Krasilovsky, and to another lawyer and Chess friend, Nate Notkin, for all the good stories.

Among the many others with whom I spoke, several contributed special help: Jane Abbott, for the Peter Herbert connection; Edna Albert, for allowing me access to early issues of *Cash Box;* Stephen Aron, who provided insights about his mother, Evelyn Aron, the founder of Aristocrat Records. Also Joe Bihari, Burt Burdeen, Robert Campbell, Bobby Charles, Malcolm Chisholm, Lucky Cordell, Billy Davis, Esmond Edwards, Richard Evans, Cynthia Fendel, Ruth and Sharon Friedman, Ward Gaines, Robert Gordon, Peter Grendysa, Gwen Kesler, Ed Komara, Dick LaPalm, Stan Lewis, Mary Nurmi, Sam Phillips, Vince Pepper, Scott Putnam, Jack Tracy, Dave Usher, Ruby Vinson, and Jerry Wexler. Jack Wiener, who built the studio at 2120 South Michigan Avenue, died while the book was in production. He provided many nuggets that enriched the Chess story.

It was a privilege and a delight to spend time with the late Lillian McMurry. Her meticulous record keeping allowed me to see firsthand what it took to run a small independent label. She was no fan of Leonard Chess but agreed to let me come to her home in Jackson, Mississippi, to get the benefit of her wisdom. I am sorry she passed away before I could put this book in her hands, even if it would have made her mad all over again.

Alan Ehrenhalt, thoughtful and stylish writer, encouraged me to turn my Chess idea into a book proposal and then gave me a useful critique. Philippa "Flip" Brophy, my agent, believed in the project from the beginning and has been a steady source of support. At St. Martin's, Cal Morgan's initial enthusiasm for the project was a great boost. When a new opportunity took him elsewhere, Elizabeth Beier stepped in without missing a beat. The attention she gave to her inherited duties is much appreciated. Her trenchant questions led to important improvements. Michael Connor, Elizabeth's genial assistant, was always available to answer questions and keep track of the mail.

The music of Tracy Nelson—the sound of a great voice and that intriguing, earthy demeanor—inspired this book. I wrote an article in 1995 about Tracy's resurgent recording career, and that story led to my rediscovering the Chess brothers. When Tracy and I talked a time or two about this project, her salty comments served as their own kind of creative fuel.

Inspiration came, too, from the memory of my father, Arnold Cohodas, a generous man of good deeds and good will, and from the memory of my grandparents, whose journey from Eastern Europe to the American Midwest paralleled the Chess family's.

Final thanks to Sylvia Cohodas, my mother, and Howard Cohodas, my brother, cheerleaders and sounding boards from beginning to end.

Abner, Ewart, 159
Ackerman, Paul, 171
"Actions Speak Louder than Words," 203
Adams, Shirley, 12
"Adulteen," 207
Afro-American musicians
    copyrights, contracts, and songwriting credits,
      36, 38, 39, 77, 77–80, 86–87, 98, 99, 130,
      307–11
    perceived exploitation of, 4, 73–74, 77–80,
      93–97, 307–11
    race and the success of rock and roll, 146–48
    See also "race" music; rhythm and blues (R&B);
      rock and roll
Afro-Americans
    black and black-oriented radio, 36–38, 45,
      213–16, 216–18
    Chicago, migration to and population of, 16,
      19–20, 45
    independent record producers, 159
    Jews, relations with, 109–10, 185–86
Ahmad Jamal Trio at the Pershing: But Not for Me
    (album), 153, 154–55, 210
"Ain't Got No Home," 132
"Ain't Nobody Here But Us Chickens," 34
Aladdin (album), 291
Aladdin records, 36, 42
Alaimo, Steve, 205, 227

Aliotta, Mitch, 283
"All I Could Do Was Cry," 186, 187, 198, 200
All Platinum, 311, 312
"All Shook Up," 144
All State Distribution, 136
Allen, William "Hoss," 61, 85, 199, 203
"Almost Grown," 164
"Always Together," 281
American Bandstand (TV show), 150, 187–88, 195,
    198
American Record Distributors, 50
Ammons, Albert, 27, 34
Ammons, Gene, 27, 50, 56, 57, 210, 301
Anderson, Clarence "Sleepy," 25
Anna Records, 162, 202
"Annie Lee Blues," 49
Apollo Records, 42
Arc Music, 79–80, 99, 116, 120, 129, 156, 158,
    163, 173, 201, 236, 260, 313, 314
    lawsuits against, 309–10
Archia, Tom, 24–25, 27, 28, 36, 37, 38, 41, 78, 81,
    153
Argo label. *See under* Chess Records
Aristocrat Record Corporation, 34–47, 47–50
    advertising, 35–36, 42, 46, 56
    distribution and promotion, 44–45, 46–47,
      48–49
    press, reviews, and public relations, 35, 47, 49

Aristocrat Record Corporation (*continued*)
  and "race" music, 34, 39, 42–43
  record distribution, 38–39
  sessions, 41–42, 43–47
  success of, 44–47
  See also Chess Records
ARMADA (American Record Manufacturers and Distributors Association), 191–92
Armstrong, Louis, 19, 26
Arnold, Billy Boy, 102, 103, 104, 109
Aron, Charles, 33, 34, 38, 43, 278
Aron, Evelyn, 43, 44, 78
  Leonard Chess, partnership with, 33, 36–40, 43–47, 47–50, 71, 278, 279
  and Aristocrat Records, 34–36
Arrow, Allen, 79, 172–73, 183, 230, 260, 262–63, 292–96
ASCAP (American Society of Composers, Authors and Publishers), 77, 154
"At Last," 188, 208
At Last (album), 188, 193
Atkins, Alex, 43
Atlantic Records, 79, 87, 121, 150, 159, 211, 271

"Baby Get Lost," 48
"Baby What You Want Me to Do," 237–38
Bacith, Esther, 300
"Back in the U.S.A.," 164
Baker, LaVern, 124
Ballard, Hank, 184, 185, 197, 198
Barge, Gene, 134, 250, 265, 287, 288, 289
Barnes, Prentiss, 98
Barnes, Sidney, 283
Bass, Fontella, 208, 246–47, 250–52, 263, 283, 285
Bass, Martha, 247
Bass, Ralph, 196–97, 236–37, 247, 263–64, 279, 288, 312
Batts Restaurant (Chicago), 141, 263– 64
Bayley, Alan, 292–96, 302–3, 306–7
Beach Boys, 236
Beatles, 236, 241–42
Bedno, Howard, 153
"Been So Long," 162
Bell, Jimmy, 41
Below, Fred, 70–71, 84, 87, 91–92, 149, 241, 265
Benjamin, Jonathan, 44
Benjamin, Louis, 205–6, 234, 261–62, 288
Benny Rides Again (album), 158
"Benny's Bounce," 57
Benson, Al, 36, 45, 50, 70, 71, 107, 127, 152, 177, 179, 217
Bernard Chalmers and Associates, 140
Bernard Lowe Enterprises, 177
Berry, Chuck, 4, 113–17, 121, 132, 133, 134, 149, 150, 272
  legal problems, 113–14, 206–8, 234
  sessions and catalogue, 115–17, 132, 133, 140, 142, 143, 144, 149, 161–62, 163–64, 164, 189, 190, 191, 202, 207, 234–36, 312
  writing credit, 308–9
Berry, Lucy, 113
"Berry on Stage," 234
Big Maybelle, 163
Big Three Trio, 81, 82
"Big Time Baby," 48
Bihari, Joe, 58, 61, 62, 72, 75, 76, 78, 86, 121, 159, 182, 184–85, 186
Bihari, Jules, 58, 62, 78, 86, 121, 159, 182, 186
Bihari, Sam, 58, 62, 78, 86, 121, 159, 182, 186
Bilbo, Theodore, 38
"Bilbo Is Dead," 38, 39, 42, 78
Billboard, 3, 121, 125, 129, 143, 145, 176, 190, 215, 220, 256, 278–79, 279, 291, 294–95
  charts, lists, and surveys, 34, 35, 45, 53, 57, 59, 60, 64, 71, 78, 86, 88, 91, 92, 117, 126, 130, 132, 133, 144, 146, 154–55, 163, 195, 198, 208, 209, 227, 239, 246, 247, 249, 251, 252, 253–54, 254, 265, 266, 271, 273, 275, 279, 280, 281, 284, 289, 290, 296, 296–97
  Chess/Checker/Argo/Aristocrat records and Chess brothers, advertising, articles, and reviews, 35, 37, 39, 42, 45, 47, 49, 50, 70, 87, 105, 112, 131, 132–33, 142, 144, 156, 157–58, 161, 163–64, 187, 188, 189–90, 193, 209, 223
  and "race" music, 34, 42–43, 45, 84, 106
"Billie's Bounce," 25
"Billy's Blues," 209
Binzer, Rollin, 281, 283, 286–87, 291, 292
Black, Bill, 145
Black and White Records, 197
"Black Angel Blues," 49
Blain, Jerry, 84, 85
Blevins, Bobby, 57
Bloomfield, Mike, 297
"Blow Wind Blow," 88
"Blue and Lonesome," 48
"Blue Suede Shoes," 146
Blues from Big Bill's Copa Cabana (album), 241
"Blues Heaven," 264, 265
"Blues in the Night," 163
Blues Rockers, 50, 71
Blues Unlimited magazine, 307–8
"Blues with a Feeling," 87–88
BMI (Broadcast Music Inc.), 77, 120, 154
"Bo Diddley," 104–5
Bo Diddley Is a Gunslinger (album), 193
Bo Diddley's Beach Party (album), 232–33
Bob Hope: The Road to Vietnam (album), 257
Bobbin label, 208
Bobby Blue Band, 67
Bonnier, Bess, 151–52
"Boogie Chillen," 67
"Boogie Woogie Blues," 78
"Book of Love," 162, 164
Boone, Pat, 129–30, 163

"Boy of My Dreams," 187
Boyd, Eddie, 41, 74, 79, 85
Bracken, Jimmy, 159
Bracken, Vivian, 159
Bradford, James, 104
Bradley, Jan, 227
Branch, Ben, 287
Brandom (publishing company), 136
Brenston, Jackie, 59, 65, 144
Brim, John, 73
British Decca
    and the Argo label, 255–56
Bronstein, Don, 165
Brooks, Glen, 27
Brount, Fred, 34
Brount, Mildred, 34, 78
Brown, Nappy, 112
Brown, Ruth, 142, 147
"Brown Eyed Handsome Man," 133, 235
Burdeen, Burt, 258, 299
Burke, Solomon, 287
"Burning Spear," 275
Burris, Ralph, 115
Burton, John Henry, 78–79, 247
Burton, Wallace, 155
"But I Do," 195, 208
"But Not for Me," 153, 154
But Not for Me. See Ahmad Jamal Trio at the
    Pershing
Butler, Jerry, 260
Butler, Silas "Buddy," 25
Butterfield, Paul, 297

Cage, James "Butch," 192
Cain, Jackie, 36
"Call It Stormy Monday," 196
Campbell, Little Milton, 208, 245, 246, 247, 248,
    272, 285, 296
"Can't Hold Out Much Longer," 70
Capital Records, 77, 136
Carey, Jake, 127
Carey, Zeke, 127, 129, 130
Carter, Johnny, 127–30
Casa Grande label, 149
Cash Box, 3, 74, 84, 100, 121, 143, 172, 190, 211,
    235, 254, 256
    charts, lists, polls, and surveys, 35, 45, 59, 60,
        64, 71, 86, 88, 91, 92, 99–100, 105, 112,
        117–18, 133, 198, 208, 209, 227, 246, 247,
        253, 260, 265, 266, 273, 275, 279, 280, 281,
        284, 289, 290, 296–97
    Chess/Checker/Argo/Aristocrat records,
        advertising, articles, and reviews, 35, 47–48,
        50, 66–67, 70, 85, 86–87, 90, 112, 138, 140,
        149, 149–50, 158, 164, 188, 191
    and "race" music, 34, 45
Caston, Leonard "Baby Doo," 82, 225–26, 249
"cat music," 106

Chamber Music of the New Jazz (album), 153
Chamblee, Eddie, 27, 28
Chance label, 98, 127–28
Charles, Bobby, 122–27, 143, 150, 163, 195, 203,
    276
Charles, Ray, 133, 163
Checker Records. See Chess Records
Chess, Celia (Cyrla Czyz) (mother), 5–6, 8, 10, 11,
    300
Chess, Diane (Marshall's wife), 282, 300
Chess, Elaine (Leonard's daughter), 22, 62, 76,
    167–68, 314
Chess, Joseph (Yasef Czyz) (father), 5–6, 8, 14,
    28–29, 300
    as a junk dealer, 13, 14, 15
    real estate ventures, 15, 22, 43
    residence (1425 South Karlov), 9–10
Chess, Kevin (Phil's son), 117, 169, 314
Chess, Leonard, 1–2
    childhood and education, 5, 10–11, 11–13
    death and funeral, 299–301
    health, 137–38, 270
    and Howlin' Wolf, 65
    marriage (Revetta Sloan) and family life, 13–14,
        62, 138, 167–69
    and Muddy Waters, 2, 40–41, 44, 44–45, 93
    musical instinct and taste, 24–28, 44, 48–49,
        51–52, 53, 71, 189, 209
    personality and expressive language of, 12,
        12–13, 28, 52, 111, 126–27, 149, 181,
        270–71, 274, 299
    philanthropy and politics, 275–79, 287–88
    religious observance, 107–8
    residence (4414 Drexel Boulevard), 14, 22
    residence (Glencoe), 138, 167
    residence (South Shore), 89
Chess, Leonard (business career)
    Evelyn Aron (Aristocrat Records), partnership
        with, 33, 36–40, 43–47, 47–50, 71, 278, 279
    business management, philosophy of, 169–71
    Cut-Rate Liquor, 14–15, 23
    financial success and entanglements, 31–32.
        See also under Chess Records
    Macomba Lounge, 2, 15–16, 22–32, 51, 278
    radio stations. See Chess brothers (radio stations)
    708 Liquor Store, 15, 23
Chess, Leonard (business career:
        Chess/Checker/Argo records)
    copyrights, contracts, and song writing credits,
        38, 39, 77, 77–80
    booking tours, 93
    distribution and promotion, 38–39, 48–50, 54,
        60–61, 75–76, 84, 88, 97, 110–11, 120, 122,
        135, 148, 193, 198–99
    Sam Philips, dealings with, 62, 64–65
    and "race" music, 34, 39, 42–43
    See also Chess Records
Chess, Mae (sister). See Silverbrand, Mae Chess

Chess, Marshall (Leonard's son), 2, 75, 83, 131, 142, 207, 242–43, 308, 313–14
on allegations of exploitation, 308, 311
bar mitzvah, 107–9
Cadet Concept, 279, 281–84, 289
and Chess Records, 60–61, 76, 89–90, 111, 154, 162, 231–32, 233–34, 235, 249, 261–63, 268, 272, 279, 288–92
and Chess Records (under GRT), 294, 295, 296–98, 302–3, 306–7
childhood and education, 13–14, 29, 31, 51, 56, 62, 168–69, 179, 231–32
CZYZ label, 314
and his father (Leonard Chess), 15, 40, 73, 79, 173, 230, 300
and his uncle (Phil Chess), 75
and Rolling Stones Records, 314
Chess, Pam (Phil's daughter), 117, 169
Chess, Philip, 2, 300
childhood and education, 6, 9, 10–11, 12, 13, 14
marriage (Sheva Jonesi) and family life, 14, 32, 155, 168–69
musical instinct and taste, 53, 145, 189
religious observance, 107–8
residence (4556 Greenwood Avenue), 22
residence (South Shore), 89
Chess, Philip (business career)
on allegations of exploitation, 311
financial success and entanglements, 31–32. See also under Chess Records
Macomba Lounge, 2, 15–16, 22–32, 51, 278
radio stations. See Chess brothers (radio stations)
real estate, 305
Chess, Philip (business career: Chess/Checker/Argo records), 50, 96
copyrights, contracts, and songwriting credits, 77, 77–80
distribution and promotion, 75–76, 85–87, 111, 119–20, 193
Alan Freed, dealings with, 85–86, 98
See also Chess Records
Chess, Revetta Sloan (Leonard's wife), 13–14, 14, 22, 67, 110, 138, 168, 300, 305, 307, 313
Chess, Sheva Jonesi (Philip's wife), 14, 22, 32, 67, 86, 155, 168, 169
Chess, Susie (Leonard's daughter), 22, 62, 314
Chess, Terry (Phil's son), 2, 117, 131, 161, 169, 270–71, 298–99, 305
Chess and Sons (junk shop), 14
Chess brothers
Afro-American musicians, perceived exploitation of, 4, 73–74, 77–80, 93–97
Afro-American musicians, friendship and social interactions with, 4, 14, 93–97
copyrights, contracts, and songwriting credits, 36, 77
Alan Freed, dealings with, 85–86, 98, 107
lawsuits, 305–6

liquor business, 15–16, 23
Macomba Lounge, 2, 15–16, 22–32, 278
and the music publishing business, 79, 163, 202
and the payola scandal, 174–75, 178–82
Sam Philips, dealings with, 62, 64–65
Universal Recording Studios, dealings with, 35, 68–69, 97–98
Chess brothers (radio stations), 4, 212–16, 216–18, 218–24, 298–99
black political and social organizations, giving access to, 223–24
Den Pals, 258, 299
and the King assassination, 286–88
L&P Broadcasting, 212–13
sale of, 304–5
WCAN (Camden, NJ), 257–58
WLUP (WSDM) FM (Chicago), 305
WNOV (Milwaukee, WI), 284–85, 304–5
WTAC (Flint, MI), 212
WYN-R, competition with, 218–22
WVON AM/WSDM FM (Chicago), 213–16, 216–18, 220–24, 258–59, 276, 284, 286–87, 298–99
Chess Records (Checker Records)
All Platinum, sale to and ownership of, 311, 312
Argo/Cadet subsidiary (jazz), 131–32, 142, 144, 150, 152–55, 155–56, 158, 162, 173, 186–89, 191, 193, 195, 199, 208, 234–35, 241, 252–55, 255–57, 280–81
Cadet Concept, 279, 281–84, 291–92
Check-mate subsidiary, 203
Chevis Music (publishing company), 203, 239, 252, 260
and country-and-western music, 97
burglary and theft, 230–31
distribution, 150, 156–59, 203–4. See also under Chess, Leonard (business career: Chess Records); Chess, Philip (business career: Chess Records)
European market, 171–72, 205–6, 234, 261–63, 288–89
family involvement, 167–68
financial success, business operations and entanglements, 57, 59–60, 66, 72–73, 88–89, 93–97, 99–100, 117, 119–21, 130–32, 135, 148–50, 154, 156–59, 169–70, 193, 201–2, 210–11, 228–29, 252, 260, 263, 288
GRT (General Recorded Tape), sale to and ownership of, 292–96, 296–98, 302–3, 306–7
long-playing records, 142–43, 157, 161–62, 165, 193
naming, 56
Marterry label, 131
Muscle Shoals studio (Alabama), 271–74, 280
office (4750 South Cottage Grove), 89–91
office and studio (2120 South Michigan), 136–37, 137–40, 141–42, 157, 203, 249–50, 312–13

office, studio, and pressing plant (320 East 21st Street), 267–69
record pressing, label printing, and album design and notes, 156, 159–61, 165, 193, 263, 267–69
See also Aristocrat Record Corporation; rhythm and blues
Chess Records (Checker Records) (artists and repertory)
advertising and promotion, 57, 66, 84, 131–32, 132–33, 142, 156, 157–58, 167, 191, 191–92, 209, 234, 235, 240–44, 256, 260–61, 291–92
catalogue and sessions, 56–57, 59–60, 64, 67–71, 74, 83–85, 87–88, 91–93, 104–5, 116–17, 120, 126, 127–30, 140–42, 142, 143–44, 148–50, 152–55, 155–56, 158, 161–62, 164–66, 186–89, 189–93, 194–95, 195–96, 198–99, 205–6, 208–10, 226–27, 232–33, 234–36, 236–37, 238–40, 241, 245–47, 247–49, 249–50, 253–55, 263–65, 272–73, 280–81, 289–90
catalogue and sessions (under GRT), 296–98
charts, lists, and surveys, 53, 57, 59, 64, 71, 88, 91, 92, 112, 117–18, 126, 227, 239, 132, 133, 144, 154–55, 170–71, 195, 198, 208, 209, 246, 247, 249, 251, 252, 253–54, 254, 260, 265, 266, 271, 273, 275, 279, 280, 281, 284, 289, 290, 296, 296–97
comedians, recording, 195–96, 205, 256–57
copyrights, contracts, and songwriting credits, 72–73, 77, 77–80, 116, 118–19, 128–29, 248–49, 264, 307–11
jazz vs. blues musicians, 56–57
house band, 225–27, 228–29
press, articles, and reviews, 66–67, 70, 85, 86–87, 90, 105, 112, 131, 132–33, 140, 144, 149, 154, 158, 163, 163–64, 165, 187, 188, 189–90, 193
unreleased songs, 74–75, 161, 235
Chevis Music (publishing company), 203, 239, 252, 260
"Chi-Baba Chi-Baba," 35, 36
Chicago
Afro-American migration to, 16, 19–20
riot of 1919, 17
South Grove Avenue ("Bronzeville") as center of Afro-American life, 16–21
Chicago American, 179, 258
Chicago Bee, 19, 27
Chicago Breakdown (Rowe), 15–16, 20–21
Chicago Daily News, 179, 221, 277, 297
Chicago Defender, 17, 18, 28, 103, 216, 217, 219
Chicago Tribune, 297
Chisholm, Malcolm, 63–64, 153, 157, 162, 165, 183
Churchill, Savannah, 131
Clark, Dick, 150, 164, 187–88
Clarke, Tony, 249

Clay, Francis, 192
Clay, Tom, 178
Cleveland, James, 239
"Close to You," 162
Clovers, 100
Club DeLisa (Chicago), 18
Club Zanzibar (Chicago), 70
Cobra Records, 140, 191
Coconut Grove ballroom (Chicago), 18
Cole, Nat King, 126, 228
Coleman, Loren, 297
Coleman, Oliver, 26
Collier, Mitty, 226–27, 239–40, 310
Coltrane, John, 210
Columbia records, 36, 41, 55
"Come Back Maybellene," 118
"Come On," 207
Coming Through the Fire (Lincoln), 110
Como, Perry, 35
"Confessin' the Blues," 113
Congo Club (Chicago), 19
Conrad Music, 260
Cooke, Carl, 238
Cooperstein, Max, 150, 153, 157, 178, 191, 204, 232, 240, 249, 250, 260, 268, 272, 287, 298
Coral Records, 99, 163
Cordell, Lucky, 221–22, 223, 299
Coronets, 86, 98
Coryell, Murali, 314
Cosey, Pete, 250, 251, 282, 289–90
Cosmic label, 162
Cosmopolitan Club (East St. Louis, IL), 114–15
Cotton, James, 190–91
Count Basie, 34, 45
Count 'Em 88 (album), 153
"Country," 134
"Crackin' Up," 164
Crawford, Ernest "Big," 41, 42, 43, 52, 53
Crawford, James "Sugar Boy," 88, 97
Crawford, Ollie, 82
Croninger, David, 213
"Cross My Heart," 280
"Crying in the Chapel," 85
Crystalette label, 131
Cut-Rate Liquor, 14–15, 23
Czyz, Cyrla. *See* Chess, Celia
Czyz, Fiszel. *See* Chess, Philip
Czyz, Lejzor. *See* Chess, Leonard
Czyz, Malka. *See* Chess, Mae
Czyz, Yasef. *See* Chess, Joseph
CZYZ label, 314

"D.B. Blues," 25
Daigre, Bertel, 223
Daley, Richard, 286, 291
Dells, 280–81, 296
Damone, Vic, 34
Daps, 131

Dave Young Orchestra, 38
David Rosen Incorporated, 178
Davis, Billy, 130, 162, 186, 194, 197–98, 200–203, 210, 225–27, 228–29, 238, 243, 245–47, 250–52, 262, 265–66, 268, 272, 280, 285, 311, 313
Davis, Miles, 154
"Dawn Mist," 48
Dawson, William L., 223
Daylie, Daddy-O, 141, 155, 178
Dayron, Norman, 297–98
Decca records, 36, 55, 163
Dee Gee Records, 151
Deep Blues (Palmer), 16
Delta Cats (Jackie Brenston and), 65
Derfler, Irv, 39, 176
DeSanto, Sugar Pie, 194–95, 238, 266
Deutsch, Hymie, Jay, and Sam, 89
Diamond, Leonard, 265, 270, 299, 311
Diddley, Bo (Ellas McDaniel), 4, 101–6, 110, 121, 209, 241–42
    acquiring his name, 103–4
    catalogue and sessions, 104–5, 112, 143, 164–65, 189, 190, 191, 193, 202, 205, 232–33, 272
    Chess Records, complaint against, 307–11
"Diddley Daddy," 112
"Diggin' My Potatoes," 85
Dion, 236
"Dirty Man," 273–74
disc jockeys
    black and black-oriented radio, 36–38, 45, 213–16, 216–18
    payola and other considerations, 61–62, 86, 174–82, 231–32
    writing credits, appropriation of, 36, 86
    See also radio
Discus (publishing company), 254
Dixon, Marie, 313
Dixon, Willie, 4, 49, 81–83, 83–85, 92, 93, 99, 120, 140, 149, 191, 199, 241, 263–65
    Arc Music, lawsuit against, 309–10
Domino, Fats, 100, 133, 147, 190
Dominoes, 106, 197
"Don't Cry Baby," 205, 208
"Don't Go No Further," 133
"Don't Mess Up a Good Thing," 247
"Don't Say Good Bye," 143–44
"Don't You Know I Love You?," 125
Donahue, Tom, 235
Dorsey, Jimmy, 146
Dorsey, Tommy, 146
Dot Records, 129, 160, 163, 211
Down Beat magazine, 151, 152, 154, 156, 157, 191, 256
Dozier Boys, 48
Dreier, Alex, 257
Dunn, Donald "Duck," 297
Dunn, John, 160

Dunn Record Pressing Inc., 160
DuSable Hotel (Chicago), 18–19, 23

East Harlem Children's Chorus, 288
Eatman, Narval "Cadillac Baby," 198–99
Eben, A. Bradley, 178
Eckstine, Billy, 26
Eddy, Duane, 190
Edmonds, Elga. See Evans, Elgin
Edwards, Esmond, 210–11, 234–35, 243–44, 252–55, 263, 268, 274–75
Edwards, Honeyboy, 68
Egalnick, Lee, 49
Eggleston, Cozy, 25, 27–28
Electric Mud (album), 289–90
Ellerbee, Linda (Linda Smith), 258–60
"Entertainer, The," 249
Epic Records, 288
Ertegun, Ahmet, 87, 100, 107, 109, 118, 150, 192, 271
Etta James (album), 209
Etta Rocks the House (album), 237
Eugene Wright and his Dukes of Swing, 48
Evans, Elgin, 53, 67, 69
Evans, Richard, 254, 274–75, 288
Evans, Sam, 60, 107, 108
"Evans Shuffle," 60
Everett, Betty, 225
Evers, Medgar, 223–24
"Everyday I Have to Cry Some," 227
"Everything I Do Is Wrong," 207

Fame studio, 271
Farmer, Art, 191, 193
Fathers and Sons (album), 297–98
Faulkner, Roland, 289
Federal Records, 196
Fenwick label, 162
Finan, Joe, 177, 180
Finfer, Harry, 148, 190, 204
Fitzgerald, Ella, 26–27, 34
Fitzhugh, McKie, 73, 107
Five Blind Boys of Alabama, 305
Five Breezes, 82
"Five Long Years," 74
Flame Club (Chicago), 41
Flamingos, 127–30, 134
Fleming, King, 195
Fletcher, Dusty, 34
"Fly Right, Little Girl," 42
"Flyin' Home," 25
Folk Festival of the Blues (album), 241
"Fool That I Am," 205
Ford, Jack, 97
Ford, Tennessee Ernie, 77
"Forty Days and Forty Nights," 132–33
Foster, "Baby Face" LeRoy, 52
Foster, Bill, 314

Four Aces, 70
Four Strings, 153
Four Tops, 200, 201
Fournier, Vernel, 26, 30, 152–55
Franklin, Aretha, 186–87
Franklin, C. L., 135
Fratto, Russ, 89, 91, 230, 268
  writing credits, appropriation of, 118–19, 130,
    308–9
Fratto's Victory Stationery, 160
Frederick, O. W., 101
Freed, Alan ("Moondog"), 85–86
  Chess brothers and, 98, 107
  payola scandal and, 174–75, 177–78, 181–82
  promotional shows and influence, 98–99, 105,
    117, 134, 145, 177
  "rock and roll" as a term, 106–7
  writing credits, appropriation of, 86, 98, 118–19,
    308
Freed, Jackie, 86
Friedman, Jake, 76
Fulson, Lowell, 97, 121, 143
Fuqua, Harvey, 98–99, 185, 188, 195, 281

Gale Agency, 117
Gann, James, 160, 199, 268, 269
Garmisa Distributing, 136
Gayten, Paul, 97, 109, 122, 126, 132, 142, 157,
  204, 232
Gems, 249, 250, 283
Gentlemen of Swing: Ramsey Lewis and His Trio,
  The (album), 155–56
"Get on the Ball Paul," 42
Gibbs, Georgia, 124
Gideon, Tony, 198–99
"Gimme What You Got," 202
Gillespie, Dizzy, 151
Glass, Paul, 136, 167
Gleason, Jackie, 146
Globe Music, 133
Go Bo Diddley (album), 165
Goldberg, Sammy, 36–38, 43
Goldner, George, 180–81
Golson, Benny, 191, 193
"Good Lookin' Woman," 43
"Good Lovin'," 100
"Good Rockin' Daddy," 184, 185
Goodman, Benny, 158
Goodman, Gene, 79–80, 99, 120, 158, 173, 260,
  307, 310
Goodman, Harry, 79–80, 99, 120, 158, 173, 234,
  260, 261–62, 310
Gordon, Herb, 204
Gordon, Mark, 188
Gordon, Roscoe, 64
Gordy, Berry, 162, 186, 202
Gordy, Gwen, 162, 202
Grayson, S. A., 37

Green, Jerome, 104, 232–33
Greer, John, 118
Gregory, Dick, 224
Grevatt, Ren, 163–64
Griggs, Sam, 86
"Grits Ain't Groceries," 296
Groove label, 118
Groovin' with the Soulful Strings (album), 275
Gross, Rod, 314
GRT (General Recorded Tape) and Chess Records
  ownership and operation, 296–98, 302–3, 306–7
  sale, 292–96
Guralnick, Peter, 303
Guy, Browley, 85
Guy, Buddy, 191, 208, 241, 262, 265
"Gypsy Woman," 42
Gysel, Dean, 277, 278

Haley, Bill, 123, 124–25, 129, 147, 163
Hall, Rick, 271, 272–74
Hampton, Lionel, 25
Hampton, Riley, 187, 188, 194, 197, 274
Hancock, Hunter, 232
Hang On, Ramsey, 254
"Hang On Sloopy," 254
Hank Ballard and the Midnighters, 184, 185, 197,
  198
Hankins, Donald, 265
"Happy Birthday Baby," 149
"Hard Day's Night," 254
Harvey and the Moonglows, 164
Hauff, Judy, 283
"Have Guitar Will Travel," 189–90
"Have You Ever Been Lonely," 42
Hawkins, Dale, 126, 150, 161
Hayes, Sherman, 35–36, 42
"Heartbreak Hotel," 146
Heftel, Cecil, 305
"Help Me," 229
Henderson, Fletcher, 25
Henderson, Robert "Hendu," 25
Henry, Clarence "Frogman," 132, 142, 150, 195,
  205–6, 208
Herbert, Peter, 310
Herman, Woody, 275
"Hey Noxema," 102–3
"Hi Heeled Sneakers," 238
Hibbler, Al, 57, 60, 126
Hill, Big Bill, 162, 217
Hines, Earl "Fatha," 25
Hines, James Earl, 184, 185
Hipsters, 102
Hoffman, Richard W., 213–14, 216
Holt, Red, 155, 165–66, 253–54
"Honey Bee," 60
"Hoochie Coochie Man," 192
Hooker, John Lee, 67, 192, 260
Hope, Bob, 256–57

Horton, Walter, 88
Hour with the Ramsey Lewis Trio, An (album), 165
"How Many More Years," 64, 79
Howlin' Wolf (Chester Burnett), 4, 62–63, 78–79, 93, 100, 121, 263
  Arc Music, lawsuit against, 309–10
  sessions and catalogue, 63–64, 64, 132, 140, 143, 162, 165, 241, 291
Hudson Chorale, 287
Hughes, Langston, 192
Hunter (reporter), 220
Hurvis, Tom, 292

"I Can't Be Satisfied," 43, 44, 45, 51, 52, 64, 244
"I Can't Believe," 131
"I Do Love You," 249
I Do Love You (album), 249
"I Don't Know," 71, 72, 73, 77, 80
"I Don't Know What I'll Do," 88
"I Feel Like Crying," 47
"I Feel Like Going Home," 43, 44, 45, 46, 52
"I Feel So Good," 190
"I Got All You Need," 264, 265
"I Got My Mojo Working," 192, 241, 298
"I Had a Talk with My Man Last Night," 239–40
"I Have a Dream," 287
I Have a Dream (album), 287–88
"I Just Want to Make Love to You," 242
"I Love Sonny Boy," 229
"I Understand Just How You Feel," 97
"I Want to Know," 194
"I'd Rather Go Blind," 273
"I'll Be Home," 128–30, 163
"I'll Be Spinning," 144
"I'm a Man," 103, 104, 105
"I'm Afraid the Masquerade Is Over," 143
"I'm in a Travelin' Mood," 47
"I'm Glad," 85
"I'm Mad," 85
"I'm Sorry," 164
"I'm Your Hoochie Coochie Man," 92–93, 93
"I'm Your Part Time Love," 226–27
"If I Can't Have You," 188
In-Crowd, The (album), 253–54
"In Love," 120
"In the Basement," 266
In the Spotlight (album), 190

Jackson, Chubby, 151, 171
Jackson, Jesse, 223, 287–88, 294
Jackson, Jump, 36, 37
Jackson, LeRoy, 25
Jackson, Mahalia, 37, 163
Jacobs, "Little Walker," 52
Jagger, Mick, 304
Jamal, Ahmad, 26, 131, 151, 152–55, 156, 158, 167, 170, 191, 193, 195, 205, 210, 253–54, 311

Jamal at the Pershing Vol. 2 (album), 193
James, Clifton, 104
James, Elmore, 191
James, Etta (Jamesetta Hawkins), 119, 235, 240
  and the Chess brothers, 229, 308, 311
  sessions and catalogue, 183–89, 191, 193, 195, 197–98, 205, 208, 208–10, 236–37, 248, 266, 272, 273, 280
Jamie Records, 148, 190, 204
jazz. *See under* Chess Records: Argo subsidiary (jazz)
Jazz at the Penthouse (album), 158
Jazz Exponents, 157
Jazztet, 170, 195
Jennings, Morris, 282, 289
Jews
  Afro-American musicians, perceived exploitation of, 4, 73–74, 77–80, 93–97
  Afro-Americans, relations with, 109–10, 185–86
  and the entertainment business, 3–4, 158–59
Jimmy Bell Trio, 48
Jimmy's Palm Garden (Chicago), 23, 37
John Henry Burton Ltd., 78
Johnnie and Joe, 144
"Johnny B. Goode," 161, 164, 236
Johnson, Eddie, 53, 67
Johnson, Harold, 27
Johnson, Johnnie, 114–15, 116
Johnson, Lonnie, 41
Johnson, Robert, 63
Johnson, Willa, 27
Johnson, Willie, 64
"Johnson Machine Gun," 42
Jones, Brian, 243
Jones, E. Rodney, 217–18, 220, 223
Jordan, Ellington, 273
Jordan, Louis, 34, 68
Jubilee label, 85, 131
"Juke," 69–70, 72, 79
"Just a Feeling," 127
"Just Make Love to Me," 93
JVB label, 135

KAAY radio station (Little Rock), 175
"Keep It to Yourself," 133
Kent, Herb, 217, 220, 221, 223, 250, 251
"Key to the Highway," 162
King, Martin Luther, Jr., 224, 276, 285–87
King Records, 42, 86, 112, 121, 159, 185, 249
"Kiss from Your Lips, A," 130, 200
"Kneel and Pray," 131
Kolax, King, 28
Krasnow, Bob, 304
KWKH radio station (Little Rock), 175
KYW radio station (Cleveland), 180

L&P Broadcasting, 212–13
"Lady Jane," 284

Landers, Wesley, 25
Langley Avenue Jive Cats, 102
LaPalm, Dick, 126, 204, 227–28, 243, 249, 252, 255–57, 260–61, 263, 268, 300
Last Request, The (album), 287
Lay, Sam, 297
Leake, Lafayette, 190, 241, 265
Leaner, Arthur, 45
Leaner, Ernie, 45, 107
Leaner, George, 107
LeBlanc, Ed, 123
Lee, Bill Doc, 238
Lee, Laura, 272, 280
Lee, Peggy, 35
Lee Andrews and the Hearts, 150
Lee Monti and his Tu Tones, 39, 42
Leftwich, Norman, 38–39
Leon, Max, 257–58
Lester, Bobby, 98–99, 185–86
"Let It Rock," 190
"Let Me In," 208
"Let's Get Together," 296
"Let's Go, Let's Go, Let's Go," 198
"Let's Go Down to the Tavern," 84
"Let's Spend the Night Together," 289
Levy, Len, 304, 306
Levy, Morris, 159, 181
Lewis, Claire, 33
Lewis, Jerry Lee, 207
Lewis, Munchy, 19
Lewis, Ramsey, 155–56, 157, 165, 170, 191, 193, 195, 253–54, 263, 279
Lewis, Stan, 84, 88, 97, 128–29, 175, 189, 268
"Like a Rolling Stone," 284
Lillian's Chicken Shack (Chicago), 19
Lincoln, C. Eric, 110
Lind, Phil, 178
Lipsius, Harold, 148
Lishman, Robert, 179–81
"Little Anna Mae," 42
"Little Marie," 236
Little Milton. *See* Campbell, Little Milton
Little Richard, 110, 147, 190
Little Walter, 67, 67–71, 79, 93, 99, 112, 121, 132, 105, 133–34
    sessions and catalogue, 83–84, 87–88, 91–92, 132, 140, 143, 161, 162
Little Walter and His Jukes, 70–71
Living Blues magazine, 73, 74
Lockwood, Robert Junior, 67
Lombardo, Guy, 34
"Long Distance Call," 60, 68
"Long Gone," 49
"Long Lonely Nights," 150
"Louisianan Blues," 60, 68
Louisville Defender, 40
"Lover Come Back to Me," 25
Lovettes, 249
"Lovey Dovey," 100

Lubinsky, Herman, 121, 159
Lymon, Frankie, 126

Mabley, Jackie "Moms," 196, 205, 209
Mabon, Beatrice Burnett, 73
Mabon, Willie, 71, 73–74, 77, 80, 85, 88–89, 99–100, 120, 121
McCarthy, Frank, 220
McCartney, Paul, 242
McClendon, Gordon, 218–19, 221
McClure, Bobby, 247
McCoy, Sid, 153
McDaniel, Gussie, 101
McElroy, Sollie, 127–30
McGuire Sisters, 99, 163
Mack, Lonnie, 236
McKaie, Andy, 312
McKinley, Flash, 238
McLin, Claude, 25, 57
McMurry, Lillian, 94–95, 120, 133, 159, 191
McNutt, Bob, 23–24
McNutt, Mary, 23–24
Macomba Lounge (Chicago), 2, 15–16, 22–32
    fire at, 51
    as a jazz venue, 26
    musical policy, 24–28
    violence, criminal activity, and drug problems at, 28–31
    well-known artists and, 26–27, 278
    women at, 29
McPhatter, Clyde, 150
McPortland, Marian, 158
McShann, Jay, 113
McVea, Jack, 34, 197
"Mad Love," 88
Main Line label, 150
Malcolm X, 224
Mallard, Sax, 66, 78, 86
Malo, Ron, 183, 203, 233, 245
"Mama Didn't Lie," 227
Mammarella, Anthony, 179–80, 210–11
"Mannish Boy," 112, 117
Markham, Pigmeat, 205
Mars, Mitzi, 85
Martin, James H., 47
Marterie, Ralph, 131
Marterry label, 131
Mascot label, 162
"Mashed Potatoes," 205
Mason, Barbara, 251
Maxwell Street Market, 21
"Maybellene," 116–17, 117, 118–19, 121, 134, 163, 308
Mayfield, Curtis, 227
"Mean and Evil Blues," 34
"Mean Old World," 71
Melrose, Lester, 41
"Memphis," 236
Memphis Slim, 48

Mercury Records, 34, 36, 39, 48, 105, 106–7, 136, 204, 272
Message from the Status Quo (album), 289
Midwest Pressing/Midsouth Pressing, 268
"Mighty Long Time," 95
Miles, Buddy, 297
Miller, Bobby, 272, 280–81
Miner, Raynard, 246, 249–52, 280–81, 288
Minhan, Ken, 290
Miracle records, 43, 48
Mitchell, Abye, 184, 186
Mitchell, Bob, 235
Mitchell, Jean, 184
Mitchell, Jutson, 27
Mitchell sisters, 185
"Moanin' at Midnight," 64, 79
Modern label, 42, 58, 62, 67, 121, 184–85
Moms Mabley at Geneva Conference (album), 209
Moms Mabley at the UN (album), 196
Moms Mabley on Stage (album), 196
"Mona Lisa," 57
"Money," 237, 248
Monotones, 162, 164
Monti, Lee, 39, 42
Moody, James, 131, 151, 195
"Moondog Symphony," 98
Moonglows, 98–99, 105, 112, 120, 121, 134, 150, 161, 190
    See also Harvey and the Moonglows
Moore, Dwight "Gatemouth," 46
Moore, Scotty, 145
Moreno, Buddy, 84
Morganfield, McKinley, 2
Morrow, Odessa, 27
Morton, Jelly Roll, 77
"Most of All," 112
Motown Records, 235
Movie Album, The (album), 279
MS Distribution Company, 136
Muddy Water at Newport (album), 192–93
Muddy Waters Sings Big Bill Broonzy (album), 190
Muhammad, Elijah, 224
Muirfield Music, 126
Muscle Shoals studio (Alabama), 271–74, 280
"Music, Music, Music," 154
"Music Goes Round and Round, The," 132
Music Sales (Memphis), 55, 57–58
"My Babe," 99, 111, 112
"My Dearest Darling," 188
"My Foolish Heart," 56, 57, 301
"My Story," 190
Myers, Dave, 70–71, 83–84, 91–92
Myers, Jack, 265
Myers, Louis, 70–71, 83–84, 91–92

"Nadine," 86, 235
Nash, Johnny, 262
Nathan, Syd, 86, 112, 121, 196–97

Nelson, Idell, 90, 142
Nelson, Nate, 127, 128, 129
Nelson, Shirli Dixon, 313
New Look, The (album), 251
Newell, Ed, 54–55
Newport Jazz Festival, 163–64, 192
"Next Door to the Blues," 209
Nighthawk, Robert, 49, 67, 83
"No Details," 235
"No Money Down," 132
"No Particular Place to Go," 235–36
"No Place to Go," 93
Nobles, Gene, 61, 85, 107
"Not Now Baby," 36
Notkin, Joey, 94
Notkin, Nate, 43, 52, 56, 63, 94, 137, 178, 193, 212, 213, 214, 293, 295
"Now's the Time," 25

"O-O I Love You," 280
"Off the Wall," 83
"Oh Baby," 93
"Oh, What a Night," 296
Okeh label, 209
One Dozen Berries (album), 161
113 Club (Chicago), 19
"Only Time Will Tell," 128
"Open the Door, Richard," 34, 197
Orioles, 85
Orr, Billy, 36
Otis, Johnny, 184, 194
"Over the Mountain," 144
Overbea, Danny, 131
Owens, Wendell, 25, 27
Oxford Music Corporation, 36

Paint It Black (album), 274–75
Palmer, Robert, 16, 42
Parham, Charles "Truck," 25
Parker, Charlie, 25
Parrot label, 127, 128
Pastels, 162
Patton, Charlie, 63
Peace (album), 291–92
Peaches (Creolettes), 184–85
Peacock label, 305–6
"Pennies from Heaven," 57
Pepper, Vincent, 214–15, 270, 305
Percy, Charles, 224
Perkins, Carl, 146, 147
Perry, J. Samuel, 305
Pershing Ballroom (Chicago), 18
Philips, Sam, 58–59, 63, 144–48, 159
    and Leonard and Phil Chess, 62, 64–65
Phillips, Dewey, 93
"Pictures of Matchstick Men," 289, 296–97
Pincus, Millie, 13
Plastic Products, 55

Platters, 134
"Please Have Mercy," 68
"Poinciana," 153–54
Pointer, Lowell, 25
"Poison Ivy," 100
Pomus, Doc, 23
"Pork and Beans," 48
Presley, Elvis, 144–48, 160
Prestige Records, 210
Price, Sammy, 192
Prima, Louis, 35
"Promised Land," 236
Pruter, Robert, 190
publishing rights, 123–24, 129–30, 309–10
Pulik, Chaske, 8
Pulik, Dvera, 6
Pulik, Morris (Moische), 7–8, 11
    as a junk dealer, 13
Pulik, Harry, 17
Pulik, Joseph (Yossel), 7–8, 17
Putnam, Bill, 37, 138, 183
Pye Records (distribution organization), 172–73,
    261–62

race music, 34, 39, 42–43, 45, 46–47
    ASCAP and, 77
    jazz vs. blues musicians, 56–57
    race and the success of rock and roll, 146–48
    rhythm and blues as new name for, 48, 106
radio
    black and black-oriented radio, 36–38, 45,
        213–16, 216–18
    and rhythm and blues (R&B), 84–85
    See also disc jockeys
Ramsey Lewis trio, 263
Randy's Record Shop (Gallatin, TN), 61, 76
Ravens, 131–32
RCA/RCA Victor, 55, 145–46, 177
"Reap What You Sow," 209
"Reconsider Baby," 97
record business
    copyrights, contracts, and songwriting credits,
        36, 38, 39, 77, 77–80, 86–87, 98, 99, 130
    long-playing records, 142–43
    race and the success of rock and roll, 146–48
    royalty rates, 94
record distribution, 44
Record Industry Association of America, 252
Record World, 254, 295
recording sessions, cost of, 35
Redcoats, 205
Redlich, Charles "Dago," 122
Reed, Jimmy, 120, 237–38, 260
Reese, Della, 126
Regal Theater (Chicago), 18
Real Folk Blues (album), 264
Republic Music, 80
"Rescue Me," 249–52, 263, 283

rhythm and blues (R&B), 48, 84–85, 106, 190
    jazz vs. blues musicians, 56–57
    See also "cat music"; Howlin' Wolf; Little
        Walter; "race" music; Rogers, Jimmy; Waters,
        Muddy; Williamson, Sonny Boy
Ricardo, Stan "Ric," 217, 220
Rich, Buddy, 195
Richards, Keith, 242, 243
Richbourg, John, 61, 85
Riley, Bud, 217
Riperton, Minnie, 283
Rivers, Johnny, 236
Roach, Max, 27, 157
"Road Runner," 190
Roberson, Bryce, 282
Robey, Don, 305–6
Robinson, Jackie, 224
Robinson, Joe and Sylvia, 307, 312
Rock, Rock, Rock (film & LP), 134, 143, 161
rock and roll, 146–47
    and as term, 106–7
    race and the success of, 146–48
"Rock and Roll Music," 149
"Rocket 88," 58–59, 65
"Rockin' Daddy," 93
"Rockin' Rockers," 57
Rogers, Jimmy (James A. Lane), 41, 52, 57, 67, 68,
    69, 70, 74–75, 143
Rolf, Gene, 50
"Roll Over Beethoven," 133, 236
"Roll With Me Henry," 185
"Rollin' and Tumblin'," 52
"Rollin' Stone," 52, 56, 57
Rolling Stone magazine, 272, 290, 307
Rolling Stones, 4, 172, 242–44
Rosen, David, 150
Ross, Gene, 27–28
Ross, Jackie, 238–39, 248, 262
Rotary Connection, 279, 281, 282–84, 291
Rotary Connection (album), 283–84
Roulette label, 159
Rowe, Mike, 15–16, 20–21
RPM, 58
"Ruby Tuesday," 284
Ruffin, David, 203

"Sad Hours," 71, 72
Sain, Oliver, 208
"St. Louis Blues," 34
Salistine, Father, 160
Salstone, Alyne, 29, 33, 36, 37
Salstone, Milt, 29, 33–35
Salvador, Richie, 268, 298, 300, 302
Samuels, Clarence, 37, 78
Samuelson, Tim, 313
Satterfield, Louis, 225–26, 282, 288, 289
Saunders, Carri, 90, 141–42, 186, 201
Saunders, Red, 187

Savoy Ballroom (Chicago), 17
Savoy records, 36, 42, 121, 159
"Say Man," 164
"Say Man, Back Again," 164
"Say No More," 35
Scaggs, Boz, 303–4
"School Day," 144
Schlacter, Marvin, 306
Searcy, Bill, 25
Sears, Zenas, 76, 107
"Security," 273
"See Saw," 200
"See You Later Alligator," 122–23, 124, 125, 129, 163
"See You Soon Baboon," 126
Segal, Joe, 152
"Selfish One," 238–39
"Seven Day Fool," 205
708 Liquor Store (708 Liquor Club), 15, 23
Shaheen, John, 212
Shaheen, Richard, 212
"Sharing You," 240
"She Moves Me," 53
Sheldon Recording Studios, 141
Sheridan, Art, 46, 50, 86, 98, 127–28
Sherman, Joe, 114
Shore, Dinah, 34
Shorr, Mickey, 151, 177, 258–59
"Shufflin' the Boogie," 34
Silverbrand, Harry, 12, 278
Silverbrand, Mae Chess, 5–6, 10–11, 12, 89, 300
Simms, Bobby, 283
Sims, Gerald, 225, 249, 282, 288, 312
Sims, Zoot, 151, 156, 166
"Sincerely," 98–99, 112, 121, 134, 163
Singer, Mattie, 164
Singular label, 162
Sir John Trio, 114
"Sitting in the Park," 249
"Sixty Minute Man," 106, 197
"Slip-in Mules," 238
Sloan, Bert, 278
Smalls, Tommy "Dr. Jive," 105
Smith, Carl, 238, 246, 249–52, 288
Smith, Milton, 126
Smith, Trixie, 106
Smith, Willie, 191
Smitty's DeLuxe tavern (Chicago), 19
"Smokestack Lightening," 132
"So Mean to Me," 208
"Something's Got a Hold on Me," 208, 237
song royalties, publishers and, 123–24, 129–30
"Soul Man," 284
Soul Stirrers, 279
Soulful Strings, 274–75
South, Wesley, 223–24
South Grove Avenue ("Bronzeville") (Chicago)

as center of Afro-American life, 16–21
Southern Christian Leadership Conference (SCLC), 287–88
Southland Distribution, 60
Spann, Otis, 87–88, 93, 104, 191, 221, 223, 241, 297
Spann, Pervis, 217, 220
Specialty records, 42
Spiegel, Art, 34–35
"Spoonful," 188
Stage Show, 146
Stan's Record Shop (Shreveport, LA), 49
"Starlite," 120
Starr, Kay, 131
Status Quo, 289
Stax label, 271
"Stay in My Corner," 281
Steele, Willie, 64
Stepney, Charles, 280, 282–83, 289
Stewart, Billy, 209, 226, 230, 247, 248–49, 265–66, 272, 280
Stidham, Arbee, 66
"Stone Crazy," 208
"Stop the Wedding," 209
"Strange Feeling," 226
Strode Hotel (Chicago), 23
Strohacker, Cynthia, 299
Strong, Barrett, 237, 248
Sugar Hill, 312
"Sugar Sweet," 132
Sullivan, Ed, 105
Sumlin, Hubert, 93
Summers, Florence, 214
"Summertime," 266
Summertime (album), 266
Sun label, 65, 159
Sunnyland Slim (Albert Luandrew), 39, 41, 41–42, 43–47
"Surfin U.S.A.," 236
"Surrey with the Fringe on Top," 153
"Sweet Little Rock and Roll," 164
"Sweet Little Sixteen," 161, 164, 172, 236
Sykes, Roosevelt, 25

Taylor, Cora "Koko," 264–65
Taylor, Robert "Pops," 264
Ted Q (disc jockey), 232
"Tell Mama," 273
"Tell Me Mama," 83
"Ten Commandments of Love, The," 164
"That's All Right Mama," 145
"That's All You Gotta Do," 97
"That's My Baby (Chic-a-Boom)," 128
"There Is," 280–81
There Is (album), 281
Theriot, Kenneth, 123
"Third Degree," 74, 85
"Thirty Days," 116, 120

This is Howlin' Wolf's New Album. He doesn't like it. He didn't like his first electric guitar either (album), 291
"This Love of Mine," 53
"This Train," 99
Thomas, Irma, 273
Thomas, Rufus, 67
Thomas, Willie B., 192
Thompson, Sonny, 49
Tibbs, Andrew (Melvyn Andrew Grayson), 37–38, 42, 47
"Tiger in Your Tank," 192–93
"Times Are Getting Hard," 50
"Toast to Lovers, A," 119
"Too Much Monkey Business," 133
"Too Pooped to Pop," 190, 202
Toscano, Eli, 140, 191
Touff, Cy, 156
Tracy, Jack, 156, 166–67, 170–71, 181, 193, 195, 204–5
"Trick or Treat," 207
"Trouble No More," 132
Trumpet Records, 95, 120, 159, 191
"Trust in Me," 188, 208
Tu Tones, Lee Monti and his, 39, 42
Tucker, Tommy (Robert Higginbotham), 238
Tuff label, 205
Turner, Ike, 62, 64
Turner, Joe, 163
"Tweedle Dee," 124
"Twenty-four Hours," 74, 79
Twist with Steve Alaimo (album), 205
2120 (album), 314
"2120 South Michigan," 244

Unart label, 288
Unbelievable (album), 266
"Uncle John," 103, 104
"Union Man Blues," 38, 42
United Distributors, 136
United Records, 103
Universal Recording Studios, 35, 68–69, 97–98, 104, 129, 148
"Up & At 'Em," 25
Upchurch, Phil, 282, 289
"Uptight Good Man," 273
Usher, Dave, 151–55, 156–59, 160, 163, 166, 172, 252

Variety, 106, 118, 175–76
Vaughan, Sarah, 45
Vee Jay Records, 89, 103, 136, 159, 260, 271
Veltone label, 194
Venegas, Kenny, 283
Vibrations, 195, 198
Violinaires, 279
Von Battle, Joe, 135

"Wabash Blues," 42
Wabash Junk Shop, 13
"Wade in the Water," 254
"Walkin' Blues," 56
"Walkin' the Blues," 120
"Walkin' the Boogie," 67
Wallace, George, 224
Waller, Fats, 19
"Wallflower, The," 184, 185
Walton, Charles, 28, 96, 221
Walton, Pete, 98
"Wang Dang Doodle," 264–65
Ware, Leonard, 294
Ward, Frank, 214–15
Waring, Fred, 140
Warren, Harry, 188
Washboard Sam, 85
Washington, Bernadine, 217, 299
Washington, Dinah (Ruth Jones), 26, 27, 34, 37, 48, 105, 106–7, 143
Washington, Ferdinand "Fats," 128–29
"Watermelon Man," 85
Waters, Geneva, 40
Waters, Muddy (McKinley Morgan), 2, 39, 40–41, 68, 94, 115, 172, 192, 263
  Arc Music, lawsuit against, 309–10
  Leonard Chess and, 2, 40–41, 44, 44–45, 93
  English bands, influences on, 241–44
  sessions and catalogue, 42, 43–47, 52, 52–53, 56, 60, 87–88, 92, 112, 120, 132–33, 140, 142, 143, 161, 162, 189, 190, 191, 192–93, 241, 244, 264, 289–90
  success, 44–46, 48–49, 51, 57, 93, 99, 117, 121, 133–34, 162
"Wa-Too-Si," 198–99
"Watusi, The," 195, 198
"Way You Move Me Baby, The," 199
"We're Gonna Make It," 246, 248
"Wear It on Our Face," 281
Weatherspoon, Fletcher, 127
Weavers, 177
Webb, Lloyd, 217, 221, 223
"Wee Wee Hours," 116
Wein, George, 192
Weinstein, Gershon, 9
Weiss, Hymie, 71–72, 159
Weiss, Sam, 159
Weizmann, Chaim, 5
Welding, Pete, 241, 290
Welk, Lawrence, 35
Wendell Owens Trio, 27
West Side Cleffs, 155
Wexler, Jerry, 79, 86, 100, 107, 118–19, 150, 159, 177, 181, 271
WGES radio station (Chicago), 36, 61
WGST radio station (Atlanta), 61
"What Will I Tell My Heart," 60
"Whatcha Gonna Do," 199

"When," 128
"When I Get to Thinking," 190
White, Maurice, 225–26, 245–46, 249, 266, 282, 288
White, Slappy, 205
White City Ballroom and Casino (Chicago), 18
"Who," 132
Wiener, Jack, 139–40, 141, 152
    See also Sheldon Recording Studios
Williams, Buster, 54–56, 57–58, 70, 84, 95, 107, 120, 159–60, 267
Williams, Margie, 232
Williamson, Mattie, 120
Williamson, Sonny Boy, II (Rice Miller), 63, 67, 68, 95, 102, 120, 133, 143, 149, 162, 165, 229
Wilson, Jackie, 186, 202
Wilson, Paul, 127
WINS radio station (New York City), 105
Winters, Pinky, 131
Witzel, Marty, 13
WLAC radio station (Nashville), 61, 76, 85
WMRY radio station (New Orleans), 88
WNOV radio station (Milwaukee, WI), 284–85

Wood, Randy, 61, 107, 129, 138, 160, 211
Wood, Roy, 301
Woods, Sonny, 90, 297
"Work With Me Annie," 184, 197
"Worried Blues," 241
Wright, Eugene, 48
Wright, Phil, 247–49, 266
WTAC radio station (Flint, MI), 212
WVON AM/WSDM FM radio stations (Chicago), 213–16, 216–18, 220–24, 258–59, 276, 284, 286–87
Wyoma, 35

"You Can't Catch Me," 116
"You Never Can Tell," 236
"You're a Fool," 85
"You're No Good," 225
"You're so Fine," 91, 92–93
"You've Got to Be Taught," 288
Young, Eldee, 155, 253–54
Young, Dave, 30–31, 38
Young, Lester, 25

Zisook, Max, 9